Q&A
Jurisprudence

Routledge Questions & Answers Series

Each Routledge Q&A contains questions on topics commonly found on exam papers, with comprehensive suggested answers. The titles are written by lecturers who are also examiners, so the student gains an important insight into exactly what examiners are looking for in an answer. This makes them excellent revision and practice guides.

Titles in the series:
Q&A Company Law
Q&A Commercial Law
Q&A Contract Law
Q&A Criminal Law
Q&A Employment Law
Q&A English Legal System
Q&A Equity and Trusts
Q&A European Union Law
Q&A Evidence
Q&A Family Law
Q&A Intellectual Property Law
Q&A Jurisprudence
Q&A Land Law
Q&A Medical Law
Q&A Public Law
Q&A Torts

For a full listing, visit www.routledge.com/cw/revision

Q&A
Jurisprudence

David Brooke

Routledge
Taylor & Francis Group

LONDON AND NEW YORK

First published 1993 by Cavendish publishing
Seventh edition published 2016
by Routledge

2 Park Square, Milton Park, Abingdon, Oxon OX14 4RN
711 Third Avenue, New York, NY 10017, USA

Routledge is an imprint of the Taylor & Francis Group, an informa business

First issued in hardback 2017

British Library Cataloguing in Publication Data
A catalogue record for this book is available from the British Library

Library of Congress Cataloging-in-Publication Data
A catalog record for this title has been requested

ISBN: 978-1-138-83368-5 (pbk)
ISBN: 978-1-138-43716-6 (hbk)

Typeset in TheSans
by Wearset Ltd, Boldon, Tyne and Wear

Contents

Preface

In this seventh edition there are new questions exploring the inter-face between jurisprudence and human rights in a current world situation bedevilled by conflicts between claims of national security and the demands of human rights.

David Brooke

June 2015

Contents

Table of Cases

.

Table of Legislation

Guide to the Companion Website

www.routledge.com/cw/revision

Visit the Law Revision website to discover a comprehensive range of resources designed to enhance your learning experience.

The Good, The Fair, & The Ugly

Good essays are the gateway to top marks. This interactive tutorial provides sample essays together with voice-over commentary and tips for successful exam essays, written by our Q&A authors themselves.

Multiple Choice Questions

Knowledge is the foundation of every good essay. Focusing on key examination themes, these MCQs have been written to test your knowledge and understanding of each subject in the book.

Bonus Q&As

Having studied our exam advice, put your revision into practice and test your essay writing skills with our additional online questions and answers.

Introduction

Professor Raz comments in his biographical note on the death of Professor Hart in *Utilitas* journal (1993):

> 'The purpose of jurisprudence is not to instruct us in the use of the word "law" but to explore the law's essential relations to morality, force and society. The task of jurisprudence is misrepresented when it is conceived as a search for the definition of the word "law". It is in fact an exploration of the nature of an important social institution.'

Examples of jurisprudential inquiry into the nature of law as a social institution include Raz's insight that all law claims legitimate and supreme authority in a territory. Whether a particular legal system has that authority is a separate question (Raz, *The Authority of Law*, 1979).

Another example is Professor Hart's argument that there are two essential conditions for a legal system to exist: that the bulk of legal officials accept the legal system that they work for and that the bulk of the population obey the law (Hart, *The Concept of Law*, 1961).

Such general and analytical jurisprudence is in stark contrast with legal theory that is preoccupied with a particular legal culture, such as Professor Dworkin's preoccupation with the correct forms of appellate argument and appellate judgment, especially in the Supreme Court of the United States (Dworkin, *Law's Empire*, 1986).

Some legal theorists are explicit that their focus is on the legal and social attributes of a few well-functioning and relatively just legal systems, as found at the present time in Western Europe, for example (Galligan, *Law in Modern Society*, 2007).

Other legal theorists have a particular issue that seems to preoccupy their writings, such as the question of how law 'binds', namely, its 'normativity' (Kelsen, *Introduction to the Problems of Legal Theory*, 1934).

Some important legal philosophers have gone straight to the foundational issues concerning law's power, such as the question as to how state power is to be justified at all through the issuance of laws. This is a major topic in jurisprudence, engaged with from Thomas Hobbes in *Leviathan* (1651) and John Locke's *Second Treatise on Civil Government* (1690) right through to modern thinkers, such as Rawls, *A Theory of Justice* (1971), and Nozick, *Anarchy, State and Utopia* (1974).

These are very interesting times for the student of jurisprudence in the context of current world events as of 2015. Old debates about the dynamic between human rights and national security have acquired an urgent significance in the context of world 'hyper-terrorism' as evidenced by the events of 9/11 in the United States and subsequent events.

Even older debates about the relationship and balance between human-created law and purported 'divine' or 'God-created' law have also acquired new traction in the context of the revival of demands for 'sharia law' in the context of the global Islamist movement.

In a speech at the 'GLOBSEC' Security conference in Bratislava, Slovakia, on 19 June 2015, the Prime Minister of the United Kingdom, Mr David Cameron, commented on some of these current dilemmas which were not apparent even 20 years ago. Referring to the massive territorial expansion of the terror group 'Islamic State' in the Middle East, Cameron said that

> 'In "Islamic State" we have one of the biggest threats our world has faced. The cause is ideological … an extremist ideology that says the West is bad and democracy is wrong … It says religious doctrine trumps the rule of law and Caliphate trumps nation State and it justifies violence in asserting itself and achieving its aims.'

The values of democracy, human rights and the rule of law need to be argued for; they are obviously not self-evident to everyone. This is one of the many tasks of jurisprudence.

The correct moral balance between legitimate national security demands and legitimate human rights demands needs to be argued for as well. Neither claims of 'national security' nor claims of 'human rights' should become too loud a drum to drown out the voice of the other.

Jurisprudence has rarely been more relevant a subject for the law, politics or philosophy student.

1 General Aspects of Jurisprudence

INTRODUCTION

This chapter offers only one question, but it is perhaps the most important question in this book. The most important general advice to any new student to the subject of jurisprudence is to identify the viewpoint of the legal theorist. Identifying the legal theorist's viewpoint on law will prevent confusion and many misunderstandings.

QUESTION 1

How does an insight into the 'viewpoint' of a legal theorist concerning law help in understanding the work of the legal theorist?

How to Answer this Question

The question concerns the general question of the role that a legal theorist's viewpoint has on the understanding of the legal theorist's theory of law. The answer identifies three general viewpoints that a legal theorist might take on the institution we call 'law':

(1) the lawyers or participant's perspective where the legal theorist seeks to explain law in terms of a lawyer's understanding of law. Dworkin and Kelsen are the best known examples of this perspective;

(2) the institutional 'engaged' perspective is where the legal theorist goes beyond the lawyer's perspective and examines law in its wider political and social perspective, but this perspective has a strong commitment to a particular type of legal system or an ideal form of law. Finnis, Galligan and MacCormick are all strong examples of this type of approach;

(3) the 'detached' institutional perspective where the legal theorist examines law in its social and political context – the 'institutional setting of law' – but has no express commitment to law or legal systems of any kind. This value-free descriptive jurisprudence is best exemplified by Professor Hart.

Applying the Law

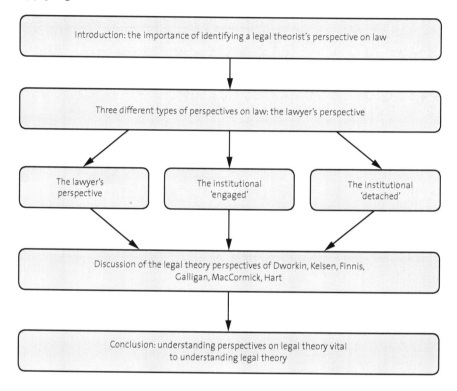

Introduction: the importance of identifying a legal theorist's perspective on law

Three different types of perspectives on law: the lawyer's perspective

The lawyer's perspective

The institutional 'engaged'

The institutional 'detached'

Discussion of the legal theory perspectives of Dworkin, Kelsen, Finnis, Galligan, MacCormick, Hart

Conclusion: understanding perspectives on legal theory vital to understanding legal theory

ANSWER

Jurisprudence can seem bewildering to the new student as a mass of theorists and theories are suddenly thrust upon them and they are expected to absorb, digest and feedback a body of knowledge that seems part philosophy, part sociology and part history, while bearing little relation to traditional law subjects.

One way of imposing order upon the chaos is to try to obtain a sense of where a particular legal theorist stands in relation to the law. Understanding the standpoint of a legal theorist makes understanding that legal theorist easier and allows the construction of a 'mind map' so that important jurisprudential scholars can fit into that 'mind map' schemata.

It is suggested that three broad standpoints could be identified in order to place a range of authors in a 'viewpoint mind map'. These authors include: Dworkin, Kelsen, Galligan, MacCormick, Finnis, Austin, Hart and Raz.

The three viewpoints or standpoint perspectives are:

(1)   participant perspectives – Dworkin, Kelsen;
(2)   institutional (or 'external') engaged perspective – MacCormick, Galligan, Finnis;
(3)   institutional (or 'external') detached perspective – Hart, Austin.

The participant perspective can also be termed the 'lawyer's perspective'. This perspective seeks to give an account of the social institution we call law from the point of view of the court-room or a judge. To a certain extent this perspective is a 'natural' one for a legal theorist to take. As Professor Raz comments in 'The Nature of Law' in *Ethics in the Public Domain* (1994):

> 'most theorists tend to be by education and profession lawyers, and their audience often consists primarily of law students. Quite naturally and imperceptibly they adopted the lawyers perspective on the law.'

The problem with the participant or lawyer's perspective on the law is that it can lead the legal theorist who adopts it to neglect important features of law because the lawyer's perspective fails to examine the law in the wider political context in which the law is moored. Two legal theorists who adopted the lawyer's perspective are Hans Kelsen and Ronald Dworkin.

Kelsen took explaining the 'normativity' or authority of the law as the backbone of his theory of law. This in itself is a question which looks at law from the lawyer's perspective – what sense, Kelsen asked, to give to claims of 'ought' in the law? As Kelsen comments in *Introduction to the Problems of Legal Theory* (1934):

> 'The Pure Theory of Law works with this basic norm as a hypothetical foundation. Given this presupposition that the basic norm is valid, the legal system resting on it is also valid … Rooted in the basic norm, ultimately, is the normative import of all the material facts constituting the legal system. The empirical data given to legal interpretation can be interpreted as law, that is, as a system of basic norms, only if a basic norm is presupposed.'

Therefore Kelsen, a person who regards a legal order as valid as opposed to a mere coercive order, presupposes a hypothetical 'basic norm' which gives 'normativity' or 'oughtness' to the legal system so interpreted as valid. Kelsen is seeking to explain what lawyers mean when they say 'the law says you ought not to do X or you ought to do X'. Kelsen's persepective is the lawyer's perspective, trying to give sense to 'lawyers' talk' of legal obligation. As Kelsen comments in *Pure Theory of Law* (1967) 'the decisive question' is why the demands of a legal organ are considered valid but not the demands of a gang of robbers. The answer to this question is that only the demands of a legal organ are interpreted as an objectively valid norm because the person viewing the legal order as valid and therefore more than a coercive order from a 'gang of robbers' is presupposing in his own consciousness a basic norm which gives validity and normative force to the legal order.

Kelsen's basic question in legal theory – what sense to give to lawyers' statements of 'legal ought' – is a question from the lawyer's perspective, but this tendency to examine the law from the lawyer's or participant's perspective is reinforced by Kelsen's methodology. Kelsen insisted that his theory was a 'pure theory of law'. He regarded it as doubly pure – pure of all moral argument and pure of all sociological facts. The view of law examined by Kelsen is free of any kind of moral evaluation, such as what moral purposes the law could serve, or sociological enquiry as for example what motivates persons to obey the law. Kelsen merely looks at the raw data of legal experience to be found in the statute books and law reports and asks: what sense to give to legal talk of 'ought'?

For a legal theory to ignore the moral and sociological realities framing the law it must be the case that that legal theory is focusing purely on the lawyer's perspective. Although Kelsen has an interesting and developed theory answering the lawyer's question of what sense to give to lawyers' talk of legal obligation, legal duty and legal 'ought', Kelsen's theory of law has little general explanatory power of the social institution called law. Moreover, by clinging so exclusively to the 'lawyer's perspective' Kelsen makes statements that, from a wider perspective, seem unjustifiable. For example Kelsen comments, in *Introduction to the Problems of Legal Theory* (1934), that:

> 'the law is a coercive apparatus having in and of itself no political or ethical value.'

Kelsen should have considered that the law can have value in itself as a means by which citizens can express loyalty and identification with their community. This point, recognised by modern writers on law such as Raz and Leslie Green, would have been lost on Kelsen – buried as he was in the lawyer's perspective.

Kelsen's theory of law was once termed by the political thinker Harold Laski as 'an exercise in logic not in life' (see Laski, *A Grammar of Politics* (1938)). We may interpret this statement by Laski as meaning that although Kelsen tries impressively to answer the question concerning the law's normativity, Kelsen has little of value to say about law as a social phenomenon generally.

The lawyer or participant viewpoint on law can be valuable but it is unreasonable to study the law solely and exclusively from the lawyer's perspective. The law must be examined, in order to get full explanatory power of this important social institution, in the wider perspective of social organisations and political institutions generally. This wider perspective may be termed the 'institutional' or 'external' perspective on law and has been the dominant viewpoint in English jurisprudence from Thomas Hobbes in the seventeenth century to Professor Hart.[1]

However, before we examine the 'institutional' perspective on law we need to examine another famous example of the lawyer's perspective – Professor Ronald Dworkin's theory of law.

Dworkin's preoccupation with his theory of law has been to answer the question: how can law be interpreted so as to provide a sound justification for the use of state coercion

....

1 Professor Hart in *The Concept of Law* (1961) used Thomas Hobbes's method of imagining society without law and then describing the benefits of law by showing how the addition of law 'cured' defects in the pre-legal order. Thomas Hobbes in Leviathan (1651) imagined society without the state and showed how the state was necessary to 'cure' the defects of the 'state of nature'.

involved in forcing the payment of compensation in a civil action at law? This is again a lawyer's question, although a different lawyer's question from Kelsen's preoccupation with the normativity of the law. Dworkin's theory of law is aimed at the justification of state coercion expressed through law. Dworkin has taken appellate case decisions as the testing ground for his theory of law which has involved the controversial proposition that the law of the Anglo-American legal system involves not just the accepted case law and statutes but also the law that includes the best moral interpretation of that law. Therefore there is a greater connection between Dworkin's lawyer's perspective and general legal theory than Kelsen's lawyer's perspective which seemed grounded on the normativity of law only. Dworkin's theory of law at least engages with the debate 'what is law?' or 'what are the grounds of law?' However, despite Dworkin's connection to wider debates in legal theory about the nature of law, Dworkin seeks to answer that question from the lawyer's perspective. Dworkin has defended his preoccupation with the courtroom[2] by observing that it is in the courtroom that the doctrinal question of 'what is law?' is most acutely answered. Dworkin comments in 'Hart and the Concepts of Law' (2006) *Harvard Law Review* Forum:

> **'Courtrooms symbolise the practical importance of the doctrinal question and I have often used judicial decisions both as empirical data and illustrations for my doctrinal claims.'**

Dworkin has often used appellate cases to support his arguments, leading to the charge that he is developing a legal theory out of a theory of adjudication. Dworkin uses the House of Lords appellate case of *McLouglinh v O'Brien* (1982) as the centrepiece for testing various theories of law, including his own theory known as 'law as Integrity' at pp. 230–240 of *Law's Empire* – Dworkin's magnum opus on legal theory from 1986. The United States appellate court decisions of the Supreme Court have been used by Dworkin, namely: the 'snail darter' case *Tennessee Valley Authority v Hill* (1978) and *Brown v U.S.* (1954) are both discussed by Dworkin in *Law's Empire* at pp. 20–23 and pp. 29–30 respectively. A case used by Dworkin in the 1960s to illustrate these arguments about the nature of law – 'Elmer's case' – is used again at pp. 15–20 of *Law's Empire*. 'Elmer's case', known properly as *Riggs v Palmer* (1883) is an appellate decision of the New York appeals court.

Dworkin's lawyer's perspective on the law and his tendency to look at the law through the prism of the courtroom has led to criticism that Dworkin has developed a theory of law out of a theory of adjudication. As Professor Raz argues in *Between Authority and Interpretation* (2009):

> **'[Dworkin's] book is not so much an explanation of the law as a sustained argument about how courts, especially American and British courts should decide cases. It contains a theory of adjudication rather than a theory of the nature of law.'**

....

2 Professor Finnis notes in his collection of essays *Philosophy of Law* (2011), p. 11 that 'Dworkin over-emphasizes the judicial, at the expense of the legislative, in law'. Finnis even says that Dworkin's account of adjudication cannot be completely accepted at p. 129: 'While we should broadly accept some main elements of Ronald Dworkin's account of adjudication, we should reject his thesis that even in hard cases there Is presumed to be a single legally right answer.'

The argument against Dworkin is that his obsession with the courtroom – the lawyer's perspective on law – means that Dworkin can miss, or fail to appreciate, essential features of law that operate in the wider social context beyond the courtroom. For example, Dworkin fails in his legal theory to account for the law's claim to authority which is an important part of the law's method of social organisation. Dworkin says a lot about the need for the law to have 'integrity' or 'fairness' but little about the law's authority. Although the integrity or fairness of the law is vital, so is the law's authority. If Dworkin had stepped back from the lawyer's perspective he might have seen this point.

The institutional perspective stands back from the lawyer's perspective, not in order to disregard it, but to examine lawyers and courts in the wider perspective of their place in the social organisation and political institutions of a society.

The 'institutional' perspective has had many representatives in the history of legal philosophy. Its influence started with Thomas Hobbes in *Leviathan* (1651) who heavily influenced Bentham (*Of Laws in General* (1782)) and Austin (*The Province of Jurisprudence Determined* (1832)). Hobbes placed law in its wider political context and argued that strong authority was needed to pacify a society, for without a common authority to keep men 'in awe' the natural tendency of man was to war with his fellow men. Once the strong authority – the 'Leviathan' (from the Book of Job, Chapter 41, Old Testament: 'Leviathan' meaning a great sea beast – so the state by analogy is something which should be overwhelmingly powerful and awe-inspiring to people) – was established then the laws were the commands of the sovereign authority designed to maintain civil peace. Hobbes thus provided an account of law in terms of political and social needs. Austin and Bentham continued this tradition. Austin and Bentham first of all identified the sovereign in a society by considering 'habits of obedience' in that society and then in the tradition of Thomas Hobbes, identified the law as the 'commands of the sovereign'. If Austin and Bentham's account of law is too 'thin', i.e. lacks explanatory power, it is not because of the 'institutional' perspective they adopted with regard to law but because the terms they employed in their description of law – 'sovereign', 'habits of obedience', 'sanctions', 'commands' – were too few in number and too simplistic to give an adequate descriptive analysis of law and legal systems.

Austin and Bentham explained the nature of the political system and then proceed to explain the nature of law by placing it within the political system. HLA Hart continued that 'institutional' tradition by examining law against the context of social and political needs. For example, Hart has a famous 'fable' in *The Concept of Law* (1961) to show the general social benefits a system of law might bring to a society governed by social rules only. Those benefits include the ability to change rules quickly through Parliamentary amendment and procedures to determine the exact scope of a social rule through the setting up of a court structure. Hart also shows how different legal rules help to plan social life out of court through laws on contract, marriages and wills, for example. Hart's approach is to show how the institution of law cannot be understood without considering law against the background of the social and political matrix that the law operates in. Therefore, the 'lawyer's perspective' on law, although valuable for some purposes, is arbitrary as the ultimate viewpoint on law if not for the simple fact that law is a social institution.

With regard to the 'institutional perspective' it is important to make a further sub-division between legal philosophers. There is (a) the 'engaged' institutional perspective and (b) the detached or 'disengaged' perspective.

The 'engaged' institutional perspective is the viewpoint of the legal theorist who seeks to give an account of law from the wide institutional perspective, placing law in its wider political and social context, but who has some sort of commitment to, or endorsement of, a particular legal system or type of legal system. Examples of this type of approach are John Finnis in *Natural Law and Natural Rights* (1980), Dennis Galligan in *Law in Modern Society* (2007) and Neil MacCormick in *Institutions of Law* (2007). Finnis regards 'the central case' of law as being a rationally prescribed ordering by those in authority for the common good of that community. Finnis uses this ideal of law ('ideal' because given human limitations it is not fully realisable) as a standard, or a lens, through which to examine actual legal systems. Indeed Finnis would say that an adequate account of modern Western democratic legal systems (which generally seek to work for the common good) is not possible unless the theorist attends to the moral reasons which cause such legal systems to come into being and be sustained. In an essay entitled 'The Truth in Legal Positivism' (in *The Autonomy of Law*, edited by Robert George) Finnis argues:

> 'the reasons people have for establishing systems of positive law and for main-taining them include certain moral reasons, on which many of those people often act. And only those moral reasons suffice to explain why such people's undertaking takes the shape it does, giving legal systems the many defining fea-tures they have.'

Therefore, while Finnis adopts the 'institutional perspective' seeking to examine law in its wider social context he does so with a commitment to an ideal form of law (**'an ordering of reason for the common good'** – the definition of law provided by the father of natural law theory: St Thomas Aquinas in the thirteenth century) and a commitment to the Western style of democratic government under the rule of law, which at least tries to govern for the common good.

In a slightly different way Dennis Galligan has a strong commitment to a certain type of law – not an 'ideal' type favoured by Finnis, but what Galligan calls **'modern legal orders'**. As Galligan notes, such praiseworthy legal systems are few in number: the societies of Western Europe, North America, parts of the British Commonwealth and occasionally elsewhere. Galligan gives a full descriptive account of such legal systems in *Law in Modern Society* (2007). Such societies are governed by a rule of law which is taken seriously by government, and there is also a 'bond of trust' between legal officials, such as police, judges etc, and the public, which is a defining mark of such modern legal orders and is absent in the corruption-soaked officialdom of the rest of the world.[3] Galligan makes it clear in his concluding paragraph that he is writing the book to further the protection of modern legal orders. Galligan writes:

'Legal orders with the features charted and discussed here are of interest and importance compared with other types of legal orders, not for reasons of western truimphalism, but because they have been effective in producing social goods that are valued in western societies and beyond. They are at the same time fragile and unstable, so that if they are to be sustained they must first be understood.'

Neil MacCormick, in *Institutions of Law* (2007), focuses on constitutional law-states ('Rechstaat' in German) and MacCormick is himself committed in his description to the basic values of those, as he calls them, 'institutional normative orders'. MacCormick seeks to uphold the values of those 'law-States', few in number in the world, which are dedicated to the values of realising peace, justice and the common good under the rule of law. MacCormick's enterprise thus resembles Galligan's: to describe the features of a small number of constitutional law states, whilst being wholly committed to the values those few law-States uphold.

There is certainly a place in legal theory for the sort of standpoint that Finnis, MacCormick and Galligan occupy but it should not be the ultimate standpoint of the legal theorist. This is where the third standpoint comes into play – the detached 'institutional' or 'external' perspective.

William Twining notes in 'Institutions of Law from a Global Perspective' (in *Law as Institutional Normative Order*, edited by Del Mar and Bankowski (2009)) that:

'pluralism of beliefs and ideologies is a fact and that legal phenomena are immensely varied and complicated'

and as such the legal theorist, if he wants to achieve great generality in his account of law and legal systems, should not become engaged with, or committed to, a particular type of legal system. Professor Hart, in *The Concept of Law*, aimed to develop a descriptive theory of law that involved the standpoint of an external juristic observer and took into account the

....

3   Professor Galligan's account of the 'bond of trust' between legal officials such as police and judges and the general public being the defining mark of modern legal orders echoes the German sociologist Max Weber's view that in the modern era legal authority depended upon public acceptance of rational rules impartially applied by legal officials and crucially that the recognised authority of legal officials only extended to the point where they complied with the legal rules, that authority stopped where official corruption began. Therefore Max Weber (died 1920) in *Law in Economy and Society* and Galligan in *Law in Modern Society* (2007) both put forward a similar idea: that the acceptance of legal authority by the general public in Western democracies depends on a delicate 'pact of understanding': that the general public will accept the law and the authority of legal officialdom but the legal officials must apply the law in an impartial and corruption free manner. This explains why legal officials such as police officers caught out in serious corruption can expect heavy prison sentences because the authorities understand that public trust and co-operation in maintaining the rule of law is seriously threatened by corruption from legal officials.

'internal point of view' of participants in a legal system but did not claim to approve of or engage with any particular legal system. Hart's external or institutional 'detached' perspective is the most appropriate for an explanation of all legal systems, whether those legal systems are wicked, weak, corrupt, inefficient, incoherent, unjust or just plain indifferent.

For many, Hart's detached perspective will be the correct one to adopt if the observer is a sociologist, a comparative lawyer, an empirical researcher, an historian or if the politics of the observer are anarchistic in outlook. It should always be remembered that even in the most benign constitutional law state, **law is a product of other people's power** and this insight should caution against too ready an endorsement of any legal system.

Hart is sometimes accused of actually endorsing law, whilst at the same time pretending to maintain a detachment from law. The problem arises because of Hart's use of a story to describe the move from a pre-legal society to a society with law, and the benefits that might bring. Some have suggested (e.g. Roger Cotterrell in *The Politics of Jurisprudence* (2003)) that Hart is endorsing and encouraging some version of the rule of law for all societies. This view of Hart is a mistake. John Gardner explains in a 2010 Research paper 'Hart on Legality, Justice and Morality':

> 'In Chapter 5 of "The Concept of Law" Hart tells his brilliant and seminal fable of the emergence of a legal system (differentiated by its secondary rules of recognition, adjudication, and change) from an imagined pre-legal or proto-legal arrangement of customary primary rules alone. As a way of making such a development rationally intelligible, his narrative emphasises the gains in efficiency and predictability that these secondary norms bring with them. Unfortunately, to the lasting confusion of many readers, he thereby makes it sound like he is extolling the virtues of the transformation from proto-law to law. Not surprisingly, he is therefore taken to task by some critics for attempting to smuggle in a political ideology under cover of his supposedly ideology-neutral explanation of the nature of law. And that political ideology seems to many, not implausibly, to be none other than the ideology of the rule of law … For all its brilliance, then, Hart's fable is afflicted by severe and damaging presentational flaws. The secondary rules, Hart should have made clear, do not automatically bring with them the rule of law and, even for believers in the rule of law, their arrival is not necessarily to be welcomed. For life without any law at all might well be better than life with law but without the rule of law. The arrival of a legal system makes some forms of oppression possible, and others easier, and there is a further step to be taken to help protect against such law-enabled and law-facilitated oppression, namely the step from having a legal system to having a legal system under the rule of law.'

Hart was well aware of the costs, as well as the benefits, of law to a society. In a key passage for understanding Hart in *The Concept of Law* Hart comments of the dangers of law:

> **'the cost is the risk that the centrally organized power may well be used for the oppression of numbers with whose support it can dispense, in a way that the simpler regime of primary rules could not.'**

Hart's stance towards law was thus one of detachment – aware of the benefits law could bring to a society, but also aware of how law could also allow the more efficient and organised oppression of the population. In other words for Hart law was 'morally risky' and scholastic detachment was the correct intellectual response. Hart maintained, in the Postscript to the second edition of *The Concept of Law*, that it was futile to look for any purpose for law beyond guiding conduct. MacCormick in 'Why Law Makes No Claims' (in *Law, Rights and Discourse*, edited by Pavlakos (2007)) claims that:

> 'Law is for the securing of civil peace so far as possible.'

This Thomas Hobbes-inspired insight into law's function by MacCormick would perhaps have been too strong for Professor Hart who would go no further with any 'inherent' purpose or function of law than to declare in the 'Postscript' to the second edition of *The Concept of Law* (1994):

> 'my theory makes no claim to identify the point or purpose of law or legal practices as such … I think it quite vain to seek any more specific purpose which law serves beyond providing guides to human conduct and standards of criticism of such conduct.'

Aim Higher

Students can gain extra marks by locating the perspective on law that a particular legal theorist takes. Is the theorist describing law from the perspective of an ideal form of law, or describing law in neutrally descriptive terms, or is the theorist praising in his description of legal systems a particular form of legal ordering such as modern Western legal orders?

NOTES

The best account on 'perspectives in legal theory' is Professor Raz's essay 'The Nature of Law' in *Ethics in the Public Domain* (1994). Professor Hart's account of his own 'general and descriptive' methodology in legal theory can be found in the 'Postscript' of the second edition to *The Concept of Law* (1994), especially at pp. 239–241 and pp. 248–249. Professor Finnis's legal methodology can be discerned in Chapter 1 of *Natural Law and Natural Rights* (1980). D Galligan's 'engaged' description of modern legal orders can be found in *Law in Modern Society* (2007) and Neil MacCormick's 'engaged' description of modern constitutional 'law-states' can be found in *Institutions of Law* (2007).

2

The Nature of Law

INTRODUCTION

The purpose of legal theory as conceived by Professor Raz is to seek to uncover and explain the nature of law, so that the explanation of law covers law wherever law is found. As Raz comments in *The Authority of Law* (1979) at p. 105:

> 'Legal philosophy has to be content with those few features which all legal systems necessarily possess.'

Two essential features of law are (1) the 'sources' thesis – that the identification of law does not depend upon a moral argument and (2) the law's claim to legitimate moral authority. This second essential and inescapable feature of law is part of the explanation of one of the key concerns in jurisprudence – the 'normativity of law'. Of course Professor Dworkin has denied that legal theory is essentially about the 'essential' properties of law but rather Dworkin conceives that the proper function of legal theory is to justify the use of state coercion through law: see Dworkin, *Justice in Robes* (2006), p. 13. For Dworkin the 'nature of law' is not as central to legal theory as he conceives it to be.

However, it is possible to talk about the 'nature of law' in terms of law's essential properties and also the role law plays in modern Western societies. The institution of law may have, in modern Western societies, a much more expansive role than law's relation to societies in the past. Law in the past may have been mainly limited to the maintenance of law and order and the regulation of a few central aspects of social life such as marriage, contracts, wills etc. However, modern law in Western societies pervades deeply into social life in a way that would have astounded our ancestors. Symbolic of that penetration of law into the social space is the ban on smoking in public places which came into effect in 2007 as a result of the **Health Act 2006**. Law regulates the social life of the community much more than in the past. This is a feature of the 'nature of law' which should not be overlooked. This chapter also examines the issue as to whether the often made claim to authority by the law is actually a part of the nature or essence of law. The final question examines whether the Nazi regime (1933–1945) in Germany had a legal system or whether its organised brutality should not be dignified with the word 'law'.

Checklist

Ensure that you are acquainted with the following topics:

■ the role of law in the postmodern social environment;
■ law's deep penetration into the social life of the nation in the modern Western state;
■ the meaning of the phrase 'normativity of law';
■ the views of Kelsen, Bentham, Hart and Raz on the 'normativity of law';
■ the relationship between the 'normativity of law' and human rationality;
■ the importance, meaning and value of the 'rule of law';
■ the question whether the often-made claim to authority by the law is really part of law's nature or 'essence';
■ the issue of whether the Nazi regime had 'law'.

QUESTION 2

Discuss the role of law in the postmodern social environment.

How to Answer this Question

Law is traditionally analysed in legal theory as having great instrumental worth in achieving mighty social goals, such as civil peace or the co-ordination of society, but law's particular role in postmodern Western societies needs consideration. The collapse of faith in modern Western democracies in religion and political ideology has left a vacuum which is partly filled by the secular law. The law thus becomes an expression of social union in increasingly fragmented societies divided on ethnic, class and financial lines. Dworkin has argued that given the fragmentation of modern societies there is a great need for the law to speak with the voice of 'integrity': so that each citizen's position in the eyes of the law is defined by the same coherent principles. Law, thus conceived by Dworkin and others, almost becomes a substitute religion, a 'belief system' for a sceptical fragmented society.

Applying the Law

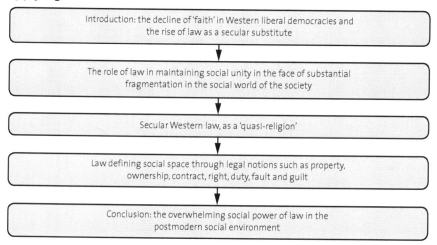

Introduction: the decline of 'faith' in Western liberal democracies and the rise of law as a secular substitute

↓

The role of law in maintaining social unity in the face of substantial fragmentation in the social world of the society

↓

Secular Western law, as a 'quasi-religion'

↓

Law defining social space through legal notions such as property, ownership, contract, right, duty, fault and guilt

↓

Conclusion: the overwhelming social power of law in the postmodern social environment

ANSWER

The law's claim to legitimate authority is not only a necessary feature of law wherever it is found but that claim by the law to an overarching authority is arguably necessary for the survival of modern Western societies in what is termed 'the post modern social environment'.

The condition of modern Western societies is such that widespread faith in political ideology, religious belief and even liberal progress itself have largely disappeared and into that 'faith' gap comes the law to provide a kind of secular certainty for people. As Bernard Lewis puts the point about religious faith in *The Crisis of Islam* (2003):

> 'most Muslim countries are still profoundly Muslim, in a way and in a sense that most Christian countries are no longer Christian.'[1]

Roger Cotterrell comments in *Law, Culture and Society* (2006):

> 'post modern ideas about the collapse of grand narratives might suggest that the authority or validity of all large-scale structures of knowledge has been put in question ... It could be argued that legitimacy through legality remains the only possibility of stable authority in the postmodern social environment' and Cotterrell comments of law's 'social power in a world that has lost faith in other discourses.'

The 'collapse of grand narratives' is a theme of postmodern writing on law, stressing how in the Western world public faith has been lost in the explanatory and justificatory power of political ideology, religious faith, even science itself. Jean-Francois Lyotard has put the matter thus: 'grand narratives have lost their credibility'. Thus in the Western world persons no longer believe in the narrative version of history provided by the Bible, Marx's 'Das Kapital' or even in the eventual solution of all mankind's problems by science. The law then provides a form of a substitute belief system for a society without shared beliefs. As the French writer Emmanuel Levy (1871–1944) comments, law is **'un substitut pratique de la religion' – a practical substitute for religion**.[2] However, although the law provides something to believe in a postmodern world, where faith has collapsed, it may not ultimately provide a real substitute for proper belief systems. As Cotterrell comments in *Living Law* (2008):

> 'in the most pessimistic post modern views, law may be all there is to believe in. But that is not much ... the endlessly pragmatic adjustment of regulation to increasing social complexity.'

---

1   Western societies may no longer be 'Christian' in terms of mass public observance of Christianity but the civilisation of the West is a product of Christianity as it affected Western societies for over a thousand years and the influence of Christianity in shaping the 'moral consciousness' of the West should not be underestimated.

2   On the idea of law or rather the idea of the 'rule of law' being a form of 'secular religion' see Lord Bingham's comment in *The Rule of Law* (2011) at p. 174: 'the concept of the rule of law ... in a world divided by differences of nationality, race, religion and wealth is one of the greatest unifying factors, perhaps the greatest, the nearest we are likely to approach to a universal secular religion.'

Indeed, modern statute law may be an appropriate object of belief for a morally empty consumer goods-obsessed modern world. As Cotterrell comments modern law's 'moral emptiness makes it a form of knowledge entirely appropriate to a morally empty world'. Modern statute law's transience, disposability and infinite adaptability mirrors the transience, disposability and infinite adaptability of the market-driven consumer society.

Naomi Mezey comments in 'Law as Culture' (2001) Yale Journal of Law and the Humanities of law's pervasive influence in modern life and the role law has in shaping modern culture:

> 'the pervasive power of law and excluding the possibility that there is an autonomous cultural realm that could be articulated without recourse to law. Here, culture is a colony in law's empire. "We live," as Ronald Dworkin puts it, "in and by the law. It makes us what we are: citizens and employees and doctors and spouses and people who own things." This version of law as culture is best exemplified by the realist insight, elaborated by critical legal scholars, that law operates even when it appears not to, that legal permissions and prohibitions are in force in the most intimate and non-legal relationships—indeed, that legal rules structure the very baseline from which we negotiate our lives and form our identities.'

Naomi Mezey points out how the Supreme Court ruling in *Miranda v Arizona* (1966) entered popular culture and shaped popular culture's understanding of the police role in interrogating suspects:

> 'The legal rule laid down in *Miranda* so effectively infiltrated cultural practice that forty years later the cultural embeddedness of *Miranda* warnings provided the justification for recognizing the constitutional status of the rule.
>
> In *Miranda*, the Court was confronted with the problem of confessions resulting from custodial interrogation practices by police that effectively infringed the privilege against self-incrimination afforded by the Fifth Amendment. The Court consciously sought a rule that would change culture in the narrow sense, by altering law-enforcement practices that ranged from the psychologically menacing to the physically brutal. By requiring that custodial interrogations begin with a warning to the suspect that "he has the right to remain silent, that anything he says can be used against him in a court of law, that he has the right to the presence of an attorney, and that if he cannot afford an attorney one will be appointed for him," the Court not only changed police practices, but also altered culture in the broadest sense – it created new meanings which circulated globally. The legal rule found its way not only into police stations, but into television stations, movies, children's games, as well as the popular imagination of Americans and foreigners alike. The *Miranda* warnings became part of culture.'

The point is made by Naomi Mezey of how law and culture are so closely intertwined in the United States, and that the cultural impact of the *Miranda* rule meant that the Supreme Court had in the *Dickerson v United States* (2000) case to recognise the *Miranda* rule as more than a 'rule of evidence' but part of the 'national culture' of the United

States which reveals just how culturally central 'law' is in the United States. Naomi Mezey said of the decision in *Dickerson v United States* (2000) which upheld the constitutional correctness of *Miranda v Arizona* (1966):

> 'The Supreme Court's reconsideration last term of its famous *Miranda* decision evinces the near-total entanglement of law and culture. At issue in *Dickerson* was whether the warnings spelled out in *Miranda* were required by the Fifth Amendment of the Constitution or were merely a prophylactic evidentiary rule meant to safe-guard constitutional rights, but not required by the Constitution itself. Despite some tough cases to the contrary the Court in *Dickerson* confirmed that *Miranda* was a constitutional decision entitled to 'stare decisis' protection and thus upheld it.

> Although the *Dickerson* majority appeared united by a commitment to 'stare decisis', it was an odd sort of 'stare decisis', in that the Court was faithful less to legal prece-dent, and more to what that precedent had come to signify in popular culture. After *Miranda*, law had transformed culture; in *Dickerson*, culture transformed law. The 'Dickerson' Court quickly and confidently declined to overrule *Miranda* because the decision *'has become embedded in routine police practice to the point where the warn-ings have become part of our national culture'*. Precisely because of its cultural ubi-quity, a decision that the Court, had been retreating from for some time was explicitly upheld, and upheld as a constitutional rule. The twist, however, is that the Court found that the warnings were constitutionally required not because the Constitution demanded them but because they had been popularized to the point that they were culturally understood as being constitutionally required.

> In *Dickerson*, the synthesis of law and culture is complete: Law became so thoroughly embedded in culture that culture became the rationale for law. While it is possible to read *Miranda* as a triumph of law over culture and *Dickerson* as a triumph of culture over law, I think such readings overlook the way in which both opinions participate in a broader narrative, in which law and culture are mutually constituted, and legal and cultural meanings are produced precisely at the intersection of the two domains, which are themselves only fictionally distinct.'

Law's social power in the postmodern social environment is that in an era of substantial social fragmentation and diversity the law of the state represents the 'last universal' – the symbol of a formal unity. Indeed Professor Dworkin draws on this idea of 'unity through the legal order' in modern Western democracies when he argues that law should have integrity as he defines the idea. Dworkin in *Justice in Robes* (2006) comments:

> 'Every contemporary democracy is a divided nation, and our democracy (USA) is par-ticularly divided. We are divided culturally, ethnically, politically and morally. We nevertheless aspire to live together as equals, and it seems absolutely crucial to that ambition that we also aspire that the principles under which we are governed treat us as equals.'

Therefore Dworkin is not merely maintaining that his vision of law as integrity is neces-sary to justify the coercive authority of the state as expressed through law, but that the very sustainability of a vastly diverse society depends on government through the rule of law.

In a 'world of strangers', which is the modern state, citizens of vastly different political, ethnic and belief systems can at least owe their primary allegiance to an impersonal, secular and impartial legal order of publicly administered rules. Leslie Green comments in 'Legality and Community' (*Oxford Journal of Legal Studies*):

> 'As other and narrower loyalties weaken citizens of modern states who have nothing else in common might look to the civic order itself as an expression of social union.'

The elevation of the law to an almost 'religious' status in modern society has been a very long process. Ian Ward comments in 'God, Terror and Law' (*Oxford Journal of Legal Studies*) of the Eighteenth Century Enlightenment:

> 'in the place of God, or at least alongside, was the law.'

For critics of Western society this deification of the law in Western societies is a symbol of deep moral crisis. The radical Islamic writer Abu Muhammed al-Maqdisi comments in his book *Democracy is a Religion*:

> 'Democracy is a religion that is not Allah's religion ... they and their followers rule according to the religion of democracy and the constitution's laws upon which the government is based ... Their master is their God, their big idols who approve or reject legislation.'

Indeed one aspect of law, namely human rights legislation, almost has the status of a 'world religion'. Indeed human rights law has been called 'the ideology at the end of history' (see Cotterrell, *Law, Culture and Society* (2006)). As John Tasioulas comments in *The Moral Reality of Human Rights* (2007): 'discourse of human rights has acquired in recent times ... the status of an ethical lingua franca'. As Professor Raz comments in *Human Rights in the Emerging World Order* (2010):

> 'human rights ... have become a distinctive ingredient in the emerging world order where they generate new channels for political action in the international arena.'

Law's power in the postmodern state derives from three factors:

(1) the widespread collapse in faith in political ideology, religion or even science to solve mankind's problems;
(2) law's backing by the coercive authority of the modern state, a coercive authority that is inescapable and ever present;
(3) the law's claim to be based on rationality, or at least the result of rational debate.

A final theme of postmodern writing on law has been on how the authority of law actually constitutes the social order. The law has the power to **'create the social'** in the consciousness of the population by shaping such ideas as property ownership, responsibility, contract, rights, fault and guilt. The authority of the law is, on this view, the very foundation of social life. This is not a particularly novel claim. Professor Raz wrote, back in 1979, in *The Authority of Law*:

> 'the law claims to provide the general framework for the conduct of all aspects of social life and sets itself up as the supreme guardian of society.'

Given that modern statute law is complex, technical and ever-changing it is not surprising that some doubt has been expressed whether natural law theory, with its emphasis on universal principles of natural law discoverable by reason, has much relevance to the image of modern statute law we are exploring here. Cotterrell in *The Politics of Jurisprudence* (2003) asks 'is natural law dead?' and penetratingly observes of the eclipse of natural law theory:

> 'The problem is that even if there are universal principles of natural law they may not offer a convincing guide or grounding for complex, highly technical, ever-changing modern law.'[3]

Law's role in the postmodern social environment as a complex, highly technical and ever-changing set of norms has the potency to test the continuing validity of one of the great schools of jurisprudential thought – namely natural law. Arguably natural law has little to say by way of guidance through so-called universal moral principles to a system of modern law that is complex, highly technical and ever-changing.

NOTES

Roger Cotterrell in *The Politics of Jurisprudence* (2003, 2nd edition) discusses the role of law in the postmodern social environment at pp. 250–257. Cotterrell returns to the same theme in *Law, Culture and Society: Legal Ideas in the Mirror of Social Theory* (2006), pp. 19–26. Cotterrell returns again to the role of law in the postmodern society in *Living Law* (2008), pp. 108–109 and see his essay on Emmanuel Levy at pp. 73–84 of *Living Law*.

QUESTION 3

Explain the 'normativity' of law.

How to Answer this Question

This question involves discussion of the important jurisprudential question of how the law is normative – the 'normativity' of law: its 'oughtness', its bindingness. The sanction-based explanation of the law's normativity offered by Bentham and Austin has been widely discredited. Kelsen's career-long efforts to explain the law's normativity through

---

3   Modern law can be highly complex and technical and the vague principles of natural law (if they do indeed exist) are very unlikely to provide any guidance at all to legislators. Lord Bingham in *The Rule of Law (2011)* comments that: 'it seems that legislative hyperactivity has become a permanent feature of our governance … the subject matter of much legislation is inevitably very complex.'

the basic norm (or 'grundnorm') occupies the greater part of his legal theory. The most satisfactory account of the law's normativity resides with Professor Hart and Professor Raz. Hart's idea, drawn from the seventeenth century's Thomas Hobbes, explains law as a 'peremptory, content-independent norm'. In other words the fact that a law is issued from an authoritative source is meant in itself to be a binding reason to obey that law on the part of citizens. As Hobbes said in Chapter 25 of his *Leviathan* (1651):

> 'Command is when a man saith do this or do not do this yet without expecting any other reason than the will of him that saith it.'

As Hart comments:

> 'For to have such authority is to have one's expression of intention as to the actions of others accepted as peremptory content independent reasons for action.'

The word 'peremptory' means just cutting off deliberation, debate or argument and the word with this meaning came into the English language from Roman law. Therefore the law-maker's expression of will is not intended to function within the hearer's deliberations as another ordinary reason for doing the act but the law promulgated by authority is intended to function as the overriding reason for doing or not doing the required or prohibited act. Professor Hart means by 'content independent' that the bindingness, the 'normativity' of the law, does not depend upon the content of the law – what the law actually commands – but rather that the 'normativity' of the law is due to its promulgation by an authority with the authority to issue laws to the populace: the 'bindingness' of the law does not depend on whether the law commands the morally good or the morally bad, but rather it is the fact of authoritative promulgation in itself that is meant to bind citizens.

Hart's account of the normativity of law (such an account of the 'normativity' of law is not found in the *The Concept of Law* (1961): where Hart merely describes the linguistic difference between being 'obliged' to do something by a gangster and being under an 'obligation' of law) found in *Essays on Bentham* (1982) resembles closely Professor Raz's idea of the law as offering the citizens 'exclusionary reasons for action'. An 'exclusionary reason' is meant to exclude other valid reasons for not complying with the exclusionary reason emanating from authority. Raz argues that law by its nature claims legitimate moral authority in that it purports to give the law's subjects exclusionary reasons for compliance with the law's edicts. Whether the law has in fact such legitimate moral authority is a different question.

The answer to the puzzle of the law's normativity lies in the law's self-image, what the law itself claims: the law claims to be a structure of legitimate moral authority and it is this claim which is intended to bind citizens and explains the 'oughtness' of law: law's 'normativity'.

Applying the Law

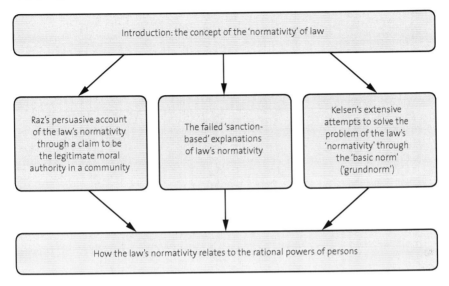

Introduction: the concept of the 'normativity' of law

Raz's persuasive account of the law's normativity through a claim to be the legitimate moral authority in a community

The failed 'sanction-based' explanations of law's normativity

Kelsen's extensive attempts to solve the problem of the law's 'normativity' through the 'basic norm' ('grundnorm')

How the law's normativity relates to the rational powers of persons

ANSWER

June 2009 marked the publication of the second edition of Professor Raz's *The Authority of Law*. The central argument of Raz's work into the nature of law has been the law's claim to authority over the society it purports to govern. The law's claim to authority is presented as a conceptual truth about the essence or nature of law wherever it is found in human societies.[4]

For Raz the law's claim to authority helps to explain a central puzzle of legal theory, namely the normativity of law. The question about the normativity of law is the question of what sense to give to the bindingness of law, its duty imposing nature. In other words, what sense can be given to the mystery 'oughtness' of law. The law is a realm of obligation and duty, the law acts not as our advisor but as an authority that must be obeyed. By framing the answer to the law's normativity in terms of what the law itself claims over its subjects, law's self-image, then Raz, by stating that the law by its nature claims legitimate authority, provides a coherent account of the law's normativity.

According to Raz the law claims to bind its subjects by offering them 'exclusionary reasons' for action. In other words it is the fact that a law has been issued from a recognised authority in that society that is meant to be taken by citizens as a standard for the conduct of the individual to the exclusion of any reasons, moral or personal that the citizen may have for non-compliance with that particular law.

4   The question whether the law's claim to legitimate authority is part of the conceptual truth about law is explored in Question 5 in this book.

Two points need to be made at this stage, concerning the alleged claim to legitimate authority of the law wherever it is found, suggested by Raz:

(1)   the fact that the law claims authority over persons in a particular society does not entail that the law actually has legitimate authority in any given society. Raz argues that the law often claims more than can be morally justified. Raz has argued that the actual legitimate reach of any legal system calls for careful reflection. Raz argues that law, by its nature, claims legitimate authority not that it in fact has such legitimate authority. A person can claim something without actually having the legitimacy to make that claim for example;

(2)   the argument by Raz that the law claims authority seems to involve a strange personification of a non-living entity. How can 'the law' claim anything in the sense that a person may make a claim? Indeed in an article entitled 'Why Law Makes No Claims' (in *Law, Rights and Discourse*, edited by Pavlakos (2007)) Neil MacCormick claims that the law is a state of affairs which cannot make claims: 'law claims nothing'. MacCormick is right in maintaining that law as such is incapable of raising, in a literal sense, any claim. In a literal sense claims can be raised only by subjects having the capacity to speak or act. However Raz means that legal officials (particularly judges) talk as if, and act as if, they have the legitimate authority which the law grants them. Law can and does raise a claim to legitimate authority for the claim is made by the law's representatives. As Raz comments in *The Authority of Law*, second edition:

> 'the law claims to have legitimate authority, in the sense that legal institutions both act as if they have such authority, and articulate the view that they have it.'

Those writers, such as Austin and Bentham, who viewed law as a species of command from a sovereign to an inferior, held that law's normativity, its 'bindingness', resided in the threat of the application of coercion from the sovereign in the light of the subject's non-compliance. However, as Raz persuasively argues in *Practical Reason and Norms* (1990) the 'sanction-based' account of law's normativity is not adequate to explain how the law binds its subjects. As Raz comments:

> 'the fact that so far as sanctions go the law is merely an auxiliary reason is not intended to belittle the importance of legal sanctions. They are a most important means of securing social co-ordination and of providing people with reasons for conforming to the law … But the fact that a law is backed by a sanction is never an exclusionary reason. It is a simple first-order reason. The inevitable conclusion is that, despite the undoubted importance of sanctions and the use of force to enforce them in all human legal systems, the sanction-directed attempt to explain the normativity of law leads to a dead-end.'

Raz's argument boils down to this: although sanctions imposed by authorities for non-compliance to laws are important, the law in fact intends its subjects to comply with its edicts because they are precisely the law's edicts irrespective of any sanction for non-compliance.

Another major attempt to explain law's normativity is to be found in Kelsen's idea of the basic norm, or in German 'the grundnorm'. Kelsen argued that it was necessary for anyone who accepted the 'normativity' of a particular legal system to presuppose that the legal system was valid, in other words for an individual to accept the normativity of a legal system he had to assume that there was a basic norm which gave normative charge to the whole legal system.[5] Neil MacCormick in *Institutions of Law* (2007) comments approvingly of Kelsen:

> 'the most basic understanding of norms ought to be in terms of the norm-user … Hans Kelsen after tackling heroically the great mystery of the ought, increasingly fell away from his initial insight.'

Kelsen explained the foundational significance of the basic norm to his own pure theory of law in *Introduction to the Problems of Legal Theory* (1934):

> 'the pure theory of law works with this basic norm as a hypothetical foundation. Given the presupposition that the basic norm is valid, the legal system resting on it is also valid. The basic norm confers on the act of the first legislator – and thus on all other acts of the legal system resting on this first act – the sense of "ought" … rooted in the basic norm, ultimately is the normative import of all the material facts consisting the legal system.'

For Kelsen the 'basic norm' gave sense to normative statements such as 'the law says X ought to be done'. Kelsen was fond of drawing parallels between his basic norm and religious faith. Although many persons do not believe in God, those persons who **do believe** in God presuppose in their religious faith the basic norm that 'God's commandments ought to be obeyed'. Similarly those who have 'faith' or 'belief' in the justified normativity of their own legal system presuppose a basic norm that the constitution of that legal system ought to be obeyed. In other words normativity like beauty is in 'the eye (or rather mind) of the beholder'. Two points need to be made concerning 'the basic norm':

(1) the basic norm is never created by any law creating body, it is not created by anyone, it is merely a presupposition of someone who believes in the legal system of a state (and for Kelsen the legal system and state were synonymous). As Kelsen explains:

> 'the Pure Theory aims simply to raise to the level of consciousness what all jurists are doing (for the most part unwittingly) when … they understand the positive law as a valid system.'

Unlike all other norms in a legal system the basic norm is not created but found in the consciousness of a person who believes the coercive order of his state is a valid legal order.

---

5   It is possible to refer to the 'grundnorm 'as the 'juristic God' the 'law deity' since some believe and some do not and only for believers does the law have 'normativity.' Law, then, is a kind of 'leap in faith' which anarchists refuse to make.

Therefore, the demands of the gangster and the taxman can be distinguished: those subject to the demands of the gangster do not presuppose such demands are valid, whereas those who are subject to the demands of the taxman can see them as valid if they see them as part of a valid legal order justified by the basic norm in the person's consciousness.

(2) Kelsen was keen to stress that it is not necessary to accept the basic norm of any legal system. Kelsen's aim was to try and explain what a person meant when they said they accepted a coercive order as a valid legal order – Kelsen's answer was deceptively simple: that person accepted the basic norm of his legal system. However Kelsen allowed for the fact that the anarchist, for example, rejected the validity of all legal systems and saw in law only coercive order. However not all persons are anarchists and Kelsen's basic norm offered an account of how a person could interpret the coercive order of his state as a valid legal order.

Kelsen seeks to explain the normativity of law by viewing the answer through the lens of how the law's subjects, the citizens, view the legal system. This is perhaps getting the issue the wrong way round and it is more fruitful to ask, with Professor Raz, what the law claims itself, the law's self-image holding the key to explaining law's normativity: the law is normative because it claims legitimate authority. Whether that normativity is justified is a separate question.

The key to the normativity of law is in the law claiming to provide valid reasons for action. Following the approach of Raz all normative phenomena, such as morality or the law, are normative because they provide persons with reasons for action. This explanation of law's normativity coheres well with the status of persons as rational agents. As John Gardner comments in 'Nearly Natural Law' (*American Journal of Jurisprudence* (2007)):

'we human beings are rational beings. We have a highly developed capacity to respond to reasons. This is an important aspect of our nature ... Our highly developed capacity to respond to reasons includes the capacity to use norms to guide our actions.'

Neil MacCormick in *Institutions of Law* (2007) comments in a similar vein that response to norms is inherent within humans:

'human beings are through-and-through norm-users, capable of achieving a kind of voluntary order among themselves by common observance of common orders.'

Indeed, MacCormick gives a definition of law in terms of normativity; law is for MacCormick 'an institutional normative order' and 'a normative order is possible, because humans are norm-users'.

The explanation of the normativity of law provided by Raz in that the law claims to provide 'exclusionary' reasons for action, i.e. legitimate authority fits the way in which law acts in the practical reasoning of rational persons to a much greater degree than the sanction backed model of law provided by Austin or Bentham or the concept of the 'basic norm' offered by Kelsen.

Indeed, following Raz's analysis, the idea of acting on reasons provided by the law not only is consistent with the actual role played by law in a rational individual's practical reasoning but indeed responding to reasons is also constitutive of being a person, for we engage with the world through our reason-driven intentions. Our rational powers, which the law employs when it directs its orders at us, are constitutive of personhood itself. Therefore the question concerning the 'normativity of law' strikes at the very essence of what it means to be a person.[6]

Aim Higher

Students can gain extra marks by noting that the 'normativity of law' is one of the most important topics in legal theory. Students will note that Kelsen's explanation of normativity in terms of the 'basic norm' (grundnorm) has attracted the most attention in terms of Kelsen's legal philosophy. Students can avoid the pitfall of thinking that the command theory of law espoused by Austin and Bentham explains the 'normativity of law' satisfactorily, when in fact that theory empties the law of normativity by making the bindingness of law turn on the existence of sanctions.

NOTES

Professor Raz's demolition of the 'sanction-based' account of normativity offered by Bentham and Austin is found in *Practical Reason and Norms* (2nd edition, 1990), pp. 161–162. Professor Hart's account of law's normativity (not to be found in *The Concept of Law* (1961): which may be regarded as one of the crucial omissions of that flawed masterwork) is to be found in *Essays on Bentham* (1982), pp. 244–258: Hart's account of a law as a 'peremptory content-independent norm' is very similar to Raz's idea of law as an 'exclusionary reason for action'. A very readable account of Kelsen's lifelong attempt to explain the normativity of law is to be found in the online and free *Stanford Encyclopedia of Philosophy*, an essay by Andrei Marmor entitled 'The Pure Theory of Law': http://plato. stanford.edu/entries/lawphil-theory/

QUESTION 4 -

Is it a conceptual truth about law, part of the essence of law, that the law always claims legitimate authority?

- -

6   Professor Raz notes In his recent book *From Normativity to Responsibility* (2011) that 'the key to normativity is in the concept of following a reason … so long as we are persons we engage with reasons' and Raz claims: 'what is the hold reasons have on us? The answer was that we cannot ignore them because we are persons … because rational powers are constitutive of personhood.'

How to Answer this Question

The law often claims authority through the actions and words of legal officials. When judges sentence a criminal to 10 years in prison this is a direct exercise of authority by the judge 'in the name of the law'. It is no use saying (as some legal theorists have done such as Neil MacCormick) that the law cannot claim anything since the law is not a living entity and only living entities can make 'claims'. The law does claim authority through legal officials such as judges acting as if they had authority given them by the law. In the same way a corporation or company can make claims through its chief executives when they for example issue legal proceedings on the company's behalf. There is nothing strange or incoherent about the proposition that the law makes claims of authority if we regard the judges and police officers making such claims as 'executives' or 'agents' of the corporation we term 'the law'.

However the crucial point is whether the law's claim to legitimate authority, which is a day-to-day phenomenon of any legal system which functions, is actually part of the 'essence' of law, part of the conceptual nature of law. Professor Raz has argued consistently that the law's claim to legitimate authority is indeed a 'hallmark' of law, part of the very essence of what law is: see Raz, *The Authority of Law* (2009, 2nd edition). Some legal theorists have taken issue with Raz's conceptual claim about the law's claim to legitimate authority. To make one point crystal clear, Raz is not saying every legal system has legitimate authority (Raz would view very few legal systems as possessing legitimate moral authority) rather that every legal system claims such authority. Professor Dworkin, in *Justice in Robes* (2006) argues that Raz has wrongly inferred from the fact that legal officials very often, daily in fact, claim authority to this fact being part of the essence or conceptual truth about law. Dworkin implies that it would be possible to have a legal system where no legal official makes any claim of legitimate authority. Raz would say that such a 'system' would not be a 'legal' system if it did not claim in any way legitimate authority. Matthew Kramer in *In Defense of Legal Positivism* (2003) tries to imagine a territory controlled by gangsters (such as the Sicilian Mafia) which held long-term sway over citizens but did not claim legitimate authority. Kramer argues if the norms issued by the Mafia were general, stable and durable then why not say it was a 'legal system?' In other words Kramer, like Dworkin, denies that the law's claim to legitimate authority is part of the very essence of law, so that its absence means a system of norms is not a 'legal' system. Raz would respond that if the Mafia did not claim legitimate authority over its territory it would remain a system of norms run by the Mafia but not a 'legal' system.

Applying the Law

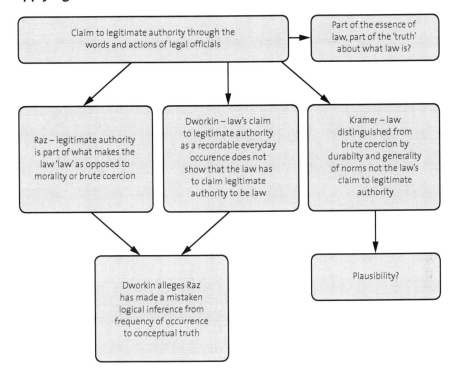

Claim to legitimate authority through the words and actions of legal officials

Part of the essence of law, part of the 'truth' about what law is?

Raz – legitimate authority is part of what makes the law 'law' as opposed to morality or brute coercion

Dworkin – law's claim to legitimate authority as a recordable everyday occurence does not show that the law has to claim legitimate authority to be law

Kramer – law distinguished from brute coercion by durabilty and generality of norms not the law's claim to legitimate authority

Dworkin alleges Raz has made a mistaken logical inference from frequency of occurrence to conceptual truth

Plausibility?

ANSWER

The argument that law by its very nature claims legitimate authority is a thesis that recurs often in the writings of Raz. In the *Authority of Law* (1979) Raz writes:

> 'The law-unlike the threats of the highwayman-claims to itself legitimacy. The law presents itself as justified and demands not only the obedience but the allegiance of its subjects.'

In *The Morality of Freedom* (1986) Raz argues in a similar vein that legal authorities 'claim a right to rule'.

In this way Raz can distinguish between the demands of a gangster and the demands of a legal system only the latter claims legitimate moral authority. Raz writes in *Ethics in the Public Domain* (1994):

> 'the significance of the law's claim to authority is ... in its distinctive moral aspect. This is a point missed ... by those who regard the law as a gunman situation writ large.'

For Raz the law's claim to legitimate authority is an important part of what turns a mere 'system of rules' into a 'legal system'. Without the law's claim to legitimate authority a system of rules would remain that and never become a 'legal system'.

Raz has always been careful to distinguish the issues of the law's claim to moral authority and whether a particular legal system has the moral authority it claims or indeed any moral authority at all. However some legal theorists, notably Ronald Dworkin (*Justice in Robes'* (1996)) and Matthew Kramer (*In Defense of Legal Positivism* (1999)), have argued that Raz is wrong to argue that it is a conceptual truth about law or part of law's essence that the law always claims legitimate authority. In other words they argue that Raz is wrong to claim that a legal system could not be a legal system without a claim to legitimate authority over the territory it purports to govern.

Professor Dworkin argues in *Justice in Robes* (1996) that although legal officials very often claim legitimate authority (for example judges sentence criminals to imprisonment in the name of lawful authority), it is not (Dworkin argues) the case that the law's claim to legitimate authority is a necessary feature for a legal system to exist. In other words Dworkin denies that the law's claim to moral authority is a conceptual truth about law, an important part of what makes a system of rules a 'legal system'. Dworkin argues in *Justice in Robes* (1996):

> 'Raz declares first, that it is part of the very concept of law that law claims legitimate authority … What can it mean to say that "the law" claims legitimate authority? He sometimes suggests that when he says that "law" claims legitimate authority he means that legal officials claim that authority; legal officials argues Raz, do this when they insist that they have a "right" to impose obligations on citizens and that these citizens "owe them allegiance" and "ought to obey the law". It is one thing to suppose that legal officials often make such claims of legitimate authority; it is quite another to suppose that unless they make such claims there is necessarily no law.'

Dworkin is saying that since Raz asserts that it is of the very essence of law that it claims legitimate moral authority and that this claim only has meaning if legal officials such as judges act and talk as if the law had such legitimate moral authority then if judges in a particular country do not actually assert that the law has legitimate authority then Dworkin argues the conclusion is that such a country has no law, which is an absurd conclusion. Dworkin is basically saying that Raz's claim that it is of the very essence or conceptual truth about law that it claim's legitimate moral authority leads to absurd conclusions. Dworkin argues that it is one thing to say that legal officials often do claim legitimate authority and another thing entirely to say that a legal system is not a legal system unless legal officials do claim legitimate authority. For Dworkin then law's claim to legitimate authority is a contingent claim (we can accept that legal officials very often do claim legitimate authority in what they say and do whilst performing their legal functions such as a judge sentencing criminals) but not a conceptual claim about the nature of law itself. In other words Dworkin leaves open the theoretical possibility of a legal system where legal officials do not make any claims to legitimate authority. Raz would deny this possibility, for him legal systems by their nature always claim legitimate authority through legal officials acting and speaking as if they had legitimate authority.

Dworkin does not deny that legal officials often make claims of legitimate authority in their work of administering the law but that it is a conceptual mistake or logical error to build the existence of such legal official claims to legitimate authority into your definition of what law is as Raz does. For Dworkin law can exist even if no legal official in that country asserts the legitimate authority of the law. This could happen if for example the population is very small, homogeneous, well integrated and culturally accustomed to obeying the law without the need for the legal officials in that country to exert claims of legitimate authority. Raz would be forced to say that such a country has no legal system despite the existence of courts, legislatures and legal officials because no legal official has to assert the legitimate authority of the legal system because the small population is very co-operative and well socialised.

Perhaps then the law's claim to legitimate authority is not, as Raz claims to the contrary, part of the essence of what law is. The law's claim to legitimate authority is therefore a contingent not a conceptual truth about the nature of law for Dworkin. Raz might reply that if a system of rules administered by courts and made by a legislature does not through its legal officials claim legitimate authority then despite appearances it is not a 'legal system' but rather a system of customary rules which helps to guide society but does not claim supreme authority over that society. In an article entitled 'Inclusive Legal Positivism' by Kenneth Himma in *The Oxford Handbook of Jurisprudence and Philosophy of Law* (2002) Himma, summarising Raz, says that for Raz part of the nature of law is the law's claim to legitimate authority. Himma says that Raz would concede that we would not notice any difference in the day-to-day functioning of a legal system called 'S' if it abandoned any claim to legitimate authority (the judges would still sit in court, the legislature would still pass laws) but Raz would argue that the abandonment of any claim to legitimate authority would mean the abandonment of 'S's' status as a 'legal' system. Whatever other names we would wish to call 'S' it cannot be called a 'legal system' if it abandoned its claim to legitimate authority. Himma says that in order to rebut Raz is to provide an example of a system of rules that makes no claim to legitimate authority yet is 'plausibly characterized' as a 'legal system'. The problem for this idea of Himma's to rebut Raz is that Raz would say to any example that could be provided of a 'system of rules' that did not claim legitimate authority but was 'plausibly characterized' as a legal system: 'It may look like a legal system with courts and legislature but if it does not claim legitimate authority it is not a legal system despite appearances.'

Matthew Kramer in a book entitled *In Defense of Legal Positivism* (1999) seeks to show that Raz is wrong in arguing that all legal systems must make a claim to legitimate authority to count as 'legal systems'. Kramer comments:

> 'Raz has erred in repeatedly insisting that an evil legal regime must claim to be morally authoritative if it is to qualify as a legal system at all (by dint of being distinguishable from the nakedly coercive sway of a gunman).'

Kramer argues that the claim to legitimate authority is 'extrinsic' to the nature of law, in other words Kramer like Dworkin argues that the claim to legitimate authority is not part of the 'nature' or 'essence' of law. Kramer argues that 'the decisive difference between law and raw coercion lies not in any such claim (to legitimate authority) but in the 'sway of norms'. Kramer explains what he means by a legal system being distinguished from a gunman 'by the sway of norms':

> 'Whereas the ascendance of a gunman over his victims typically involves situation-specific orders rather than any general decrees of standards, a regime of law must involve the reign and application of general norms if it is to be properly classifiable as a regime of law.'

Kramer develops his idea of an evil legal system being distinguished from the orders of a gangster by the 'sway of norms' rather than a claim to legitimate authority. Kramer says:

> 'Whereas a gunman almost always issues his orders to a highly limited set of people for a highly limited stretch of time, a system of governance that counts as a fully-fledged legal regime will have imposed its requirements through various sorts norms (statutes, regulations, judicial principles, and so forth) that typically apply to indefinitely numerous people for long periods of time. Those norms together cover a far, far wider range of behaviour than do the usual instructions of a gunman.'

So for Kramer what distinguishes an evil legal system from the demands of a gangster is the 'sway of norms' – the fact that the gunman's direction of his victim's behaviour is typically much more limited in its scope and much less systematic or regularised in its occurrence than the norms of a legal system. Laws, by contrast, extend to general classes of people and to general modes of conduct, and they typically last for long periods.

Kramer can then move from his argument that what distinguishes a legal system from the demands of a gangster is the 'sway of norms' and not any claim to legitimate author-ity to an argument that it is possible to imagine a legal system that does not claim legiti-mate authority. Kramer asks us to imagine an organised-crime syndicate such as the Mafia which might well exert control over most aspects of life in a certain region, with dictates that are just as broadly applicable and lasting as the mandates of a legal system. Kramer asks us the crucial question: 'whether a designation as a legal system should be withheld simply because the crime syndicate does not claim to moral worthiness i.e. makes no claim to legitimate authority?' Kramer argues that a claim to moral legiti-macy is not a decisive factor. Instead for Kramer the key factors in distinguishing a legal system are the generality and durability of the Mafia's norms, and the institutional regu-larity of the application of those norms. Kramer comments:

> 'if the Mafia's system of exerting far-reaching control over people's lives does indeed very substantially partake of the key qualities (of generality and durability) and if it also meets some relevant test for efficacy (such as obedience by the bulk of the population) then it ought to be classified as a legal system.'[7]

---

7   It seems intuitively implausible to say that a Mafia system of social control (as may have actually hap-pened in Sicily in the past) is a 'legal system'.

Kramer admits that 'the notion of an organized-crime syndicate as a legal regime may initially seem outlandish' but says that the 'strangeness' of the notion derives chiefly from the unlikelihood that such a syndicate will indeed establish a system of social control that exhibits the essential features of law. Kramer says that gangsters do not usually rule over virtually all aspects of social and individual life in a given region and even if they do manage to gain comprehensive control, they are likely to retain such power for too brief a period to develop a full-blown legal regime with its formal and institutional characteristics. However Kramer says that should, however implausible, the Mafia come to exert comprehensive reign over the populace of some territory via norms that are general and durable and regularly applied, the evil reign of the syndicate should be designated a legal system irrespective of a claim by the Mafia to legitimate moral authority. Raz would say in response that until the 'Mafia system' in control of a territory actually asserts legitimate moral authority, in other words until the Mafia claim legitimate authority there is not a 'legal system' only very well organised coercion.[8]

Common Pitfalls

Professor Raz is not simply arguing that the law very often makes claims of legitimate authority but that the law's claim to legitimate authority is part of the conceptual truth about what law is. Also Raz is not saying all legal systems actually have legitimate authority only that all legal systems claim legitimate authority. The issue of whether a particular legal system has the authority it claims has to be answered by looking at the socio-political structure of the society in which that legal system operates.

NOTES

Professor Raz in *The Authority of Law* (2009, 2nd edition) claims at p. 331: 'I have argued that the law claims to have legitimate authority, in the sense that legal institutions both act as if they have such authority, and articulate the view that they have it'. Professor Dworkin's rebuttal of Raz's view is to be found in *Justice in Robes* (2006) at pp. 199–200. Dworkin comments against Raz: 'It is one thing to suppose that legal officials often make such claims (of legitimate authority); it is quite another to suppose that unless they make such claims there is necessarily no law.' Matthew Kramer's views against Raz on this topic are found in *In Defense of Legal Positivism* (1999) at pp. 92–98. Kramer says what distinguishes law from the demands of a gangster is in the generality and durability of norms of a legal system, what Kramer terms the 'sway of norms' and definitely not any claim to legitimate authority.

....

8   Professor Raz has made the claim that the law's claim to legitimate authority for a very long time. In *The Authority of Law* (1979) Raz comments at p. 30: 'for it is an essential feature of law that it claims legitimate authority'.

QUESTION 5

Did the Nazis have law?

How to Answer this Question

Law as a concept has certain connotations of equality, fairness and justice, what Marx called 'the conception of right' which is part of the general understanding of what law is. The issue then is: is it right to dignify the Nazi terror machine with the words 'law' and 'legal system?' Gustav Radbruch, a German jurist who had lived through the horrors of Germany's Nazi past, believed that an exaggerated German conception of 'legality' and concern for 'correct procedures' at the expense of moral content of orders had contributed to a legal atmosphere where too few German lawyers had stood up to the Nazi regime. Radbruch, after the Second World War, argued that as part of the conception of legality, what was 'legal' should include basic principles of humanitarian morality. Radbruch argued that if a law violated fundamental principles of humanitarian morality it was not a 'law' and that consequently the Nazis did not have a 'legal system'. Professor Hart argued that this was misguided and it was better to say, to avoid confusion that the Nazis had 'law', that it had no moral force because it was radically evil. Lon Fuller argued that the procedural defects of Nazi law that such laws were often secret, demanded the impossible were internally inconsistent with one another meant that we cannot say Nazi norms formed a 'legal system'. Professor Dworkin provides the most subtle response to whether Nazis had law in that Dworkin insists that 'context' is vital: if we are saying that Nazi law was one strand in the historical story we call 'law' then plainly the Nazis had law. If, however, Dworkin says we are trying to make an 'interpretive' judgment about whether Nazi law provided any moral justification for Nazi coercion we have to say that the Nazis did not have law, if we mean by 'law' a social practice designed to justify the coercive power of the state – clearly Nazi law did not provide any moral justification for Nazi crimes.

Applying the Law

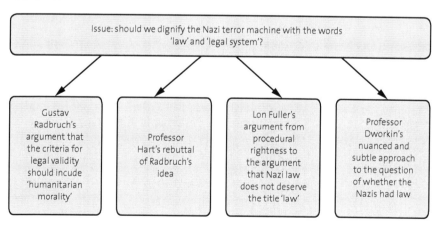

Issue: should we dignify the Nazi terror machine with the words 'law' and 'legal system'?

| Gustav Radbruch's argument that the criteria for legal validity should include 'humanitarian morality' | Professor Hart's rebuttal of Radbruch's idea | Lon Fuller's argument from procedural rightness to the argument that Nazi law does not deserve the title 'law' | Professor Dworkin's nuanced and subtle approach to the question of whether the Nazis had law |

ANSWER

The Nazi regime in Germany (1933–1945) has become, since the Second World War, an archetype for state evil, perhaps the most barbarous tyranny the world has seen. The question that has arisen for jurists is: did the Nazis have law? The concept of law has certain connotations of justice, procedural due process and fairness which seem wholly inappropriate to bestow on the Nazis regime of organised brutality and mass extermination of the innocent. Yet the Nazis did have courts, lawyers, statutes and legislatures, can it be wholly right to say that they had no law, no legal system?

The debate must begin with the views of Gustav Radbruch (1878–1949) a prominent German legal theorist[9] who, in the aftermath of the Second World War, famously argued that a sufficiently unjust or evil legal rule loses its status as a valid legal norm. For Radbruch, writing after the horrors of Nazi rule had ended in 1945, a legal rule or for that matter a legal system which violated fundamental precepts of humanitarian morality was not law or a legal system at all. As Brian Bix comments in 'Radbruch's Formula and Conceptual Analysis':

> 'The Second World War and the evil done during that period in his native Germany, often under the rubric of law, deeply affected Radbruch. In works written right after the war, Radbruch offered ideas about the connection between the moral merits of a purported legal rule and its legal validity, that would become highly influential.'

Radbruch wrote in *Statutory Lawlessness and Supra-Statutory Law* (originally published 1946):

> 'Where there is not even at attempt at justice, where equality, the core of justice, is deliberately betrayed in the issuance of positive law, then the statute is not merely "flawed law", it lacks completely the very nature of law. For law, including positive law, cannot be otherwise defined than as a system and an institution whose very meaning is to serve justice.'

Therefore, revolted by the experience of Nazism and convinced as a lawyer himself in Germany that Nazi judges were able to apply evil law because of their trained instinct to separate legal from moral questions, Radbruch after the war reconsidered his pre-war 'positivist' position that a law was a law irrespective of its moral defectiveness. Professor Hart, who considered Radbruch's post-Second World War views in Hart's 1958 article 'Positivism and the Separation of Law and Morals' commented that Radbruch believed the dominant

---

9   Gustav Radbruch is sometimes termed a 'natural lawyer' because he makes the ultimate legal validity of legal norms turn on whether they conform to principles of 'humanitarian morality'. However Radbruch is not in the tradition of natural law thinkers such as Thomas Aquinas, John Locke or Sir William Blackstone who all believe that human law derives all its authority from a link to God given 'natural' law. Radbruch is not a natural law theorist but rather puts forward a stark and simple principle for humanitarian judicial decision: if a legal rule violates principles of basic humanitarian morality then the judge should not apply it, indeed the judge should not recognise such a rule as law if it violates humanitarian morality. Gustav Radbruch has not so much a 'theory of law' as a principle for humanitarian judicial decision making.

legal theory in Germany before the war that 'law is law' had in some way contributed to the rise and dominance of the Nazi regime. Hart commented in his 1958 article:

> 'Radbruch had concluded from the ease with which the Nazi regime had exploited subservience to mere law – expressed, as he thought, in the positivist slogan "law as law" (Gesetz als Gesetz) – and from the failure of the German legal profession to protest against the enormities which they were required to perpetrate in the name of law, that "positivism" (meaning here the insistence on the separation of law as it is from law as it ought to be) had powerfully contributed to the horrors. His considered reflections led him to the doctrine that the fundamental principles of humanitarian morality were part of the very concept of Recht or Legality and that no positive enactment or statute, however clearly it was expressed and however clearly it conformed with the formal criteria of validity of a given legal system could be valid if it contravened principles of morality … the doctrine meant that every lawyer and judge should denounce statutes that transgressed the fundamental principles not as merely immoral or wrong but has having no legal character, and enactments which on this ground lack the quality of law should not be taken into account in working out the legal position of any given individual in particular circumstances.'

Therefore Radbruch had, in Hart's phrase, a 'striking recantation' of his pre-War view that law is law and no amount of moral turpitude can alter the status of a law duly passed as a law. Hart expresses in his 1958 article 'sympathy' for Radbruch's passionate demand that the German legal conscience should open itself up to the demands of humanitarian morality by adopting his post-Second World War view that humanitarian morality is part of the criteria of legal validity. However Professor Hart expressed his deep scepticism that the widespread juristic belief in pre-war Germany that 'law is law' had anything to do with the rise of the Nazis as Radbruch alleges. Hart comments:

> 'there is an extraordinary naivety in the view that insensitiveness to the demands of morality and subservience to state power in a people like the Germans should have arisen from the belief that law might be law though it failed to conform with the minimum requirements of political morality.'

However Hart admits that the slogan 'law is law' and the subsequent distinction between law and morals acquired a 'sinister character in Germany'.

Hart believes that the 'truly liberal answer' to any sinister use of the slogan 'law is law' is not to say the slogan is wrong and that 'law is not always law' but rather to admit that 'law is law' but to say as Hart does: 'Very well (law is law), but that does not conclude the question. Law is not morality; do not let it supplant morality'.[10]

Therefore for Hart, liberal enlightenment is to see the question of whether a rule is a law and the question of whether there is a moral obligation on citizens to obey or on judges

---

10 The legal philosophy of Professor Hart (1905–1992) can be explored in Questions 9, 10, 11, 12 and 15 of this book, Chapters 3 and 4.

to apply that law, as two very different questions. For Hart the Nazis had law but such immoral law in such an immoral system that there was no question of any moral obligation to obey or apply such evil laws. For Radbruch the gross immorality of Nazi law deprived Nazi law of the status 'law' and hence no question of moral obligation ever arose. It might be thought that the dispute Hart had with Gustav Radbruch over Nazi 'law' was purely academic, after all both Radbruch and Hart deny totally any moral force to Nazi 'edicts' or 'law'. However the debate had significance at a practical level in a number of cases after the Second World War in the courts of the democratic Federal Republic of Germany (West Germany as it was known). Hart explains in his 1958 article:

> 'After the war Radbruch's conception of law as containing in itself the essential moral principle of humanitarianism was applied in practice by German courts in certain cases in which local war criminals, spies, and informers under the Nazi regime were punished. The special importance of these cases is that the persons accused of these crimes claimed that what they had done was not illegal under the laws of the regime in force at the time these actions were performed. This plea was met with the reply that the laws upon which they relied were invalid as contravening the fundamental principles of morality.'

Professor Hart cites one of these cases decided by a West German court on 27 July 1949 and known in jurisprudential literature as the 'Nazi woman informer' case. In 1944 a woman, wishing to be rid of her husband, denounced him to the authorities for insulting remarks he had made about Hitler while on leave from the German army. The wife was under no legal duty to report his acts, though what he had said was apparently in violation of statutes making it illegal to make statements detrimental to the government of the Third Reich. The husband was arrested and sentenced to death, apparently pursuant to Nazi statutes, though he was not executed but was sent to the fighting front-line. In 1949 the wife was prosecuted in a West German court for an offence which could be described as illegally depriving a person of his freedom. This was punishable as a crime under the German Criminal Code of 1871 which had remained in force continuously since its enactment. The wife on trial pleaded that her husband's imprisonment was pursuant to the Nazi statute of 1934 and therefore since she acted under law passed by the Nazis in 1934 what she did by informing on her husband was no crime when she did her act in 1944. The West German court held that the Nazi statute under which the woman acted was no law since the statute 'was contrary to the sound conscience and sense of justice of all decent human beings'. The woman informer was therefore guilty of procuring the deprivation of her husband's liberty by denouncing him to the Nazi authorities for insulting Hitler. This reasoning was followed in many other cases in West Germany courts after the Second World War.

Professor Hart argued that the 'wisdom' of the line of reasoning adopted by the West German courts in these cases to deny the legal validity of Nazi law completely – in other words for the post-war courts Nazi law was not law. Hart said this could only lead to confusion, better he said to accept that Nazi law was law but that it lacked moral authority. Hart said that to punish the 'Nazi woman informer' the West Germans should have introduced a frankly retrospective law so that the Nazi law the woman acted under would have been overridden by retrospective law introduced after 1945 allowing for the punishment of the 'Nazi informer woman'. Hart was keen to keep the question of whether a rule was a 'law' entirely distinct from questions of moral obligation to obey law. Hart thought, as he said in *The Concept of Law* (1961), that to keep people clear headed in the face of the law's demands they should not regard the fact that a rule is a 'law' as being conclusive on the question of whether to obey it or not. For Hart the best way to combat tyranny was to say 'that is the law' but the question of whether we should obey it is a separate question. Hart thought Radbruch's approach, although admirable in intention, was to confuse the issue by making principles of humanitarian morality part of the criteria for legal validity. Better, Hart says, to admit Nazi law was law but that its gross immorality meant that it had no moral bindingness. Hart wrote in *The Concept of Law* (1961) that we should never accept that because a rule is a law that we should therefore reason we have to obey it. Hart wrote in 1961:

> 'What surely is most needed in order to make men clear sighted in confronting the official abuse of power, is that they should preserve the sense that the certification of something as legally valid is not conclusive of the question of obedience, and that, however great the aura of majesty or authority which the official system may have, its demands must in the end be submitted to a moral scrutiny.'

The approach of Gustav Radbruch in importing into the criteria of legal validity some notion of principles of humanitarian morality, so that much of Nazi law was not 'law' on Radbruch's analysis, has a theologically based counterpart in the writings of the great eighteenth century judge and jurist Sir William Blackstone (1723–1780). Blackstone wrote his famous *Commentaries on the Laws of England* (1765–1769) which were an important summary and rationalisation of English law. Blackstone wrote that any human law which violated the God-given natural law (a natural law which could be discerned by reason which God had given man to understand his law) had no legal validity whatsoever. Blackstone wrote: 'no human laws are of any validity, if contrary to the natural law'. Radbruch imported morality into the criteria for law by way of 'humanitarian morality'. Blackstone imported morality into the criteria for law by way of God-given 'natural law' binding across the world and at all times and on all persons. John Austin, a nineteenth century legal positivist forerunner of Professor Hart, attacked Sir William Blackstone's strong natural law view, that the criteria for law included universal principles of natural law. Austin argued that the existence of a law is one thing, its moral merit is a separate question. In a way Austin's nineteenth-century attack on Sir William Blackstone is a forerunner of Hart's critique of Radbruch. Both Austin and Hart want to say that legal validity is one issue, the moral merit of particular laws or the moral merit particular legal systems is a separate question.

There is a more subtle 'natural law' position to that offered by Sir William Blackstone – that seriously unjust laws which violate the natural law are not law at all. John Finnis in his classic restatement of the classical natural law tradition *Natural Law and Natural Rights* (1980) argues that the central case or focal case of law and legal systems is to order and co-ordinate the community for the common good. Evil laws (or evil legal systems) are therefore not the 'central' cases of law but rather peripheral or degenerate forms of law since these forms of law are not intended to co-ordinate the community for the common good. These 'peripheral' or 'degenerate' forms of law therefore lack much or any of the moral bindingness of the central case of law which is for the co-ordination of the common good. Finnis can then use his analysis to say that Nazi law was law but in a very degenerate sense (Nazi law may have been passed in accordance with certain legislative procedures and applied by Nazi judges) of the word 'law'. Given the extreme degeneracy of Nazi law there was a positive moral obligation to resist it rather than apply it in court.

There is yet another position on the question of whether Nazi law was law. This is the position of Lon Fuller (1902–1978) who argued that because Nazi laws often violated important principles of legality then often Nazi law did not deserve to be called law at all. Fuller argued in 'Positivism and Fidelity to Law: A Reply to Professor Hart' (1957–1958) *Harvard Law Review* that before we can call Nazi law 'law' as Hart suggested: 'it is unwise to pass such a judgment without first inquiring with more particularity what 'law' itself meant under the Nazi regime'.

Fuller argued that the Nazis, in order to achieve their odious ends, often passed 'secret laws' 'retroactive laws' and laws that were overturned just on the say-so of Hitler. Fuller suggested that:

> 'throughout his discussion Professor Hart seems to assume that the only difference between Nazi law and English law is that the Nazis used their laws to achieve ends that are odious to an Englishman.'

For Fuller gives several examples of the many ways in which the Nazis had corrupted the instrument of law, not just used it for evil purposes. Fuller writes of the profusion of retrospective laws and secret laws (in which, for example, killings in concentration camps had been made lawful by secret enactment). Another corruption of law was the willingness of Nazi courts to ignore any statute, even those enacted by the Nazis themselves, if this suited their convenience or they feared 'displeasure from above'. Fuller is not saying because Nazi law was evil it was not 'law'. Rather Fuller is saying that the Nazi legal system was so degraded in the way it operated compared to a standard legal system that it hardly deserved to be called a legal system. Nazi laws were so debased in their formal qualities (apart from their evil content) that in the most extreme cases they might not, argued Fuller, be considered laws at all. The historical evidence supports Fuller's claim that the very abnormal functioning of the Nazi legal system calls into question whether it could be considered to be a representative of the 'genus' or 'species' called 'legal system' as the name for a system of interrelated authoritative rules in a society. In *The Third Reich* (1999) edited by Christian Leitz, Albrecht Tyrell comments of the Nazi legal regime:

> 'After his emigration from Berlin to the United States in 1938, Ernst Fraenkel, lawyer and later political scientist, used his personal observations to describe the Nazi system of power fittingly as a "dual state" (Doppelstaat). This meant that the Nazis condoned the existence of a "normative state" (Normenstaat) which as a rule, respected established or new laws alongside a "prerogative" state which, if necessary,

ignored the very same laws. The rule of law was not guaranteed any longer as the "prerogative state" repressed it further and further. The continued existence of a legal framework proved to be advantageous to the Nazis. Not only did it allow the superficial pacification of everyday life, but it also gave the Nazis a semblance of legality.'

When the Nazis intervened in the legal apparatus their priority was to combat opponents of the regime. Special decrees and courts ensured that 'political criminals' were increasingly removed from normal legal procedures. When using the bureaucratic and legal apparatus Hitler was not bound to legal norms. Hitler could issue a personal order to countermand any law. After the murder of over 70 Nazis in the Roehm purge Hitler declared that 'the supreme court of the German people ... consisted of myself'.

The question follows Fuller's analysis: was the procedural defectiveness of Nazi law so extreme and so pervasive that we should not accord it the title 'a legal system?' Certainly this is a different line of attack from Radbruch who argued that the moral defectiveness of Nazi law robbed it of any status as 'law'. Fuller's attack is different, looking at the gross procedural defects of Nazi law, e.g. secret laws, retrospective laws, non-applied laws when convenient to the Nazi regime, the ability of Hitler to override any law with a personal order. These procedural or due process defects of Nazi law could be thought so grave that the only conclusion is that Nazi law was not really 'law' but organised gangsterism for odious political ends. Nazi law with its systemic procedural defects was so far from the standard legal system as not to count as 'law' at all. Fuller gave a list of eight 'principles of legality' of a legal system in good shape (we can see that Nazi law often failed to come close to these basic features of a standard legal system):

❖ The legal rules must be general and apply to all persons. The protection of Nazi law did not extend to Jews for example.
❖ The legal rules must be promulgated – no secret laws. The Nazis made extensive use of secret laws.
❖ Retroactive rulemaking and application must be minimised. The Nazis used retroactive law whenever convenient.
❖ The legal rules must be understandable. The Nazis ran a double state or doppelstaat of ordinary law and Nazi law so no citizen knew for sure which laws applied.
❖ The legal rules should not be contradictory. A double or doppelstaat involved inevitable contradictions between laws.
❖ The legal rules should not be impossible to obey. Nazi laws which forbade marriage between Jews and non-Jews were obviously impossible for some couples to obey.
❖ The legal rules should remain relatively constant through time. Hitler could overrule any legal rule with a personal order.
❖ There should be a congruence between the legal rules as announced and as applied.
❖ The Nazi courts would often not apply legal rules when it was convenient to the Nazi party not to follow the legal rules.

Professor Dworkin has, in writings from *Law's Empire* (1986) to *Justice for Hedgehogs* (2011), perhaps given the most nuanced and subtle response of all jurists to the question as to whether the Nazis had law. Indeed Dworkin tackles the issue directly at pp. 101–104 of *Law's Empire* in a section entitled 'Did the Nazis have law?' Dworkin argues that some legal philosophers have argued that in some nations there is no law, in spite of the existence of familiar legal institutions like legislatures and courts because the practices of these institutions are too wicked to deserve that title of 'law'. The argument is we honour the Nazis too much by bestowing on their organised brutality the word 'law'. Dworkin says such a claim, that the Nazis had no law despite the existence of courts and legislatures, is understandable if we accept that legal theory is what Dworkin calls 'interpretive'. Legal theory, according to Dworkin aims to show how the social practice of law, legality, or the rule of law (all mean roughly the same) can justify state coercion as expressed through law. Nazi law stands totally condemned because no interpretation of it can provide any justification whatsoever for Nazi coercion expressed through Nazi law. Nazi law was too evil in itself within a totally evil regime to submit to any interpretation that can find justification for what was expressed through Nazi law. Therefore it is plausible to argue that the Nazis did not have 'law' if law is understood as a way of justifying coercion by the state. However Dworkin says that it is also possible to understand the legal philosopher who says the Nazis did have law. Dworkin says such a claim is 'pre-intepretive'. The legal philosopher who claims the Nazis had law is not to be taken to be arguing that Nazi law actually justified Nazi coercion. Rather the legal philosopher who claims Nazi law was law is arguing that with its courts and legislatures Nazi law was 'one historical realization' (in Dworkin's words) of the 'general practices and institutions from which our own legal culture also developed'. In other words if we take Roman law as the 'parent' legal system then Nazi law with its courts and practices is one historical manifestation of that historical phenomenon we call 'law' dating back to the classical world of Greece and Rome. Therefore Dworkin concludes that the answer to the question of whether the Nazis had law is both no and yes. Dworkin argues that our language and idiom are rich enough to allow a great deal of discrimination and choice in the words we pick to say, and our choice of words will therefore depend on the question we are trying to answer and the context in which we speak. Dworkin concludes his discussion of whether the Nazis had law in *Law's Empire* by saying:

> 'We need not deny that the Nazi system was an example of law because there is an available sense in which it plainly was law. But we have no difficulty in understanding someone who does say that Nazi law was not really law, or was law in a degenerate sense, or was less than fully law.'

Dworkin says that the legal philosopher who says that the Nazis did not have 'law' are making sceptical interpretive judgments that Nazi law lacked features crucial to flourishing legal systems whose rules and procedures do justify coercion. This judgment, that the Nazis had no law, is 'a special kind of political judgment for which his language, if the context makes this clear, is entirely appropriate'. Dworkin has said in the later *Justice for Hedgehogs* (2011) gives an interpretive denunciation of Nazi law that Nazi edicts were not 'law' in the interpretive sense of justifying Nazi state coercion. Dworkin says:

> 'The hideous Nazi edicts did not create even prima facie or arguable rights and duties … It is morally more accurate to deny that these edicts were law.'

Professor Dworkin has given the most persuasive answer to the question of whether the Nazis had 'law'. Dworkin argues that the Nazis had 'law' in the sense that it shared historically familiar features with other legal systems in history such as courts and legislatures. However, Dworkin also says that, from a morally interpretive point of view, the Nazis did not have 'law' as nothing in Nazi law could ever justify the vile coercion of the Nazi state. If the ultimate point of law is to provide a justification for coercion by the state then on this account the Nazis did not have 'law'.

NOTES

Professor Hart's essay 'Positivism and the Separation of Law and Morals' deals with Hart's response to the views of Gustav Radbruch. It was originally published in the 1958 *Harvard Law Review* and is now essay 2 in Hart's *Essays in Jurisprudence and Philosophy* (1983). Martin Krygier deals with Fuller's views on Nazi law in 'The Hart-Fuller Debate, Transnational Societies and the Rule of Law' in a collection of essays entitled *The Hart-Fuller Debate in the Twenty-First Century* edited by Peter Cane (2010). Professor Dworkin has returned to the issue of whether the Nazis had law on a number of occasions. Dworkin deals with the topic in *Law's Empire* (1986) at pp. 101–104. In *Justice in Robes* (2006) at p. 4 Dworkin suggests: 'we might deny for various reasons, that the Nazis had a legal system'. In his 2011 book *Justice for Hedgehogs* Dworkin again examines the issue of what Dworkin calls 'Evil Law' at pp. 410–412, Dworkin argues: 'The hideous Nazi edicts did not create even prima facie or arguable rights and duties. It is morally more accurate to deny that these edicts were law.'

3

Legal Positivism

INTRODUCTION

Legal positivism is the name given to a great school of juristic thought, which includes such luminaries of philosophy as Hobbes (1588–1679), Bentham (1748–1832), Austin (1790–1859) and Professor HLA Hart (1907–1992). The main feature of legal positivism is its insistence that the law of a society be identified purely by 'social facts' and that one does not need a moral argument to work out the content of the law – what the modern legal positivist, Professor Raz, calls 'the sources thesis'. The legal positivist does not deny that law is very often influenced by morality, or even that there are necessary connections between law and morality but legal positivism argues that it is better to analyse the social practice we call 'law' without importing into our analysis any view of what the ultimate moral function of law is: in other words we should analyse law without 'rose-tinted spectacles' such as how 'necessary' law is for society, for such a 'rose-tinted' view could distort the actual reality or 'essence' of law.

The questions in the chapter include definitions of legal positivism, discussion of the 'command theory' of law, Professor Hart's restatement of legal positivism and the attack on the doctrine of legal positivism from Professor Ronald Dworkin. In addition there are questions on Professor Raz, the leading legal positivist, and Professor Galligan's attempt to analyse 'modern Western legal orders'.

Checklist
Ensure that you are acquainted with the following topics:
■ the definition of legal positivism;
■ the virtues and drawbacks of the 'command theory' of law;
■ Professor Hart's definition of law as 'a union of primary and secondary rules';
■ the methodology of Professor Hart;
■ the contribution of Professor Raz to legal positivistic thought;
■ the attack on legal positivism by Professor Dworkin;
■ Professor Galligan's analysis of 'modern Western legal orders'.

QUESTION 6

What do you understand by 'legal positivism'?

How to Answer this Question

The question calls for a discussion of the great school of juristic thought called 'legal positivism'. The origins of legal positivism are usually taken to be with Bentham (1748–1832) and Austin (1790–1859), but the tradition can be dated as far back as Thomas Hobbes (1588–1679).[1] The essence of legal positivism is not a denial of the 'natural law' claim that law and morality are heavily interlinked; it is rather that the identification of the law is not dependent on moral argument but that it depends on social facts alone – what Professor Raz (the leading living legal positivist) calls the 'sources thesis'. The legal positivist will point to the function of law in providing authoritative co-ordination of human activity as justifying the necessity of law being clearly and crisply identified from social facts such as Parliamentary enactment and judicial precedent. The *locus classicus* of legal positivistic texts is *The Concept of Law* (1961; 1994, 2nd edition) by Professor Hart, which sought to reinvigorate the legal positivist tradition from the defects of earlier 'command theories' propagated by Bentham and Austin. The main attack on legal positivism has not come from traditional natural law; indeed, Professor Finnis (author of *Natural Law and Natural Rights* (1980)) accepts the legal positivist 'sources thesis', but from the courtroom-driven vision of the American Professor, Ronald Dworkin. Dworkin argues that legal positivism cannot account for the fact that legal argument in the higher appeal courts in the USA and UK often has recourse to moral arguments to support propositions of law. Dworkin's attack on legal positivism remains controversial, as does his denial of the central methodological claim of legal positivism that there can be descriptive legal theory only with no justificatory ambitions towards law.

Applying the Law

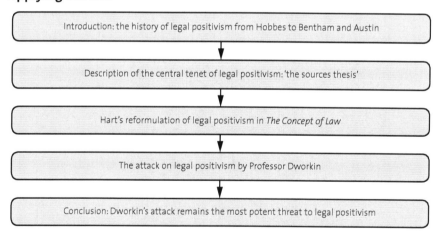

Introduction: the history of legal positivism from Hobbes to Bentham and Austin

Description of the central tenet of legal positivism: 'the sources thesis'

Hart's reformulation of legal positivism in *The Concept of Law*

The attack on legal positivism by Professor Dworkin

Conclusion: Dworkin's attack remains the most potent threat to legal positivism

---

1   Hobbes's seventeenth century 'command theory of law' although influential on Bentham and Austin must be clearly distinguished from those nineteenth-century command theorists. For Hobbes the obligation to obey the sovereign power and its laws stemmed from an antecedent agreement by citizens to obey the sovereign in exchange for protection by the sovereign. Therefore the obligation of citizens to obey the law stems for Hobbes from the 'pact of protection' between sovereign and citizens. Much cruder is the legal theory of Bentham and Austin who located the obligation on citizens to obey the sovereign in the threat of punishment (sanctions) imposed by the sovereign.

ANSWER

In his important essay 'Authority, law and morality' (reprinted in *Ethics in the Public Domain* (1994)), Professor Raz comments that Professor Hart was the torch-bearer of a 'great tradition'. That 'great tradition' is legal positivism. The great figures of the tradition of legal positivism are usually considered to include Bentham (1748–1832), Austin (1790–1859), Herbert Hart (1907–1992) and Joseph Raz. However, the true philosophical origins of legal positivism probably reside in the great seventeenth century philosopher, Thomas Hobbes (1588–1679). For Hobbes, the law was an exercise in the expression of the sovereign will. As Hobbes commented: 'The civil laws are the commands of him who hath the chief authority for direction of the future actions of his citizens'. On this view of the law, the laws are essentially rules laid down and upheld by the sovereign and the sovereign is the person or persons with effective authority in a society. The law represented for Hobbes the sovereign's will and judgment as to what the law's subjects, the citizens, must do. The Hobbesian conception of law, 'the command theory', was later developed by the two great positivist thinkers of the nineteenth century, Jeremy Bentham and John Austin. Austin developed and popularised Bentham's approach and Austin's account became the more influential, given the fact that Bentham's writings on this subject were not published until after the halfway point of the twentieth century.

However, Bentham's views are of note because they reveal a legal positivistic distaste for judge-made law in contrast to the certainties and forward-looking nature of legislation. Indeed, it was Bentham who first used the term 'judge-made law', using it as a term of abuse and contempt for English common law. As Gerald Postema comments in 'Philosophy of the Common Law' (in *Oxford Handbook of Jurisprudence and Philosophy* (2002), edited by Coleman and Shapiro), Bentham spent a large part of his life trying to undermine the grip of the common law on lawyers in England. Bentham compared judge-made common law to the way people train dogs; as he commented: 'When your dog does anything you want to break him of, you wait till he does it, and then beat him for it. This is the way you make laws for your dog, and this is the way the judges make law for you and me'. The retroactive and reactive nature of the common law compared unfavourably with statutory codification. Bentham favoured statutory codification, which looked to the future and not the past. Bentham's aim (which he hoped to extend beyond England to other countries, such as the United States) was to create a complete code of laws which he eventually called the 'pannomion' (meaning 'all the laws'). Legislation (or codification) fits better the 'commands of the sovereign' model of law than the vagueness and uncertainties of the common law, which Bentham derided in the following terms: 'A law is to be extracted (from common law) by every man who can fancy that he is able; by each man perhaps a different law'. Arguably, English law has moved in a general direction that Bentham would have approved of. One of the long-term processes witnessed by the twentieth century in the legal system of England and Wales was the transition from the common law dominated system of the nineteenth century to the statute dominated system of the twenty-first century. Statute, not common law, is generally how new legal rights and duties are now created in England and Wales.

A landmark in the legal positivist tradition was the publication of Austin's *The Province of Jurisprudence Determined* in 1832. Austin's conception of law was that the law was essentially the result of the 'commands of the sovereign'. The law of any society with a 'sovereign' was to be identified by asking two fundamental questions: (a) who is the 'sovereign'? (Austin believed every organised society had a 'sovereign' who obeyed no other authority and was itself obeyed by the bulk of the population), and (b) what has the sovereign commanded? In this simple way the law of any society could be distinguished from the norms of morality, religion and custom of that society. Therefore, legal positivism recognises that the virtue of law is that it forms a public and dependable set of standards for the guidance of officials and citizens whatever the disagreements in that society over the dictates of morality, religion or custom. The method by which legal positivism distinguishes law from other systems of norms (such as morality) is by the stipulation that the law is to be identified by 'social sources' – that is, the law can be identified by asking certain questions about human behaviour (such as 'what has the sovereign commanded?').

This doctrine – that the law can be identified by reference to social facts alone, and that law is not identified by engaging in a moral argument – is called 'the sources thesis' by Professor Raz. The 'sources thesis' has been identified by Raz as the key doctrine of legal positivism. Raz states in *The Authority of Law* (1979) that the legal positivist thesis is that what is law, and what is not, is a matter of social fact; he states further that a jurisprudential theory is acceptable only if its test for identifying the content of the law and determining its existence depends exclusively on facts of human behaviour, capable of being described in value-neutral terms, and applied without resort to moral argument. Other legal positivists have differed somewhat in the exact test to be used to identify the law, and the history of legal positivism as a doctrine can be seen partially as a more and more sophisticated attempt to capture the essence of a proper test for law.

'The command theory' of Bentham and Austin was effectively replaced by the 'rule of recognition' of Hart's analysis (in essence, that the identification of law was to be made upon the observance of the behaviour of legal officials and how they identified legal rules in their society) as the test for the identification of law. Both the 'command theory' and the Hartian 'rule of recognition' are examples of Raz's 'sources thesis' – that is, that the law of a society is to be identified by social facts alone.

Legal positivists do not deny that law is influenced by morality at many points and, indeed, Professor Raz has denied that the heart of legal positivism is about denying necessary connections between law and morality. When Austin commented 'the existence of law is one thing; its merit and demerit another', this should not be taken to mean that legal positivism denies the connections between law and morality, but merely that the identification of law is a separate question from its moral merit. As Raz comments (in 'About Morality and the Nature of Law' (2006)) there can be no doubt that there are necessary connections between law and morality and that legal positivism does not deny this. However, the most potent criticisms of legal positivism all emanate from the view that legal positivism fails to accept fully the intimate connections between law and morality. The attack on legal positivism comes in two main forms. First, there is the 'natural law' view that law and legal systems can be properly understood only if it is understood that the point or ultimate value of legal systems is a moral function – that law is the primary means by which civil society is co-ordinated and ordered for the benefit of the 'common good'. This 'natural law' critique suggests that legal positivism gives a very 'thin' and underdeveloped view of the concept of law. The legal positivist could suggest that he does not deny law's 'higher functions' but that his main thesis that law is identified by social facts alone is unaffected by the whole 'natural law' apparatus. Indeed, plausibly a legal theorist could assent to the truth of legal positivism whilst developing a fully fledged 'natural law' theory, as Professor Finnis has done in *Natural Law and Natural Rights* (1980).

The second attack on 'legal positivism' is not possible to reconcile with the legal positivist tradition as it asserts that the central idea of positivism, that law is identified by 'social sources' alone, is fundamentally flawed. The leading proponent of the attack on the legal positivist 'sources thesis' is Professor RM Dworkin, as exemplified in his *magnum opus* on legal theory, *Law's Empire* (1986). Dworkin has argued that legal positivism cannot properly account for legal argumentation by lawyers and legal decision by appellate judges in so-called 'hard cases' where the source based law does not provide a clear answer. Dworkin argues that the law consists not merely of the settled legal rules but also legal principles, which are identified not from the 'social sources' but from the moral interpretation of settled law. Dworkin, in his theory of law, makes the identification of law at least partly dependent on moral interpretation carried out by the law's interpreter – the appellate judge. This argument, if true, undermines the central positivist tenet of the 'sources thesis'. As Raz comments in an essay 'Two Views of the Nature of the Theory of Law' (2001) (see Hart's 'Postscript: Essays on the Concept of Law' (2001)), if Dworkin's theory of law is correct then Hart's theory is flawed at its foundations. The focus of Dworkin has been very much on appeal cases where legal positivism has had difficulty in explaining the moral driven nature of legal argumentation in 'hard cases'. However, Dworkin has probably overestimated the amount of controversy in legal cases where, most frequently, the argument of counsel concerns not the law but the facts of the case. Yet Dworkin does seem to capture the judicial atmosphere in hard cases; indeed, the natural lawyer, Professor John Finnis (who accepts legal positivism's 'sources thesis' in *Natural Law and Natural Rights*) comments that we should broadly accept some main elements of Ronald Dworkin's account of adjudication in appeal cases (see Finnis, 'Natural Law: The Classical Tradition' in *The Oxford Handbook of Jurisprudence and Philosophy of Law* (2002)).[2]

The legal positivist tradition explains well the role of legislation in society. Raz comments that the law is a structure of authority and that the normal exercise of political authority is by the making of laws and legally binding orders (see *The Morality of Freedom* (1986)), and legal positivism can explain the rule-governed and appellate-controlled operations of

2 Professor Finnis does reject Dworkin's idea that in every hard case there is one right answer waiting to be discovered. Finnis argues that there will often be more than one reasonable legal answer to a legal question in a 'hard case' even if there are plainly wrong answers.

the lower courts, such as the magistrates' court, county court and Crown Court. Indeed, Hart commented in *The Concept of Law* (1961) that, in great measure, the prestige gathered by the courts is from their unquestionably rule-governed operations over the vast, central areas of the law. However, legal positivism has an underdeveloped account of legal argumentation and legal judgment in appeal cases where the law runs out compared to Dworkin's rich and nuanced account, which seems to capture the judicial scene where legal argument and moral standards often are interwoven. Legal positivists could argue that the nature of legal argumentation in 'hard cases' in the Anglo-American legal systems was never the focus of legal positivism, which aimed to give a general account of the concept of law as it appears to people in all cultures where law appears. Although it can be accepted that legal positivism is, in the words of Hart, not tied to any particular legal system, but seeks to give an explanatory and clarifying account of law as a complex social and political institution with a rule-governed aspect (see Hart, *The Concept of Law* (1994, 2nd edition)), legal positivism does have an implicit theory of judicial adjudication in 'hard cases'. For example, both Raz and Hart think that the existence and content of law depend on social facts and not on moral considerations but, given the unforeseeability of the facts of future cases and the lack of clarity of language, then the law is riddled with gaps, leaving judges with significant discretion to make law. As Hart commented in *The Concept of Law*, in every legal system a large and important field is open for the discretion of courts. Where legal questions turn on moral argumentation the judges are not controlled by law and they have discretion to make 'new law'. Of course, in making new law judges must proceed carefully by analogy with decided cases and consider what the will of Parliament may be on the matter, as pointed out by Hart in *The Concept of Law* (1994, 2nd edition). However, this characterisation by legal positivists of judicial decision in 'hard cases' has been criticised by Dworkin as 'wholly inadequate' (see 'Hard Cases' (1975), reprinted in *Taking Rights Seriously* (1977)). Dworkin has argued that judges in hard cases should not be nor are 'deputy legislators' but should 'find' the law to any 'hard case' by re-interpreting the existing law in the best moral light possible with an acceptable level of consistency with decided law. Even if Professor Dworkin overstates somewhat the amount of interpretation needed in the law, where in most cases the law can be understood and applied without the need for Dworkinian interpretation the fact remains that Dworkin's legal theory represents the greatest challenge to the tradition of legal positivism currently debated.[3]

3　Professor Raz in his essay 'Authority, Law and Morality' in *Ethics in the Public Domain* (1994) comments that Dworkin's legal theory makes some of the law 'hidden' waiting to be discovered by the Dworkinian interpreting judge. Raz says if the law's main function is to provide authoritative guidance to persons then how can law provide this authoritative guidance if part of the law is 'hidden' from public knowledge?

Common Pitfalls

Students can avoid the pitfall that legal positivism argues that there is no necessary connection between law and morality – the so-called 'separability thesis'. Students can gain extra marks by arguing that legal positivists such as Raz and Gardner argue that there are necessary connections between law and morality, such as (a) the law by its nature always claims moral authority (b) the language of law and morality are virtually identical with terms such as 'rights' 'duties' and 'normative' in both discourses of law and morality. Students can also gain extra marks by arguing that the central claim of legal positivism is 'the sources thesis' – that the content and existence of the law is made without resort to a moral argument.

NOTES

The reader should first approach 'legal positivism' through the pages of the greatest legal philosopher of the twentieth century, Professor Hart, in *The Concept of Law* (1961), especially Chapters 2–5 of that book. The most readable account by Raz of legal positivism is the essay 'Authority, law and morality', (1985) The Monist, reprinted in *Ethics in the Public Domain* (1994).

Dworkin's frontal attack on legal positivism can be gathered from the article 'Hard cases' (1975), republished in *Taking Rights Seriously* (1977). Hart's reply to Dworkin's criticisms can be found in the 'Postscript' to *The Concept of Law*, published in the second edition in 1994 and edited by Raz and Bulloch. A very useful essay 'Legal Positivism' by Leslie Green is to be found in the online and free *Stanford Encyclopedia of Philosophy* (http://plato.stanford.edu/).

QUESTION 7 --

Has the 'command theory' any virtue as a theory of law?

How to Answer this Question

The 'command theory of law' is widely considered to have been effectively demolished by Professor Hart in *The Concept of Law* (1961). However, it is possible to see valuable insights in this theory, as Hart himself recognised. The 'command theory' of Austin (1780–1859) and Bentham (1748–1832) saw a clear conceptual separation between the identification of law and the claims of morality, which remains the basis of legal positivism today (see Raz's 'sources thesis'). The 'command theory' also captures valuable insights into the relationship between law, power and coercion which may reflect the reality of power even in so-called 'democracies'.

Applying the Law

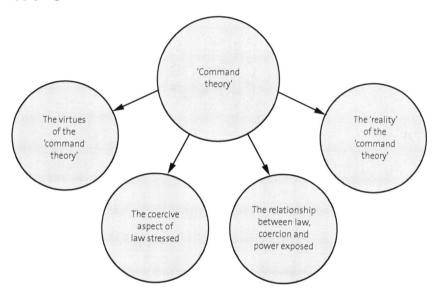

ANSWER

The 'command theory' of law dominated jurisprudence in the nineteenth century through the writings of John Austin (1790–1859) and owes its philosophical origins to two giants of philosophy, Thomas Hobbes (1588–1679) and Jeremy Bentham (1748–1832).

Jeremy Bentham was a product of the Eighteenth Century Enlightenment or 'age of reason'. The Enlightenment was an attack on old habits of thought which were alleged to rest on the dark forces of superstition, irrationality and religion. One doctrine which came under attack during the Enlightenment was the doctrine of natural law which had been the dominant jurisprudential doctrine before the Enlightenment. Bentham and other Enlightenment thinkers such as Montesquieu attacked the idea that there was a universal natural law applicable to and binding on all mankind, created by God and discoverable through reason and which formed a basis for the promulgation and authority of man-made law. Bentham argued that the natural law was 'a mere work of the fancy' having no basis in reality and that it was not a God-given natural law which gave man-made law its authority but rather human authority alone which established the authority of man made law.[4] In other words human law was merely the result of the 'commands of the sovereign' and did not derive its authority from any link to a mystical and fictitious 'natural law'.

---

4   Bentham was reflecting a strong atheistic element to the Eighteenth Century Enlightenment reflected in such philosophers as David Hume (1711–1776) who derided Christianity and looked back for inspiration to the pagan 'virtue' theories of Aristotle and others of the ancient classical world who taught that people could train themselves through habits of action and thinking to have virtues such as self-control and courage.

It is important to take note of the historical context in which Bentham formulated his 'command theory of law'. Bentham was keen to refute the idea of natural law thinkers such as Grotius that there could be property rights in the 'natural law sphere' even before man-made law had spoken. For Grotius the ultimate origin of the right of property was that God at creation had given the earth to mankind and so there could be 'natural' rights of property before the say-so of man-made law. For Bentham this natural law doctrine was to be completely rejected. For Bentham, following Hobbes and Hume, only such goods and property that had been assigned to a man by positive law (man-made law) could be said to belong to him. For Bentham property and man-made law were born together and there could be no property rights before man-made law had spoken and therefore for Bentham natural law theory was to be rejected. Indeed natural law theory went into a steep decline in the nineteenth century following the Enlightenment attack of Bentham and others and natural law theory only revived in importance in the twentieth century. For Bentham the man-made law derived its authority not from God or the natural law but from the fact of promulgation by a sovereign – the law was the 'commands of the sovereign' – no more, no less.

It is now seen as a theory whose account of law is too simplistic and too 'thin' to account for the important legal phenomena that we find in complex legal systems. However, on reconsideration, the 'command theory' does have some valuable insights into the relationship between law, coercion and power.

Early in his career, Austin came under the influence of his mentor, Bentham, although Austin's work on legal theory was more influential, especially *The Province of Jurisprudence Determined* (1832). In the great tradition of legal positivism, Austin sought to give a general descriptive account of all legal systems. As to what is the heart of the concept of law, Austin's answer is to say that positive law (that is, man-made or 'posited' law) is the 'commands of a sovereign'. Positive law consists of those commands laid down by a sovereign to be contrasted with those dictates of religion or morality. The 'sovereign' is defined as a person or collection of persons who receives habitual obedience from the bulk of the population but who does not habitually obey any other person or institution. When, in a law case, the 'commands' (the laws) do not determine the issues, Austin had no objection to judicial law making which Austin called 'highly beneficial and even absolutely necessary'. Judge-made law could be accommodated within the 'command theory' by regarding such law as the 'tacit' commands of the sovereign, who then affirms those fresh judicial law making acts by not repealing them; those judicial acts of law making then become 'the commands of the sovereign'. Austin is therefore in the tradition of legal positivism (see Hart and Raz) in according a limited law-making discretion to the judiciary.[5] Bentham objected to judicial law making and would have such disputed legal questions referred back to the legislature for decision.

---

5 Austin desired much more codification of law than there was in his time: see Roger Cotterrell, *The Politics of Jurisprudence* (2003). However Austin proved more realistic than Bentham in that it was never possible to fully codify all the law.

The 'command theory' makes the identification of the law of a community depend on social facts: one does not need to make a moral argument to identify the law; it is enough merely to identify the 'sovereign' (the sovereign is identified by looking at patterns of obedience in the bulk of the population) and then ask 'what has the sovereign commanded?' Even though Professor Hart ultimately rejected the 'command theory' as a satisfactory description of law (Hart said in *The Concept of Law* that the simple model of law as the sovereign's coercive orders fails to reproduce some of the important features of a legal system) he does maintain, in the legal positivistic tradition, that the law is identified by social facts alone and that this insight was provided by Austin following Hobbes and Bentham. As Hart comments, in *Essays on Bentham* (1982), the 'command' theory's conceptual separation of law and morality is a permanently valuable insight which should be retained when the 'command' (or 'imperative') theory is discarded. That the law is identified independent of morality not only reproduces the way the law in modern societies appears to many citizens but also permits the construction of a general theory of law applicable to every society where law is found. Therefore, the 'command theory' is the source not only of the 'sources thesis' but also the view that the ambitions of legal theory are universal, in that it aims to describe law as a specific type of social organisation wherever it is found. For both Raz and Hart, the 'sources thesis' and the 'universality' of legal theory are important themes.[6]

The 'command theory' builds the idea of a sanction into the very idea of law. A 'command' involves an expressed wish from a 'superior' that something be done or not done by an 'inferior' and a sanction to be imposed if that wish is not complied with. In the understanding of citizens, the image of the law conjures up pictures of police, judges and prisons. As Professor Galligan writes, in *Law in Modern Society* (2007), the coercive aspect of law colours the common perception of law and how people talk about it. People rely upon the law because of the assumption that the law will ultimately use coercion to protect them or enforce their rights. Coercion is then a significant feature of modern legal systems, which Austin in the 'command theory' captured well. Indeed, Professor Hart, the foremost critic of the Austinian 'command theory', can be criticised for underplaying the importance of coercion to modern legal orders in *The Concept of Law*. The 'command theory' captures the inherent coerciveness of many systems of law and the importance of power to the maintenance of the state. Austin's conception of law and legal systems perhaps captures in a cynical way the relationship between law, coercion and power in modern states. Austin's 'command theory' is a theory of the 'rule of men' of government using law not as an instrument for the realisation of the 'common good' but as a way of controlling populations for the ultimate benefit of those few in real power. As John Locke realised, in his *Treatise on Civil Government* (1690), there is a tendency in some human beings to strongly aim for power; as Locke wrote: 'human frailty, apt to grasp at power'. The 'command theory' conceives law not as a specific method for the co-ordination of the

----

6   By the term 'universality of legal theory' is meant the idea that legal theory should aim to provide an account of the essential elements in law and legal systems wherever they are found. This type of legal theory epitomised by Professor Hart can be strongly contrasted with legal theory which limits it's attention to a particular type of legal system (e.g. Galligan's 'Law in Modern Society' or McCormick's 'Institutions of Law') or an ideal type of legal system (e.g. Finnis in 'Natural Law and Natural Rights').

common good as natural lawyers, such as John Finnis would have us believe in *Natural Law and Natural Rights* (1980), but rather the Austinian conception sees law as an instrument of power in which a 'superior' authority addresses the 'inferior' mass of humanity not necessarily for the true benefit of the 'inferior' mass of the people.

NOTES
The Stanford Encyclopedia of Philosophy (http://plato.stanford.edu/) has a free online and very useful essay on John Austin written by Brian Bix in 2005. The critical analysis of Austin's 'command theory' given by Professor Hart in Chapters 2–4 of *The Concept of Law* (1961) should be examined carefully. Professor Hart's more positive remarks on 'the command theory' can be found in his *Essays on Bentham* (1982).

QUESTION 8
Explain how later legal positivists, such as Hart and Raz, criticised Austin's 'command theory'.

How to Answer this Question
The 'command theory', despite its virtues, has fundamental and near fatal flaws as an explanation of the concept of law. Professor Hart (1907–1992), in *The Concept of Law*, exposed the weaknesses of the 'command theory' in that Austin's theory failed to account for the reality and complexity of legal phenomena, such as the variety of legal rules which cannot all be reduced to the 'commands' of the sovereign and the 'internal' point of view of legal officials in a legal system. Professor Raz added to the weight of criticisms of the 'command theory' in that the old Austinian theory cannot account for the law's claim to legitimate authority, such a claim of authority being a central feature of the law's method of social organisation.

Applying the Law

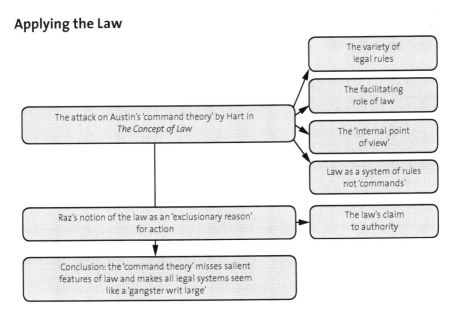

ANSWER

It is now widely accepted that Austin's 'command theory' account of law is inadequate as an explanation of key legal phenomena. Although not without critics in the nineteenth century, the mortal blow to the 'command theory' was delivered by Professor Hart in *The Concept of Law* (1961) where, in Chapters 2–4, Hart effectively demolishes the edifice of the Austinian account of law. Hart argues persuasively that Austin's model of law as 'the sovereign's coercive orders' failed to reproduce some of the key features of a legal system. There are two main angles of attack on Austin: (1) the different kinds of rules in a modern legal system which cannot be reduced to 'commands' and (2) the 'internal aspect of rules'.

Hart points out that there are important categories of legal rules (other than the criminal law) where the model of laws as commands – orders backed by threats – fails completely, since these rules perform a different social function from commanding behaviour. Legal rules defining the ways in which valid contracts, wills or marriages are made do not require persons to act in certain ways whether they wish to or not. Such laws do not impose duties or obligations. Instead, they provide individuals with facilities for realising their wishes to create new rights, duties and relationships within the coercive framework of law. Hart comments that the power conferred on individuals to mould their legal relations with others – by, for example, contracts, wills and marriages – is one of the great contributions of law to social life and it is a feature of laws obscured by representing all law as a matter of orders backed by threats. Perhaps an important criticism of Austin's 'command theory of law' is that it does not capture the totality of the relationship expressed through the law between the modern liberal state and its citizens. The law certainly has important coercive aspects, but the law is also an enabler and facilitator for the autonomous citizen to shape his life through meaningful choice offered by the law through the legal institutions of contract, marriage and probate. Austin gives the reader the model of the 'submissive, inferior citizen' through law. Hart gives the reader the more benign and realistic portrait of the 'autonomous citizen' through law. As Professor Raz comments (in an article in 2003, 'Between authority and morality') even fairly straightforward legal institutions like contract law enable the creation of business relationships which would not exist outside institutional contexts – for example, neither corporations nor intellectual property could exist outside the law. The law makes a significant and decisive contribution to the realisation of the moral goal of the autonomous citizen under law.

Austin's view of the law as 'coercive commands from a sovereign' neglects another important social fact of modern legal systems – namely, that many of the legal officials and some citizens actually accept the law without being coerced into compliance. This is the 'internal point of view' which Hart sought to understand and which is completely missed by the 'command' account of law. The central message of Hart is that law must be understood from the 'internal' point of view. This 'internal point of view' is the way of thinking of someone who treats a legal rule as a reason for action. Austin's account of law, with its emphasis on coercion, cannot account for the view of many officials of a legal system who regard the existence of a legal rule as a 'reason for action' independent of any threatened sanction for non-compliance.

More generally, Hart commented in *The Concept of Law* that the model of laws as commands should be replaced by an idea of law as a system of rules for the guidance of officials and citizens alike, both in and out of court.[7] The notion of law as a series of 'commands' cannot account for the conduct guidance feature of law whereby persons use law as standards for conduct as well as using the law to plan their lives. Hart's central conception of law as 'the union of primary and secondary rules' has been very influential and must be taken to have effectively replaced the view of laws as being 'commands of the sovereign'.

Although Professor Raz is a legal positivist and accepts the 'sources thesis', he believes that the Austinian model of law is fundamentally flawed because it cannot account for the 'authority of law'. Professor Raz points out that a central feature of law is that it claims authority. The existence of a sanction is not supposed to be the primary reason why the law insists it should be obeyed. The law claims itself to be 'an exclusionary reason for action' in that the law claims binding force for itself to the exclusion of any reasons for non-compliance the citizen may have. The existence of a sanction is merely an auxiliary (supporting) reason for obeying the law. As Raz explains, in his 1975 book *Practical Reason and Norms*, the fact that so far as sanctions go the law is merely an auxiliary reason is not intended to belittle the importance of legal sanctions. Sanctions are an important way of securing social co-ordination and of providing persons with reasons for conforming to the law.[8] However, the sanction-based attempt to explain the authority of law leads to a dead end, says Raz. So it is the fact that the law has been promulgated by the legitimate authority (such as Parliament) which is intended by the lawmakers to be the exclusionary reason for the obedience of citizens, and the sanction attached to the law is only a supporting reason for the recalcitrant. Raz claims that the law's claim to supreme authority within a territory is a significant and distinctive feature of the law's method of social organisation; this is missed by the Austinian model of law, which sees the law ultimately as the tool of a 'gangster writ large'.[9]

NOTES

The critique of Austin in Hart's *The Concept of Law* (1961) is justly famous (see Chapters 2, 3 and 4) but Raz's account of 'exclusionary reasons' should be examined in *Practical Reason and Norms* (1975). Raz's important essay 'Authority, Law and Morality', (1985) The Monist, reprinted in *Ethics in the Public Domain* (1994), should also be consulted.

....

7   Hart's account of modern law as a system of publicly promulgated and administered rules guarded by a cadre of specialist legal professionals is very similar to Max Weber's much earlier account of modern law in *On Law in Economy and Society*.

8   Sanctions to obey the law will grow in importance as the traditional bonds that hold society together and produce conformity to law such as family, ethnic identity and religion substantially weaken.

9   Some could argue that what distinguishes law from the demands of a gangster is the 'sway of norms' (see Question 5 in this book) in that a gangster normally orders only a few people about whereas legal systems do so for millions of persons. Raz would insist that what distinguishes law from a gangster is that law claims legitimate authority for its demands.

QUESTION 9

Was Professor Hart engaged in mere description of the concept of law when he wrote *The Concept of Law* in 1961?

How to Answer this Question

An issue currently forming one of the main controversies in jurisprudence is whether it is possible to have a descriptive account of the concept of law, or rather whether all legal theorists are committed to some ultimate view as to the point, value or purpose of law. Professor Hart (1907–1992) has always maintained that his analysis of law has been from a detached 'external' point of view, even if he acknowledges that legal theory must take into account the 'internal committed' point of view of participants in the legal system. The recognition of the 'internal point of view' has a major role to play in Hart's *The Concept of Law* (1961).[10] However, acceptance of the reality of the 'internal point of view' does not entail personal acceptance of the legitimacy of law from the legal theorist himself. Hart must be correct because an anarchist (Hart is not an anarchist) who denies the legitimacy of all coercive law could still give an account of a modern legal system, including the 'internal' point of view. However, Professor Dworkin has argued that all meaningful theories of law are driven by a view of law's point or function and that this entails a 'justification' of law in liberal democracies. Professor Raz has sought to defend Hart by arguing that general descriptive legal theory is possible despite Dworkin's assertions.

Applying the Law

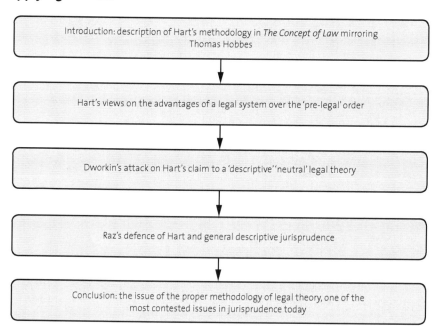

Introduction: description of Hart's methodology in *The Concept of Law* mirroring Thomas Hobbes

Hart's views on the advantages of a legal system over the 'pre-legal' order

Dworkin's attack on Hart's claim to a 'descriptive' 'neutral' legal theory

Raz's defence of Hart and general descriptive jurisprudence

Conclusion: the issue of the proper methodology of legal theory, one of the most contested issues in jurisprudence today

---

10 A new edition of Hart's *The Concept of Law* (3rd edition) appears in 2012 with an explanatory introductory essay by Leslie Green.

ANSWER

Professor Hart (1907–1992), in the preface to *The Concept of Law* (1961), comments that his aim has been to further the understanding of law, coercion and morality as different but related social phenomena and that the book can be viewed as an essay in descriptive sociology. Certainly, Hart's jurisprudence is not tied to a particular legal system but aims to give a general account of the concept of law as it has appeared in different human societies. The key question is whether a general descriptive theory of law is possible, as Hart asserts, or whether even Hart's legal positivism was driven by some contestable view of law's function or value and is therefore a view of law that can be contested by rival theories of law, such as that propounded by Professor Dworkin.

As well as attacking Austin's concept of law, Hart also builds his own theory out of the ashes of the 'command theory'. As Hart comments, Austin's account of law is the record of a failure and there is plainly need for a fresh start. That fresh start is introduced on pp. 89–96 of *The Concept of Law* in which Hart invents a story designed to show the value to any 'pre-legal' society of having a legal system. The story is not intended by Hart to describe any historical reality but rather is meant to illustrate how a pre-legal system might benefit from a legal system. The story begins in what Hart calls a pre-legal society, which is governed purely by rules of obligation – a set of commands and prohibitions. Hart points out the social defects of such a regime and how the addition of secondary rules to the primary rules of obligation cures the defects of the pre-legal order. The methodology of Hart here is interesting as it recalls the work of Thomas Hobbes (1588–1679) in his work *Leviathan* in 1651, in which Hobbes, as a conceptual device, imagines a society without any central authority, such a situation being termed by Hobbes 'the state of nature'. The defects of 'the state of nature' – which include a perpetual state of war as man fights man and an ever-present risk of violent death – are cured by the establishment of an absolute authority through a social covenant when each person acquiesces to absolute authority which, in turn, guarantees the safety of person and property.

In the spirit of Thomas Hobbes, who asked us to imagine the horrors of life without state authority, Professor Hart asks us to consider life without law and how the introduction of secondary rules helps to cure the defects of the pre-legal order. There is no claim by Hart that pre-legal societies ever did exist; rather, as for the Hobbesian 'state of nature', the Hartian 'pre-legal society' serves as an analytical or conceptual device in order to better illustrate an important point. Hart points out the defects of a pre-legal regime. Those defects in the pre-legal order are threefold: (1) uncertainty, (2) static quality – an inability to change the rules, and (3) inefficiency.

As Hart explains in *The Concept of Law*, the rules by which the pre-legal society lives will not form a system but will simply be a separate set of standards without any identifying mark. Therefore, as Hart rightly points out, if doubts arise as to what the rules are or as to the precise scope of some given rule, there will be no procedure for settling the doubts by reference to an authority set up by secondary rules to determine the issue. This is the defect of uncertainty cured by the addition to the primary rules of secondary rules concerning the establishment, authority and jurisdiction of courts. A second defect is the static character of the primary rules. There will be no means in the pre-legal order of deliberately adapting or eliminating old rules in the light of changing circumstances. The remedy for this defect is the addition of secondary rules concerning the introduction, variation and repeal of primary rules. The third defect of the pre-legal order is inefficiency of that society as disputes arise as to whether a rule has or has not been breached. Again, the introduction of secondary rules to set up courts to deal quickly and authoritatively with the question of breach of the primary rules is the remedy for the pre-legal problems.

Hart argues that the introduction of secondary rules to deal with the three main defects sees the emergence of a recognisable legal order and, in a key phrase of Hart, the concept of law may be most illuminatingly characterised as 'a union of primary and secondary rules'.

For Hart, the most important secondary rule is the 'rule of recognition'. This rule specifies some feature or features, possession of which by a purported rule is a conclusive indication that the rule is a legal rule and not only a mere rule of morality, custom or religion. As Hart says, where a secondary rule of recognition is accepted and used for the identification of primary rules of obligation, then that situation is the foundation of a legal system. This all seems as if Hart was, in value-neutral terms, merely describing the benefits to a society of adopting a legal system over a pre-legal order of simple primary rules. However, Hart has a firm view of the value of law, which is related to the co-ordinating virtues of clarity and certainty that law provides to a society. For Hart, a legal system provides a settled, public and dependable set of standards for private and official conduct which cannot be called into question by any person's sense of morality or policy. If Hart had identified other defects in the pre-legal order – such as that the regime of primary rules does not provide any forum for discussion as to whether the primary rules form a set of coherent principles – then Hart might have been led to a different account of legal order, one in which adjudication in 'hard cases' was a prominent feature of his theory of law.

Indeed, Professor Dworkin believes that Hart and other legal positivists are driven by a contestable vision of the value of law and that Hart is not merely presenting a description of the concept of law for use by sociologists or historians of legal systems. Dworkin, in an important article for students of jurisprudence entitled 'Hart's Postscript and the character of political philosophy' (in the 2004 *Oxford Journal of Legal Studies*), has argued that proper legal theory is concerned with the interpretation of law so as to justify its use as the mechanism by which the state's monopoly on the use of legitimate force is expressed. Dworkin rejects Hart's view that whilst Dworkin is engaged in the important but narrow issue of how judges should decide hard cases, Hart simply describes these activities in a general and philosophical way and describes them as a detached observer from the outside. Dworkin insists that legal positivism – in particular, Hart's legal positivism – is driven by ethical claims about the value of law. As Dworkin states, legal positivists all stress the role of law in substituting crisp direction for the uncertainties of morality and custom. For Bentham, the law's efficiency would be undermined if the identification of law was made to turn even in part on moral argument, since persons disagree about the requirements of morality; the consequent disorganisation in the identification of the law would produce chaos, thought Bentham. Hart wrote that law cures the inefficiencies of a mythical pre-legal state of custom. Raz argues that the essence of law is authority and that authority through law is undermined if the identification of law, even partly, depends on moral argument. For legal positivists, from Hobbes to Bentham to Hart and Raz, the idea of law makes social co-ordination possible, so positivism insists that morality should and does play no role in identifying true claims of law. Dworkin concludes that legal positivism has appeal only when its underlying views of the function of law are brought out because mere description of the concept of law is not possible.[11]

Dworkin's views of the purposes of legal theory are hotly contested in Hart's 'Postscript' to *The Concept of Law* (1994, 2nd edition) and in the jurisprudential writings of Raz. Hart, in his 'Postscript', claims that his account of law is descriptive in that it has no justificatory aims – it does not seek to commend law to anyone. Hart comments that his legal theory is descriptive and general in a way Dworkin's theory of law is not, as Dworkin's theory is addressed to the particular culture of Anglo-American law. As contributors in a recent book celebrating Hart's contribution to legal thought maintain (*The Legacy of HLA Hart* (2008), edited by Kramer and Grant), Hart always said that legal philosophers themselves need not adopt the internal perspective of a committed participant in a legal system but that the best vantage point for a legal philosopher was to analyse law from a detached 'external' point of view, even though the astute legal philosopher will attend to the 'internal' point of view – the 'outlook' of the persons who are being subject to philosophical enquiry without the legal philosopher sharing that 'internal' point of view himself. Hart comments that he finds it hard to follow why Dworkin appears to rule out general and descriptive legal theory as at best 'useless', in Dworkin's word, to describe legal theory. Indeed, Hart has a strong ally in Professor Raz who believes that the true purpose of legal theory is to be general and value-neutral in approach. In an article published in 2004, 'Can there be a theory of law?', Raz comments that legal theory is an attempt to explain the nature of a certain kind of social institution and that law as a concept occupies a central role in our understanding of our own and other societies.[12] Raz comments that the inquiry of true legal theory is universal in that it explores the nature of law wherever it is to be found, not merely a justification of the Anglo-American legal system as found in Dworkin's 'localised' legal theory.

The question as to whether legal theory can be usefully descriptive or must inevitably have some justificatory purpose is one of the most contested issues in legal theory today. In this issue not only the content of jurisprudence but its whole methodology and its purpose are in contest. It is perhaps the 'holy grail' of jurisprudential questions.

....

11   Professor Dworkin argues that a 'pre-interpretive' description of law is possible but that such an account is not interesting or useful. Dworkin claims that legal positivists offer no evidence to support their claims to explain 'all' legal systems: see *Justice in Robes'* (2006) at p. 212 where Dworkin says:

> 'legal positivists celebrate positivism as an accurate description of the very concept of law or as the most illuminating theoretical description of legal phenomena over time. But they offer no empirical evidence that might support large generalizations about the forms and histories of legal institutions.'

12   Therefore for Raz, legal theory is not an arid and uninteresting part of philosophy but can improve our self-understanding of our own culture through examination of a central cultural creation: the law.

NOTES

The preface to the original *The Concept of Law* (1961) by Professor Hart should be consulted, as should the 'Postscript' by Hart to the second edition of *The Concept of Law* (1994), for Hart's own views as to his aims in legal theory. The most important source for Professor Dworkin's views on the proper methodology for legal theory is the essay 'Hart's Postscript and the Character of Political Philosophy' (2004) *Oxford Journal of Legal Studies*, vol 24, no 1, pp. 1–37. Raz's views can be found in his essay 'Can There be a Theory of Law?' (2004) available on Raz's website (http://josephnraz. googlepages.com/home). A useful discussion of the 'methodological' debate in legal theory between Dworkin on the one side and Hart and Raz on the other can be found in Andrei Marmor's essay 'The Nature of Law' (2007), to be found on the online and free *Stanford Encyclopedia of Philosophy* (http://plato.stanford.edu/).

QUESTION 10 ---

How have later legal theorists sought to improve upon Hart's analysis in *The Concept of Law* (1961)?

How to Answer this Question

Professor Hart only intended *The Concept of Law* published in 1961 to be a student text in the Clarendon Law Series of which he was the editor. It is ironic that *The Concept* as it is known in jurisprudential circles has come to be treated as Hart's *magnum opus* or masterwork on legal philosophy, when it was only meant to function as an introductory student text. Hart moved away from cutting edge work in legal philosophy after 1961 in favour of topics such as 'Causation in the Law' and 'Punishment and Responsibility'[13] so *The Concept of Law* came to be viewed as Hart's defining work in pure jurisprudence. As Nicola Lacey points out, in her very readable biography of Hart: *The Nightmare and the Noble Dream* (2004), Hart's aim was to present his own theory of law as an accessible student text. Lacey quotes Hart's notebook written at the time (1961) on his aims with the publication of *The Concept of Law*:

> 'My ambition … is to dispel forever the definitional will o' the wisps – the search for 'definitions' of law – by showing that all that can be done and is important to do is to characterise the *Concept* of law by identifying the main elements and organization of elements which constitute a *standard* legal *system*.'[14]

Therefore *The Concept of Law* (1961) should be read as an effort to provide a general and descriptive account of the main elements of a standard legal system. It is not correct then

....

13   Professor Hart did publish on legal philosophy after 1961 most notably in the collection of essays *Essays on Bentham* (1982) and *Essays in Jurisprudence and Philosophy* (1983) and published a rebuttal of Dworkin's arguments in the 'Postscript' to the second edition of *The Concept of Law* in 1994.

14   Hart in *The Concept of Law* second edition 'Postscript' (1994) maintained that his legal theory was both 'general' and 'descriptive' in other words an attempt to describe the main elements of a general or standard legal system.

for Professor Finnis in his various writings to suggest that his own 'ideal theory of law' – a rational system of norms for the co-ordination of the common good – is an improvement on Hart's theory. Hart's descriptive value-neutral account of law, not commending the institution of law to anyone was a radically different jurisprudential enterprise to Finnis's description of law from the standpoint of an approved ideal form of law – see *Natural Law and Natural Rights* (1980). Of course Hart's theory of law in *The Concept of Law* (1961) is by no means perfect. Hart in his description of a standard legal system says too little about the subtleties of common law adjudication which Professor Dworkin so ruthlessly exploited in subsequent years and led to Hart becoming somewhat preoccupied with his American critic so that nearly all Hart's 'Postscript' to the second edition of *The Concept of Law* (1994) is taken up with replying to Dworkin's criticisms of Hart's own legal theory. Indeed in the 'Postscript' Hart says a lot more about common law reasoning in 'hard cases' that was omitted in the original *The Concept of Law*. Other writers have used Hart as a starting point, including Dennis Galligan in *Law in Modern Society* (2007) who refers to Hart's 1961 work as 'a classic'. Whatever subsequent critics have said about Hart's work in *The Concept of Law* (1961) it will always have the status of reviving serious philosophical interest in the philosophy of law. Hart is the modern heir of the legal methodology adopted by Bentham, which is what Hart terms in 'Essays on Bentham' as the 'sane and healthy centre of legal positivism' – the calculatedly neutral approach to the definition of legal and social phenomena.

Applying the Law

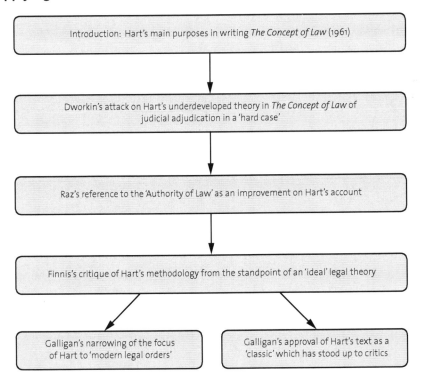

ANSWER --

Hart's *The Concept of Law* (1961) is widely considered to be the canonical text of modern jurisprudence. The book in many ways represented 'year zero' for jurisprudence, a new start after the failures of Austinian jurisprudence which had dominated English jurisprudence for over a century. As John Finnis comments in 'Natural Law: The Classical Tradition' (in *The Oxford Handbook of Jurisprudence and Philosophy* edited by Coleman and Shapiro 2002):

> 'Late twentieth century legal theory's paradigm text is called 'The Concept of Law ... Hart might more accurately, if less elegantly, have called his book "A New and Improved Concept of Law".'

It is somewhat ironic that Hart's book should have this 'central text' status since the book was originally conceived by Hart as a book for undergraduate students, a product of his lecture notes at Oxford University. The aim was to produce his own theory of law as an accessible student text. In his biographical note for Hart in the *Oxford Dictionary of National Biography*, Tony Honore comments of Hart's book:

> 'his aim was to give beginners in jurisprudence a book that that was more than a catalogue of great names spiced with superficial comments on their theories. Instead they would be introduced to the main issues in the subject of which two stood out: the relation of law to brute force on the one hand and morality on the other.... For writers on jurisprudence criticism of Hart at once replaced criticism of Austin as the starting point of their thinking. It seeks to lay bare the structure of modern legal systems and to show what it is that separates them from other forms of social control such as brute force or morality.'

So a 'student text' became treated as Hart's major work in legal theory and this trend was confirmed by the fact that Hart, quite early on, abandoned major work in legal theory in favour of other pursuits such as academic administration (Hart was President of Brasenose College, Oxford), editing Bentham's copious works and writing on other aspects of law such as *Punishment and Responsibility* (1968).

Hart is sometimes criticised for not analysing in *The Concept of Law* the role of the common law with its conflicting principles in the 'rule' dominated analysis of law found in *The Concept of Law*. Brian Simpson, drawing on his deep knowledge of the common law, argued that Hart's analysis of a legal system does not fit the 'muddle' of the common law (see 'The Common Law and Legal Theory' in *Oxford Essays in Jurisprudence* (1973)). Brian Simpson further criticises Hart in his comments (Michigan Law Review 2005) that:

> 'the book (*The Concept of Law*) devotes virtually no attention whatever to the working of the common law tradition: indeed the common law does not appear in the index and is hardly mentioned in the entire book.'

It may be said that Hart was overly influenced by the 'legislation model' of law so beloved of the 'command theorists', Austin and Bentham, and also by Kelsen's legislation slanted legal theory and that as a consequence Hart adopted the view that law is fundamentally a matter of varied but still legislated 'rules'. However, to defend Hart against this charge of neglecting the common law's place in the legal system, we may return to the point that Hart was interested in describing a 'standard' or 'archetypal' legal system and in such an archetype, the common law may not necessarily be a feature. It is wise to remember that Hart, in his legal theory, was concerned with generality of scope, aiming to describe a 'standard' legal system and was not in the business of giving an accurate definition of the Anglo-American legal systems with its common law element.

Hart's text in *The Concept of Law* was used as the basis for the launch of Professor Dworkin's own anti-positivistic theory of law, such as the article 'The Model of Rules' (1967) which heavily criticised Hart's notion that law could be understood as a system of different kind of rules. Dworkin argued through a number of articles and finally in his book *Law's Empire* (1986) that, contrary to Hart's analysis, law could not be identified in the form of a master rule or recognition, but rather that the law of the Anglo-American legal system was identified through the moral interpretation of existing law. However a way has been suggested to defend Hart from Dworkin's attack, whilst acknowledging that judges in the Anglo-American legal system sometimes use moral arguments to identify the law. Jules Coleman in a 1982 article 'Negative and Positive Positivism' argues that in the Anglo-American legal system there is an 'accepted social practice' among judges that where the law is unclear then the case will be decided by the moral interpretation of existing law. This 'accepted social practice' amongst judges to decide cases in that way is itself part of the rule of recognition. Moreover, because that 'accepted judicial practice' of using morality to identify law is true only of certain legal systems then the legal positivist argument of Hart, that law everywhere is identified by reference to sources, is unaffected. Hart can therefore agree with Dworkin that certain legal systems recognise a judicial social practice where difficult cases are resolved by reference to moral arguments but that it is the 'social practice' that gives such moral arguments their legitimacy and not the moral principles themselves as Dworkin argues. This 'inclusive legal positivism' suggested by Coleman was given approval by Hart in the second edition of *The Concept of Law* (1994).

However, some legal positivists, such as Professor Raz, reject 'inclusive legal positivism' in favour of a hardline 'exclusive positivism'. For Raz the identification of law can never turn on a moral argument for the very essence of law is that it is an exercise in authority to replace the moral reasons underlying the legal directive with the finality of law's authority. If citizens had to employ moral arguments to work out the content of the law then this would undermine the very point of the law, which is to replace the uncertainties of morality with the crisp authority of law. Raz has stood fast to the 'sources thesis' namely that the existence and content of the law can be determined without resorting to any moral argument.

Raz has generally been sympathetic to Hart's *The Concept of Law* but a few points of distinction need to be made. First of all Raz maintains a harder version of legal positivism than Hart. Raz believes morality plays no part in the identification of law (although Raz agrees that law is often heavily influenced by morality), whereas Hart is prepared to accept a softer version of legal positivism where in some jurisdictions accepted judicial practice allows morality some place in the identification of law in hard cases. Secondly, Hart in *The Concept of Law* correctly pointed out that there was a crucial difference between the demands of the taxman and the gangster and that this distinction was captured in the difference between 'being obliged' and 'being under an obligation'. However although Hart noted descriptively the legitimacy of law's demands over the demands of a gangster, apparent also in Hart's idea of the 'internal point of view' of someone who endorses a legal order as valid irrespective of sanctions for non-compliance, Hart did not fully bring out the point that the law by its nature claims legitimate authority. It was Raz, in works such as *The Authority of Law* (1979) who firmly made the point concerning law's authority that law is differentiated from the brute force of the gangster by law's claim to authority. In a development of the legal positivist tradition, of which Hart himself represented a significant improvement over Austin's 'command theory', Raz comments in *The Authority of Law*:

> 'Put in a nutshell, the law is a system of guidance and adjudication claiming supreme authority within a certain society.'

This is a definition which Hart was feeling towards in *The Concept of Law* but perhaps because of his dislike of 'definitions' of law he was not as crisp on the point of the law's authority as he should have been in *The Concept of Law*.

Perhaps because Hart was writing *The Concept of Law* primarily for a student audience then his analysis of law and legal systems can seem simplistic. A good example of Hart's simplistic reduction of legal systems to a basic level of description is Hart's claim that:

> 'law may most illuminatingly be characterized as a union of primary rules … with … secondary rules.'

This alleged 'key' to understanding law and legal systems offered by Hart is similar in its distorting simplicity to Austin's claim that the 'key' to jurisprudence was understanding law as 'the commands of the sovereign' a view of law which Hart was at such pains to reject in *The Concept of Law*.

The simplistic reduction by Hart, in *The Concept of Law*, of the institution of law to a system of primary and secondary rules **'will not do'**, as MacCormick comments in *Institutions of Law* (2007). As a final analysis of legal systems the reducing of legal systems to a union of primary rules and secondary rules about those primary rules is inadequate even as an explanation for Hart's undergraduate students in 1961. On this account of legal systems provided by Hart, the law is not distinguished from sporting organisations or social clubs that also have basic primary rules of permitted and prohibited conduct but also have secondary rules specifying the procedure for the variation or elimination or replacement of the basic primary rules. Hart had, therefore, failed to distinguish between law and sporting or social clubs in his account of legal systems as consisting of a union of 'primary and secondary rules'. Indeed Hart commented in *The Concept of Law*:

'"a legal system is a complex union of primary and secondary rules…" and that such a union of rules is: "the heart of a legal system".'

Hart could have added that such a union of rules is also the heart of a sporting association or social club. Hart therefore failed in one of his tasks in *The Concept of Law* (1961) which was to distinguish law from other social institutions. Hart's 'key' to understanding law does not provide in its structure a way of distinguishing legal systems from organised sports. For the source of this biting criticism of Hart's theory of law, which holds that Hart does not distinguish legal systems from sporting clubs, see Professor Dworkin in the *Harvard Law Review* Forum (2006): 'Hart and the Concepts of Law'.

Professor Finnis in *Natural Law and Natural Rights* (1980) took Hart's analysis in *The Concept of Law* as the starting point for his breathing of new life into the old tradition of natural law theorising. As Finnis has commented in 'On Hart's Ways: Law as Reason and as Fact' (in *The Legacy of HLA Hart* (2008), edited by Kramer *et al.*), Hart's work:

'is a standing invitation to develop legal theory's critical account and promotion of those considerations of justice, of concern for the common good and make law salient as a means of governance.'

For Finnis, Hart's account of a modern legal system found in *The Concept of Law* (1961) is incomplete because Hart did not, in his descriptive account of law, tie that description to the 'central case' of a legal system, which is an ordering of reason for the common good. Finnis believes that an adequate description of those legal systems which work for the common good (such as modern Western democracies) cannot be given without attending to the moral purposes of those legal systems, which is to further the common good. For Finnis the human institution we call 'law' has a specific moral purpose, namely the common good of a community. For Finnis **the 'central case'** or 'central example' legal system is an arrangement rationally prescribed by those responsible for the community for the common good of its members. Hart in *The Concept of Law* famously introduced the 'internal point of view', the point of view of participants in a legal system who accepted the law as a valid set of standards for conduct. Hart famously said 'acceptance' of law by legal officials could be based on habit, a wish to conform, calculations of long term interest etc. Finnis argued in *Natural Law and Natural Rights* that the 'central case' of the internal point of view was the legal official who accepted the law because he saw a moral duty to uphold the legal order for the common good of the community. Therefore Finnis seeks to improve Hart's analysis by seeking to widen and deepen the description of a legal system by reference to an 'ideal' type of legal system, namely a legal system that is working for the common good. Of course Hart himself was seeking to describe law and legal systems in descriptive social-scientific terms, as he famously said in the Preface to the original *The Concept of Law*, the book could read as an essay in 'descriptive sociology'. Indeed in the 'Postscript' to the second edition of *The Concept of Law* Hart commented:

'like other forms of positivism my theory makes no claim to identify the point or purpose of law and legal practices as such…. In fact I think it quite vain to seek any more specific purpose which law as such serves beyond providing guides to human conduct and standards of criticism of such conduct.'

Ultimately, then, it is not possible to see the work of Finnis as an 'improvement' upon Hart for Hart was aiming at general, even universal, coverage of legal systems morally good, morally bad or indifferent whereas Finnis was aiming at an account of those few legal systems working genuinely for the common good. In other words Finnis's work is 'engaged' with law as a social institution, Hart's work is 'disengaged' from law as a social institution and it is absurd to see Finnis's work as an improvement upon Hart's *The Concept of Law*.

Another legal philosopher who sought to 'improve' upon Hart's account in *The Concept of Law* is Dennis Galligan who, in 2007, published *Law in Modern Society*. Galligan aims to give a rich descriptive account of what he calls 'modern legal orders' – the few legal orders, mainly of Europe, North America and the former British Empire such as Australia, where the rule of law is virtually fully realised. Galligan pays his respects to Hart's *The Concept of Law* by commenting:

> 'his account is illuminating, has acquired the status of a classic, and on the whole has stood up to critics.'

However, by narrowing his focus to the few 'modern legal orders', Galligan hoped to bring out certain crucial features missed by Hart in his general account of all modern legal systems. As Galligan notes:

> 'In modern legal orders, officials have special relations with citizens … A noticeable aspect of Hart's account is that, while officials are placed at the centre, citizens are relegated to the margins. For Hart a legal system in its essentials consists of general obedience to law by the people and acceptance by officials of the rules of the system. The idea of citizens needing only to obey, while officials accept, may be justified in a very general way in relation to legal systems generally, but hardly matches the character of modern legal orders and needs to be reconsidered.'

For Galligan in *Law in Modern Society* the special relations between citizens and officials is one of the defining features of a modern legal order and explains legal doctrines such as the separation of powers, judicial review of executive action and the possibility of bringing civil actions, such as false imprisonment against the police for example.[15] Galligan argues that in Hart's concern in *The Concept of Law* to settle on a description of law wide enough to cover all legal orders from the good to the bad to the intolerable, Hart had to take account of legal systems sustained by legal officials with the barest support of the people – hence the criticism that Hart's account is 'legal official centred'.

However, Galligan argues in practice that in order for legal systems to be stable over the long term they need the support, not just the obedience, of the people. As Galligan comments:

> 'the support (not just the obedience) of the people is essential to preserve any form of rule, no matter how strong. In its absence or loss, inherent instability or fragility will be manifest.'

---

15 The **Bribery Act 2010** is a modern attempt to bolster public trust in legal and other officials.

Galligan is clearly in the business of justifying and supporting the great social benefits that modern Western legal orders bring in terms of social peace and prosperity. Although valuable this is very different legal theory from Hart's in *The Concept of Law* who aimed to describe legal systems in terms which would cover the very wide range of human situations and societies where law appears.

However, it may be that Hart was right in his analysis to focus on legal officials in his account of a legal system and that Galligan is unduly romantic and optimistic in his description of the 'bond of trust' between legal officials and citizens in a modern legal order. In an article in 2010 (*Oxford Journal of Legal Studies*) Michael Wilkinson argues:

> 'Is it in the nature of modern society for subjects to become alienated from their laws? Do the features of modern society tend to distance subjects from genuine engagement with the law and can this be seen in the way modern law becomes official, specialised and institutionalised? There may well be something about modern society that promotes a retreat by the subject to the private sphere, and the adoption of a limited and deficient sense of acceptance of law that is purely self-interested or sheep-like.'

This vision of modern Western society and its legal system is far removed from the 'bond of trust' between legal officials and citizens that Galligan said characterised modern legal orders. Perhaps Hart, in his unromantic and realistic way, was correct to give an account of law in terms of the acceptance by legal officials of legal norms. Citizens in anonymous, massive consumerist Western societies can view the legal order as remote, technical and arcane. Law is, then, on this pessimistic view a 'distinctively official practice' – an account which Hart caught well in *The Concept of Law*.

Hart was well aware of the risks involved in the institution of law and refused to be 'romantic' (as Finnis and Galligan are 'romantic' about law in their different ways: in the sense that they tend to view law through 'rose-tinted lenses') about law.

Law has of course been used for hideous oppression in the past but law also brings with it other forms of dangers as Leslie Green argues in 'The Inseparability of Law and Morality':

> 'the necessary moral hazards of law include not just better organized and more efficient instruments of oppression; but also new forms of oppression: the alienation of community and value, the rise of hierarchy, domination by experts, and the docility of those who are bought off by the goods that legal order brings.'

Given the moral hazards of instituting a system of law then it was wise of Hart to seek to frame his explanation of law in terms of an institutionalised normative system resting on a consensus of thought and action amongst legal elites. Hart was right to distance himself from any 'romantic' view of law that seeks to give an account of law from the standpoint of some alleged ideal, whether that ideal be 'Law as Integrity' (Dworkin), 'law as an ordering of rationality for the common good' (Finnis) or 'a bond of trust' between legal officials and citizens in a 'modern legal order' (Galligan).

HLA Hart in *The Concept of Law* (1961) aimed to give his students a 'road map' of the main features of a legal system without offering himself any endorsement of such a system. Hart's 'general and descriptive' purposes can be seen in the following features he highlighted:

(1) The different types of legal rules performing differing functions, some rules prohibitory such as the criminal law but some enabling and facilitating the lives of citizens such as laws on contract, wills and marriage.

(2) The 'internal' point of view of legal officials and some citizens who accept the legal rules as valid for a variety of reasons – self-interest, habit, a desire to conform but at least an acceptance of the law going beyond a fear of sanctions

(3) The 'rule of recognition' as the criteria for validity in a legal system differentiating the law from morality, social custom and other social rules. Hart provided an account of how the rule of recognition is identified – through observing the actions and attitudes of legal officials and an account of its importance – Hart said that the rule of recognition was the knot of the legal system.

(4) The minimum necessary conditions for a legal system to exist which Hart defined as (a) acceptance by legal officials of the rule of recognition and hence the legal system, (b) obedience to the law by the bulk of the population.

(5) The general benefits that a legal system can bring to a society which Hart explains in his famous 'fable' of the pre-legal society which, by adding the institution of law to the pre-legal social rules, gains the benefits of certainty, efficiency and adaptability in the handling of the basic rules of the pre-legal society.

(6) Hart stressed how law is used in society to plan and organise life out of court.

However, in all this description of law and legal systems generally Hart was not committing himself (unlike other theorists such as Dworkin or Finnis) to a view that law was 'a good thing' or 'intrinsically valuable'. Although he was not an anarchist Hart could have been an anarchist sociologist writing *The Concept of Law* as a rough guide for his students as to what a legal system was and its possible benefits, but in the end reserving judgment as to the inherent value of law to society knowing that law is 'morally risky'. Hart was, above all, keen not to romanticise legal phenomena. As Hart said in *Essays in Jurisprudence and Philosophy* (1983):

'The identification of the central meaning of law with what is morally legitimate, because oriented towards the common good, seems to me in view of the hideous record of the evil use of law to be an unbalanced perspective, and as great a distortion of the opposite Marxist identification of the central case of law with the pursuit of the interests of a dominant economic class.'

Given man's inherent moral imperfection and a consequent tendency in human affairs for things to go badly then Hart may have been correct to have said that the institution of law itself could be used for evil purposes as equally as good purposes.

However, a conservative thinker might argue that it is precisely because of mankind's inherent moral imperfection that law and government are a necessity and that therefore law cannot be separated from the realisation of the common good through law's restraining of the evil impulses within mankind. As Anthony Quinton comments on the traditions of conservative thought in England:

> 'The consequence of men's moral imperfection is that men, acting on their own uncontrolled impulses, will on the whole act badly, however elevated their professed intentions may be. They need, therefore, the restraint of customary and established laws and institutions, of an objective and impersonal barrier to the dangerous extravagance of subjective, personal impulse.'

Therefore on the conservative reading of human nature, which is not purely inspired by the Christian religion's doctrine of 'original sin' but was also shared by the atheistic Thomas Hobbes and David Hume from observation of human nature, **law and government are accepted as necessities** given the moral imperfection of mankind. Perhaps then there is **a closer connection** between the institution of law and the realisation of the common good than Professor Hart allowed for in his legal philosophy: the institution of law is a necessity given the inherent human tendency to do the morally bad rather than the morally good. Anthony Quinton expressed the point well about the necessity of government and law in *The Politics of Imperfection* (1978):

> 'the conservative … locates the need for government in the propensity for anti-social conduct that is to be found in every-one … His ideal government has to be strong, since it has to control a universal impulse.'

The institution of law, given the unpleasant realities of human nature, is then tied to the realisation of the common good in a way which is much more in tune with the views of natural lawyers such as Finnis in *Natural Law and Natural Rights* (1980) than Professor Hart's detached social-scientific approach to law found in *The Concept of Law* (1961).

Aim Higher

Students can gain extra marks by noting how, even to the very end of his writings (see the 'Postscript' to the second edition of *The Concept of Law* (1994)). Hart maintained that his purpose in legal theory was general and descriptive with no agenda to justify or recommend law to anyone. Students can avoid the pitfall of thinking that Hart was, in *The Concept of Law*, arguing for the moral superiority of law over a pre-legal order. Hart merely pointed out some very general benefits of the institution of law, whilst at the same time recognising the risks law can bring in terms of the organised coercion of the population.

NOTES

Professor Hart's reply to Dworkin's criticisms of Hart's theory of law is best seen in 'The Postscript' to *The Concept of Law* (1994, 2nd edition) edited by Bulloch and Raz. Galligan's praise of Hart can be found in *Law in Modern Society* (2007), pp. 6–18. Nicola Lacey's insightful biography of Hart: *A Life of H.L.A. Hart: The Nightmare and the Noble Dream* (2005) has good material on *The Concept of Law* at pp. 221–233.

QUESTION 11 --

Has Dworkin, in his theory of law, successfully overcome the appeal of legal positivism?

How to Answer this Question

Professor Dworkin has for 40 years ('The model of rules', his first attack on legal posit-ivism, appeared in 1967 and has been reprinted in *Taking Rights Seriously* (1977)) been the most erudite and eloquent critic of the tradition of legal thought we call 'legal positivism'. Dworkin initially attacked the account of judicial adjudication in appeal cases offered by legal positivism – namely, that the judge has an inescapable law making function. This characterisation of the judicial role in a 'hard case' (where settled law does not dictate an answer) was severely criticised by Dworkin, who developed his own 'gapless' theory of adjudication and law in response. By the time of *Law's Empire* in 1986, Dworkin had broad-ened his attack on 'legal positivism' to suggest that it offered a poor vision of the value and potential of law in a modern liberal democracy compared to Dworkin's own vision of 'law's empire', namely, 'law as integrity'. The debate between Dworkin and modern legal positivists, such as Professor Raz, continues today but Dworkin's vision of law represents the most complete and serious attack in legal thought on the legal positivistic tradition.

Applying the Law

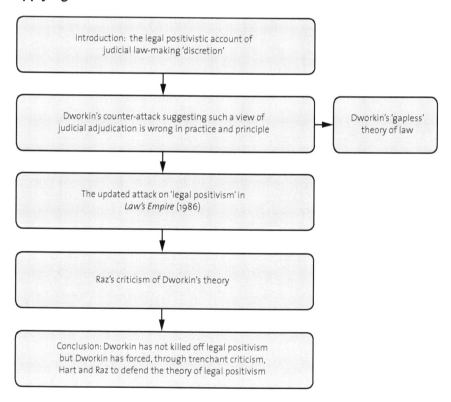

Introduction: the legal positivistic account of judicial law-making 'discretion'

Dworkin's counter-attack suggesting such a view of judicial adjudication is wrong in practice and principle

Dworkin's 'gapless' theory of law

The updated attack on 'legal positivism' in *Law's Empire* (1986)

Raz's criticism of Dworkin's theory

Conclusion: Dworkin has not killed off legal positivism but Dworkin has forced, through trenchant criticism, Hart and Raz to defend the theory of legal positivism

ANSWER

Ronald Dworkin's attack on legal positivism as the reigning theory of law, from Austin and Bentham in the nineteenth century to Professor Hart in the mid-twentieth century, has been complex, shifting and sometimes persuasive. The original attack by Dworkin was on Hart's conception of legal positivism and what Dworkin took to be the inadequacies of the legal positivist account of judicial adjudication in 'hard cases', as exemplified in Dworkin's influential articles, 'The Model of Rules' (1967) and 'Hard Cases' (1975), both collected in *Taking Rights Seriously* in 1977. The fact that Hart was never focally interested in describing the judicial role in a 'hard case' (a case where the settled legal rules do not dictate an answer) in *The Concept of Law* (1961) was never acknowledged by Dworkin, and the true scope and methodology of legal theory remains a contested issue between Dworkin and the legal positivists today (see, for example, Dworkin's article on the methodology of legal theory in *Oxford Journal of Legal Studies* 2004).

Dworkin's core idea in his attack on the legal positivistic conception of law is that the idea that the law is solely identified by social sources is wrong and fails to capture the reality of legal argumentation and judicial judgment in 'hard cases' at appeal court level. Dworkin holds that what he calls the 'true grounds of law' include the best moral interpretation of existing law. If Dworkin is right then he has indeed overcome Hart's legal positivism where the 'grounds of law' are to be determined without recourse to moral argument but depend on a master factual test – 'the rule of recognition'. As a later positivist, Professor Raz comments (in his essay 'Two Views of the Nature of the Theory of Law' (2001) – see *Hart's Postscript: Essays on the Postscript to the Concept of Law*, edited by Professor Jules Coleman) that if Dworkin is right to maintain that his theory of law is correct, then Hart's theory of legal positivism is flawed at its foundations. The main issue then is whether Dworkin is correct? We can accept that Hart's and Dworkin's understanding of the character of legal philosophy differ and that Hart views his own theory as a general description of law as a type of social institution (and this 'internal point of view' of Hart's conception of his own theory deserves some weight) whereas Dworkin's focus is on Anglo-American adjudication in 'hard cases', but this difference in approach does not mean that Dworkin's theory and Hart's legal positivism can be reconciled.

Dworkin argues, in an article called 'Hard Cases' (1975), that legal positivism provides a theory of hard cases. When a particular lawsuit cannot be brought under a clear rule of law, laid down by some institution in advance, then the judge has, according to legal positivism a 'discretion' to decide the case either way. The judge, for the legal positivist, must create new law – legislate when the law runs out. For the legal positivist, the law begins and ends with the sources – the statutes, cases and conventions. Beyond the sources lies judicial discretion and judicial legislation in 'hard cases'. Dworkin argued that this theory of adjudication inherent within legal positivism is wholly inadequate. Dworkin built his immense reputation as a legal theorist by constructing an alternative theory of judicial adjudication to that offered by legal positivism, a theory of adjudication which found its most mature expression in *Law's Empire* (1986). Legal positivism is sometimes defended from Dworkin's attack by pointing out that Hart's legal positivism was concerned with a general and descriptive account of law and was not concerned with the judicial role in 'hard cases' – indeed, judicial adjudication in hard cases receives only passing reference in the whole of *The Concept of Law*. Professor Finnis writes, in *Natural Law and Natural Rights* (1980), that Dworkin's theory of law offers guidance to the judge as to his judicial duty in a 'hard case'. Hart's theory of law is a descriptive account offered to historians to enable a history of legal systems to be written. Finnis believes that Dworkin's debate with positivists such as Hart and Raz miscarries because Dworkin fails to acknowledge that Hart and Raz have no intention in their legal positivist theories of law to offer solutions to 'hard cases' disputed amongst competent lawyers.

However, against this view of Finnis we can argue that legal positivism does have a theory of 'hard cases' implicitly, even if 'hard case' adjudication is not the main or even subsidiary focus of legal positivist legal theory. We have seen that legal positivism limits the law by stipulation to the 'social sources' so that the law can perform its various functions of social co-ordination through authoritative directives. Inevitably, as the law is a bounded institution, there will be gaps in the law and here the judge has a limited law-making function, say legal positivists. Indeed, Professor Hart, in his 'Postscript' to *The Concept of Law* (1994, 2nd edition), went to some length to defend a theory of judicial law creation in 'hard cases' from Dworkinian attack. 'Hard cases' might not be central to legal positivism, but legal positivism has a theory of 'hard cases' anyway. For Dworkin, an acceptable legal theory must provide a plausible account of certain features; Dworkin finds in adjudication that, even in 'hard cases' where the 'sources' run out, the lawyers and judges argue as though there are legally binding standards to be applied. Dworkin's theory of law therefore emerges from his theory of adjudication. It may be questioned whether a theory of adjudication should not follow a theory of law. Whilst, for the legal positivist, the central legal figure is the law-maker or legislator, the central legal figure for Dworkin's theory of law is the law's interpreter: the appellate judge. Although the focus of the two theories is different, there is a small but crucial overlap between the theories concerning 'hard cases'. Dworkin has found his ground to attack legal positivism and has consistently attacked legal positivism because it fails to capture the reality of judicial adjudication in 'hard cases'.

Dworkin starts from the idea that legal positivism is both wrong as a description of 'hard case' adjudication and also politically objectionable. Judges, in the Anglo-American legal system, when they give judgment in 'hard cases' talk as if they were 'finding' the law, not 'inventing' new rights and duties. However, we can counter this argument of Dworkin by commenting that, for reasons of political acceptability, unelected judges should talk as though they are 'constrained' by law rather than owning up to their exercise of discretion in actually making law. Indeed, judges sometimes do admit that they make law, as Professor Hart points out in his 'Postscript' to *The Concept of Law* (1994). Hart comments that judges of the stature of Oliver Wendell Holmes and Cardozo in the United States, or Lord Macmillan, Lord Radcliffe or Lord Reid in England, have insisted that there are legal cases left incompletely regulated by the law where the judge has an inescapable law-making task.

Professor Dworkin has several political arguments for the view that judges should not legislate in even the hardest 'hard case'. In a democracy the power to make new law is not vested in judges but in Parliament. The law-making power should not be exercised by unelected judges. Hart responds by commenting in the 'Postscript' that the fact that judges should be entrusted with law-making powers to deal with disputes which the law fails to regulate may be regarded as a necessary price to pay for avoiding the inconveniences of alternative methods of regulating them, such as reference to the legislature; the price may seem small if judges are constrained in the exercise of these powers and cannot introduce wide reforms of the law, but only rules to deal with the specific issues thrown up by particular cases. In any case the legislature has final control over judicial legislation and may repeal or amend any judge-made law that Parliament finds unacceptable. These responses by Hart, in the second edition of *The Concept of Law* (1994), considerably take the 'sting' out of Dworkin's attack on legal positivism that judges should not make law. Hart is also determined to point out that, on his theory of judicial legislation in 'hard cases', when judges make new law it should be in accordance with principles or underpinning reasons recognised as already having a footing in the existing law. Judges in 'hard cases' do not and should not 'push away' their law books and start to legislate without further guidance from the law. However, there is still the need to legislate new law since, in any hard case, different principles may present themselves and a judge will often have to choose between them, relying like a conscientious legislator on the judge's sense of what is best in terms of new law.

Dworkin, however, has been insistent that in complex legal systems, like the Anglo-American systems, the law never runs out and that a judge, if clever enough, can always find the 'right answer' already within the existing law to any 'hard case'; this can be understood as the 'gapless' theory of law, to be contrasted with legal positivism as exemplified by Hart and Raz who regard the law as riddled with gaps. Hart, in *Essays in Jurisprudence and Philosophy* (1983), comments that Dworkin's theory of law as a gapless system of entitlements is a 'noble dream'.

Dworkin's attack on legal positivism is not just on its theory of judicial legislation but on its whole theory of law, especially the legal positivist idea that there is a single master test for law in the form of a 'rule of recognition'. Dworkin argues that there is no master test which can be devised which could capture all the legal principles in a complex legal system and, even if such a new 'rule of recognition' could be devised, it would not perform the function that the legal positivists require of it – to sharply distinguish law from other social standards. Dworkin comments, in *Taking Rights Seriously*, that if we treat principles as law, we must reject the legal positivist view that the law of a community is distinguished from other social standards by some test in the form of a master rule. Dworkin argues for a much more expansive conception of the scope of legal considerations than do the positivists. For Dworkin, the law (at least in the USA and UK), encompasses not only court decisions and legislation but the totality of the law seen by the interpreting judge as an internally coherent and consistent set of individual rights and duties. This view of law obliterates the legal positivist view of judicial legislation in 'hard cases'. It must be said that Dworkin's theory of law represents the most influential and subtle attack on legal positivism in current legal theory. It is therefore wrong for Brian Leiter (in an article in *Rutgers Law Journal* 2005, called 'The End of Empire') to comment that Dworkin's theory of law and adjudication is implausible, badly argued and largely without philosophical merit. As the respected legal theorist, Professor Finnis argues (in *The Oxford Handbook of Jurisprudence and Philosophy of Law* (2002)) we should broadly accept at least some of the main elements of Ronald Dworkin's account of adjudication. Indeed, Gerald Postema (in an article entitled 'Philosophy of the Common Law', in *The Oxford Handbook of Jurisprudence and Philosophy* (2002)) comments that Dworkin's 'interpretive' account of legal reasoning may be the best available characterisation of the intellectual process in common law reasoning.

Dworkin's core concept is that the distinction between the law and moral standards is much more blurred than legal positivism says that division is. For Dworkin, the identification of law in 'hard cases' depends in part on a best moral interpretation of existing law. Professor Raz comments, in *The Authority of Law* (1979) that Professor Dworkin has opted for the most conservative interpretation of the judicial role. Judges on Dworkin's view, according to Raz, are not entitled to assume a reforming role. The judges on Dworkin's view, according to Raz, must rely in 'hard cases' only on analogical arguments which perpetuate and extend the existing legal ideology. However, to defend Dworkin from Raz, the Dworkinian judge may come up with the best moral interpretation of the law that has never occurred to previous judges and the 'reforming' judge through Dworkinian interpretation could take the law into new territory.

A legal principle exists, according to Dworkin, if that principle follows from the best moral and political interpretation of past judicial and legislative decisions in the relevant legal areas. What is interpretation of law? The judge must apply two central criteria in assessing the acceptability of legal principles discovered in the law. Those judicial criteria are 'fit' and 'justification'. The judge must choose as the 'right legal answer' that legal principle which 'fits' the law to a 'satisfactory' level (that is, the legal principle is consistent with past legal decisions to a certain degree) and which also illustrates the law in the best moral light. There are several consequences which follow from Dworkin's theory of adjudication:

(a) Judges do not and should not legislate in a 'hard case' because in the existing law the 'one right answer' is potentially to be found in every case, at least in complex legal systems such as the UK and the USA.

(b) The law is not applied retroactively to the litigants by the judge but the law is already in existence, for Dworkin, waiting to be found by the judge in a 'hard case'.

(c) There is always, according to Dworkin, one legally right answer to cover the 'hard case' that 'fits' the previous law well enough and justifies the law in the best moral light possible. A real life judge might identify the 'wrong' legal principle but this does not alter the fact for Dworkin that 'the one right answer' already exists in the existing legal materials. An ideal judge called 'Hercules' by Dworkin in his legal writings (such as *Law's Empire* (1986)) always finds the 'one right answer' in every 'hard case' however real life judges make mistakes.

The Dworkinian characterisation of adjudication in 'hard cases' has come under criticism. Professor Finnis (in an article in 1987 'On Reason and Authority in Law's Empire') has the following trenchant criticisms of Dworkin's notions of 'fit' and 'justification' as the governing criteria in adjudication in a 'hard case'. Finnis comments that Dworkin provides no guidance as to how much 'fit' a legal principle has to have with previous legal decisions before it is acceptable as a legal principle for application in a 'hard case' – what is the threshold level of 'fit' in a 'hard case'? Finnis also comments that Dworkin provides no means of balancing the two criteria of 'fit' and 'justification' against each other so that the judge in a 'hard case' is provided with little concrete guidance on how to apply the Dworkinian method of adjudication in a 'hard case'.[16] Finnis also comments that in a 'hard case' there will often be more than one answer which is a 'correct' legal answer, even if many answers will be clearly wrong on the criteria of 'fit' and 'justification', and that it is wrong to say that there will always be 'one right answer', as Dworkin does.[17]

Whatever the indeterminacy and vagueness of Dworkin's theory of adjudication, Dworkin's aspiration is a 'noble dream'. Dworkin, in *Law's Empire*, comments that he asks judges to assume, so far as this is possible, that the law is structured by a coherent set of principles about justice, fairness and procedural due process, and that judges should enforce these standards in the fresh cases that come before them so that each citizen's situation is fair and just according to the same standards. Such a legal system turns that society into a community of principle. In *Law's Empire*, Dworkin's own Empire is extended from the small but important colony of 'hard case' adjudication to the large country of the justification of the authority of the state and the moral obligation by the citizen to obey the law.[18] Dworkin has expanded his theory of law, known as 'Law as Integrity', to answer some of the major questions of political philosophy. Dworkin writes in *Law's Empire* (1986) that a political society that accepts integrity as a virtue in the courts and legislation becomes a special form of community, special in a way that promotes that society's moral authority to assume and deploy a monopoly of coercive force. Dworkin now takes this as the central task of legal theory that a theory of law must explain how the law provides a general justification for the exercise of coercive power by the state. Therefore, from a theory of adjudication in 'hard cases', Dworkin has not only developed a theory of law, but also a theory for the moral legitimacy of the state itself. Professor Hart

....

16 Finnis in his 1987 article 'Reason and Authority In 'Law's Empire' collected in Finnis's *Philosophy of Law* (2011) comments that often in a hard legal case there will be 'no uniquely correct answer' where there is an identifiable set of two or more options/answers. In such a situation the judge must choose but not thinking in choosing he has chosen the uniquely correct answer to the legal problem in the case. Finnis says that even Dworkin's superhuman judge 'Hercules' could not justifiably claim unique correctness for his answer to a hard case.

17 Finnis said in his 1987 book review of *Law's Empire* by Dworkin, 'Reason and Authority In Law's Empire' that Dworkin 'identified no criteria, however sketchy for specifying when "fit" is "adequate" that is, for locating the threshold of fit beyond which the criterion of soundness would prevail.'

18 Finnis In his 1987 book review of Dworkin's *Law's Empire* (Finnis' book review is collected in *Philosophy of Law* (2011)) comments that Dworkin's defence of the legitimacy of political authority is 'very thin' depending on the similarity allegedly between the obligations of family and friendship and the obligations of belonging to a political community such as the United States of America. The point against Dworkin is that family and friendships differ enormously from the obligations of citizenship in a country.

never claimed to have such justificatory aims in *The Concept of Law*; he was merely trying to describe the essential features of a familiar social institution – the law.

There is one more major criticism of Dworkin's legal theory and that is from Hart's heir in the legal positivist tradition, Professor Raz. Raz has criticised Dworkin's theory of law as being inconsistent with a central feature of law – namely, its claim to authority (see Raz's essay, 'Authority, Law and Morality', reproduced in *Ethics in the Public Domain*). Dworkin's theory of law undermines the guidance function of law by making the content of the law depend somewhat on controversial moral interpretation of settled law. As Raz comments, much of the law of a country may, according to Dworkin, be unknown. Yet it is already legally binding, waiting there to be discovered by the judge in a 'hard case'. Hence, the 'hidden' law is neither, nor is it presented as being, anyone's judgment on what the law's subjects ought to do. Raz holds that Dworkin's theory is inconsistent with the authoritative nature of law. The law is a structure of authority; it is in the business of telling people what they must do. This conduct guidance function of law, the key to its method of social organisation, is undermined by Dworkin's theory of law. Raz thinks that the key problem for Dworkin is that his theory is a theory of law developed out of a theory of adjudication. Raz argues that legal philosophy must stand back from the lawyers' perspective, not in order to ignore it, but in order to examine lawyers and courts in the wider perspective of social organisation and political institutions generally, which is what Hart tried to do in *The Concept of Law*.

Professor Dworkin's subtle, influential and wide-ranging attack on the legal positivism of Hart has not killed off the theory as Hart killed off the 'command theory' of Austin, but legal positivism remains alive and kicking as the continued influence of both Professors Hart and Raz illustrates.

Common Pitfalls

Students can avoid the pitfall of thinking that legal positivists such as Raz and Hart have no answer to Dworkin's claim that judicial law-making is anti-democratic since judges are unelected. Students can gain extra marks by pointing out that Raz and Hart argue that judicial law-making is very different from Parliamentary legislation because: (a) judges engage in small scale improvements to the law not whole-scale reforms; (b) judges on the whole avoid law-making in areas of political or social controversy; (c) judges have to make their law reforms fit in with existing legal principle: judges in making new law have to have regard to 'legal reasoning': making sure the new judge created law fits with the existing law as far as possible; (d) Parliament has final control, overturning any judge-made law it finds objectionable. All these factors take the 'sting' out of Dworkin's criticisms that judicial legislation is objectionable because anti-democratic Judicial law-making is a very different process compared to Parliamentary legislation, and the 'anti-democratic' criticism loses much of its force when the differences are fully appreciated.

NOTES

The best starting point for Professor Dworkin's initial attack on 'legal positivism' is to read two essays collected in *Taking Rights Seriously* (1977), namely 'The Model of Rules' and 'Hard Cases'. The response of Professor Hart to many of Dworkin's criticisms can be read in 'The Postscript' to the second edition of *The Concept of Law* (1994) edited by Raz and Bulloch.

In *The Oxford Handbook of Jurisprudence and Philosophy of Law* (2002), edited by Coleman and Shapiro, Gerald Postema, in an essay entitled 'Philosophy of the Common Law' pays tribute to Dworkin's work on the judge's task in common law adjudication, commenting:

'There is much to be said for Dworkin's characterisation of this process as an account of an important part of common law reasoning.'

Professor Raz's criticisms of Dworkin's legal theory, from a modern legal positivistic background, can be found in the essay 'Authority, Law and Morality' (1985) The Monist, reprinted in the collection of Raz's essays, *Ethics in the Public Domain* (1994).

A useful summary of the changing nature of the debate between Dworkin and legal positivism can be found in the online and free essay 'The Nature of Law' (2007) by Andrei Marmor in the *Stanford Encyclopedia of Philosophy* (http://plato. stanford.edu/)

QUESTION 12

Discuss Professor Raz's contribution to legal theory.

How to Answer this Question

The contribution of Professor Raz to legal philosophy has been immense. Raz has restated and recast the traditional central legal positivistic position, that law is identified by 'social sources' only, by tying that thesis to the function of law as a type of social organisation which claims legitimate supreme authority within a territory. Raz has also defended legal positivism from the trenchant attacks of Professor Dworkin by emphasising the 'authoritative' nature of law. Raz has also stressed the importance of law to the realisation of the goal of personal autonomy for citizens through the creation of legally protected rights and interests. A skeleton plan is suggested.

- ❖ the role of law in furthering and upholding the value of personal autonomy;
- ❖ conclusion, the law is not just a structure of authority but a vital support for personal freedom.

Applying the Law

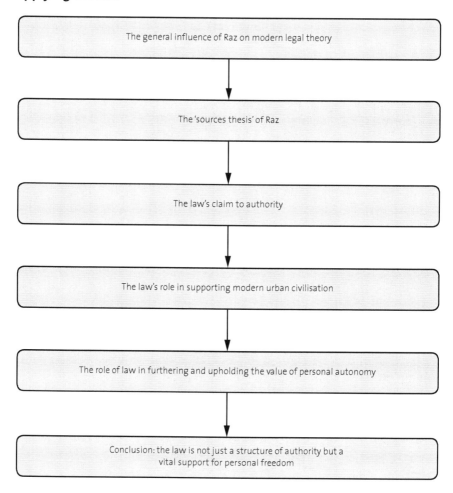

The general influence of Raz on modern legal theory

The 'sources thesis' of Raz

The law's claim to authority

The law's role in supporting modern urban civilisation

The role of law in furthering and upholding the value of personal autonomy

Conclusion: the law is not just a structure of authority but a vital support for personal freedom

ANSWER

Professor Joseph Raz is perhaps the best known legal philosopher who generally supports the main ideas of the legal positivistic tradition. His best known work in legal philosophy is his collection of essays in *The Authority of Law* (1979) but Raz's legal philosophy includes *The Concept of a Legal System* (1970), *Practical Reason and Norms* (1975) and essays in *Ethics in the Public Domain* (1994). Raz has also written widely on moral, political and ethical philosophy, including *The Morality of Freedom* (1986) and *Practice of Value* (2003).

In an article in *The Oxford Journal of Legal Studies* (2005) Leslie Green writes, in 'Three Themes from Raz', that the widespread interest in jurisprudence is testament to the great influence of Raz and that, to find another legal philosopher who has not only produced an indispensable body of work but who has influenced so many legal scholars, one has to go back to Professor Hart.

It is not possible in the space provided to do full justice to the richness of Raz's legal theory, but a few important 'Razian' themes will be highlighted.

Raz defends the central tenet of legal positivism that the law of a community is identified by reference to social sources alone – the 'sources thesis', as Raz terms it. The basic argument of Raz is that law, by its nature, claims to be a legitimate practical authority for its citizens. However, to be an authority, Raz claims, legal rules must be able to guide citizens without any evaluation needing to be taken concerning the moral reasons that the law claims to replace. Therefore, Raz concludes, the content of law must be ascertainable without resort to moral argument. The 'service conception' of authority, in which the law aims to make citizens better comply with right reason, is used to justify a hard line legal positivism in that Raz argues that it is not in the nature of law to contain moral tests for the content and validity of legal rules. A theory of law such as Professor Dworkin's (see *Law's Empire* (1986)), which makes moral judgments part of the grounds of law, undercuts and undermines the inherent claim to authority that law makes for itself.

Raz claims in *The Authority of Law* (1979) that a normative system is a 'legal system' only if it claims to be authoritative and to occupy a position of supremacy within society – in that the law claims the right to legitimise or outlaw all other social institutions. For Raz, the law is a system of guidance and adjudication claiming supreme authority within a certain society.[19] This 'definition of law' represents an evolution in the legal positivistic tradition from the 'law as commands' view of Austin and Bentham, and the later Hartian view of 'law as a union of primary and secondary rules' (see *The Concept of Law* (1961)).

Indeed, 'the authority' of law is a key feature for Raz for whom the law's claim to authority is a significant and distinctive feature of the law's method of social organisation. Therefore, following Raz's analysis, the legal positivist thesis that the law is identified solely by reference to social sources is a necessary and inevitable consequence derived from the very nature of law itself, especially the law's institutionalised, conduct-guiding, authoritative character.

The basic underlying function of the law, for Raz, is to provide publicly ascertainable standards by which members of the society are held to be bound[20] and by which legal standards cannot be made non-binding by moral argument either by citizens or officials. The 'sources thesis' identifies the law as a kind of human institution which is of crucial importance to the regulation of social life.

....

19 Raz captures well the idea of law claiming supreme authority in a society by saying in *The Authority of Law* (2009, 2nd edition): 'a normative system is a legal system only if it claims to be authoritative and to occupy a position of supremacy within society – in that the law claims the right to legitimize or outlaw all other social institutions.'

20 Because the authoritative guidance of conduct is seen by Raz as the basic function of law – law is a complex web of reasons for action or non-action then Raz is suspicious of legal theories such as Dworkin's (*Law's Empire* (1986)) which argue that the law depends partly for its existence on controversial judicial interpretation. Raz thinks that Dworkin makes some of the law 'hidden' until found by judicial interpretation and this 'hidden' law cannot therefore function as reasons for action.

When the 'source-based' law runs out in a 'hard case', Raz, like earlier legal positivists such as Austin and Hart, believes that the judge has an inescapable law-making function.[21] For Raz, the law begins and ends with the 'sources' – beyond the 'sources' lies judicial discretion to make new law.

Raz not only believes that the law is the primary means by which political authority is expressed, but that without the intervention of the law personal autonomy as a moral ideal would be very difficult to realise for the majority of citizens. As Raz has written (in a 2003 article 'Between Authority and Morality: First Storrs Lecture') law and legal institutions have made possible the whole urban civilisation as we know it over the last century or two. Personal autonomy is the capacity to make significant 'life choices' for oneself. As Raz writes (in an article 'Autonomy, Toleration, and the Harm Principle' (1987)) the ruling idea of personal autonomy is that persons should make their own lives. The autonomous person is a part author of his own life. The ideal of personal autonomy is the vision of persons controlling, in some degree, their own destiny, fashioning it through successive decisions throughout their lives. To be autonomous, a person must not only be given a choice but he must be given an adequate range of options. The autonomous person is the one who makes his own life. The law's role in fostering and protecting personal autonomy is vital for Raz. Part of the function of legal rights not to be enslaved, falsely imprisoned or assaulted is that the law forms a protective bastion enabling an individual to achieve his own ends in a life he shapes himself. However, not only does the law bestow protective 'negative' rights on persons, it also bestows 'positive' legal rights which allow the autonomous life to be lived by offering legally protected choices to marry, travel or make contracts, for example. For Raz, the goal of personal autonomy is partly dependent on an adequate range of choice and the law protects that range of choice by offering protected 'rights' to X as well as rights to be protected from various harms.

Raz wrote, in an important article in *Ratio Juris* (1992) 'Rights and Individual Well-being', that the law protects freedom of religion, freedom of speech, freedom of association, of occupation, of movement, of marriage not because it is important that persons should practice religion, get married or travel, but because it is important that persons should decide for themselves whether to do so or not. Through the legally protected rights, such as a right to marry or a right to travel or worship religion, the individual can fashion his own life, be the part author of his own life.

In summary, although Raz has a distinctive conception of the law as a structure of authority and, as Raz notes, authority involves essentially the power to require action, the law

---

21 Raz in *Ethics In the Public Domain* (1994) comments that he certainly believes there is a role for judicial law-making, at p. 358:

> 'Mine is not the theory that courts should have no share in making and developing the law. I am an advocate, not an opponent, of both judicial discretion and judicial power to set precedents, which between them give the courts considerable law-making power.'

has a more benign face than merely telling people what to do. The law has, for Raz, a crucial role in securing, through protected and protective legal rights, the moral ideal of personal autonomy.

NOTES

A good starting point for an overview of the juristic thought of Raz is Leslie Green's article 'Three Themes from Raz' in *The Oxford Journal of Legal Studies* (2005). The essay by Raz, 'The Claims of Law' in *The Authority of Law* (1979), should be consulted for the idea of the law's claim to authority. Many of Raz's recent essays can be found on his own personal website by going to http://josephnraz.googlepages.com/home. His 2003 article 'Between Authority and Morality: First Storrs Lecture' is particularly useful on the role of law in supporting urban civilisation. The link between law and personal freedom is explored in Raz's book *The Morality of Freedom* (1986).

QUESTION 13

Has the law any intrinsic value beyond its great instrumental benefit to society?

How to Answer this Question

This question concerns the issue as to whether the institution of law has any value in itself, independent of any instrumental benefit law may have to society. Traditional legal theory has usually tended to view law in purely instrumental terms, seeing law as the instrument of the state to achieve civil peace (Hobbes in *Leviathan* (1651)) or as co-ordinating society for the common good (Finnis in *Natural Law and Natural Rights* (1980)) to give two prominent examples of law's instrumentality. The famous Austrian jurist Hans Kelsen, in *Introduction to the Problems of Legal Theory* (1934) positively asserted that law had no value in itself beyond the goals that law could achieve for society. Kelsen said:

> 'The law is a coercive apparatus having in and of itself no political or ethical value, a coercive apparatus whose value depends, rather, on ends that transcend the law qua means.'

However a number of legal theorists, most notably Professor Raz, have asserted that law can be a focus for the identification of a person with his society. Since the law is the political voice of a community then the law can be a means by which a person self-identifies with his own society through an attitude of 'respect for the law'. Kelsen's extreme view is therefore in need of modification. Law has a dual aspect: instrumentally important to achieve societal goals but also potentially intrinsically important as a focus for the self-identification of citizens with their society.

Applying the Law

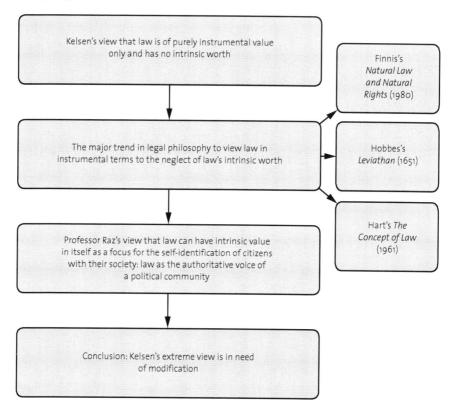

Kelsen's view that law is of purely instrumental value only and has no intrinsic worth

The major trend in legal philosophy to view law in instrumental terms to the neglect of law's intrinsic worth

Professor Raz's view that law can have intrinsic value in itself as a focus for the self-identification of citizens with their society: law as the authoritative voice of a political community

Conclusion: Kelsen's extreme view is in need of modification

Finnis's *Natural Law and Natural Rights* (1980)

Hobbes's *Leviathan* (1651)

Hart's *The Concept of Law* (1961)

ANSWER

The great Austrian jurist, Hans Kelsen (d 1973) was firmly of the view that law was only of purely instrumental value to a society. Kelsen wrote on this matter in *Introduction to the Problems of Legal Theory*:

> 'the law is a coercive apparatus having in and of itself no political or ethical value, a coercive apparatus whose value depends rather on ends that transcend the law qua means.'

Kelsen, to bring the point home, commented further:

> 'Law is a means, a specific social means, not an end' and also that the law is 'a specific social means, not an end.'

This instrumentalist approach to law's authority in society, propagated by Kelsen, has dominated jurisprudence – the idea that law is there to achieve mighty social goals, but has no intrinsic worth itself – like a piece of cheap cutlery such as a fork which can be put to the great end of eating food but has no real value in itself. Bentham elevated legislation far above the common law (which Bentham despised) because of legislation's superior ability to co-ordinate society, so as to maximise utility. Professor Hart in *The Concept of Law* (1961) regarded the emergence of law to a pre-legal society as bringing instrumental benefits of certainty, efficiency and adaptability in terms of legal rules of that society. Thomas Hobbes in *Leviathan* (1651) regarded the law of the sovereign power as a mighty instrument for achieving the supreme goal of civil peace over the anarchic 'state of nature' without law. Professor Raz has written extensively on how the authority of law brings instrumental benefits to society and individuals through the guidance of reason and expertise as expressed by policy-makers through law.[22]

However it is clear that the instrumentalist conception of authority is not the whole picture. It is possible to view the law as a public order of rules loyalty to which by citizens can be seen as a valuable way of showing commitment to a particular political community whose law the citizen loyally obeys. As Raz comments in *Between Authority and Interpretation* (2009): the law 'is the authoritative voice of a particular community'. As Raz further explains:

> 'the law and its institutions are among the central constituents of a community: a political community ... in being partly constitutive of a community which is normally a focus of identification, the law can be intrinsically valuable.'

It is important to be clear about what Raz is saying here. Raz is not denying that many persons in Western societies actually feel a sense of profound alienation from their own society and legal system and who therefore feel unable to identify with the law of their society. Raz also insists that the sense of identification or respect for their own legal system or law that is valuable for some citizens is not a morally obligatory position to take, even in a liberal democracy. The issue is one of choice:

> 'I can choose to identify with my own society by identifying with the legal system of that society. This is entirely optional but such a choice has value for me if I choose to identify with the law. However the anarchist who despises all State law is entitled to his stance in the sense of not being required to identify with the law of his own society even if he must obey the law.'[23]

Raz comments in *Between Authority and Interpretation* (2009):

> 'identification with a community depends on our ability and willingness to accept the standards which these communities endorse as our own ... Given the importance of political communities in the life of their members, an ability to

....

22 Raz comments of the instrumental benefits of law in *Authority: Readings in Social and Political Theory* (1990) at p. 6: 'I believe that the primary arguments in support of political authority rely on its expertise (or that of its policy making advisers) and on it's ability to secure social coordination.'

23 The German anarchist Gustav Landauer declared that:

> 'The state is not something which can be destroyed by a revolution, but is a condition, a certain relationship between human beings, a mode of human behaviour; we destroy it by contracting other relationships, by behaving differently' (Colin Ward, *Anarchism: A Very Short Introduction*, p. 8).

For anarchists such as Gustav Landauer, the very possibility of 'self-identification' with the law would have seemed abhorrent.

identify with one's political community is intrinsically valuable. Any account of the law which disregards that aspect of it is incomplete. To understand the nature of the law we have to understand its role as partly constitutive of a political community and therefore as an object for identification, as playing an important role in people's sense of who they are.'

The extent to which the law has intrinsic value depends crucially on the particular cultural and political mix in a particular society. In the United States the Supreme Court is venerated by many Americans, but ignored by many as well.[24] The common law of England may in the past have held intrinsic value for some English persons. Raz writes in *Ethics in the Public Domain* (1994) that Professor Hart disliked **'the excessive veneration in which the law is held in common law countries'**.

The discussion has shown that the original view expressed by Kelsen – that the law has instrumental value – only has to be modified in the light of the observation that law can have a value inherent in itself beyond any instrumental value the law undoubtedly possesses. This inherent value of law is found in those societies where some citizens voluntarily adopt an attitude of 'respect for law' out of a sense of self-identification with their society, of which the law is the authoritative product of the political institutions of that society. To that extent the law can have an 'inherent' value.

NOTES

Hans Kelsen's view that law was purely of instrumental value – 'a coercive apparatus', can be found in his *Introduction to the Problems of Legal Theory* (1934) at p. 31. Professor Raz's view that law can have intrinsic as well as instrumental value can be found in his *Between Authority and Interpretation* (2009) at pp. 102–106.

QUESTION 14

Professor Galligan claims in *Law in Modern Society* (2007) that the 'bond of trust' between legal officials and citizens in modern Western legal orders is a distinctive feature of those legal systems. Is he correct?

How to Answer this Question

The 'bond of trust' between legal officials such as judges, police and civil servants and the public is claimed by Professor Galligan to be a 'defining mark' of Western legal orders. Those Western legal orders could be numbered as less than 20 in the world and include the United States, Australia, United Kingdom and France for example. The 'bond of trust' between legal officials and citizens is really an important aspect of the more wider 'rule of law' where legal officials enjoy no special immunities, are not generally corrupt and can

---

24 Roger Cotterrell notes of the centrality of the United States Supreme Court in American cultural life: 'The centrality of the judge in the negotiation of law's relations with morality ... a Supreme Court has ultimate authority to interpret a written constitution and bill of rights which are, themselves, seen as the repository of political and moral values.'

be trusted to carry out their duties expeditiously and efficiently. There a number of legal doctrines which underlie this 'bond of trust' including in the United Kingdom a new **Bribery Act of 2010**. Professor Hart in his account of the standard legal system *The Concept of Law* (1961) did not give an account of (1) the 'bond of trust' in modern Western legal orders and (2) how important not just the obedience of the population is to the survival of any state but the active support of most of the population. However Hart would not have regarded the 'bond of trust' between legal officials and citizens as part of a 'standard legal system' indeed if a poll is taken of the current legal systems of the world and the official corruption in those legal systems then the 'standard legal system' would show a 'lack of trust' between legal officials and citizens not a 'bond of trust'. Even in modern Western legal orders the 'bond of trust' is problematic for the young, ethnic minorities, the travelling communities, the so-called 'underclass'. As Robert Reiner points out in *The Politics of the Police* (2000) certain groups in society become 'police property' because of their low socio-economic status such as illegal drug addicts, alcoholics, the long term unemployed. Reiner explains:

> 'A category becomes police property when the dominant powers of society leave the problems of social control of that category to the police. They are low-status, power-less groups whom the dominant majority see as problematic or distasteful … The prime function of the police has always been to control and segregate such groups, and they are armed with a battery of permissive and discretionary laws for this purpose … The concern with 'police property' is not so much to enforce the law as to maintain order using the law as one resource among others.'

This sociological analysis by Reiner forces us to modify any glib assertion of a 'bond of trust' between legal officials and citizens in modern legal orders such as the United Kingdom.

Applying the Law

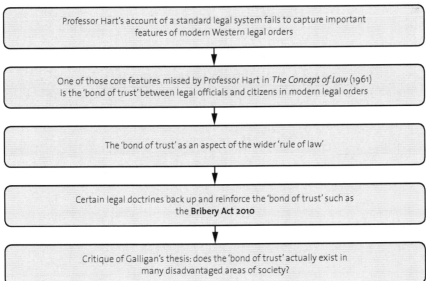

Professor Hart's account of a standard legal system fails to capture important features of modern Western legal orders

One of those core features missed by Professor Hart in *The Concept of Law* (1961) is the 'bond of trust' between legal officials and citizens in modern legal orders

The 'bond of trust' as an aspect of the wider 'rule of law'

Certain legal doctrines back up and reinforce the 'bond of trust' such as the **Bribery Act 2010**

Critique of Galligan's thesis: does the 'bond of trust' actually exist in many disadvantaged areas of society?

ANSWER

Professor Galligan in *Law in Modern Society* praises Hart's book *The Concept of Law* (1961) as a 'classic' which should be used as a starting point for an analysis of 'law in society'. Galligan comments:

> 'Hart … positively claims an interest in the social context of law, which shows itself in two ways. The more fundamental is that his description of law is based on and reflects faithfully the social experience of law. Added to this is the further claim to being a descriptive sociology suggesting that his theory of law could be read also as a sociological account of law. Taken as a whole they are good reasons for using "The Concept of Law" as a way of beginning of law in society.'

However Galligan's methodological focus is much narrower than Hart's. Hart in *The Concept of Law* (1961) aimed to provide an account of the main elements of a standard legal system whilst providing cautionary advice. That cautionary advice included warning that the existence of a legal system whilst bringing certain benefits to society in terms of certainty and efficiency in the application of rules also allowed for better organised coercion of a population. Hart also said that it would be wiser to keep law and morality distinct so that the certification of a rule as legally valid was not conclusive of the question whether we should morally be obliged to obey that law. Despite certain words of cautionary advice Hart's intention in writing *The Concept of Law* (1961) was to provide an account of the main elements of a standard legal system grounded in Hart's knowledge of social experience. Galligan does not take as his focus in *Law in Modern Society* (2007) the standard legal system as found in the historical record of humanity but rather the historically specific and few in number legal systems termed by Galligan 'modern legal orders'. These 'modern legal orders' include the legal systems of Western Europe, United States, Canada, Australia, New Zealand and the United Kingdom. Galligan points out that 'the bond of trust' or 'special relationship' between citizens and legal officials such as judges, police, civil servants, magistrates and other legal functionaries is a strong characteristic feature of 'modern legal orders' and a feature that Hart in his search for generality overlooked. Galligan comments in *Law in Modern Society* (2007):

> 'In modern legal orders, officials have special relations with citizens … A noticeable aspect of Hart's account is that, while officials are placed at the centre, citizens are relegated to the margins. For Hart a legal system in its essentials consists of general obedience to law by the people and acceptance by officials of the rules of the system. The idea of citizens needing only to obey, while officials accept, may be justified in a very general way in relation to legal systems generally, but hardly matches the character of modern legal orders and needs to be reconsidered.'

Galligan notes of 'modern legal orders' of Western liberal democracies that the powers of legal and political officials are constrained by their social relations with citizens expressed in a series of doctrines which together form a distinctive normative structure of a liberal democratic state. These doctrines include the rule of law, separation of powers between judiciary, legislature and executive, judicial review of executive action or in some jurisdictions judicial review of legislation, and the full accountability of legal officials to the law. For Galligan 'the bond of trust' between legal officials and citizens is an especially important feature of modern legal orders. Galligan writes of the distinction between Hart's conception of a reasonable mature legal system and the 'modern legal order'. For Galligan:

> 'That distinction lies in the bond of trust between governors and the governed, and the social good in government and administration being conducted according to the terms of the bond … It is the specifically legal expression of a set of social relations between citizens and officials that is unique to a few modern legal orders. Its practical expression is to be found in the combination of general principles of constitutional law, and the very specific and often technical doctrines of administrative law.'

Galligan's idea of 'a bond of trust' between legal officials and citizens is certainly one of his leading and guiding ideas for Galligan's analysis of 'modern legal orders' as terms them. Galligan comments:

> 'the special relations between citizens and officials are one of the defining features of a modern legal order, and the stance from which the actions of officials are to be understood.'

Galligan claims that in modern legal orders legal officials are largely motivated by a disinterested motive to uphold the common good. In a significant way Galligan's idea of disinterested legal officials toiling for the common good has a strong echo of the natural lawyer John Finnis's idea of the 'central case' legal system being the one where legal officials work for the preservation of the common good through upholding the legal system. However Finnis describes an 'ideal' or 'central' case legal system whereas Galligan describes an actual living reality – the modern legal orders of Western Europe and North America.

Galligan comments in *Law in Modern Society* (2007) of the need for legal officials to take a disinterested moral attitude to the upholding of modern legal orders:

> 'While all recognizably legal orders are directed at providing certain social goods, the distinguishing mark of modern legal orders is the unique combination of the social goods of security and stability, the positive provision of welfare and the restriction of activities through regulation, and finally the containment of official power. The interest in securing these social goods provides legal officials and others with a set of reasons for accepting the legal order, the corollary being that unless they subscribe to those reasons, modern legal orders will fail. Unless there is a shared foundation of disinterested commitment to advancing and protecting the social relations particular to modern societies, the legal order will lose its bearings.'

A key element of the 'bond of trust' between legal officials and citizens in modern legal orders is the idea 'that government is restrained by its relations to citizens, that every person has rights'.

The 'bond of trust' between legal officials and citizens in modern legal orders is says Galligan vital to winning the support of the people and hence vital to the stability of modern legal orders. Galligan comments of the distance of his analysis from Professor Hart's in *The Concept of Law* (1961):

> 'In Hart's concern to settle on a description wide enough to cover all municipal legal orders, from the good to the bad to the intolerable, Hart had to take account of legal systems sustained by officials with the barest support of the people. As long as officials accept the law as binding and act accordingly (Hart said), it does not matter for legal theory that the people do not share the internal point of view, do not accept the system as a binding legal order.'

However Galligan is insistent that the long-term stability of a legal system depends on the 'bond of trust' between legal officials and citizens being maintained and that mere obedience of the population might work for a time to sustain a regime but that the active support of the population not just obedience is essential to the long-term survival of a legal system. The Soviet Union survived under dictatorship for 70 years (1917–1991) but eventually 'people power' brought the communist system crashing down all over Eastern Europe. Galligan comments:

> 'the support (not just obedience) of the people is essential to preserve any form of rule, no matter how strong. In its absence or loss, inherent instability and fragility will be manifest.'

Galligan comments on the collapse of the communist system in Eastern Europe between 1989–1991:

> 'The recent collapse of regimes throughout central and eastern Europe has revealed how fragile those apparently impregnable orders were; and it is surely no coincidence that all were based on the rule of the few, with officials accountable to the few rather than to a legal order.'

The question remains though: is the 'bond of trust' between legal officials and citizens in a modern legal order merely an academic exaggeration or a reality of social experience in those societies? A cynic might argue that those groups who experience the sharpest conflict with the hard edge of the state represented by the police (the visible symbols of lawful activity on the streets) such as young people, the homeless, certain members of ethnic minorities do not feel any 'bond of trust' with the police rather the opposite – hostility of varying degrees of intensity. The middle classes and liberal elites (such as academics like Galligan) might indeed feel 'a bond of trust' with their representatives in the legal order but the 'marginalized' such as the 'underclass' might 'experience' the legal order as control and subordination. Indeed in a revealing research study 'Policing as Social Discipline' (1997) Satnam Choongh comments:

'The police equate "legal discipline" with their own identity – the 'dross' must continually demonstrate that they accept without reservation the sacrosanct nature of police authority and dominance … For many police officers, a challenge to police authority represents a challenge to the social fabric of society, a rejection of fundamental values. Therefore, a significant amount of police activity is dictated by the need to send a message to these communities, namely that challenge, resistance and a lack of general respect for the police will always incur punishment.'

This 'punishment' by the police over the 'dross' who challenge police authority takes place mainly at the police station. Choongh comments:

> 'the police station is … a location of immense symbolic importance … it is an integral and essential aspect of a social disciplinary model of control.'

The police power to detain a suspect for questioning gives the police the mechanism they need to exercise authority over the 'dross'. Choogh comments of the police power of non-consensual interrogation:

> 'The police value their right to interrogate because it empowers them to attack the very notion of the suspect as an autonomous being … Coercing a suspect to engage in dialogue … is something which the police can do to a suspect whether the suspect likes it or not … The importance which the police attach to their power of interrogation is at least partly explicable by the police desire to control "obnoxious" individuals and communities. It provides them with a means by which to communicate their dislike of and power over these elements in the social order.'

There does not appear to be much of a 'bond of trust' between social groups who challenge police authority and the police who use legal powers such as detention and questioning to 'discipline' those social groups perceived by the police as a threat to their hegemony on the streets.

Jeremy Waldron, in an essay entitled 'Legal Pluralism' in *The Hart-Fuller Debate in the Twenty-First Century* edited by Peter Cane (2010) comments that legal order can bring with it a 'specialist executive apparatus' to administer the legal rules of a society which can lead to 'alienation' of ordinary people from the legal rules which govern their lives. Waldron comments:

> 'As secondary practices of interpretation and rule-change become established, both those practices and the primary rules they validate may begin to seem increasingly distant from ordinary people's ways of life.'

Therefore 'alienation' of many citizens from the legal order may characterise modern legal orders as much as Galligan's much vaunted 'bond of trust' between legal officials and citizens.

However despite the above mentioned scepticism about how widespread in the 'policed population' is the 'bond of trust' between legal officials and citizens of modern legal orders, the legal order of the United Kingdom contains many legal doctrines and legal rules designed to shore up such public trust in legal officials. For example legal officials such as police officers can be prosecuted in the criminal courts for perjury (giving false evidence deliberately on oath) contrary to the **Perjury Act 1911**, or for the common law offence of perverting the course of justice by fabricating or 'planting' evidence. Police officers and other legal officials can also be criminally prosecuted for the old common law offence of 'misconduct in a public office'. This common law offence is interesting because the judicial authorities make it clear that the essence of the offence is a public official betraying the trust of the public which echoes Galligan's idea of the 'bond of trust' between legal officials and citizens in a modern legal order. In the leading case of *R v Bembridge* (1783) Lord Mansfield spoke of 'a man accepting an office of trust' and that punishment for misbehaviour in that public office 'is essential to the existence of the country'. In the recent case of *R v Belton* (2010) the Court of Appeal said that:

> 'the central theme of the authorities was that a man accepting an office of trust concerning the public was answerable criminally for misbehaviour in his office. If conduct was so serious as to affect the public trust, a prosecution might follow.'

The police or other legal officials could also face criminal prosecution under the new **Bribery Act 2010**[25] for receiving bribes in the performance of their duties. The usual criminal law such as the law on assaults and theft also apply to police officers and other officials – there is no immunity stemming from holding public office in the United Kingdom. In the civil law, police officers and other legal officials can be sued for assault, battery, false imprisonment and malicious prosecution. The Chief Constable of Police remains vicariously liable for the torts of his officers under the **Police Act 1996**. Police officers and other legal officials can be sued for 'misfeasance (misconduct) in a public office' in tort. Exemplary damages are available in the civil law to punish police officers and other legal officials for 'oppressive, arbitrary or unconstitutional' action against citizens above and beyond the usual compensatory damages – see *Kuddus v Chief Constable of Leicestershire Constabulary* (2001).[26]

'The 'bond of trust' between legal officials and citizens is certainly an important feature of modern Western legal orders as the foregoing discussion of the many legal doctrines in

---

25   **The Bribery Act 2010** creates criminal offences of giving or receiving bribes in the performance of public functions. The **Bribery Act** states concerning offences relating to the giving of bribes: A person ('P') is guilty of an offence if either of the following cases applies:

> (a) P offers, promises or gives a financial or other advantage to another person, and (b) P intends the advantage – (i) to induce a person to perform improperly a relevant function or activity, or (ii) to reward a person for the improper performance of such a function or activity.

Offences relating to being bribed: A person ('R') is guilty of an offence if any of the following cases applies: where R requests, agrees to receive or accepts a financial or other advantage intending that, in consequence, a relevant function or activity should be performed improperly (whether by R or another person).

26   Exemplary or punishment damages available in the civil law are an exception to the principle that civil damages should compensate leaving punishment to criminal law. However the House of Lords in *Kuddus* (2003) were of the opinion that exemplary damages had an important constitutional role in deterring police abuse of power – although Lord Scott dissented from the majority view.

UK law attempting to bolster that trust. Indeed modern legal orders of the Western world can be contrasted with legal orders such as Russia where corruption amongst public officials is rampant. As the *Daily Telegraph* commented in 2012:

> 'Under Putin (the Russian President) politicians like him from the security services have pillaged the country (Russia). His long period in power is a reminder that a state without constraints becomes a gangster.'

Aim Higher

The highly influential German sociologist Max Weber said in 'On Law in Economy and Society' that in the modern age of the twentieth century, legal authority came from the application of consciously made 'rational rules'. Weber said that the authority of legal officials was 'legitimate in so far as it corresponds with the norms' of the legal system. Weber was arguing that the only possible basis of legitimacy for a legal system in the modern era was official action justified by rational impartially administered legal rules. Galligan echoes Weber when Galligan says that the 'bond of trust' between legal officials and citizens is the hallmark of modern western legal orders for indeed if citizens did not generally trust legal officials to follow legal rules impartially then it is difficult to see what legitimacy western legal orders could have. Modern western legal systems do not base their authority on 'tradition' (as Weber put it) such as religious texts like the Koran or Bible or on the 'charismatic' leadership (another category of Weber) of an individual such as Adolf Hitler who could overrule any legal rule in Germany by his own personal orders. Modern western legal orders base their authority on the power of consciously made rational rules administered impartially by anonymous legal officials (Weber) this is the heart of Galligan's idea of the 'bond of trust' between legal officials and citizens in modern western legal orders.

NOTES

Professor Galligan's *Law in Modern Society* (2007) contains a good critique and praise of Hart's 1961 *The Concept of Law* as well as developing Galligan's ideas about the distinctiveness (such as the 'bond of trust') of modern legal orders. Robert Reiner's account of certain socio-economic groups and vulnerable individuals becoming 'police property' is to be found in Reiner's classic sociological account: *The Politics of the Police* (2000, 3rd edition) at pp. 93–94. Satnam Choongh *Policing as Social Discipline* (1997) gives a different perspective to relations between police and the policed to Galligan's model of benign 'trust' in *Law in Modern Society* (2007).

INTRODUCTION

Today's natural lawyers, such as John Finnis, view law from the perspective of its ultimate moral function which is taken to be the ability of law to co-ordinate human activity for the common good. This perspective can be contrasted with the tradition of legal positivism which seeks to examine the concept of law without attending to law's ultimate moral purpose which for Finnis, Robert P George, Mark Murphy and others in the natural law tradition is to co-ordinate society for the common good. Which perspective on law, legal positivistic or natural law, gives a more truthful or more rounded perspective on the social institution and cultural artefact we call law is a matter of intense jurisprudential debate today.

Checklist
Ensure that you understand the following topics: ■ natural and positive law contrasted; ■ natural law as an aspect of Divine providence; ■ the link between natural law and modern legal systems (the 'common good' view of law); ■ Finnis's self-evident human goods; ■ the disagreements in the present era between legal positivists and natural law theorists.

QUESTION 15

In the present era what are the significant disagreements between legal positivist theorists and Natural law theorists?

How to Answer this Question

Legal philosophers in the natural law tradition tend to take a very positive and upbeat view of law's potential to further the common good of society. In the more theologically based versions of natural law such as represented by St Thomas Aquinas (1223–1273) human law is part of the divine plan for mankind where the rulers use human law to concretise or instantiate the requirements of the God given natural law. Until natural law is determined '*determinatio*' by human law we would not know what to do. The example of the rule of the road is a central example. There is nothing intrinsically valuable in driving on the left as opposed to the right and yet an authoritative human enactment is needed to settle the issue. Natural law thus, is not like a vending machine of legal statutes but takes takes a significant amount of human choice to yield positive human law. Natural law specifies that we should pay heed to physical safety but it requires human determination or choice to decide on whether we all drive on the left or the right or the speed limit is set at 60, 70 or 80 miles per hour on the motorway. Another very good example of the need for human *determinatio* is the selection of appropriate judicial punishment for criminal offenders. The natural law specifies that criminal offenders should be punished but judges must decide through choice the exact punishment. John Finnis argues at p. 178 of *Human Rights and Common Good* (2011) that natural law dictates that a criminal offender should be punished to subject them to something (punishment) 'contrary to their will' and by this act of state punishment *the advantage the offender gained by preferring their own will to that required by law is cancelled out*. However the natural law leaves it to judicial choice what the exact punishment of an offender shall be. Finnis comments in *Human Rights and Common Good* (2011):

> 'In human punishments, on the other hand, penalties must be chosen by the judge from a range. There is no "natural" measure of punishment, that is to say, no rationally determinable and uniquely appropriate penalty to fit the crime. Punishment is the (natural law) tradition's stock example of the need for *determinatio*, a process of choosing freely from a range of reasonable options none of whichh Is simply rationally superior to the others.'

Natural law thinkers thus stress that we cannot make sense of law fully unless we pay central attention to the moral reasons that cause a legal system to be instituted, maintained and pursued by legal officials. Those moral reasons are centrally those for the pursuit of the common good through the co-ordinative functions of law. It is hardly surprising that thinkers in the natural tradition such as John Finnis (see *Natural Law and Natural Rights* (2011, 2nd edition) argue that attention to the moral reasons that underlie legal officials actions is the central standpoint to view law and legal systems since the natural law tradition has always argued that human 'positive' law derives its moral authority from its derivation from principles of (God-given) natural law or in Finnis's terminology 'principles of practical reasonableness'. Legal positivism on the other hand seeks to examine law without reading into law any intrinsic moral purpose beyond the guidance of human conduct. The tradition of legal positivism seeks neither to condemn law (unlike the philosophical anarchists such as Robert Paul Woolf condemn law) nor praise law (unlike the tradition of natural law represented by Aquinas and Finnis who take the view that law 'is the primary and proper means of co-ordinating civil society). Legal positivism as a tradition of intellectual thought represented by Professor Hart in *The Concept of Law* (1961) seeks to represent law 'as it is' with no agenda aimed at the destruction or commendation of law as a social institution.

Applying the Law

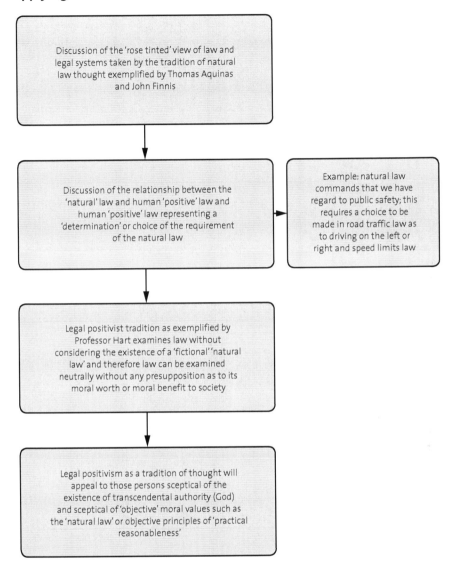

Discussion of the 'rose tinted' view of law and legal systems taken by the tradition of natural law thought exemplified by Thomas Aquinas and John Finnis

Discussion of the relationship between the 'natural' law and human 'positive' law and human 'positive' law representing a 'determination' or choice of the requirement of the natural law

Example: natural law commands that we have regard to public safety; this requires a choice to be made in road traffic law as to driving on the left or right and speed limits law

Legal positivist tradition as exemplified by Professor Hart examines law without considering the existence of a 'fictional' 'natural law' and therefore law can be examined neutrally without any presupposition as to its moral worth or moral benefit to society

Legal positivism as a tradition of thought will appeal to those persons sceptical of the existence of transcendental authority (God) and sceptical of 'objective' moral values such as the 'natural law' or objective principles of 'practical reasonableness'

ANSWER

The Thomist[1] natural law tradition views state law as 'the primary proper means of co-ordinating civil society' (Finnis, 1998, 255). An alternative formulation of the natural law position concerning the inherent relationship between law and the good is offered by

1 'Thomist' is a shorthand expression for the natural law tradition initiated by St Thomas Aquinas (1225–1273).

Finnis: 'Law is a kind of ongoing plan for common good' (Finnis, 2011, 12). The insight of Raz that all state law claims legitimate authority as a distinct method of social organisa-tion could be endorsed by a philosophical anarchist even if the philosophical anarchist denied that any state law possessed such legitimate authority. Raz writes about legal the-ory's search for what is significant and important about the social institution of law: 'But in claiming that these features are important one is not commending them as good. Their importance can be agreed upon by anarchists who reject any possibility of legitimacy for such institutions' (Raz, 1994, 220). As Liam Murphy comments on Raz's methodology in seeking to pick out the significant in law and legal systems without endorsement of those significant features:

> 'Raz seeks the deep structure of the concept of law by exploring the implications of what can be uncontroversially be asserted about it … the apparently uncontroversial starting point for Raz's account is that it is implicit in the concept of law that 'every legal system claims that it possesses legitimate authority.' (Murphy, 2001, 381, 382)

Given that, as Twining notes, 'pluralism of beliefs and ideologies is a fact and that legal phenomena are immensely varied and complicated' (Twining, 2009, 24) then it may perhaps be wiser for the legal theorist to develop as Professor Hart did in *The Concept of Law* (1994, 239, 240) a descriptive/evaluative analysis of legal systems rather than seek to morally endorse the institution of law generally (Finnis (1980; 2011)) or morally endorse particular legal systems (Dworkin (1986; 2006)). Hart himself was aware (although Hart's critique of the moral risks of law is quite mild compared to the the philosophical anar-chists' fierce condemnation of law) of the 'morally risky' nature of law. Hart wrote in *The Concept of Law* of the downside as well as the benefits legal order can bring to a pre-legal society: 'the cost is the risk that the centrally organized power may well be used for the oppression of numbers with whose support it can dispense, in a way that the simpler regime of primary rules could not' (Hart, 1994, 202). Falling short of the co-ordinated organised outright oppression that a legal order can threaten to a society, modern vast bureaucratic legal systems can also bring other moral hazards such as alienation of sub-stantial parts of the population 'policed' by the legal system, weakening of ancient local norms and customs by the intrusion of general state law norms, the rise and dominance of elite professional legal and political classes or elite cadres in society and citizens' pas-sivity in the face of the impersonal, over-sized legal machine and sheep-like acceptance of the legal and political order through the material goods and comforts of a consumer society that legal-political order can bring.

Given the variety of quality of legal phenomena in the world and the inherent moral risk-iness of legal systems then it might be wise to adopt a Hartian detached legal positivistic approach to the analysis of law and legal systems committed to no moral endorsement of the social institution called 'law' even if one also rejects the extremity of the philo-sophical anarchist position which sees law as intrinsically bad. The leading exponent of the natural law tradition in the twenty-first century, John Finnis argues that a proper evaluation of differing legal systems cannot be properly given unless the theorist attends to the moral reasons which would induce legal officials to bring into being and maintain legal order as opposed to other social conditions such as arbitrary domination by a dictatorship or forms of anarchistic society. Finnis comments of the legal theorist's need to evaluate the superiority in terms of justice of law over arbitrary rule and anarchy as forms of social living:

> 'Hart and Raz would respond that descriptive analysis of law's character as instrument can proceed without evaluating the diverse purposes and uses to which the instrument is put. But this response seems insufficient. For law's characteristic purport as obligatory and authoritative … itself proposes an evaluation and critique of alternative social conditions (anarchy, arbitrary domination). There cannot be an adequately inward understanding or analysis of what characterizes diverse legal systems … without an understanding of the ways law's characteristic features themselves manifest a critical evaluation of, and value-affirming constructive response to, the sorts of injustice or other lesion of human good which are inherent in lawlessness of every kind.' (Finnis, 2011, 165,166)

The fundamental point Finnis makes against the legal positivist methodology of Hart and Raz is that their attempt to evaluate law and legal systems from a descriptive/neutral standpoint miscarries unless attention is given to the theorist to the moral reasons why legal ordering would ever be preferred to arbitrary domination or anarchy. In other words for Finnis (Finnis, 2008, 17) the legal positivist cannot carry through his descriptive/evaluative project of analysing law and legal systems because the legal positivist such as Hart (1994) falls short of giving an account of why legal officials will have strong moral reasons for bringing into existence maintaining and defending legal systems. The Hartian project of the descriptive/evaluation of law and legal systems focused on the instrumental benefits, not the moral benefits, that a legal system might bring to a pre-legal society in terms of certainty, adaptability and efficiency by the addition of secondary legal rules to the primary rules of obligation of the pre-legal system (Hart, 1994, 79–99). Finnis comments critically on the Hartian project: 'Hart … truncated his enquiry into legal reasons' (Finnis, 2008, 17). These salient 'legal reasons' for Finnis drive a concern for the common good that causes legal officials to create, maintain and defend legal systems to further the common good. Hart commented that the societal situation where legal officials accept a legal system on moral grounds 'will be most stable when they do so' (Hart, 1994, 203) but Hart referred to a number of other non-moral motivations for legal officials to accept a legal system for those legal officials to adopt the 'internal point of view' of a person who accepts a system of norms as valid. These 'non-moral' reasons of legal officials to accept a legal system as mentioned by Hart include 'calculations of long term interest … an unreflecting inherited or traditional attitude … or the mere wish to do as others do' (Hart, 1994, 203). These non-moral reasons would not be considered by Finnis to be the 'central case' reasons that motivate legal officials to accept and support a legal system (Finnis, 2008, 17) and therefore Hart's descriptive/evaluative analysis of legal systems miscarries at a crucial point for Finnis.

However if a legal theorist wanted great reach in his legal theory covering many legal systems in history it may be wise to define law's most basic function as 'the preservation of civil peace as far as possible' rather than to link the 'central case' system of law to that ordering which seeks the 'common good' as Finnis has done in his neo-classical natural law writings such as *Natural Law and Natural Rights* (1980) or *Aquinas* (1998). The realisation of 'civil peace through law' is certainly an important aspect of the 'common good' but even in those legal systems blatantly and obviously not geared to the common good of all persons in that society (such as the slave-owning Roman Empire or eighteenth-century British legal order dedicated to the protection of property of the elite from the depredations of the lower orders) the maintenance of civil peace through law was the fundamental aim of the legal system. The Roman legal system and eighteenth-century British legal system were, above all else, dedicated to the maintenance of civil peace as far as possible. Nothing caused more alarm to the Roman or British elites than a threat to the breakdown of civil order. Therefore it might be more accurate, historically at least, to describe the 'central case' or 'focal' legal system as a system of coercive promulgated rules whose main function is the preservation of civil peace as far as possible. It is not historically accurate to argue, as Finnis does, from his classical natural law background that 'the central case of law' is an ordering for the 'common good'. Finnis might deny that his claim is actually historically accurate but rather a description of an 'ideal' form of law but the problem then is his choice of words – saying as Finnis does that the 'central case of law' is that ordering for the 'common good' has an implication of historical accuracy about it since law and legal systems are not just abstractions but have been living realities in history. Finnis should have chosen his words more carefully to avoid confusion, instead of saying that the 'central case of law and legal systems' is an ordering for the 'common good' (which invites comparison with the historical human experience of law and legal systems) Finnis should have said that the 'ideal' or 'perfected potential' of law and legal systems is that ordering which is for the 'common good'. Finnis should have said that the 'realised potential' for law is that ordering of public rules which is for the common good. Indeed Finnis has had to clarify what he meant by asserting that the 'central case' of law is for the common good. Finnis comments in *Philosophy of Law* (2011) that saying that the 'central case of law is that which is for the common good':

> 'The sense of the thesis is the sense in which the doctor says "You need medicine", meaning something which by its nature is curative, without for a moment claiming or imagining that what has been served up as medicine "through the ages" has always, or generally, or even usually been curative.'

Therefore the claim of Finnis (the pre-eminent neo-classical natural lawyer) that the 'central case' of law is that which is for the 'common good' is definitely not an historical claim about law's use in history but refers to an ideal potential use of law to unlock and promote the common good of a society subject to law. Given that Finnis has had to clarify the situation it would have been better for him not to have used the phrase 'the central case of law' when referring to his 'ideal' form of law because his talk of the 'central case' of law and legal systems is ambiguous in meaning between an historical claim about law's use in human history and an ideal claim about law's realisable potential to further the 'common good' of society. The claim for example that the 'central cases' of surrealistic painting were by Salvador Dali and Magritte is an historical claim about a particular time in the history of modern art. The critic of modern art is saying 'as a matter of historical experience' the paintings by Dali and Magritte were the central examples, the 'central cases' of the art movement known as surrealism. Finnis could have appreciated that his claim in *Natural Law and Natural Rights* (1980) that the 'central case' legal system was an ordering for the common good could easily be read as an historical claim about the use of law in human history,where law has only rarely been used for the common good and therefore the 'central cases' of law and legal systems has definitely not been employed for the 'common good'. More historically accurate than the claim of Finnis that the 'central case' of law is for the common good is the claim that the 'central case' of law and legal systems is that coercive ordering designed to 'secure civil peace as far as possible'. Most, if not the vast majority, of the legal systems in human history have had as their basic function the securing and maintenance of civil peace. Indeed the Roman legal system valued civil order above all else. The Roman legal system is sometimes termed the 'parent' legal system because of its breadth throughout the classical world from Hadrian's Wall in England to the deserts of North Africa and because for the first time in human history the idea of a legal system as a system of rights and duties was established by the Roman legal system. The Romans saw the 'pax romanus', the Roman peace, as absolutely essential to the Roman Empire.

The fact that the very first and most important function of law and government is the preservation of civil order is attested to by many political sources. William Whitelaw was Conservative Home Secretary in July 1981 at the time of serious rioting in many English cities. Whitelaw said In the House of Commons on 16 July 1981:

> 'It is the duty of every Government to underline, and act on, their fundamental responsibility to uphold the rule of law.'

Lord Liverpool, Prime Minister 1812–1827, had to deal with serious civil unrest in Britain following the return of soldiers from the wars with Napoleon in 1815. Lord Liverpool commented on the duty of government to stifle civil disorder (taken from Professor Norman Gash's 1984 biography of Lord Liverpool):

> 'The fear of the mob invariably led to arbitrary government and the best friends of liberty were therefore those who put down popular commotion, and secured the inhabitants of the country in the peaceable enjoyment of their rights.'

Lord Liverpool was here arguing that civil disorder and the great fear of it by ordinary citizens can lead to the rise of an extremist government who, whilst restoring civil order, might not respect liberties of the people as they should be respected by government. It is better, Lord Liverpool argued, to put down disorder firmly by firm repressive measures which will protect the life, property and liberty of ordinary citizens from the mob, than to allow disorder to continue with the inevitable result that an extremist government, such as a dictatorship, comes to power which puts down disorder and restores order – but at a huge cost, namely the dictatorship has little respect for the traditional liberties of the citizens.

There are generally two unfortunate consequences of a breakdown in civil order in a country or part of a country:

(1) The most violent, destructive and dangerous elements in society are given a 'free hand' to do what they will. The violent, destructive and dangerous elements in society are attracted to a situation of disorder as moths are to a light.

(2) The most vulnerable in society, the young, the old, females, the disabled and the weak suffer most from a breakdown in civil order as lacking the means or the will to defend themselves they are prey to the worst elements in society.

The basic duty of any government is to protect the vulnerable in society from attack.

From August 1946 through to late 1947 there was widespread civil disorder in parts of India as the colonial power Britain lacked the will or the manpower to enforce order after the Second World War and as Indian independence approached in August 1947. The disorder was motivated by communal hatred between Hindus, Sikhs and Muslims as it became clear that the British were leaving for good and that India was to be partitioned between India and a new state, Pakistan. The worst parts of India affected were the states of Punjab and Bengal. The leader of the Indian nationalist party 'The Congress' was Jawaharlal Nehru who later became Prime Minister of India, 1947–1964. Nehru wrote from East Bengal in mid-October 1946 (quoted in Stanley Wolpert's 'Shameful Flight: The Last Years of the British Empire in India', 2006):

'A vast area of Bengal has ceased to have any Government functioning, any security, and has just become the happy hunting ground of the worst elements in the community.'

Nehru continued on the impact of this breakdown on the weak and vulnerable especially:

'Mass slaughter, arson, burning of human beings, rape, abduction on a large scale and all manner of other horrible things are happening.'

There has been a discernible tendency in recent years in legal theory to down play the differences between the legal positivist tradition and the natural law tradition exemplified by Finnis. It is now accepted that natural lawyers can accept the legal positivist 'sources thesis' (Finnis, 1996, 204) without compromising the coherence of their own natural law apparatus. Contemporary legal positivists such as Gardner (2001, 223) unreservedly accept that there are many necessary connections between law and morality so the old shibboleth concerning the separation of law and morality as marking the alleged division between natural lawyers and legal positivists is no longer generally accepted. In addition there is a tendency among some legal theorists to deny the relevance of labels such as 'legal positivism'. Raz, in the preface to the second edition to *The Authority of Law* comments: 'that we should move away from ways of classifying theories of law which serve to obscure rather than clarify' (Raz, 2009, vii) and 'the classification of theories into legal positivism and others is misleading and unhelpful' (Raz, 2009, 317). Raz is joined in his dislike of the practice of attaching misleading labels to complex legal theories by

MacCormick who comments of the old fashioned distinction between legal positivism and natural law theory: 'it is better to reject the aforesaid dichotomy as based on a misleading account of the history of ideas than to trouble responding to the question: 'Are you a positivist or natural lawyer?' (MacCormick, 2007, 279) and that: 'In truth, such dichotomies are rarely revealing of any important truth' (MacCormick, 2007, 278).

However two points can be made about the 'closing of the gap' between legal positivism and natural law theory. The first point is that historically the contrast between the traditions of legal positivism and natural law has been a significant one. Mark Murphy comments: 'Legal positivism has defined itself by setting itself in contrast with natural law' (Murphy, 2005, 22) and Murphy provides a clear historical example of such a contrast, between the legal positivist 'command theories' of Bentham and Austin who both viewed the validity of law solely in terms of the social facts of what the 'sovereign commanded' and Blackstone's overly strong natural law view that a human law which violated the universal law of nature was not a law: 'Austin and Bentham took as their primary targets Blackstone's seeming affirmation of the strong natural law thesis' (Murphy, 2005, 23). The second point concerning the 'closing of the gap' between the legal positivist tradition and the natural law tradition is that is a fundamental and arguably unbridgeable methodological divide between the legal positivism of Hart and Raz on the one hand and the natural law theory of Finnis on the other. Finnis (Finnis, 2011) has proposed an optimistic and upbeat view of law's potential to secure human goods in comparison with other social conditions such as arbitrary domination or the anarchistic commune as part of the legal theorist's very account of the social institution called law. Hart (Hart, 1994) and Raz (1994; 2009) in their different ways seek to give an evaluative account of law and legal systems which is not dependent on the premise 'legal ordering is morally superior compared to other social conditions'. The premise 'legal ordering is morally superior compared to other social conditions' is the premise of most natural law theory and therefore this is the heart of the disagreement between legal positivism and the natural law tradition. The legal positivist in their approach to the analysis of law do not presume state law is morally bad (the philosophical anarchist position) or morally good (the natural law tradition). Legal positivism aims to pick out what is significant in law and legal systems without moral approval or condemnation. Julie Dickson in 'Legal Positivism: Contemporary Debates' in *The Routledge Companion to Philosophy of Law* (2012) comments of legal positivism as a tradition of philosophical investigation into the nature of law:

> 'As legal positivism is an inquiry into certain aspects of the nature of law it should also not be viewed as a thesis about what qualities it would be morally or politically beneficial for law to possess ... Nor does legal positivism offer any explicit or implicit commendation or condemnation of law ... Legal positivism comes not to praise, recommend, advise, condone or condemn: it aims to tell it like it is about some aspects of the nature of law, and so help us better to understand this vitally important and far-reaching social institution with which we are all so familiar, and which plays a significant role in our lives ... Legal positivism is implicitly committed to illuminate certain aspects of law's nature.'

Therefore legal positivism stands as a legal theory somewhat between the two opposing poles of classical natural law theory and philosophical anarchism. Classical natural law theory seeks to commend law to us, philosophical anarchism seeks to condemn law.[2] Legal positivism seeks neither the commendation of law or condemnation of law – it seeks merely to explain law's nature.

Aim Higher

Legal positivism seeks neither to praise the institution of law nor condemn the institution of law. Of all approaches to law, legal positivism is the closest to sociology and the social sciences, seeking to analyse law in a neutral, non-ideological way. The great practitioner of this approach was Professor Hart whose 'The Concept of Law' (1961) with its analysis of law as public rules administered by legal officials echoes strongly Max Weber's analysis of modern law as a 'rational technical apparatus' in Weber's book *On Law in Economy and Society*. Natural law theorists would never limit their analysis of law to Hartian or Weberian terms in which law is seen as 'a rational technical apparatus' but would insist on giving an account of law which attended to law's moral purpose of securing, maintaining and furthering the moral common good of society.

NOTES

For a very recent survey of Legal Positivism see the essay by Julie Dickson: 'Legal Positivism: Contemporary Debates' in *The Routledge Companion to Philosophy of Law* (2012) edited by Andrei Marmor. For a survey of natural law thinking see Brian Bix: 'Natural Law: The Modern Tradition' in *The Oxford Handbook of Jurisprudence and Philosophy of Law* (2002) edited by Jules Coleman and Scott Shapiro. *Mark Murphy: 'Natural Law in Jurisprudence and Politics', Cambridge Studies in Philosophy and Law* (2006) and *Mark Murphy: Natural Law Theory: The Blackwell Guide to the Philosophy of Law and Legal Theory* (Oxford: Blackwell Publishing, 2005). *John Finnis' collection of essays: 'The Philosophy of Law'* (2011). MacCormick's (2007) *Institutions of Law: An Essay in Legal Theory* (Oxford University Press, 2007). J Raz essay 'Authority, Law and Morality' in *Ethics in the Public Domain* (1994).

QUESTION 16

What is the relevance of natural law theory today?

How to Answer this Question

The tradition of 'natural law' theory is often misunderstood as having little in common with the mainstream of jurisprudence or being concerned with crass slogans, such as 'An unjust law is not a law'. However, properly understood, the tradition of natural law

---

2   On the topic of philosophical anarchism see Questions 21 and 22 in Chapter 6 of this book.

going back to Thomas Aquinas has much to offer legal theory by providing a moral basis for the criticism and guidance of the activities of judges, legislators and citizens. The 'big picture' perspective of natural law thought, as exemplified by Professor Finnis in *Natural Law and Natural Rights* (1980), offers an antidote to the 'narrowness' of some legal theory dominated by, for example, what happens in the courtroom. It is perfectly possible to grasp the essence of natural law theory without subscribing to the theological underpinnings of much natural law thought. Therefore, in a secular 'post religious' society, natural law theory can have continued relevance today. A skeleton plan is presented as follows:

Applying the Law

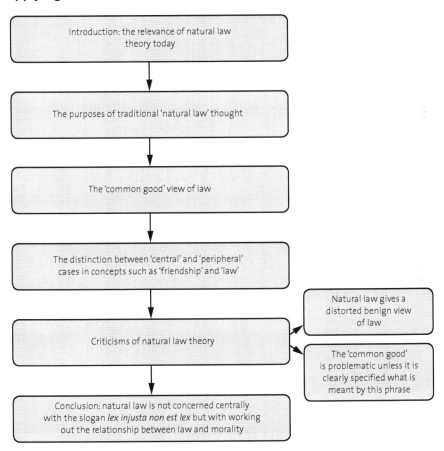

Introduction: the relevance of natural law theory today

The purposes of traditional 'natural law' thought

The 'common good' view of law

The distinction between 'central' and 'peripheral' cases in concepts such as 'friendship' and 'law'

Criticisms of natural law theory

Natural law gives a distorted benign view of law

The 'common good' is problematic unless it is clearly specified what is meant by this phrase

Conclusion: natural law is not concerned centrally with the slogan *lex injusta non est lex* but with working out the relationship between law and morality

ANSWER

The tradition of natural law theory can appear to be somewhat detached from the mainstream of analytical jurisprudence – represented by legal positivism or Ronald Dworkin's theory of law – which asks questions concerning the nature of a legal system or the nature of common law adjudication. Natural law theory appears at times to be remote from such issues as its concerns seem much more high flown, relating to the connections between the cosmic order, divine will, human reason and law.[3]

However, natural law theory does have a significant contribution to make to mainstream jurisprudence. As Brian Bix comments (in an essay entitled 'Natural Law: The Modern Tradition', in *The Oxford Handbook of Jurisprudence and Philosophy of Law* (2002)) perhaps the most important idea brought to jurisprudence by modern natural law theorists is that a view of law that recognises law's higher moral aspirations gives a fuller understanding of the institution of law than legal theories which are merely content to describe law (for example, legal positivism – see Hart, *The Concept of Law* (1961)) or to focus on one important feature of law (for example, Dworkin's account of common law adjudication – see *Law's Empire* (1986)).

The insight that modern natural law theory offers to contemporary legal theory is that the human institution of law can only be fully understood if we understand the ultimate moral value of law to human society. In the words of the central figure in natural law theory, Thomas Aquinas (1225–1273): 'Law is an ordinance of reason for the common good.' This basic insight is lost if we merely focus on describing the crucial elements of law and a legal system or concentrate too fully on common law adjudication. As Aquinas pointed out, there is an intimate connection between the institution of law and the proper (as in the sense of morally correct) governance of society: 'Law is the primary proper means of co-ordinating civil society.' This view of the 'bigger picture' than that provided for by mainstream jurisprudence is perhaps the greatest contribution natural law theory can make to legal theory today. As Professor Finnis comments (in his modern restatement of natural law theory, *Natural Law and Natural Rights*), the true tradition of natural law theory is not about the rather obvious insight that morality often affects the law but, instead, is about pointing out the true requirements of morality to provide a rational basis

....

3   Criticisms of 'natural law' philosophy fall into four broad camps: (1) A denial of the existence of 'a natural law' such as Bentham who called it a 'mere work of the fancy. In a secular age people tend to get impatient with claims of an objective non-visible 'natural law' (2) Even if there is a natural law what guidance does it provide to the formulation of very technical complex modern legislation even if the natural law could provide guidance to law-makers in the field of moral law such as the law on abortion or suicide? (3) The natural law can be used as an ideological cover for any unjust regime that tries to justify itself by reference to the 'natural law'. As Alf Ross, the Scandanavian jurist said in *On Law and Justice*:

> 'Like a harlot, natural law is at the disposal of everyone. The ideology does not exist that cannot be defended by an appeal to the law of nature. And, indeed, how can it be otherwise, since the ultimate basis for every natural right lies in a private direct insight, as evident contemplation, an intuition. Cannot my intuition be just as good as yours? The historical variability of natural law supports the Interpretation that metaphysical postulates are merely constructions to buttress emotional attitudes and the fulfillment of certain needs.'

(4) Natural law theorists often speak about law co-ordinating the 'common good' of society (see, e.g. Finnis, *Natural Law and Natural Rights* (2011, 2nd edition) but is the 'common good' a realisable aim? Is not society a pack of conflicting and competing group and individual interests and government's task is to mediate between conflicting sections of society divided on class, ethnic, regional and work-related lines? In other words the 'common good' is an illusion masking real and deep conflicts in society.

for the activities of legislators, judges and citizens. This is linked to the ultimate purpose of natural law theory which is to show, according to Finnis, how law and legal institutions can be justified – on what conditions, and to criticise those legal institutions by showing the ways in which they are defective. The natural law theory of Professor Finnis is not then merely descriptive of law (as in the tradition of legal positivism) but is normative (guidance giving), similar to Dworkin's legal theory, although the theory of Finnis looks at the whole institution of law rather than the narrow issue of 'a judge in a hard case' that has preoccupied Dworkin's legal theorising for, as Finnis comments, the tradition of natural law theorising is not characterised by any particular answer to the question of what a judge should do in a 'hard case'.

The 'natural law tradition' has been around for thousands of years and can be traced to Ancient Greece (Aristotle) and Rome (Cicero). St Augustine, in the fifth century, was an important figure in the development of a specifically Christian natural law doctrine, but the key historical figure was Thomas Aquinas in the thirteenth century. As Mark Murphy comments (in 'The natural law tradition in ethics' in *Stanford Encyclopedia of Philosophy* (2008)) we should take Aquinas's natural law theory as the central case of a natural law theory, given his influence at the time (for example, Pope John XXII in the fourteenth century was a canon lawyer and devotee of Aquinas) and in the present day (Professor Finnis wrote a commentary on the moral, legal and political thought of Aquinas in 1998). Indeed, the continuing influence of the thought of Aquinas can be seen in a recent work, *St Thomas Aquinas and the Natural Law Tradition* (edited by Goyette, Latkovic, and Myers, 2004) where, in the introduction, the authors comment that we are in the midst of a great revival of interest in natural law. Much of this thinking, say the authors, is traced in one degree or another to the thoughts of St Thomas Aquinas.

For Aquinas there are two key features of the natural law, as discerned in his work, *Summa Theologica*. The first feature looks at God's role as the giver of the natural law; the natural law discovered by the reason of man is just one aspect of divine providence. The second feature looks at things from the human perspective as the human recipient of the natural law. The 'natural law' constitutes the principles of practical rationality – those principles by which human action is to be judged as reasonable or unreasonable. From God's point of view, natural law is seen through its place in the scheme of divine providence and, from the human point of view, the natural law constitutes a set of naturally binding and knowable rules of reason.

There is a crucial point to be made. The natural law is discernible without divine revelation but purely through human reason. As Thomas Aquinas pointed out, the first principles of natural law are self-evident to the human mind but knowledge of the existence of God is not self-evident to the human mind and is only known through supernatural grace. 'Original sin' (a key 'natural law' doctrine), inherited by all persons from birth, has so clouded man's reason that knowledge of the divine creator can only come through divine revelation. Given that the natural law and natural law theory can be understood, assented to and analysed without considering the question of God's ultimate existence, it may be tempting to ask in a secular 'post Christian' age whether natural law theory really needs to argue for the existence of God at all. The central point of the theory of Finnis in *Natural Law and Natural Rights*, that the law is a specific and social human institution for the maintenance, protection and realisation of the 'common good' of society, can be grasped and assented to by even the most militant atheist or secularist or humanist. However, the ultimate connection between 'natural law theory' and the existence of God cannot be broken for the following reasons: first, just because natural law theory can be understood, analysed and applied without referring to the question of the existence of God it does not mean that no further explanation of the origin of natural law is available or that the existence and nature of God is not that explanation. Second, the founders of Christian natural law theory – in particular, St Augustine (*The City of God*) and St Thomas Aquinas (*Summa Theologica*) – would not have regarded as intelligible a theory of natural law without the existence of divine providence for mankind. The 'internal point of view' of St Augustine, St Thomas Aquinas, and even modern writers such as Finnis who see an unbreakable link between the existence of God and the natural law, must be considered when assessing natural law theory. However, Finnis dismisses as a 'phantom' the view of Kai Nielsen (in 'The myth of natural law', in *Law and Philosophy*, edited by Hook (1964)) that natural law concepts are totally dependent for intelligibility on the view that God exists. Natural law theory can be understood in terms acceptable to an atheist even if many natural law theorists posit God as the ultimate origin of natural law.

Exactly how modern natural law theory relates to modern society will now be sketched. Professor Finnis, in his groundbreaking work *Natural Law and Natural Rights* (1980) rescued the natural law tradition from many misconceptions that had grown up over the centuries, such as the slogan *lex injusta non est lex* ('an unjust law is not a law') which does not represent the natural law tradition according to Finnis.

Finnis identified a number of self-evident 'human goods' which are self-evident to human reason. The integration into life and ordering of these basic goods over a lifetime is an important aspect of human well-being. These goods are seven in number: life, knowledge, play, friendship, religion, practical reasonableness and aesthetic experience (enjoyment of nature or art). It may be observed that some of these 'self-evident' goods are rather 'bourgeois' in character and their supposed 'universality' can be questioned.

The law, for Professor Finnis, comes in the following way to regulate human society: when many human beings as exist in a society try to pursue these 'self-evident' goods there will be inevitable conflicts and co-ordination problems which only practical authority can resolve. The law is the expression of the judgments and decisions of that practical authority. The point or function of human law is to facilitate the common good as connected to the realisation of the self-evident goods in human life by providing authoritative rules (laws) that solve the conflicts and co-ordination problems that arise in connection with many persons pursuing the 'self-evident' goods. Finnis comments in *Natural Law and Natural Rights* that the term 'law' refers to rules made by an effective authority for a community and supported by sanctions in accordance with the rule-guided courts. These legal rules and legal institutions are directed to the reasonable resolving of the community's co-ordination problems for the common good of that community. In order to effectively solve co-ordination problems, the law must be clearly and certainly identified by legal officials, civil servants and officials. Therefore, the natural lawyer, Professor Finnis, defends the legal positivist thesis that the law is identified from social sources. The argument is this: to perform the moral function of solving society's co-ordination problems for the benefit of the common good, the law must be clearly ascertained from human sources and no moral argument should cloud the identification of the law.

Therefore, the identification of the law independent of a moral argument is necessary for the central moral function of law: to co-ordinate human behaviour for the common good. The adoption of the legal positivist 'sources thesis' by the leading contemporary natural lawyer, Professor Finnis, supports the observation by the legal positivist, Raz (in his article 'About morality and the nature of law' (2006)), that it is a mistake to make the division between 'legal positivists' and 'natural lawyers' the basic division in legal philosophy. In distinction to Professor Hart's analysis in *The Concept of Law*, Professor Finnis goes beyond an analysis which purports only to describe law as a social phenomenon and social institution. Professor Finnis seeks to give an account of law from the central or focal case of law as a human institution designed to further the common good. This technique of seeking an explanation of a concept by focusing on the 'central' or 'focal' example of that concept rather than seeking a definition which will include 'peripheral' examples of that concept can be traced back to Aristotle (384–322 BC). So there are central cases, as Aristotle insisted, of friendship (lifelong friends, for example) and more or less peripheral cases (such as business friendships, casual or work friendships). There are central cases of constitutional government (such as the United Kingdom) and there are peripheral cases (such as Hitler's Germany). As Finnis, following Aristotle, points out, there is no point in restricting one's explanation of the central cases to those features present also in the peripheral cases. The description of the 'central cases' should be as conceptually rich and complex as is required to answer all relevant questions about these central cases. There-fore, Finnis, in *Natural Law and Natural Rights*, takes as his perspective for description the central case of law: the morally just legal system working for the common good. Finnis believes that a fully complex and adequate description of the concept of law cannot be given without analysing law through the prism of the ultimate function of law: to order civil society for the common good.

Professor Hart, in *Essays in Jurisprudence and Philosophy* (1983), criticises Finnis for believ-ing that the 'central' case or 'focal' case of law is that which is for the 'common good'. Pro-fessor Hart comments that, in view of the horrors of human history and the evil use of law, then to say that the central meaning of law is that which is for the common good is an unbalanced perspective and as great a distortion of reality as the opposite Marxist identification of the central case of law with the pursuit of the interests of a dominant economic class. However, to defend Finnis against this trenchant criticism by Professor Hart, the interest of Finnis is in the ideal form of law, the potential of the idea of law to unlock and further the common good. Finnis is interested in the idea of law as a moral ideal, not the historical reality of the use of law which, as Hart correctly points out, has often been used for evil ends. Only by living in an ordered community under the rule of law can the common good be properly realised.

As Finnis comments in the very first sentence of *Natural Law and Natural Rights*, there are human goods that can be secured only through the institution of human law. For example, a taxation system which is fair and efficient, and is necessary to provide social services for the old and vulnerable in society, is one obvious advantage of a society under law. Natural law theory does not dictate what the precise level of taxation shall be in a particular society as this will depend on many changing economic and social factors, but natural law theory does stipulate adequate social service provision through an effective and fair taxation system. As Finnis comments, if material goods are to be used efficiently for human well-being there must normally be a regime of private property. However, the precise rules of such a regime of private property are not settled by natural law theory. Those in lawful authority must choose the particular rules of taxation, private property and contract, for example, but once the choice is made it becomes authoritative for officials and citizens alike. For Finnis, in a morally just legal order, the law represents the choices (the determination-concretisation by rational choice) of lawful authority to further the common good. The rulers' choice from a range of reasonable options determines what thereafter is just for those subject to their authority. There arises a moral obligation on citizens to obey the law. The citizens' obligation to obey is a duty not, strictly speaking, owed to the rulers themselves but rather to, if anyone, their fellow citizens in fairness since the law of a just state represents a seamless web of social co-ordination and fairness (see Finnis's article, 'Law as Co-ordination' (1989)).

Finnis comments, in his commentary on Aquinas (*Aquinas: Moral, Political and Legal Theory* (1998)), that the central case of law is co-ordination of willing subjects by law which, by its fully public character, its clarity, generality, stability and predictability, treats them as partners in public reason. Aquinas, according to Finnis, understands the state precisely as the type of community fitted to securing goods which are only well secured by general and published laws employed with impartiality and coercive force. Aquinas holds that governments themselves are not above the law but are appropriately regulated and limited by law. This is reflected in two important moral truths: (1) that government is for the common good, not for the advantage of the rulers, and (2) that no-one has any 'natural right to govern'.[4]

Aquinas originally based his argument for authority on the superiority in wisdom and intelligence that some would have, compared with others in their society. Whilst this is an important consideration in his later works, Aquinas added the more fundamental consideration that social life needs common policy and common action which cannot be achieved in a group whose members have many ideas about priorities – proper co-ordination requires authoritative choice and that can only come from proper authority. We have

....

4   The view of Thomas Aquinas that no one had a natural right to rule went against the prevailing ideology of that time (the thirteenth century in Europe) that certain families possessed a 'royal bloodline' which meant that they had a 'Divine,' God-given right to rule: the 'Divine right of Kings' ideology. Max Weber in 'On Law in Economy and Society' comments: 'Every highly privileged group develops the myth of its natural, especially its blood superiority.'

already considered the criticism of Professor Hart, that in the light of the horrors of human history the identification of the 'central case' of law with the co-ordination of society for the common good is an historical distortion. Further criticism can be made of the natural law 'common good' concept of law – namely, that in our conflict-ridden societies there is too much observable conflict to identify the 'common good'. This is the thrust of the criticism by Leslie Green, in *The Authority of the State* (1988), of the 'common good' conception of law. Green comments that there is 'zero-sum' conflict between individuals and classes over power, status and other goods in which there is no 'common good', but merely winners and losers. Also, there are areas of less sharp but still conflicting interests over such public goods as clean air. The combined result over all this inevitable conflict in society is to leave little room for the 'common good'. Natural law theory's 'common good' view of law can be criticised as utopian and unrealistic in the light of the many real conflicts which beset all modern democracies. Government should be seen on the model of 'managing grievances' within society rather than the high flown concept of the 'common good': such a phrase masks real and deep divisions in society. The utopianism of natural law theory should be set against the harsh realities of politics, for as Benjamin Disraeli, Lord Beaconsfield (1804–1881), the nineteenth-century Prime Minister of Britain once said: 'Politics is the art of the possible'.[5] The pursuit of the 'common good' by government through law is much more impinged upon by social, political and economic factors than 'natural law theory' would have us believe.

This discussion of natural law theory will conclude by examining a supposed central tenet of natural law theory – namely, that *lex injusta non est lex* (an unjust law is not law). St Augustine comments in one of his dialogues that 'a law that was unjust would not seem to be a law'.

St Thomas Aquinas rather more carefully commented that morally bad laws are not law in the 'focal' or 'central' sense but are still 'law since they have the character of law in one important respect – they are the command of a superior to his subordinates'. Therefore, Aquinas carefully avoids saying that 'an unjust law is not a law'. Professor Finnis, in *Natural Law and Natural Rights*, adopts the formulation of Aquinas on this issue. Finnis does not deny legal validity to unjust laws but argues that they are not law (an ordinance of reason for the 'common good') in the central 'focal' or flourishing sense of the word 'law'. Indeed, Finnis argues that the main focus of natural law theory, properly understood, has never been the false slogan 'unjust laws are not laws' but rather that the main concern of a proper theory of natural law has been to explore the requirements of natural reason for a community under the rule of law.

---

5 Of course the Disraelian phrase: 'Politics is the art of the possible' can be used to justify minimalist government action, can be used to justify governmental apathy.

Aim Higher

Students can gain extra marks by pointing out that there may be an inescapable con-nection between law and the pursuit of the common good, in that given the essen-tial selfishness of human nature then the institution of law is a necessity to act as a restraint on destructive human impulses. Students can avoid the pitfall of thinking that natural law theory endorses the principle 'an unjust law is not a law' because modern natural law theorists, such as Professor Finnis, do not endorse the view of St Augustine that an unjust law is not a law, but rather argue that an unjust law is still a law but that the moral obligation to obey that unjust law may be severely affected by its unjustness. Finnis, in *Natural Law and Natural Rights*, denied that the proverb 'an unjust law is not a law' in any way characterised the tradition of natural law thought.

NOTES

The modern *locus classicus* of natural law thought remains *Natural Law and Natural Rights* (1980) by Professor John Finnis. Finnis wrote a detailed commentary on the thought of the father of natural law theory, St Thomas Aquinas (1225–1273) in 1998, *Aquinas: Moral, Political and Legal Theory*. A good commentary on natural law thought can be found in the online and free *Stanford Encyclopaedia of Philosophy* with the entry on 'The natural law tradition in ethics' being written by Mark Murphy (http://plato.stanford.edu/). Criticisms of 'natural law theory' can be found in Hart's *Essays in Jurisprudence and Philosophy* (1983) and L Green, 'Law, Co-ordination and the Common Good' (*Oxford Journal of Legal Studies* (1983)) and also in Green's *The Authority of the State* (1988). Essays on 'Natural Law' in *The Oxford Handbook of Jurisprudence and Philosophy of Law* (2002), edited by Coleman and Shapiro, should be consulted. The first essay in that collection is by John Finnis: 'Natural Law: The Classical Tradition'. The following essay is by Brian Bix: 'Natural Law: The Modern Tradition'. Professor Finnis has also written a useful entry on 'Natural Law Theories' (2007) in the online and free *Stanford Encyclopaedia of Philosophy*.

QUESTION 17

Is Professor Dworkin a 'natural lawyer?'

How to Answer this Question

Professor Dworkin is noted in his legal theory for his hostility to the central idea of legal positivism – that the existence and content of law can be worked out without a moral argument. Dworkin argues the contrary position, namely that:

> 'people who argue about the content of law draw on moral considerations in a way that positivism cannot explain' – see *Justice in Robes* (2006) at p. 187.

Dworkin's hostility to legal positivism's 'sources thesis', through his insistence that moral-ity forms part of the grounds of law (the identification of law), have led some people to assert that Dworkin is a 'natural lawyer', or at least a 'weak natural lawyer'. However, on true reflection, Dworkin's work in legal theory should not be placed within the tradition of natural law thought, with its emphasis on a universal moral law discerned by reason which Dworkin has never subscribed to, let alone the theological underpinnings of the natural law tradition. Dworkin's work on common law appellate court reasoning places him instead in the tradition of classical common law thought, and in many ways Dworkin is a 'common law romantic' for he views the common law as providing from within itself, through the process of constructive interpretation by the judge, nearly all right answers to hard questions that need decision by the appellate courts.

Applying the Law

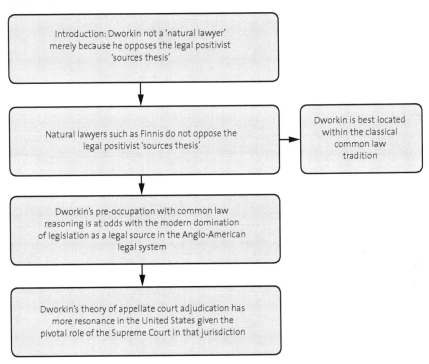

Introduction: Dworkin not a 'natural lawyer' merely because he opposes the legal positivist 'sources thesis'

Natural lawyers such as Finnis do not oppose the legal positivist 'sources thesis'

Dworkin is best located within the classical common law tradition

Dworkin's pre-occupation with common law reasoning is at odds with the modern domination of legislation as a legal source in the Anglo-American legal system

Dworkin's theory of appellate court adjudication has more resonance in the United States given the pivotal role of the Supreme Court in that jurisdiction

ANSWER

Professor Dworkin has sometimes been termed 'a natural lawyer', perhaps because of his jurisprudential hostility to the central tenet of legal positivism – namely the 'sources thesis' that law is identified by reference to social sources alone and that therefore a moral argument is not required to work out the content of the law. There seems to be an assumption that because Dworkin, in his legal theory, makes the identification of law depend on a moral reading of existing law, therefore Dworkin is anti-positivist and ergo a natural lawyer. There is a fundamental fallacy in this argument. First of all some natural lawyers actually subscribe to the legal positivist 'sources thesis'. Professor Finnis, who breathed new life into the 'natural law tradition' in 1980 with the publication of *Natural*

Law and Natural Rights, has given his powerful assent to the legal positivist 'sources thesis' since, in order to perform its essential task of defending, maintaining and promoting the common good of society, the law must be crisply identified from social sources such as legislation, common law or custom. As Finnis writes in 'The Truth in Legal Positivism' in *The Autonomy of Law: Essays on Legal Positivism* (1996):

> 'since the whole of a human community's existing law … custom, legislation, judgments – can all be identified by lawyerly historical methods, without 'moral argument.'

The implications of this are that Finnis, the natural lawyer, is at one with legal positivists from Hobbes in the seventeenth century to Raz in the twenty-first century in holding that the judge must exercise a law-making function when the legal sources run out. As Finnis argues:

> 'when the sources yield no determinate solution all concerned have the responsibility of supplementing the sources to fill the gap by a choice guided by standards of fairness and other morally true principles and norms.'

Therefore Dworkin is very much on his own amongst present day leading legal theorists in asserting that the common law itself can find the solution to any novel legal problem by the constructive moral interpretation by the judge of existing law. There is nothing particularly tied to the natural law tradition in Dworkin's theory, indeed Finnis writes in *Natural Law and Natural Rights* that the natural law tradition has not been characterised by the answer as to what a judge should do in a 'hard case', when the legal rules do not provide a definite answer. It is strange that Dworkin should ever have been considered a 'natural lawyer' merely on the ground that he disputed the legal positivist 'sources thesis'. However Kent Greenawalt, in the collection of essays edited by Robert P George, referred to above, comments:

> '**weak natural law is the term I attach to Dworkin's views … Dworkin has consistently maintained that judges deciding difficult cases must rely on principles that have a sort of mixed moral and legal status. These principles do not owe their status as law to having been authoritatively posited on any particular occasion.**'

However, as we have seen assenting to the legal positivist 'sources thesis' is not inconsistent with the natural law tradition, and indeed Dworkin's professed liberalism seems somewhat out of kilter with mainstream natural law views that abortion, pornography and homosexuality are 'sins' that the state ought to discourage. Indeed Dworkin has defended a right to pornography (see *A Matter of Principle* (1985)), asserted the rights of homosexuals and a right to abortion. Also, natural lawyers dating back to Thomas Aquinas in the thirteenth century have traditionally asserted a realm of natural law or natural reason which is not human in origin and from which positive human law is derived or, in the terminology of natural lawyers, human law is a 'determination' of the natural law – a concretisation or determination of the natural law. Dworkin in his legal writings over 40 years has never written of his support for the view that there is a universal and eternal natural law to be discovered by the use of reason, which applies to all persons in all ages, let alone the traditional natural law belief that the natural law is the product of transcendental authority (i.e. God).[6]

Therefore it is a serious mistake to categorise Dworkin as a 'natural lawyer', whether weak or otherwise. Dworkin, in his liberal atheistic beliefs, cannot be assimilated to the natural law tradition and the only foothold that can be made to place Dworkin in the 'natural law' camp is due to Dworkin's jurisprudential belief that the identification of law depends on moral evaluation of that law. However this foothold is tenuous because, as previously argued, whether law is identified purely by social sources or partly by morality is not part of the natural law tradition. As Robert P George argues in *In Defense of Natural Law* (1999):

> 'the role of the judge as law-creator reasonably varies from jurisdiction to jurisdiction according to each jurisdiction's determinationes.'

and:

> 'Some people who are loyal to the tradition of natural law theorizing are tempted to suppose that Professor Dworkin's position is the one more faithful to the tradition. This temptation should, however, be resisted ... natural law theory treats the role of the judge as fundamentally a matter for determinatio (determination or concretization), not for direct translation from the natural law.'

Professor Dworkin is best characterised not as some adjudicative version of a natural lawyer but rather as being a subtle, persuasively argued modern representative of the classical common law tradition. Dworkin, in support of his theory of adjudication called 'law as integrity', has drawn a parallel between the incrementalist approaches of judges at common law and the development of, what Dworkin calls, 'the chain novel'. In the 'chain novel' a different writer writes a different chapter of the same book with the aim of producing a readable coherent product. The 'chain novel' is a kind of literary 'parlour game' and is meant to mirror the development of the common law over generations of different judges. Each writer (judge) must take the preceding chapters (decided cases) and develop the story (the common law) to make his own contribution the best it can be, consistent with the other chapters. In this metaphor Dworkin seeks to mirror how judges develop principle out of earlier decisions, in much the same way as Lord Atkin did in *Donoghue v Stevenson* (1932).

---

6   In the modern era natural law theories of an objective universal moral order not created by God but 'part' of the world are put forward. Michael Moore believes that 'nothing exists answering to a personal conception of God'. However in Moore's judgment, the non-existence of God is perfectly compatible with morality's objectivity. Michael S Moore argues in an article entitled 'Good Without God' in *Natural Law, Liberalism and Morality* (1996) edited by Robert P George that belief in an 'objective' moral order can be held without belief in God. Moore thinks that 'values' including moral duties are natural and 'impersonal' qualities of things in the world, like 'wetness'. Values are like 'wetness' a quality 'in the world' only different because values give 'objective reasons to act'.

As Dworkin comments in *A Matter of Principle* (1985), aiming his fire at judges who, in their common law decisions, seek to ignore previous legal decisions in the search for justice or policy:

> 'A judge's duty is to interpret the legal history he finds, not to invent a better history.'

Dworkin uses the case of *McLoughlin v O'Brien* (1982) to support his arguments for a theory of the common law driven by judicial adherence to principle not policy. Indeed in *McLoughlin v O'Brien* Lord Scarman gives a statement of the common law method which strongly echoes Professor Dworkin's theory of the common law. Lord Scarman commented:

> 'whatever the court decides to do, it starts from a baseline of existing principle and seeks a solution consistent with or analogous to a principle or principles already recognised … The distinguishing feature of the common law is this judicial development and formation of principle … By concentrating on principle the judges can keep the common law alive, flexible and consistent, and can keep the legal system clear of policy problems which neither they, nor the forensic process which is their duty to operate, are equipped to resolve. If principle leads to results which are thought to be socially unacceptable, Parliament can legislate to draw a line or map out a new path.'

Professor Dworkin, consistent with this judicial view of the common law method expounded by Lord Scarman, has always denied judges the legitimate power to make law in the name of 'policy' and has maintained that the richness of the common law gives the judge in a 'hard case' the resources to find the 'right answer' located within the existing legal history – if that legal history of cases is subject to 'constructive interpretation' by the judge. However, the fact that Lord Scarman was in a minority of judges and that most English judges think that policy has a role to play in the determination of cases suggests that Dworkin's theory of adjudication is a theory of how judges ought to decide cases, rather than a correct descriptive account of how they actually do decide cases.

Dworkin has called his theory of adjudication 'law as Integrity' which can be summarised by quoting from *Law's Empire* (1986):

> 'Law as integrity asks judges to assume, so far as this is possible, that the law is structured by a coherent set of principles about justice and fairness and procedural due process and it asks them to enforce these in the fresh cases that come before them, so that each person's situation is fair and just according to the same standards.'

Dworkin should be viewed as part of the classical common law tradition that elevates the common law as part of, and a driver of, a community's morality and also sees the common law as rich enough to find a 'legal' solution to any issue that comes before the courts for adjudication. Indeed Dworkin's implicit affinity with classical 'common law' thought is made explicit in *Law's Empire* where Dworkin refers with great approval to Lord Mansfield's celebration of the common law that: 'the law works itself pure' (see *Omychund v Barker* (1744)). The connection between Dworkin's conception of the common law and Lord Mansfield's view that the common law works itself pure is explained by Dworkin in *Law's Empire*:

'Sentimental lawyers cherish an old trope: they say that the law works itself pure. The figure imagines two forms or stages of the same system of law, the nobler form latent in the less noble, the impure, present law gradually transforming itself into its own purer ambition … never worked finally pure, but better in each generation than the last. There is matter in this mysterious image, and it adds to both the complexity and the power of law as integrity.'

Having allied himself with classic common law thought it is hardly surprising that Dworkin has been termed a 'common law romantic' by D Dyzenhaus and M Taggart in *Common Law Theory* (2007). Certainly Dworkin has always seemed focused in his legal theory on common law adjudication. Indeed the very first sentence of *Law's Empire* (1986) starts:

'It matters how judges decide cases.'

Four hundred pages later in the same book comes the statement:

'The courts are the capitals of law's empire, and the judges are its princes.'

For Dworkin the common law, if viewed as a coherent sytem of rights and duties, can provide the solution to any novel problem at law, i.e. through the constructive interpretation by the judge of previous common law decisions the common law works itself pure – it develops more 'integrity' over time through the successive efforts of generations of judges.

As a result of viewing the law through the prism of common law appellate adjudication Dworkin has been criticised for developing a theory of law from a theory of adjudication. As Professor Raz comments in *Between Authority and Interpretation* (2009):

'his book (Law's Empire) is not so much an explanation of the law as a sustained argument about how courts, especially American and British courts should decide cases. It contains a theory of adjudication rather than a theory of the nature of law.'

Raz would argue that since law is an important social institution and a cultural phenomenon, it should be examined from the 'institutional' perspective – how law operates in the context of its societal and political setting. The 'lawyer's' perspective of Dworkin, looking at law from what goes on in the courtroom or more specifically what goes on in an appellate judge's mind, is getting things the wrong way round. A theory of law should be developed, followed by a theory of adjudication, not the other way round as Dworkin implies. Indeed Dworkin makes a double mistake in his focus on the common law's courtroom adjudication for (1) law as a social institution should be studied by standing back from the lawyer's perspective and (2) common law is in the present era very much subordinated to legislation as a legal source, although judicial adjudication has a special resonance in the United States where the Supreme Court acts as a guardian of the United States Constitution.[7]

---

7 Roger Cotterrell in *The Politics of Jurisprudence: Second Edition* (2003) comments at p. 252 that in the United States 'law has remarkable cultural centrality'.

In England at least Dworkin's preoccupation with common law adjudication seems at odds with the domination of legislation as a legal source, as Roger Cotterrell comments in *Living Law* (2008):

> 'The old common law image of law distilled from community experience and moral-ity, brought to the court in litigation, has to co-exist with the modern and in many ways much more powerful image of enacted positive law, handed down "from above" in the form of statutes and other law produced from non-judicial sources.'

Cotterrell is keen to make clear 'the considerable tension between the modern concept of enacted positive and the older idea of common law as found by judges. English law has seen a long "cold war" between these two conceptions, in which common law thought has fought a lengthy rearguard action in a battle of ideas'.

Dworkin may best be characterised as a jurist who has given a modern and subtle inter-pretation to classical common law thought, but at a time when legislation, not the common law, in England is the much more dominant legal source. However Dworkin's focus on appellate court reasoning as his focus for a theory of law may have much more resonance in the United States where the Supreme Court regularly adjudicates on great moral-political questions and where the United States Supreme Court (unlike the Supreme Court in the United Kingdom) has the final authoritative say to settle controver-sial moral-legal questions.[8]

Aim Higher

Students can gain extra marks by pointing out that Professor Dworkin has little in common with the classical natural law tradition but has much in common with clas-sical common law thought where Dworkin shares the view of old writers, such as Lord Coke, that the common law is a rich enough resource to provide sound answers to any novel legal question if the judge is skilful enough in his search. Students can avoid the common pitfall which argues that because Dworkin is 'anti-positivistic' and makes morality part of the grounds for identifying law that therefore Dworkin is a 'natural lawyer'.

NOTES

Kent Greenawalt discusses his view that Dworkin is 'a weak natural lawyer' in 'Too Thin and Too Rich: Distinguishing Features of Legal Positivism' in *The Autonomy of Law*, edited by Robert P George (1996) at p. 5. Dworkin defends his own legal theory in *Justice in Robes* (2006), see pp. 187–188 and pp. 234–239. Dworkin comments: 'I want to oppose the idea that "law" is a fixed set of standards of any sort'. Roger Cotterrell discusses Dworkin's theory of law in *The Politics of Jurisprudence* (2003, 2nd edition) at pp. 160–174.

---

8 The United Kingdom could in the future develop 'strong form' judicial review as in the United States. Whether this is a good idea or not is explored in Question 28, Chapter 7 of this book.

5

Law and Ideology

INTRODUCTION

The view that law is best understood as ideological camoflauge for the social, political and economic interests of the ruling elites has been a powerful form of discourse about law and cannot be ignored by any serious student of the nature of law. The idea that law disguises reality by presenting an ideal of equality, justice and procedural due process which masks wider and deep social and economic inequalities informs the writings of Marx, Engels and Lenin. The view that law induces a consciousness restricting 'servility of mind' informed the writings of the 'anarchist aristocrats' Bakunin and Kropotkin.

Checklist

Ensure that you understand the following topics:

- the meaning of the phrase 'law as ideology';
- the use of law as an ideological device In the criminal law of eighteenth-century England;
- the approach to law of anarchism and marxism contrasted;
- the influence of the ideology of the Eighteenth Century Enlightenment on modern conceptions of state and law.

QUESTION 18

Discuss what is meant by 'law as ideology'.

How to Answer this Question

The crude understanding of the law of a liberal capitalist society is to view it as the will of the dominant class written into legislation. However, a much more subtle understanding of law is provided by Marx and EP Thompson who both assert that the law does contain elements of fairness and equality which are realised in practice but that the law functions as ideology by covering and distorting the true reality of socio-economic realities in society.

EP Thompson, in his 1975 book *Whigs and Hunters*, does pay tribute to the real achievement of the 'rule of law' in the English common law which has helped radicals and dissenters obtain real political advances by using the law.

Applying the Law

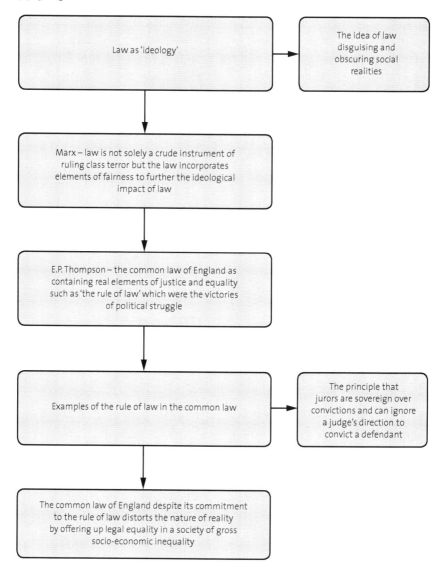

Law as 'ideology'

The idea of law disguising and obscuring social realities

Marx – law is not solely a crude instrument of ruling class terror but the law incorporates elements of fairness to further the ideological impact of law

E.P. Thompson – the common law of England as containing real elements of justice and equality such as 'the rule of law' which were the victories of political struggle

Examples of the rule of law in the common law

The principle that jurors are sovereign over convictions and can ignore a judge's direction to convict a defendant

The common law of England despite its commitment to the rule of law distorts the nature of reality by offering up legal equality in a society of gross socio-economic inequality

ANSWER

The basic point of those who accuse the law of liberal capitalist states of being 'ideology' is the idea of law as a source of manipulation: 'law cloaks power' in the words of the French sociologist Foucault. Arguing that law is ideology, as the anarchist and Marxists have done, is to argue that the law has a role in justifying unequal economic and social relations by obscuring the reality of such relations. The function of ideology is to distort reality but to present itself as the reality. Christine Sypnowich argues on ideology in the Stanford Encyclopedia of Philosophy:

'Ideology conserves by camouflaging flawed social relations, giving an illusory account of their function or rationale, in order to justify and win acceptance of them'.[1]

However it should not be thought that Marx and Engels viewed the law simply as a tool to oppress the working classes and poor. Marx and Engels realised that in order to better perform its work as justifying ideology then the law of liberal capitalist states must have a certain amount of formal justice in it, the law's claim to defend all persons equally was not just empty rhetoric but had a real basis to it even if the equality of the law masked the cruelty and unfairness of wider social and economic inequalities. Marx talked about the law of liberal capitalist states having an ideology of 'the conception of right' by which formally all persons were equal before the law. Marx said it would offend the 'conception of right' 'if a code of law is the blunt, unmitigated, unadulterated expression of the domination of a class'.

Indeed the powerful and rich elites themselves come to believe somewhat in their own ideology, persuaded by the rhetoric of the law that it is a just and fair order, and hence the strength of law as ideology is given strength and durability because the elites themselves come to believe in the ideology of law as a realm of justice, equality and fairness. Marx commented in his work *The German Ideology* that the consent of the masses of the people to law and governance in liberal democratic states will not be available if the ideology of the law bears no relation to actual reality: to function successfully as ideology the law must deliver partly at least on its commitment to fairness, justice and equality. Marx in *The German Ideology* has a crucial metaphor or image for ideology: reality, real social relations appear upside down in ideology, similar to the photographic process provides an inverted image in a 'camera obscura'. The 'inverted image' of the photographic process is a version of reality but it is a distorted version of reality since it is upside down. The 'inverted image' of reality than ideology delivers in law is that 'some' equality, 'some' fairness is delivered by law but at the expense of distorting the wider picture of social and economic reality: which is gross inequality.

Therefore the more subtle versions of 'law as ideology' admit the extent to which the law of a liberal democratic state has elements of both class-based manipulation and genuine equality and fairness for all persons. This analysis leads to the conclusion that the ideals of legality in the ideological presentation of the law are not wholly illusory but are actually to be found in the law even if in a partial and incomplete form. Law then, according to the more sophisticated Marxist analysis, is not simply the will of the ruling class elevated

---

1 Ideological constructions in the past to justify authority include: (1) The 'Divine Right' of rulers, that all political authority derives from God as asserted by St Paul in chapter 13 of the Epistle to the Romans. 'All power is of God': a stock claim justifying the authority of rulers; (2) the 'aristocratic' principle that a class of persons by 'breeding' education and social class are the only people 'fitted' to exercise political leadership; (3) the 'charisma' of an individual leader such as Adolf Hitler the 'Fuhrer', or Chairman Mao 'the great helmsman' of China: these 'special' individuals alone allegedly have the 'insight' or 'wisdom' to guide 'their' people.

into legislation even if it is the ruling class who ultimately benefit from the law's claim to universal equality. Law of modern Western capitalist states cannot be viewed simply as a bald instrument of class oppression, as some of the cruder Marxist analysis would have it. Ideology must ultimately work in the consciousness of those subject to it and to work on the consciousness of the masses the law cannot be viewed simply as an instrument of class warfare. If the law is viewed simply as class warfare by the masses, then the experience of the French and Russian Revolutions tells us what happens to ruling elites who lose the obedience of their social inferiors.

EP Thomson, the Marxist historian, has argued in *Whigs and Hunters* that in order for liberal capitalist law to function successfully as ideology, then the law must deliver some genuine justice. As Sypnowich comments:

> 'if law trumpets justice, equality and freedom, then it must succeed in realizing these ideals, however imperfectly, in order for law to function as ideology.'

As EP Thompson comments:

> 'The forms and rhetoric of law acquire a distinct identity which may, on occasion inhibit power and afford some protection to the powerless.'

Thompson, a Marxist, was keen to defend the achievements of the seventeenth century constitutional struggles in England against those left-wingers who denigrated the legal protections won in that era such as jurors who could deliver verdicts against the evidence in oppressive prosecutions, a judiciary that could not be dismissed by the executive, and legal remedies such as the writ of habeas corpus. Such achievements then helped to provide some protection to English democratic and radical movements over the following centuries. Although EP Thompson said in *Whigs and Hunters* that the actual operation of English law often fell short of its own rhetoric of equality the 'idea' of the rule of law present in English law was 'an unqualified good'. Thompson said:

> 'there is a difference between arbitrary power and the rule of law ... the imposing of effective inhibitions upon power and the defence of the citizen from power's all-intrusive claims.'

The more subtle and persuasive accounts of 'law as ideology' are not going to be content with the facile and simplistic comment that 'law is a mask for power' but instead argue that the law of, for example the United Kingdom, does contain important elements of fairness such as the 'rule of law' ideal as EP Thompson admits. The English common law did have real elements of justice, a classic example being the traditional power of the jury in the common law of England to acquit a defendant against the weight of the evidence and the wishes of the government and judges. Lord Devlin in an article in the 1991 Law Quarterly Review entitled 'The Conscience of the Jury' points out: 'the jury is the creation of the judges at common law. They endowed it for better or worse with all its powers. Power resides in the last word'. Judges at common law gave juries the 'power of the last word' enabling juries to acquit a defendant against the weight of the evidence and defy the government. As Devlin makes clear it was the common law judges who gave the jury such power:

> 'Lord Mansfield[2] said (in the *Dean of St. Asaph* case 1784) that the jury had it in their power to do wrong. But in truth they have no power except what the judges give them. Jailors listen to judges, not to juries; a verdict has no legal effect until it is embodied in a judge's order.'

In 1724 Chief Justice Pratt in *R v Jones* 'it was never yet known that a verdict was set aside by which the defendant was acquitted'. In the 1784 *Dean of St. Asaph* case, Lord Mansfield said that 'a judge could tell the jury how to do right, but that they had it in their power to do wrong, which is entirely between God and their own consciences'. In these words Lord Mansfield recognised the sovereignty of the jury in English criminal trials – the jury had the 'last word' whether the defendant was convicted of the charges they faced. Devlin describes the *Dean of St. Asaph's* case 1784 as 'the most important case in English law not to be discussed in the textbooks'. Lord Mansfield, described by Lord Devlin 'as the greatest of English judges' said in the *Dean of St. Asaph's* case that the jury had the power to do wrong by delivering a 'perverse' acquittal against the evidence and that that matter was entirely between God and their own consciences. However this' power to do wrong' was given to the juries by judges at common law, part of the liberty-favouring aspect of the common law of England which EP Thompson acknowledges as a legal reality from his Marxist perspective. The power of the jury granted by judges to bring in a verdict of not guilty (which cannot be challenged by the government) against the weight of the evidence means that political prosecutions, that is prosecutions motivated by a political agenda can always be countermanded by the jury bringing in a not guilty verdict against a defendant: this is a solid achievement for the rule of law created by the judges themselves, which any reasonable Marxist ideologue has to acknowledge as a genuine aspect of English common law.

However for Marxists, such as EP Thompson, the law despite its elements of fairness and equality, is ultimately an ideological weapon of the ruling classes for the law successfully, indeed very successfully, distorts and obscures the reality in society of much wider socio-economic cruelties and injustices beyond the law.

NOTES

The best account of 'Law and Ideology' is in Christine Sypnowich's article 'Law and Ideology' in the free online Stanford Encyclopedia of Philosophy: http://plato.stanford.edu/entries/law-ideology/

....

2 Lord Mansfield sat on the bench as Chief Justice for 30 years and single-handedly fashioned a 'commercial law' for a growing British Empire. Paul Halliday in *Habeas Corpus: From England to Empire* (2010) comments that Lord Mansfield retired in late 1786 after taking up judicial post in 1756. Lord Mansfield was replaced by Lord Kenyon who had a 'more circumscribed sense of judicial self' than Lord Mansfield possessed. Lord Mansfield was a great judge but that is always how he saw himself.

EP Thompson's account of the rule of law in English common law is in his 1975 book *Whigs and Hunters*. Douglas Hay's classic article 'Property, Authority and Criminal Law' is to be found in the second edition of *Albion's Fatal Tree* (2011) which shows how the criminal law was utilised ideologically by the English eighteenth-century ruling elites. Lord Devlin explores how the judges gave the jury the 'final word' over convictions in English courts in 'The Conscience of the Jury' (1991) Law Quarterly Review.

QUESTION 19

Contrast the anarchist and Marxist attitudes to the state and its laws.

How to Answer this Question

Both anarchism and Marxism grew out of the Enlightenment and both sought a radical refashioning of society through the abolition of the capitalist state and its laws. The 'stateless' socialist society was therefore the ultimate goal of both the anarchist Bakunin and Marx himself. However there was radical disagreement between anarchists and Marxists on how to achieve the stateless socialist society, a disagreement so bitter that Marx had Bakunin expelled from the International Working Men's Association in 1872. The anarchist believed that the workers revolution which both they and the Marxists believed essential should be immediately followed by the abolition of the state and the building of the stateless socialist society. The Marxists believed that an intermediate stage of indeterminate duration called 'the dictatorship of the proleteriat' was necessary to secure the social conditions for the 'withering away of law'. The Marxists believed that the workers revolution which destroyed the capitalist state would still be under threat from counter-revolutionary forces and therefore the 'vanguard of the communist party' the intellectual elite would with the support of the workers seize control of the state machinery in order to crush the enemies of the revolution. The anarchist aristocrat philosophers Bakunin and Kropotkin thought strongly that the 'dictatorship of the proleteriat' would not be temporary but would solidify into a new omnivorous state authority and therefore the stateless society would be aborted. History proved the anarchists correct for the Soviet Union continued for 70 years after the revolution until its dissolution in 1991. The anarchists and Marxists also disagreed on the tactics to achieve the much anticipated workers revolution. Although Bakunin was against individual acts of terrorism other anarchists believed that through individual acts of anarchist terrorism the workers would be inspired to revolution hence the idea of 'the propaganda by the deed', that ideas were inspired by deeds, that the idea of revolution would be planted in the heads of the workers by successful anarchist terrorist acts. Europe and the United States suffered a wave of anarchist inspired terrorist violence from about 1880 to 1920 helped by the discovery of dynamite in 1866. Marxists such as Leon Trotsky were vehemently opposed to terrorist violence as a means of inspiring the much hoped for workers' revolution. Trotsky was not moved by any concern for the 'sanctity of life' in his opposition to terrorist violence rather his opposition to terrorism was based on practical concerns: (1) terrorism was not effective as one assassinated police chief or government minister would be replaced the next day by his deputy; (2) the workers were demotivated to organise themselves by terrorist violence because terrorist violence gave the illusion that freedom from capitalist exploitation would come from a small band of anarchists armed with revolvers and dynamite rather than through workers strikes and workers revolution; (3) terrorist anarchist violence only produced more police repression of the socialist workers movement.

Applying the Law

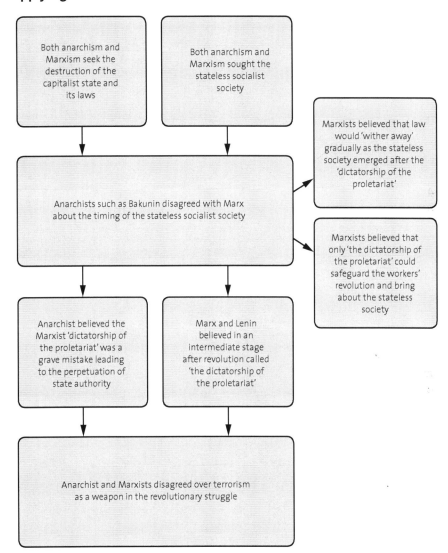

Both anarchism and Marxism seek the destruction of the capitalist state and its laws

Both anarchism and Marxism sought the stateless socialist society

Marxists believed that law would 'wither away' gradually as the stateless society emerged after the 'dictatorship of the proletariat'

Anarchists such as Bakunin disagreed with Marx about the timing of the stateless socialist society

Marxists believed that only 'the dictatorship of the proletariat' could safeguard the workers' revolution and bring about the stateless society

Anarchist believed the Marxist 'dictatorship of the proletariat' was a grave mistake leading to the perpetuation of state authority

Marx and Lenin believed in an intermediate stage after revolution called 'the dictatorship of the proletariat'

Anarchist and Marxists disagreed over terrorism as a weapon in the revolutionary struggle

ANSWER

In theory the anarchists and the Marxists agreed that the ultimate goal of the revolution was the stateless socialist society even if anarchists and marxists disagreed over tactics such as the use of terrorist violence and the so-called temporary and transient 'dictatorship of the proletariat'.

Anarchist activity in the late nineteenth century went much further than anarchist periodicals such as *Commonweal* and *The Torch* and the polemical books, pamphlets and articles of Bakunin and Kropotkin. There was a wave of anarchist inspired terrorist violence, the infamous 'propaganda of the deed'. The arrival of anarchist terrorism in Europe and the United States after 1880 was due to a despairing belief that the mass insurrection of the workers needed to overthrow the capitalist system required by anarchists and marxists alike required a spark or beacon to action in the form of individual acts of terrorism. An early Italian internationalist, Piscane argued that the 'propaganda of the idea' was empty because 'ideas result from deeds, not the latter from the former'. The theory was that impressed by the murderous deeds of anarchist terrorists the masses would take anarchist ideas seriously.

There was nothing explicit in philosophical anarchist thought which mandated such terrorist violence and indeed Bakunin who died in 1876 had always advocated mass insurrection of the workers not terrorist bombings and shootings. However at the 1881 international anarchist conference in London, Kropotkin and others agreed that terrorist acts could be justified in the hope of sparking the workers revolution that all anarchists and marxists hoped for. As a consequence of bombings of bourgeois symbols of culture (helped by the discovery of dynamite in 1866) and assassinations of elite figures across Europe, anarchism was not an obscure political belief but the serious subject of discussion in the respectable press such as *Blackwood's Magazine*. Between 1881–1920 there was a wave of anarchist assassinations of public figures throughout Europe and the United States including President McKinley in the United States in 1901. The terminus of the anarchist terrorist wave is usually dated at 1920 with the anarchist bombing of the financial centre, Wall Street in New York which killed 38. Theatres, opera houses, cafes and stock exchanges were hit as symbols of the hated bourgeois civilisation. Anarchism today is seen as an interesting if marginal political philosophy but back in the 1890s (the peak decade for anarchist terrorism) 'it was much more difficult for anyone then to see the positive significance of anarchism than it is now' (Watt, 2000, 122). Joseph Conrad, who immortalised anarchists in London in his 1907 political thriller *The Secret Agent*, wrote to his friend, the novelist Galsworthy, that anarchism was a 'manifestation of human nature in its discontent and imbecility' (Bradbury, 1988, 96). Eventually most anarchists realised that political terrorism was not having the desired sparking effect on the masses but merely led to severe police repression and the influence of the October 1917 Revolution in Russia showed that it was the organised revolutionary power of the masses and not individual acts of terrorism that counted, terror only brought about police repression. This police repression even occurred in otherwise liberal Britain where the anarchist 'Autonomie' club near Tottenham Court Road in Soho, London was permanently closed down in 1894 by the Metropolitan police following the accidental self-killing of a 26-year-old French anarchist Martial Bourdin whilst carrying a bomb in Greenwich Park in south east London.

Britain, due to its self-proclaimed Victorian liberal status as the 'asylum of nations', had been something of a haven for foreign revolutionaries such as Lenin, Kropotkin, Bakunin and even Stalin (Bradbury, 1988, 82), but after the Bourdin explosion even the British police lost patience with the anarchists and the legislative tide began to turn against former hospitality to foreign revolutionaries. The **Aliens Act of 1905**, the first modern act to regulate alien immigration into Britain was passed not due to domestic fear of foreign anarchists (always relatively small in number) but mainly as a response to the great influx into London, in particular, of Jewish refugees from Russia and Eastern Europe fleeing persecution from the late 1880s onwards and a concern with the impact such an influx was having on the wages and jobs of native workers especially in the East End of London (Pellew, 1989, 370). However the 1911 Aliens (Prevention of Crime) Bill was a response to foreign anarchist activities in London. Pellew comments:

> 'the first of these events was the much-publicized murder of a policeman in Tottenham by two alleged anarchists. The second of these, which occurred in December 1910, was the famous Sidney Street affair in which, after an attempted robbery by a gang of foreign burglars, the alleged criminals were run to ground in Sidney Street, Mile End Road ... the uproar and anti-anarchist feeling aroused by the combination of foreign burglars and firearms convinced even Churchill (who as Home Secretary had been unable to resist rushing to the scene of action) of the necessity for legislation to strengthen the hands of the authorities against foreign criminals.'

The 1911 Aliens Bill, amongst other provisions, required all aliens to be licensed to carry firearms, and it also obliged British judges to explain why they had not recommended expulsion from the country in cases of criminal conviction of aliens (Pellew, 1989, 382). However the Bill never became an Act of Parliament because of the pressure of domestic and international crises on the government. Eventually, on 5 August 1914, the outbreak of the First World War revived the urgent need for new alien legislation and the Aliens Restriction Bill (which replaced the **Aliens Act 1905**) was as Pellew comments: 'debated, passed and signed by the monarch all on the same day' (Pellew, 1989, 382).

The eventual disillusionment of anarchists with individual acts of political violence had been foreshadowed by a severe denunciation of the use of political terrorism to achieve revolutionary ends by Leon Trotsky. Trotsky in an article of 1911, before the anarchist wave of terrorism had ceased, argued that such acts of individual terrorism were counter-productive to the revolutionary cause. Trotsky wrote:

> 'Whether a terrorist attempt, even a 'successful' one, throws the ruling class into confusion depends on the concrete political circumstances. In any case the confusion can only be short-lived; the capitalist state does not base itself on government ministers and cannot be eliminated with them. The classes it serves will always find new people; the mechanism remains intact and continues to function. But the disarray introduced into the ranks of the working masses themselves by a terrorist attempt is much deeper. If it is enough to arm oneself with a pistol in order to achieve one's goal, why the efforts of the class struggle? In our eyes, individual terror is inadmissible precisely because it belittles the role of the masses in their own consciousness, reconciles them to their powerlessness, and turns their eyes and hopes toward a great avenger and liberator who some day will come and accomplish his mission. The more 'effective' the terrorist acts, the greater their impact, the more they reduce the interest of the masses in self-organisation and self-education.' (Trotsky, 1911)

It was not only over the tactic of terrorist violence to achieve the revolutionary uprising that anarchists and Marxists disagreed. Bakunin, the leading anarchist before his death in 1876 and Marx disagreed about where the revolution would first occur with Marx prophesising that the most industrial countries would be the scene of the first workers' revolutions. Berlin remarks:

> 'The unsystematic and wayward Bakunin predicted more accurately than his great rival Marx the circumstances in which the revolutions by the dispossessed would occur. He saw that they were liable to develop not in the most industrialised societies on an ascending curve of economic progress, but on the contrary, where the majority of the population was near subsistence level, and had the least to lose by an upheaval, that is, in the most backward regions of the world, inhabited by primitive peasants in conditions of desperate poverty, where capitalism was weakest-Spain, Russia.' (Berlin, 1990, 241)

However the greatest disagreement between the anarchists and the Marxists was over the issue of the timing of the disappearance of the state following the successful revolution. In Marx's 'Critique of the Gotha Programme' he argued that whatever form the state took it would be an instrument of coercion. Therefore communism which rejected coercion also rejected the state and its laws. However, although the stateless socialist society was the shared ultimate goal of anarchists and Marxists the crucial difference and a difference that led to the split between Bakunin and Marx in 1872 by the expulsion of Bakunin from the International Working Men's Association, was over the timing of the disappearance of the state and its coercive laws. The anarchists were adamant the once the revolution successfully overthrew the capitalist order then the state should be immediately abolished. The marxists agreed with the anarchists that the goal was the abolition of the state but in contrast the marxists justified a transitional period of indeterminate length following the revolution when the 'dictatorship of the proletariat' would use the state to defend the revolution and crush the class enemies of the workers and then the state and the need for laws would 'wither away'. Sypnowich comments: 'With Engels as his authority, Lenin argues that the state is a product of the irreconcilability of class antagonisms and will wither away with the abolition of classes' (Sypnowich, 1987, 320). Lenin argued that the state would have only a revolutionary transient role in defending and consolidating the revolution. Bakunin, although he died in 1876 predicted (correctly as it turned out) that the Marxist 'dictatorship of the proletariat' following a successful workers' revolution would only lead to new state tyranny and not the stateless utopia (Shatz, 1990, 178, 179). Capitalist exploitation, Bakunin argued, would be replaced by a new 'red terror' controlling the masses if the institution of the state was allowed to survive the revolution. Kropotkin's death in Russia in 1920[3] led to an outpouring of anarchist grief at

---

3 Kropotkin was a noted explorer when young and explored remote parts of Siberia where his contact with nomadic people far from the influence of the Russian state may have sparked his interest in anarchism: society without the state. For the traditional nomad is the perfect 'anarchist' – totally independent of the state wandering between national boundaries as the seasons of nature demand.

his funeral as thousands attended[4] which then sparked a Bolshevik crackdown on anarchist groups in Russia. Ironically Kropotkin, like his countryman and fellow aristocrat Bakunin, had written in 1920 shortly before his death of the dangers of the 'socialist state': 'the attempt at introducing the new society by means of the dictatorship of one party is doomed to be a failure' and that the new Soviet regime represented the survival 'of an unlimited, omnivorous authority' (Shatz, 1995, 257).

In Sypnowich's phrase 'the rehabilitation of the superstructure' (Sypnowich, 1987, 322) namely the state and its coercive apparatus developed dramatically under Stalin. As Sypnowich comments:

> 'The systematic use of political and legal resources no longer figured as a short-term measure of revolutionary society, but as an established feature of the socialist phase in the development of Soviet communism.' (Sypnowich, 1987, 323)

The 'withering away' of the socialist state was under Stalin predicated upon world revolution so that only under those conditions could the socialist state relax its guard and allow itself to wither away. The Stalinist era writer Vyshinsky commented:

> 'when communism triumphs throughout the world, we shall consign (law and state) to the museum of antiquities, together with the ax of the stone age and the distaff.' (Sypnowic, 1987, 323)

Stalin himself declared at the 18th party congress in March 1939 that 'the withering away of our socialist state' (Letwin, 2005, 240) could not take place in the Soviet Union because such an outcome could only happen when communism had triumphed in all countries of the world. Therefore from Stalin onwards the old ideology of a temporary 'dictatorship of the proletariat' to secure the gains of the revolution hardened into a new justification of the state based on realpolitik. The Soviet state could not safely dissolve itself until all the world had embraced communism and thus the old anarchist fears of 'the dictatorship of the proletariat' leading ultimately to a new form of permanent state coercion was fully borne out by history. Indeed under the Brezhnev era the Soviet state was decreed an 'all people's state', a supposed permanent reality until its dissolution in 1991. The 1977 Constitution decreed:

> 'Having fulfilled the tasks of the dictatorship of the proletariat, the Soviet state has become an all-people's state … a socialist all-people's state which expresses the will and interests of the workers, peasants and intelligentsia, the working people of all the nations and nationalities of the country.' (Sypnowic, 1987, 324)

---

4   Anarchism as a political doctrine was always at its most popular in Russia and Spain: the most underdeveloped and 'peasant' societies of Europe in the early twentieth century. Anarchism may have made more sense in peasant societies remote from central government and used to running their own affairs rather than in highly organised industrialised societies such as England.

NOTES

For anarchist thought see the following three works: Bakunin, *Statism and Anarchy* (1990), edited by Marshall Shatz. Kropotkin, *The Conquest of Bread and Other Writings* (1995), edited by Marshall Shatz. Marshall Shatz has an article entiled 'Anarchism' in *The Oxford Handbook of the History of Political Philosophy* (2011), edited by George Klosko.

Leon Trotsky's denunciation and condemnation of terrorism in the revolutionary struggle is entitled 'Why Marxists Oppose Individual Terrorism', originally published in 1911 and now to be found on-line at: www.**marxists.org/archive/trotsky/1911/11/tia09.htm**

For Marxist thought on the state and its laws see Christine Sypnowich's article 'The "Withering Away" of Law', Studies in Soviet Thought 33 (1987), 305–332. Shirley Letwin also examines Marxist attitudes to law in her book *On the History of the Idea of Law* (2005).

Joseph Conrad's attitude to anarchism in the late nineteenth century can be found in Ian Watt's *Essays on Conrad* (2000). Malcolm Bradbury's book *The Modern World: Ten Great Writers* (1988) Secker and Warburg has useful information on Conrad's attitude to anarchism.

Isaiah Berlin in his collection of essays *The Crooked Timber of Humanity: Chapters in the History of Ideas* (1990) examines the political thought of the anarchist Bakunin and Marx himself.

On Edwardian legislation to restrict immigration see: Jill Pellew, 'The Home Office and the Aliens Act 1905', *The Historical Journal*, vol 32, no 2, June 1989, pp. 369–385.

6

Authority

INTRODUCTION

The related, but distinct, questions concerning the justification of state authority and the moral obligation to obey the law are crucial and enduring questions of political philosophy and legal theory. The question as to how the authority of the state is to be justified has drawn the attention of philosophers of the stature of Hobbes (1588–1679) and Locke (1632–1704), and the question continues to be debated between 'philosophical anarchists' and defenders of the possibility of legitimate state authority such as Professor Raz. The question of the moral obligation to obey the law first taxed Socrates (470–399 BC) (as reported in Plato's *Crito*), as he debated whether to flee the judgment of death that the state had passed on him. The question of the moral obligation to obey the law has occupied virtually every leading legal philosopher from Finnis and Raz to Dworkin and Greenawalt. The questions in the chapter consider how state authority is to be justified, if at all, and whether there is any general moral obligation to obey the law.

Checklist

Ensure that you are acquainted with the following topics:

- the 'social contract' theories of state authority propounded by Hobbes and Locke;
- the challenge to state authority presented by 'philosophical anarchism';
- the 'normal justification thesis' for legitimate state authority given by Professor Raz;
- the attempt to ground a moral obligation to obey the law variously on 'consent', 'gratitude', 'fair play' and 'associative obligations';
- the special moral obligation to obey the law of public office holders;
- the denial of a general moral obligation to obey the law by Raz;
- the argument of the conservative authoritarian tradition in political philosophy from St Augustine to Thomas Hobbes that the state and its laws are an indispensable necessity;
- the role of the *Leviathan* in Thomas Hobbes's political philosophy;
- how Professor Nozick justifies the 'minimal state' from the anarchist challenge;
- how the 'character' of leading politicians Is a 'philosophical' issue.

QUESTION 20

Critically examine how the authority of the state is to be justified.

How to Answer this Question

Professor Raz (in the essay 'Legitimate authority', collected in *The Authority of Law* (1979)) commented that there is little surprise that the notion of authority is one of the most controversial concepts in legal and political philosophy, since the concept of authority has a central role in any discussion of legitimate forms of social organisation. The attempt to justify political authority starts with the end of Bible-based arguments for political authority in the mid-seventeenth century. Both Hobbes (1588–1679) and Locke (1632–1704) attempted to justify political authority through the emergence of authority from an anarchic 'state of nature'. In modern times, the whole notion of political authority has come under severest attack from the school of thought known as 'philosophical anarchism'. The 'normal justification thesis' for justifying political authority given by Professor Raz can be viewed as the most persuasive rebuttal of the challenge posed by philosophical anarchism to the possibility of legitimate political authority. A skeleton argument is given.

Applying the Law

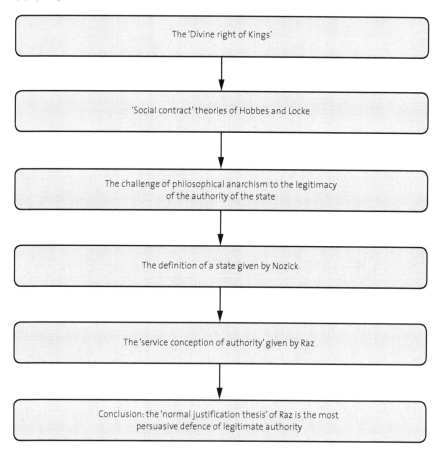

The 'Divine right of Kings'

'Social contract' theories of Hobbes and Locke

The challenge of philosophical anarchism to the legitimacy of the authority of the state

The definition of a state given by Nozick

The 'service conception of authority' given by Raz

Conclusion: the 'normal justification thesis' of Raz is the most persuasive defence of legitimate authority

ANSWER

In *The Authority of the State* (1988) Leslie Green comments that all modern states claim authority over their citizens and that the state's authority claims to be supreme. Indeed, as a form of social order, the state is distinctive in claiming supreme and wide authority over the lives of citizens. Widespread belief in the legitimacy of state authority can itself strengthen the stability of the state in question. For these interrelated reasons it is a crucial question in jurisprudence and in political philosophy to determine when a belief in the authority of a state is justified, and if such justification is possible at all.

The connection of this question with the subject of jurisprudence is not difficult to understand. The authority of the modern state is typically expressed through the laws and legal directives of those in authority. The study of the authority of the state is crucially linked to how that authority is usually expressed, namely, through law. As Raz comments in *The Morality of Freedom* (1986), the normal exercise of political authority is by the making of laws and legally binding orders. As Raz notes in his essay, 'The Claims of Law' (in *The Authority of Law* (1979)): 'The notion of authority is inextricably tied up with that of law … for it is an essential feature of law that it claims legitimate authority'. Therefore, the concept of authority plays a crucial part in our understanding of the concept of law.

The attempt to justify political authority is an ancient one and can be traced back to Plato's (428–347 BC) philosophical work, *Crito*, when Socrates debates whether to flee Athens or face execution. However, the usual starting point for discussion of the legitimacy of the authority of the state is the once-powerful doctrine that political authority had been ordained by God and was, for that reason, legitimate. Christian doctrine held that rulers existed as a result of Divine will, the key text being St Paul's Epistle to the Romans (Chapter 13, verses 1–2): 'For there is no authority except from God, and those that exist have been instituted by God. Therefore he who resists the authorities resists what God has appointed.' This Christian doctrine justified the 'Divine right' of Kings in an era when the Bible was paramount.[1] Therefore, James I (1566–1625) of England and Scotland, in his 1598–1599 work *Basilikon Doron*, wrote for his son that 'God made you a little God to sitte on his throne, and rule over other men'. This doctrine of the 'Divine right' of Kings also justified another observation of James I that he could not be subject to the law since it was his law. However, the English Civil War (1642–1651), culminating in the execution of Charles I in 1649, effectively ended the power of the 'Divine right of Kings' as a justification of political authority. Indeed, the Bible itself was used to justify the execution of Charles I since he was 'a man of blood', a Biblical concept; this was used to undermine his Divinity and justify his execution.

Thomas Hobbes, who had lived through the English civil war and revolution, wrote his secular justification for political authority, called *Leviathan*, in 1651. As the leading historian of the seventeenth century, Christopher Hill, commented in *The World Turned*

---

1   Shakespeare referred to the ideology of the 'Divine right of Kings' when in his 1597 play *Richard II* the character John of Gaunt says (Act 1 Scene 2) of the King: 'God's substitute, His deputy anointed in His sight … for I may never lift an angry arm against His (God's) minister.'

Upside Down (1972), anyone in 1651 who was convinced by the arguments in Hobbes's *Leviathan* would no longer find it possible to look to the Bible alone for answers to political problems. The work of Hobbes in *Leviathan* can be seen as a decisive break with the past as it sought to justify political authority in secular terms. Hobbes, having lived through the political disintegration of the English civil war period, asked the reader in *Leviathan* to imagine society in a 'state of nature', a condition of society without government; as Hobbes comments, the state of nature is 'the time men live without a common Power to keep them all in awe'. In this 'state of nature' there is a continual fear and danger of violent death as man fights against man and human life is 'solitary, poor, nasty, brutish and short'. As Hobbes comments: 'All men in the state of nature have a desire and will to hurt, they are in that condition which is called War.'

Hobbes characterises the natural condition of humankind as a mutually unprofitable state of war of every person against every other person and, since Hobbesian persons value self-preservation above all else, there will emerge the beginnings of political power as each person submits to some mutually recognised public authority who will protect person and property. However, this central authority must have absolute power, according to Hobbes, in order to prevent society from falling back into the anarchic 'state of nature'. So the way out of the desperate 'state of nature' is for men to make a 'social contract' and establish a very strong state to keep peace and order. Hobbes can be criticised for exaggerating the horrors of the 'state of nature', for having an 'obsession' with the risks of violent death in the 'state of nature' and for proposing absolute authority as the only alternative to the horrors of the 'state of nature'. Indeed, Hobbes can be criticised for replacing the horrors of the 'state of nature' with the horrors of absolute authority in the hands of one ruler. However, despite these criticisms, the writings of Hobbes mark a decisive shift away from justifying political authority on the basis of the Bible to some sort of secular 'social contract'. Hobbes, often in his own era described as an atheist, did, however, share the prevailing 'Calvinistic' religious view that the depravity of man in his 'natural state' necessitated an authoritarian state. (The Calvinistic view was that 'original sin' had depraved and distorted human nature and that only the few 'elect' of God would be saved – from the teachings of John Calvin (1509–1564).) The evil majority must be controlled, kept in subordination, or anarchy would result, said both the secular Hobbes and religious men like Oliver Cromwell (1599–1658).

John Locke (1632–1704) followed Hobbes in postulating a 'state of nature' followed by a 'social contract' to establish political authority but, unlike Hobbes, Locke accepted legal limits on government and accepted that those in authority could be removed if their actions threatened the property of men. Locke argued, in contrast with Hobbes, that the executive may forfeit its rights if it endangers the stability of property. Hobbes thought that any revolution against the authority of the sovereign must dissolve society into anarchy. Locke held that society could continue to exist even if the men of property found it necessary to change the sovereign, as they did in 1688.[2] In the *Second Treatise of*

---

2 For extended discussion of the ways in which John Locke is 'the father of liberalism' see Question 27, Chapter 6 of this book.

Civil Government (1690), Locke comments that legitimate civil government is instituted by the explicit consent of those governed. What counts as legitimate consent is a matter of dispute amongst political philosophers but the important point is that, despite Locke's own religious Christian faith, his theory of political authority is a further development of the 'social contract' theory of authority away from explicit reliance on the Bible as the source of political authority. As Christopher Hill comments, in *The English Bible and the Seventeenth Century Revolution* (1993), the political revolution starting with the execution of Charles I shattered the universal acceptance of the Bible as an infallible text the pronouncements of which were to be followed implicitly. As Karl Marx commented, 'when the bourgeois transformation had been accomplished, Locke supplanted Habbukuk (of the Old Testament)' (from *Selected Works of Marx and Engels* (1935)).

The question of the justification of political authority has continued to be fiercely debated in the modern era. Indeed, the great attempt to justify a 'minimal State' by Robert Nozick in *Anarchy, State and Utopia* (1974) uses the old device used by Hobbes and Locke of the 'state of nature' to show how a legitimate state might evolve without infringing individual rights. Although Nozick's explanation of the kind of state that emerges from 'the state of nature' differs radically from the view of the state propounded by both Hobbes and Locke, the basic methodology is the same – namely, to see what defects in the 'state of nature' the emergence of a state might cure. As Nozick observes, 'state of nature' explanations of the emergence of states have punch and illumination in political philosophy. Nozick also gives us a useful definition of what a state is when he comments, in *Anarchy, State and Utopia*, that a state claims a monopoly on deciding who may use force when it says that only the state may decide who may use force and under what conditions: the state reserves to itself the sole right to pass on the legitimacy and permissibility of any use of force within its boundaries; furthermore the state claims the right to punish all those who violate its claimed monopoly of force. It should be noted that the law's claim to a monopoly on the use of force, which has been recognised as the defining mark of a state by political philosophers from Max Weber (1864–1920) to Robert Nozick (1938–2002), is part of the definition of a state but does not justify the authority of the state. Force secures authority and enables it to be effective but force does not justify authority. The mere fact of possession of effective force in a territory may have justified authority for Thomas Hobbes in *Leviathan* (1651) but few philosophers have followed Hobbes in so holding. The horrors of the English civil war so conditioned Hobbes that he equated the fact of authority with the justification of authority. However there is something of a proper justification for state authority in the 'Leviathan' of Hobbes beyond the mere assertion that effective authority exists so therefore it is legitimate. For Hobbes authority, 'The Leviathan', was only legitimate if the state authority honoured the 'pact of protection' guaranteed to all citizens by the all mighty state in return or exchange for citizens giving complete obedience to the state. Hobbes accepted the old Latin proverb '*homo homini lupus*' – 'man is a wolf to man' (a summation of man's inhumanity to man) and the state by offering protection of all against all justified its awesome possession of absolute power. The question is: does the mere fact that the state guarantees security of citizen's property and persons in itself justify the depositing of complete power in the hands of the Hobbesian-Leviathan State?³

The greatest challenge to the attempt to justify political authority has come from the tradition of political thought known as 'philosophical anarchism'. As Robert Nozick observes, the fundamental question of political philosophy, one that precedes questions about how the state should be organised, is whether there should be any state at all and that, if valid, anarchist theory undercuts the whole subject of political philosophy. The *locus classicus* of the philosophical anarchist tradition is to be found in the work of Robert Paul Woolf in his *In Defense of Anarchism* (1970). Following Kant (1724–1804), Woolf argues that persons are endowed with reason and free will and, as such, persons have a duty to themselves to be autonomous. It is therefore the primary moral duty of each person to form his own judgment on matters concerning himself. However, as Woolf observes, to recognise the authority of another is to surrender one's own judgment to his and, as a result, if the person submits to the state and accepts its claim to authority then he loses his autonomy. The rational and autonomous person does not ignore the state's commands, says the philosophical anarchist; he will treat them as requests or advice, but not as binding orders. As Robert Woolf comments, for the truly autonomous man there is no such thing, strictly speaking, as a command and as long as we recognise our responsibility for our actions, and acknowledge the power of reason within us, we must acknowledge the continuing obligation to be the authors of the commands we choose to obey. For Woolf, the philosophical anarchist, the defining mark of the state is authority, the right to rule. The primary obligation of man is autonomy, the refusal to be ruled. There is, for Woolf, no resolution of the conflict between the autonomy of the individual and the authority of the state and that, in so far as a person fulfils his obligation to make himself the author of his decisions, he will resist the state's claim to have authority over him. Woolf concludes that the concept of a legitimate state is empty and that philosophical anarchism is the only reasonable practical position for an enlightened man.

This challenge of philosophical anarchism to the legitimacy of the state is a serious challenge for it denies the possibility of any justification of state authority, whether that justification is 'social contract' or otherwise. Recognition of authority does involve in some way a 'surrender of judgment' by the citizen and the whole concept of authority is a social relation of domination and subordination between a superior and a subject. Perhaps the philosophical anarchists, such as Robert Paul Woolf, have a point that there is something inherently troubling about the notion of authority. The question is, does this troubling intuition make all political authority illegitimate? Professor Raz, in *Ethics in the Public Domain* (1994), makes the following claim about legitimate governments: that they claim the right to rule us by right reason, that is to take over from us the task of deciding what we should do on certain matters. Does it follow that the philosophical anarchist is right and that there cannot be legitimate government over autonomous people? Raz, in defending the notion of legitimate authority, denies against Woolf that autonomy means never handing over to anyone the right to decide for a person on any matter. Raz

---

3   For extended discussion of Hobbes' political philosophy see Question 27, Chapter 7 of this book.

comments that a person does not abandon his autonomy when he authorises an agent to represent him in a sale or in some complex commercial negotiations. A person, says Raz, does not abandon his autonomy when joining a trade union which has power to reach binding agreements concerning one's wages and conditions of employment. A person, argues Raz, does not surrender his autonomy by appointing an attorney to conduct a lawsuit on his behalf. Raz, drawing an analogy with the legitimate state, says that these are just a few of the innumerable occasions on which people find it reasonable to give up their right to decide for themselves on certain matters. Raz concludes that the philosophical anarchist attack on the notion of authority is a misconception. As Raz comments, one way of wisely exercising one's autonomy is to realise that, in certain matters, one would do best to abide by the authority of another.

As long as government leaves significant areas of personal choice to the decision of the individual citizen, then over matters such as taxation and health and safety policy the state can exercise legitimate authority based on its superior expertise and ability to co-ordinate human action. Indeed, the argument for legitimate authority is bolstered by the observation that a functioning liberal state is needed for the realisation of personal autonomy, as Raz notes in *The Morality of Freedom* (1986). The law protects and promotes personal autonomy by protecting and promoting certain fundamental rights, such as the right to marry, the right to travel and the right make contracts, as well as protecting personal autonomy through laws against violence and false imprisonment.

It is true that it is possible to have an over-reliance on authority and when this happens a person does, to some extent, forfeit his own humanity. This 'dehumanising' effect of authority concerned the 'father' of philosophical anarchism, William Godwin (1756–1836), who argued 'where I make the voluntary surrender of my judgment … I annihilate my individuality as a man' (*An Enquiry Concerning Political Justice* (1793)). However, as Scott Shapiro comments, while the dangers of reliance on authority are real it is important not to exaggerate them. The world is simply too complex for anyone to live a life in Western society completely unaided by experts who typically advise governmental authority (see 'Authority' in *The Oxford Handbook of Jurisprudence and Philosophy of Law*, edited by Coleman and Shapiro (2002)).

The most persuasive justifications of modern political authority point to the ability of authorities to co-ordinate human activity for the common good and on the superior expertise of those authorities in such areas as economic policy, health and safety policy, defence policy, foreign relations with other states, etc. There are many problems of great importance to the orderly conduct of any society of complexity. There will be a range of possible solutions to those problems. There is a need for authority to designate the chosen options – there is a need for decision. Professor Finnis has argued, in *Natural Law and Natural Rights* (1980), that the ultimate basis of a ruler's authority is that he has the responsibility of furthering the common good by stipulating solutions to the community's co-ordination problems. Raz, the legal positivist, agrees with Finnis, the natural lawyer, that the ability of government to co-ordinate action for the common good is a core justification for modern political authority (see Raz, *Practical Reason and Norms* (1975)).

Raz has developed perhaps the most persuasive justification for modern political authority, namely, the 'service conception'. The 'service conception' of authority reminds us that the function of authorities is to serve the governed. Raz argues that authority can be legitimate if by complying with the authority the subjects are better able to follow the moral reasons that otherwise apply to them. Raz calls the 'service conception' of authority the 'normal justification thesis' for authority in that it is not the only way to justify political authority but is the 'normal justification' of authority.

Raz gives two main ways in which a political authority can meet 'the service conception', the 'normal justification thesis'. In a collection of essays entitled *Authority*, edited by Raz (1990), Raz mentions two primary arguments in support of political authority: (1) the expertise of government and its policy-making advisers in such matters as consumer protection legislation; and (2) the ability of government to secure social co-ordination.

Both of these are aspects of the 'service conception' of authority in that the authority, by relying on its expertise in certain areas and its ability to co-ordinate human activity, can enable citizens to better conform to the requirements of morality, such as the duty to help those in need, than if the citizens were to decide for themselves.

Raz comments that the expertise of government is most clearly seen in consumer protection legislation, the regulation of the pharmaceutical industry, laws to secure safety at work or on the roads. The ability of government to co-ordinate is most evident in the provision of public goods (clean air and water, for example). Both factors, superior expertise and an ability for co-ordination, are present, says Raz, in most cases of justified governmental action. This is fundamentally an instrumental approach to justifying authority. There is no appeal here to any 'social contract', real or imagined, that appealed to Hobbes and Locke in the seventeenth century; the basis of legitimate authority is in getting citizens to better conform to right reason. The 'service conception' of authority propounded by Raz has intuitive appeal because it justifies authority only to the extent that it serves the governed. A lot of the feelings of misgiving and unease, which philosophical anarchists trade on, about authority disappear when legitimate authority is understood from the viewpoint of Raz – that legitimate authority is there to help citizens do the right thing in reason. Raz's 'service conception' of authority helps to meet the challenge of philosophical anarchism to the legitimacy of any state. The philosophical anarchist uses the powerful intuition that submission to political authority constitutes a breach of a person's personal autonomy. After all, authority involves essentially the power by the authority to require action on the part of the subject. However, if submission to authority is not global but leaves significant choice in the hands of the citizen, and if submission to authority is only justified by the idea that authority exists to serve the governed, then the philosophical anarchist challenge to authority is largely met.

Professor Raz, in a 2005 lecture, 'The problem of authority: revisiting the service conception', returned to the topic of the justification of authority and its relation to autonomy. Raz gives the example of decisions about the safety of pharmaceutical products, which are not the sort of decisions which people should make for themselves rather than follow authority which has superior expertise on the matter. However, Raz admits there are many decisions in life – such as who to marry, where to live, whether to do this job or that job – where it is better to decide for oneself unaided by authority. Raz concludes by saying that the primary point of authority is to improve conformity with reason. The normal understanding of authority is that it does involve a hierarchical relationship involving an imposition on the subject. The unease which these facts of authority can induce in us are somewhat dissipated by the Razian 'service conception' of authority which explains how authority can be legitimate if it serves the public good.

Aim Higher

Students can gain extra marks by pointing out that Hobbes is the true father of modern political philosophy with his *Leviathan* in 1651. Hobbes was rational and secularist in his approach, not using any argument from the Bible to justify his political conclusions but basing his arguments on rationally observed principles. Students can avoid the pitfall of thinking that 'anarchism' is merely a violent political movement without realising the existence of 'philosophical anarchism' which is non-violent but teaches that a rejection of the state is the only position for a reasonable enlightened person. To gain extra marks, students will note the truth of Weber's statement that authority strives for acceptance not submission.

NOTES

The political thought of both Hobbes and Locke is captured in essays in the online and free *Stanford Encyclopedia of Philosophy* (http://plato.stanford.edu/): 'John Locke' is covered by William Uzgalis; 'Locke's Political Philosophy' is examined by Alex Tuckness; 'Hobbes's Moral and Political Philosophy' is examined by Sharon A Lloyd and Susanne Sreedhar.

The general concept of 'Authority' in the *Stanford Encyclopedia* is examined by Tom Christiano.

The general philosophy of Hobbes can be further explored in a collection of essays: 'Perspectives on Thomas Hobbes' (1988, reprinted 2002) edited by Rogers and Ryan. The general topic of 'Authority' is examined by Leslie Green in his book, *The Authority of the State* (1988), as well as in the collection of essays edited by Professor Raz called *Authority: Readings in social and political authority* (1990); the introduction in that volume by Professor Raz is particularly valuable. An account and explanation of 'the normal justification thesis' for legitimate authority is given by Raz in the early chapters of *The Morality of Freedom* (1986).

QUESTION 21 -

Examine how the question of the moral obligation to obey the law has been treated by philosophers.

How to Answer this Question

The issue of the obligation to obey the law has attracted much philosophical thought from the time of Socrates (470–399 BC) (see *Crito* by Plato) to the present day. There have been many candidates put forward to justify such a general moral obligation based on the 'consent' of the governed, the 'gratitude' of the governed to the state, duties based on 'fair play' and the need to 'support just institutions', to give the major examples. However, all of the attempts to justify a general moral obligation have been found to be defective and the better view probably resides with Professor Raz who denies any general moral obligation to obey the law but argues that the moral obligation to obey the law varies from person to person. A skeleton answer is sketched.

Applying the Law

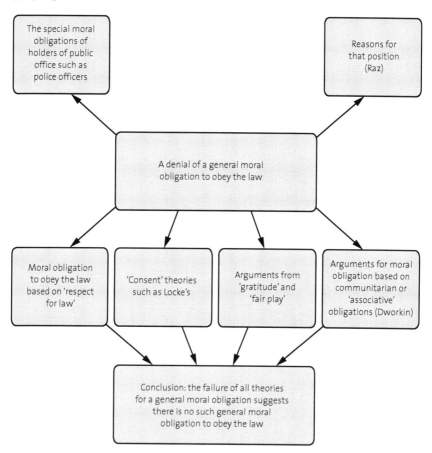

ANSWER

It may at first sight appear obvious that there is an obligation to obey the law in a liberal democratic state. As Klosko comments, the feeling that we have a moral obligation to obey the law is one of our deepest intuitions (quoted in 'Law and Obligations' by Leslie Green in *The Oxford Handbook of Jurisprudence and Philosophy of Law*, edited by Coleman and Shapiro (2002)).

However, the surprising consensus of opinion among legal philosophers today is that citizens do not have a general moral obligation to obey the law; such obligation as exists varies from person to person.

Professor Raz, the leading proponent of the view denying a general moral obligation to obey the law, comments that there are risks, moral and other, in uncritical acceptance of authority (*The Authority of Law* (1979)).[4] Raz argues that often persons do have a moral obligation to obey individual laws based on concern for others, trying to avoid setting a bad example and the need for social co-ordination, but Raz denies any unthinking general moral obedience to any legal system, no matter how virtuous. Whilst defending the idea of legitimate authority from the philosophical anarchists, Raz comments that the question of moral obedience to a legal system is a different question and he seems to take on board the insight of philosophical anarchism (see Robert Paul Woolf's *In Defense of Anarchism* (1970)) concerning a person's moral independence from the legal system under which he exists. Raz argues that the extent of the moral duty to obey the law in a relatively just state varies from person to person. There is, says Raz, a common core of cases regarding which the moral obligation exists and applies equally to all. Some duties based on the co-ordinative argument (for example, the moral duty to pay lawful taxation), and on the avoiding of setting a 'bad example' (for example, avoiding political terrorism) are likely to apply equally to all citizens. Beyond this core, says Raz the extent of the moral obligation to obey the law will vary greatly among persons. The Prime Minister's moral obligation to obey the law will be much stronger, due to his high office, than the average citizen. For example, as Kent Greenawalt comments, persons who have taken an oath to obey the law are under a much stronger moral obligation to obey the law than the average citizen. Persons such as police officers, judges, magistrates and government ministers of the state who voluntarily assume positions of official responsibility have promised to uphold the law and perform their duties in a lawful manner. As Greenawalt concludes, although most citizens make no promise – like undertaking to obey the law – some persons do engage to obey in a general way and such promises have moral force and constitute a substantial moral reason for obedience ('Promissory Obligation', in *Authority*, edited by Raz (1990)).

It is necessary to understand Raz's argument denying a general moral obligation to obey all the laws of even a relatively just state on the following concern based on historical

---

4   Raz comments on the dangers of 'an uncritical attitude towards the law'. This fear was perhaps best exemplified in Nazi Germany where a German legal culture of excessive respect for 'legality' led to a culture where the legal challenges to Nazi Germany were not as they should have been, easing the rise of Hitler's terror machine. This issue is discussed in fuller depth in Question 6, Chapter 2 of this book.

experience, in that too often in the past, the fallibility of human judgment has led to submission to authority from a misguided sense of duty where this was a morally reprehensible attitude (Raz, *The Authority of Law* (1979)).

Raz is a defender of the idea of legitimate authority against philosophical anarchists, but believes the question of moral obedience to law is a separate though related issue. Generally, persons should take the existence of a law from legitimate authority very seriously because those in authority usually have superior knowledge and expertise on matters requiring law than ourselves. However, the superior wisdom and expertise of those in legitimate authority cannot, according to Raz, justify a general moral obligation to obey the law. Raz goes on to identify one possible source of a general moral obligation to obey the law for some persons: this is the situation where an individual voluntarily accepts such an obligation as a way of identifying with his society. Raz comments that the government and the law are official organs of the community. If the government and law represent the community and express its will justly, then a natural indication of a member's sense of belonging is one's attitude toward the community's laws. Such an attitude Raz terms 'respect for law'. This is the belief that one is under a moral obligation to obey because the law is one's law, and the law of one's country. However, such a belief binds only those who choose to adopt such a 'respect for law', says Raz. There are many who do not feel this way about their country and the law of their country. Alienation from country and law is a sad and widespread fact of modern states. As Raz comments in *The Morality of Freedom* (1986), those who consent to respect the laws of a state have a moral obligation to obey the laws of that state. But not everyone does have this attitude. Obligations undertaken through consent or respect are voluntary obligations; they bind only those who undertake them. It cannot ground a general moral obligation to obey the law. Those who do not voluntarily place themselves under the authority of relatively just governments are under only a partial and qualified obligation to obey the law. In particular, they have a moral obligation to obey the law where that is necessary for social co-ordination. However, as Raz concludes, a general moral obligation to obey the law is the result of a special relationship between an individual and his state; however, by no means everyone has this attitude towards their own state.

The modern view of most legal theorists is that there is no general moral obligation to obey the law but, for many years, the 'traditionalist' view was that there is a prima facie moral obligation to obey the law of a reasonably just state. A modern legal theorist who does argue for a general moral obligation to obey the law of a reasonably just state is Professor Finnis, the natural law author of *Natural Law and Natural Rights* (1980). Finnis argues from 'fairness' to a general moral obligation to obey the law. In a 1989 article, 'Law as Co-ordination', Finnis argues that the law presents itself as a seamless web of rights and duties by forbidding its subjects to pick and choose; all the subjects of the law are put in like case and linked to each other by that network of protections and other benefits which the law secures for each by imposing restraints on all. Finnis argues that the point of law is not merely to ensure the survival of government; part of the point of law is to maintain real fairness between the members of a community. This is why there might be a general moral obligation to obey the law because of the fairness we owe to others in the community governed by law. We benefit as individuals from others obeying the law; therefore, we owe our fellow citizens in the community a general moral obligation to obey the law. Insightfully, Professor Finnis locates the moral obligation to obey the law not to the rulers of society but to our fellow citizens – the law is a web of fairness. However, Finnis also believes that not endorsing a general moral obligation to obey the law will undermine the effectiveness of law as well. In his 1998 book, *Aquinas*, Finnis writes that picking and choosing among the law's requirements will inevitably undermine the law's protection of rights and interests. However, this argument for a general moral obligation to obey the law from the consequences to the effectiveness of the legal system of disobedience must face the fact that most legal systems function in the light of many acts of disobedience. Many unlawful acts such as trespass, breach of contract and breach of copyright do not threaten the effectiveness of a robust legal system.

The traditional argument for a general moral obligation to obey the law has been based on 'consent' or 'social contract'. For most of the history of liberal democracies the dominant theory about why citizens are morally obligated to obey the law has been social contract. The citizen has an obligation to obey the law because he has in some way 'consented' to the authority of government. The history of 'social contract' theories of obligation to obey really start with John Locke's account of social contract which makes a citizen's relationship to the state like that of a promisor: the citizen has made something like a promise to obey the law. Locke (1632–1704) based the citizen's obligation to obey the law on an implied consent to authority. This 'implied consent' for Locke is stated (in *The Second Treatise on Civil Government* (1690)) to arise when any citizen remains within the country: the 'very being of anyone within the territories' of a government amounts to tacit or implied consent. This is obviously a very weak argument in favour of a moral obligation to obey the law – that the citizen fails to emigrate to build a new life from scratch under a foreign flag. Indeed, the philosopher David Hume (1711–1776) commented on Locke's theory of obligation to the state that a poor peasant or artisan has no free choice at all to leave his country. Remaining in a country cannot be taken to render tacit agreement to obey the laws. Citizens remain in a country because of family, career, friends and culture, among other reasons. No one can maintain with a straight face that a refusal to emigrate constitutes tacit consent to the laws of that country. Indeed, the citizen under Locke's theory has no real choice at all since if he leaves one country he merely puts himself under the sovereignty of another country and so the problem arises again; 'consent to law or emigrate': perpetual emigration is the only solution to the dilemma posed by Locke's theory. There are more promising avenues of exploration for 'tacit consent' than Locke's 'remaining in the territory' argument. Tacit consent to the laws of the realm could arise from (a) voting in elections, or (b) receipt of benefits from the state, such as housing, transport systems, pension, education, etc.

With regard to voting, an argument based on 'tacit consent' could be that the very act of voting implies a recognition of the legitimacy of the state and its laws and that, therefore, an implied promise to abide by the laws of that state could be developed from the act of voting – a participation in government. Such a theory for a general moral obligation to obey the law faces formidable objections. As a preliminary point, voting could not amount to any form of 'consent' in Australia, where voting is mandatory and required by law. A more universal objection is the reality that many millions of citizens do not vote whether due to inertia, objection to the political system, or whatever. Therefore, 'voting' cannot ground a general obligation to obey the law that would reach all citizens. Perhaps the killing objection to voting as a ground of moral obligation to obey the law is that the act of voting is not understood as involving any undertaking as to obedience to the law. Voting in an election is not like an oath of office; it is merely an act of political preference.

An argument for a general moral obligation to obey the law based on benefits received from the state is a more fertile line of argument than either 'residence' or 'voting' as a basis for 'tacit consent'.

The argument based on 'gratitude' for benefits received from government is not a recent one. It has an ancient lineage. Socrates (470–399 BC) mentions the gratitude he feels for the benefits he has received from the Athenian state when he explains why he will not disobey, by escaping, the ruling of the jury that sentenced him to death (Socrates' dilemma is recounted in Plato's *Crito*).

In a modern setting, the argument from gratitude for benefits received from government to a general moral obligation to obey the law can be stated as follows: although citizens differ greatly in the amount of benefits they receive from government, all liberal democratic governments do confer substantial benefits on all citizens, such as a transport system, police force, education, social services, clean water and other utilities. As a general principle of morality, when a person accepts benefits from another, that person therefore incurs a debt of gratitude towards his benefactor. If, for example, someone saves my life then only a moral idiot would say that I was under no debt of gratitude to that life saver. Therefore, the argument goes, showing obedience to the law is the best way of showing gratitude to the state for benefits received. But there are a number of objections to the argument from 'gratitude' for benefits received from government. In the ordinary course of life, if someone confers benefits on me without any consideration of whether I want them I have no obligation to be grateful towards my unsolicited benefactor. Robert Nozick, in his 1974 book *Anarchy, State and Utopia*,[5] gives some striking examples to show that there is no obligation of gratitude for benefits received which are not solicited by the recipient. Nozick says if each day a different person on your street sweeps the entire street, must you do so when your time comes? Even if you don't care that much about a clean street? Nozick, in addition, imagines a brilliant lecture from a philosopher from the back of a sound truck in a suburban street. Nozick asks do all those who hear it – even all those who enjoy and profit by the brilliant lecture – owe the philosopher a lecture fee? Of course, they do not owe him a lecture fee, says Nozick. In the same way, the most important benefits of government – such as a transport system – are provided for citizens without the citizens ever asking for them.

A more fruitful argument to a moral obligation to obey the law is based on 'fairness'. Professor Finnis, we saw earlier, had a variation on this theme when he argued that the

---

5   Robert Nozick's political philosophy is discussed in Question 28, Chapter 7 of this book.

moral obligation to obey the law is owed to our fellow citizens in 'fairness'. This is the so-called argument from 'fair play' first explained by Professor Hart in an article entitled 'Are there any natural rights?' (*Philosophical Review* (1955)). Hart basically argues that a person who has accepted the benefits of a scheme of mutual co-operation is then bound by a duty of fair play to do his part and not to take advantage of the free benefits by not co-operating. This obligation of fair play seems to arise most clearly within small, tightly knit voluntary co-operative enterprises such as working men's clubs, sporting and religious organisations. Can the duty of fair play really be adequately extended to modern societies of millions of persons where they hardly know their neighbours?

The next argument for the general obligation to obey the law is the argument that there is a moral duty to support just institutions. The American philosopher, John Rawls, argued such a duty in his 1971 book, *A Theory of Justice*. Rawls argued that reasonable people recognise a natural moral duty to support reasonably fair and just institutions. Most liberal democratic states have reasonably fair and just legal orders; therefore, there is a general moral obligation to support those institutions by general moral obedience to the law in those societies. Raz accepts that the most common theme to liberal political theorising on authority is that the legitimacy of authority rests on the duty to support and uphold just institutions as, following Rawls, the duty is now usually called ('Authority and Justification', in *Authority*, edited by Raz (1990)). Raz rejects the attempt to found a general moral obligation to obey the law on the moral duty to uphold reasonably just institutions. Raz comments (in *The Morality of Freedom* (1986)) that the duty to uphold reasonably just institutions may entail an obligation to obey certain of the more politically sensitive laws such as laws against the use of political violence. However, Raz says it is an exaggeration to suppose that every breach of the law threatens, by however small a degree, the survival of government or of law and order. Moreover, Raz argues, if we take seriously the duty to support reasonably just institutions, this will entail duties far above those of obedience to the law. Lawful strikes may threaten the fabric of a society much more than many unlawful acts. So a person wanting to support the institutions of government would abstain from lawful strikes, etc. Indeed, the duty to support reasonably just institutions would entail a duty to play a part in political participation in government.

The criticisms of Raz of the argument from a duty to support reasonably just institutions to the moral obligation to obey the law can be summarised in two propositions: (1) many breaches of the law – such as acts of trespass, breach of copyright – have no implications for the stability of government; and (2) the full implications of the moral duty to support reasonably just institutions could entail such onerous and oppressive duties as actual political participation to support the state.

The failure of many of the traditional arguments for the general moral obligation to obey the law has led some legal scholars in the last 20 years to try to base a moral obligation to obey the law upon the idea that 'membership' of an 'associative' ideal, such as 'society', grounds such an obligation. At the heart of the 'associative' approach is the idea that political obligation is a form of non-voluntary obligation similar to obligations owed to family members. Professor Dworkin, in *Law's Empire* (1986), has the most well-known explanation of this theory. Dworkin argues that political association, like family and friendship, is in itself pregnant of obligation. Dworkin argues that a state which accepts 'integrity' (treating all citizens as equals under the rule of principle in law and legislation) thereby becomes a 'special' kind of community which justifies a moral obligation to obey the law of that 'society under the rule of law as integrity'. This view of Dworkin does fit with a common intuition of many persons who do think of themselves as members of political societies who have an obligation to obey their polities' laws. The true essence of 'associative obligation does not rest on any fictitious social contract or gratitude but on a feeling of "belonging"'.

Just as many persons feel a sense of belonging and obligation to family members they never chose to belong to, therefore, the argument goes, there is a moral obligation to obey the law of a fair society that a person never chose to be born into. There are problems, though, with trying to base a moral obligation to obey the law on the model of family obligations:

(a) Members of modern political societies lack the close relationships with each other that family members typically share. The family is a very small close-knit unit. A political society is massive in number, anonymous and alienating to many persons.

(b) Many families have a developed sense of paternalism and surveillance of its members which would be unacceptable in a modern liberal democratic state.

(c) A philosophical anarchist would argue that a person's sense of 'belonging' to his state is as a result of false consciousness and that no state is ever legitimate.

(d) Many persons feel a strong sense of 'belonging' to groups which challenge the authority of the state (for example, religions or radical political ideologies).[6]

'Associative obligations' are often competing with each other and this is why, ultimately, any appeal to 'communitarianism' as a ground of moral obligation to obey the law must fail.

The history of attempts to justify a general moral obligation to obey the law is a history of ultimate failure and perhaps the cumulative failure of all the theories from Locke in the seventeenth century to modern-day theories, such as Dworkin's 'associative' theory, suggests that there is no general moral obligation to obey the law and that any moral obligation varies from person to person in society.

George Klosko in *Political Obligations* (2005) has argued for a general moral obligation to obey the law based on citizens receipt of essential public goods from the state. Klosko writes:

'One of my governing assumptions is that the overwhelming majority of inhabitants of modern societies do not prefer to live in the woods or some remote outpost. (Persons want acceptable lives) and by "acceptable" lives I mean lives in modern

---

6 Islamic fundamentalists often claim that their allegiance to the 'umma', the worldwide Muslim community is far superior in strength to their allegiance to any nation state. Dworkin's theory of political obligation is in trouble when faced with religious obligations higher than, or in conflict with, the secular national state.

industrial societies, as we know them. These societies are relatively safe, have functioning economies, and allow a wide range of occupations, activities and modes of life. "Acceptable" lives are led by persons who are integrated into such societies and take advantage of the amenities they provide.'

Klosko goes on to write:

'the organised force of society, in the form of the State, able to be channeled in different directions is itself arguably indispensable to acceptable life. A number of public goods are required for acceptable lives and private or non-State provision of these goods will not work adequately therefore traditional States possessing both authority and a monopoly of force are necessary for acceptable lives. To have a safe and secure environment, an economy that functions healthily, efficient transportation and communication and other "essential services" require a high degree of efficient coordination which Klosko argues only an organised modern democratic State can provide.'

Klosko's conclusion is as follows:

'Because we need public goods supplied by the State in order to lead acceptable lives, we all have obligations to support their production. Political obligations are based on the principle of fairness. Political obligations are rooted in receipt of essential public goods from the State.'

Klosko's argument is essentially a variant on the argument from gratitude for benefits received from the state but with the emphasis that such benefits are 'essential' to the living of 'acceptable lives' by citizens. A critique of such an argument might focus on the consumerist and materialistic driven vision of many of those 'acceptable' lives in modern Western societies. An even stronger critique would argue that modern Western democratic states far from producing 'acceptable' lives for their citizens actually produce morally corrupting and spiritually stultifying effects on their citizens: materially rich but spiritually empty wastelands. It is by no means as obvious as Klosko seems to imply that the 'essential' nature of modern Western states to the living of 'acceptable lives' by citizens actually produces a general moral obligation to support those Western industrial democracies.

NOTES

In the online free *Stanford Encyclopedia of Philosophy* (http://plato.stanford.edu/) there are a couple of useful essays on the issue of moral obligation to obey the law. 'Political Obligation' is by Richard Dagger; 'Legal Obligation and Authority' is by Leslie Green. In *The Oxford Handbook of Philosophy and Law* (2002), edited by Coleman and Shapiro, there is an essay by Leslie Green called 'Law and Obligations', which is a survey of the issues in this area. In the collection of essays, *Authority* (1990), edited by Professor Raz, there is an essay by Kent Greenawalt called 'Promissory Obligation: The Theme of Social Contract', which is particularly valuable. The best collection of various essays on this topic from writers as diverse as Robert Paul Woolf to Joseph Raz is to be found in: *The Duty to Obey the Law: Selected Philosophical Readings* (1999), edited by William A Edmunson.

QUESTION 22

Is the 'character' of political leaders a philosophical issue?

How to Answer this Question

The problem of 'dirty hands' in politicsm, which is that the duties of high political office sometimes require politicians to order morally distasteful courses of action. The assassination of Osama Bin Laden in May 2011 on the orders of Barack Obama, President of the United States, can be viewed as a 'quintessential' Presidential decision, an archetypal political decision. A decision that could have had enormous geo-political consequences if the attempt to kill Bin Laden went wrong but was also 'morally risky' as well involving risks to the lives of innocent civilians as well as United States military personnel. Given the duties of political office in terms of safeguarding the security of the citizens of the country politicians need to have both virtue and ruthlessness. Such people will be rare. There is also a concern with the types of persons attracted to politics, the 'love of power' is not an attractive personality trait. Also in reaching the top of politics and 'staying in office' require character traits of ruthlessness, professionalism and ambition which call into question the characters of politicians. Liberal political theory such as Rawls' *A Theory of Justice* (1971) has tended to treat politics and persons as abstract concepts dealt with by abstract principles but in abstraction from questions of character. Character and the character traits we want politicians to have (e.g. political courage, strong will, self-control) and citizens to have (self-control, work ethic, loyalty to the state, law-abidingness) are vitally important as they can determine in the long run whether liberal democratic states of the kind supported by Rawls in *A Theory of Justice* (1971) actually can survive. No state can survive general lawlessness in the population and widespread corruption by political officials especially not fragile liberal states.

Applying the Law

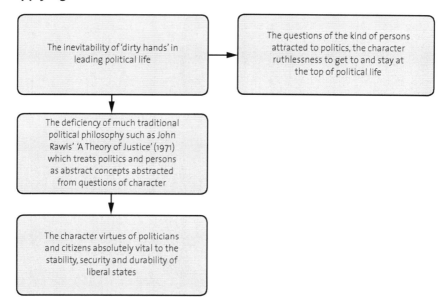

The inevitability of 'dirty hands' in leading political life

The questions of the kind of persons attracted to politics, the character ruthlessness to get to and stay at the top of political life

The deficiency of much traditional political philosophy such as John Rawls' 'A Theory of Justice' (1971) which treats politics and persons as abstract concepts abstracted from questions of character

The character virtues of politicians and citizens absolutely vital to the stability, security and durability of liberal states

ANSWER

In an essay entitled 'Politics and Moral Character' (1981) the eminent philosopher Bernard Williams asks: 'What sorts of persons do we want and need to be politicians?' There is a problem from the outset concerning the 'character' of politicians because of the kind of people who self-select themselves for political life. As Bernard Williams comments:

> 'It is widely believed that the practice of politics selects at least for cynicism and perhaps for brutality in its practitioners.'

Shakespeare in Henry V1, Part 3 alluded to the fact that, for a few people the gratifications of political power is all that will satisfy their craving for domination. Richard of Gloucester comments:

> 'Then, since this earth affords no joy to me But to command, to check, to o'erbear such As are of better person than myself, I'll make my heaven to dream upon the crown.'

So there is a problem with the 'kind of people' who go into political life: political power for some persons is an intoxicating brew. The next level concerns the politician's journey to the top of what Disraeli called the 'greasy pole' of politics. To reach the top of the 'greasy pole' might well involve deception, dirty tricks and ruthlessness towards others perceived in the way. Bernard Williams comments:

> 'Except in very favoured circumstances, it is likely to be the case that getting to the top of the political system will require properties which, while they need not at all necessarily be spectacularly undesirable or even regrettable, may nevertheless lean in the direction of the kind of ambition and professionalism which does not always make for the best judgment, moral or practical.'

So we have already identified two key stages in the life of a politician which might involve concern about 'moral character': (1) the kind of person who self-selects for political life; (2) the kind of person who has to exhibit a certain ruthlessness and ambition to get to the top of Disraeli's 'greasy pole'. Bernard Williams in a 1983 interview with *The Center Magazine* referred to the well-known phenomenon of 'rising politicians' making deals to advance their careers but also letting other people down, 'selling out' people who are no longer useful to them. Williams comments of the damaging moral effect on a politician's moral character of 'letting too many people down' by broken promises. Williams comments:

> 'if politicians do enough of that (letting people down) they will end up as hollow persons who can no longer be themselves, good or trusted as politicians.'

There is a third key stage in the life of a politician which also raises profound concerns about moral character and that is the duties and responsibilities of high political office combined with the desire of political leaders to stay in office. The first issue concerns the duties and responsibilities of high political office: political leaders to fulfil their duty to protect the public may well have to sanction political or military activity which necessarily involves the politician getting 'dirty hands'. The problem of political leaders getting 'dirty hands' was first canvassed in the philosophical literature by the American political philosopher Michael Walzer in a 1973 essay 'Political Action: The Problem of Dirty Hands'. Walzer said that the politician who took an 'absolutist' view of morality and therefore refused to politically order the morally dubious course of action was probably not fit for political office and should stay in private life where he could maintain his moral purity at no cost to the public. Walzer commented of the politician who refuses to get his hands dirty in the moral sense:

> 'If he remains innocent chooses the "absolutist" side … he may also fail to measure up to the duties of his office which imposes on him a considerable responsibility for consequences and outcomes.'

The politician who holds high office such as President or Prime Minister has an overriding duty stemming from his office to secure the safety of the public. This inescapable responsibility may involve the taking of morally dubious activity such as the political ordering of the assassination of foreign terrorist targets in foreign countries by the military. This does involve questions about the moral character of politicians: we might require politicians who are willing, in the name of the security of the people, to take morally dubious decisions and such willingness might require a certain ruthlessness and lack of remorse in the politicians so ordering those morally dubious actions. This need stemming from the 'duties of office' for top politicians to be both virtuous and ruthless may be referred to as 'Machiavelli's paradox': that too much virtue in a politician is actually a vice, unfitting him for political leadership and the awesome responsibilities of top political office. The implicit premise here is that only a very few individuals have the flexibility of character needed in a top-level politician to be both virtuous and ruthless when that is required for public safety, the character of most people being too fixed to allow for the requisite flexibility of character required of high political office. 'The Florentine' (from Florence, Italy) Niccolo Machiavelli had said in *The Prince* (1531) that a political leader must strive to be as virtuous as possible but when necessary for the security of the state the political leader must change and behave ruthlessly and against Christian virtues such as humility, truthfulness and kindness by employing cruelty and deceit in the service of the state. Machiavelli said:

> 'he (the politician) should not depart from the good if it is possible to do so, but he should know how to enter into evil when forced by necessity … And so it is necessary that he should have a mind ready to turn itself according to the way the winds of Fortune and the changing circumstances command him … he will be able and know how to change to the opposite.'

In addition to the burdens of the duties of high office, top politicians desire to 'stay in office' and to get re-elected and therefore those politicians might get involved in political activity which is morally dubious such as concealing information or 'dirty campaign tricks' against opponents. Even the most morally virtuous politician will realise that private morality cannot always be duplicated in public office. In order to protect the public some governmental secrecy is essential in order for example to prevent vital security information falling into the wrong hands such as terrorist. Private morality demands general truth telling, but the duties of public office means that secrecy, the non-disclosure of information or outright lying might be often required in government.

We have therefore identified a number of key areas where the character of politicians is in issue: (1) the decision to enter politics, (2) the climb up the 'greasy pole' of politics, (3) the duties of public office to protect the public from attack which might require the morally dubious course of action such as assassination of foreign terror suspects, (4) the duty of government to be secretive in some respects in order to protect the public and (5) the desire of elected politicians to stay in office which might involve 'dirty tricks' against political opponents.

The fact that politicians must play 'roles' to reach the top of the 'greasy pole' of politics was well captured by Shakespeare in Henry VI Part III where Gloucester illustrates to the audience how he will win political power by the playing of various deceptive 'roles':

> 'Why, I can smile and murder whiles I smile, And cry "content" to that which grieves my heart, And wet my cheeks with artificial tears, And frame my face to all occasions, I'll play the orator as well as Nestor, Deceive more slyly than Ulysees could, I can add colours to the chameleon, Change shapes with Proteus for advantages, And set the murd'rous Machiavel to school. Can I do this and cannot get a crown? Tut, were it farther off, I'll pluck it down.'[7]

The famous United States actor and director of films, Orson Welles was asked in an interview on the 'Parkinson' television interview show in 1974 about the 'stature' of politicians in the wake of the 'Watergate' scandal concerning the then President of the United States, Richard Nixon who was forced to resign from office in late 1974. Orson Welles directly made a connection between political life and acting but denied that political acting was necessarily deceitful and that we accept as part of our 'culture' that politics is a form of 'acting'. Orson Welles said:

....

7   The speech of Richard of Gloucester in Shakespeare's play *Henry the VI*, Part III needs some explanation: 'Nestor' was a Greek leader during the Trojan Wars reputed for eloquence. 'Ulysses' was Greek hero of the Odyssey and noted for his ability to deceive opponents. 'Proteus' was a Greek Sea-god with the power to take on all kinds of shapes to evade being questioned. 'Machiavel' is a reference to Machiavelli, whose short book *The Prince* (1531) was widely believed to advocate separating morals from the exercise of power.

In the play *Richard III*, Shakespeare again refers to the cunning deceitfulness of politicians when he makes King Richard exclaim: 'And thus I clothe my naked villainy/With odd old ends, stolen forth of Holy Writ/And seem a saint when most I play the devil.'

Another playwright, John Webster, a contemporary of Shakespeare, also had a caustic view of the deceitfulness of politicians in his two plays *The White Devil* and *The Duchess of Malfi*. Webster writes in his plays of the inherent cunning of successful politicians: *The White Devil*, John Webster: 'O they have wrought their purpose cunningly, as if they would not seem to do it of malice. In this a politician imitates the devil'. Act 3, scene 3.

The Duchess of Malfi, John Webster: 'A politician is the devil's quilted anvil; He fashions all sins on him, and the blows are never heard.' Act 3, scene 2.

'Politicians are not natural crooks, they are actors and actors are neither men nor women. Actors belong to a third sex. Actors are actors and one aspect of it is the political game, but that kind of acting is not lying so long as it refers to and reflects and exalts the essential common ideals of a culture. Those performances are part of our culture even though they are performances and even though some of the actors themselves may be cynical about their performances.'

Bernard Williams comments that the individual who does not wish to choose to do the morally disagreeable is not fitted for public life as a politician. Williams comments:

'If the politician is going to take the claims of politics seriously and if he is going to act at anything except a modest and largely administrative level of responsibility, then he has to face at least the probability of situations of this kind … He may even have, as a few seem to have, a virtue or moral cunning which drives such situations away. But it is a predictable and probable hazard of public life that there will be these situations in which something morally disagreeable is clearly required. To refuse on moral grounds ever to do anything of that sort is more than likely to mean that one cannot seriously pursue even the moral ends of politics.'

Williams comments about the life of politics:

'A certain roughness is to be expected by anyone who understands the nature of the activity, and it is merely misunderstanding to go on about it in a way which might be appropriate to more sheltered activities.'

At root politics is a brutal business involving, as it must, winners and losers, it is not for the faint hearted of character.

Another eminent political philosopher Thomas Nagel examined the problem of politicians and moral character in 'Ruthlessness in Public Life' in *Mortal Questions* (1979). Nagel comments that holding public office can 'produce a feeling of moral insulation' in the sense that the politician feels he or she is the agent of vast impersonal forces or the servant of institutions larger than any individual. The politician in high office can feel release from moral restraints which is significantly liberating. The strange effect produced by high political office on politicians in creating what Nagel calls 'a slippery moral surface produced by their roles or offices' is reason enough to have concerns about the moral character of politicians. Nagel comments: 'The office he occupies gets between him and his depersonalized acts'. It is easy for the politician who orders a military strike on foreign lands far away not to feel emotionally the suffering of the people he has caused by ordering such an attack. The politician's high office, his Presidency for example, acts as a buffer between the politician's decisions and the consequences of those decisions. Nagel goes on to argue that: 'the exercise of power in whatever role is one of the most personal forms of individual self-expression, and a rich source of purely personal pleasure'. Therefore not only does the holding of high political office tend to distance the politician from experiencing personally the horrible moral consequences of his actions and decisions but the taking of momentous actions and decisions which could cause the suffering of others is a source of personal pleasure to the politician since political decision is an intensely personal form of self-expression. Nagel comments:

> 'The pleasure of power is not easily acknowledged, but it is one of the most primitive human feelings-probably one with infantile roots. Those who have had it for years realise its importance only when they have to retire.'

Nagel is probably right when he says that the enjoyment of political power is immense. Henry Kissinger, President Nixon's Secretary of State in the 1970s said that 'power is a great aphrodisiac' meaning that the opposite sex were attracted to very powerful men. Indeed power is far more than an aphrodisiac, Frederick Forsyth has said that: 'power is the most demonic narcotic in the world. It makes heroin look like asprin'.

Another United States Secretary of State, Dean Acheson, Secretary of State to President Truman in the late 1940s said:

> 'Leaving high office is like the end of a great love affair – a void left by the disappearance of heightened sensibilities and focused concerns.'

Nagel comments further on the purely personal pleasure derived from holding high political office:

> 'Despite their grave demeanour, impersonal diction and limited physical expression, holders of public power are personally involved to an intense degree and probably enjoying it immensely ... the exercise of power is a primary form of individual expression, not diminished but enhanced by the institutions and offices on which it depends.'

The fact that the exercise of political power is such a source of personal satisfaction is reason enough to doubt the characters of those who would find satisfaction in this way. Also the politician to be successful and command the support of the public must, as Michael Walzer points out, express a confidence in his own judgment which would seem like sheer arrogance in non-political walks of life. Again, what kind of person has the near complete confidence in their own judgment that politicians profess to have?

From consideration of the personal pleasures to be gained from high political life, which should warn us about the moral character of politicians, Nagel then covers similar ground to Michael Walzer and Bernard Williams. Nagel comments that because of the duties of his high office, the politician has a 'heightened concern for results' than ordinary persons. The elected politician of high office has duties to the people which give him an acute anxiety about results and consequences of his decisions. Public institutions are designed to serve purposes much larger than those of particular individuals or families. Nagel comments that: 'public obligations differs systematically from that of private ones' and that a result of this chasm or great divide between private obligations and public duties is that public duties 'warrants methods usually excluded for private individuals and sometimes it licenses ruthlessness'. The dropping of the atomic bombs on the Japanese cities of Hiroshima and Nagasaki in August 1945 by the United States can be viewed as a particularly extreme example of the possible need for 'ruthlessness in public life'.

Public institutions such as the Government of the United States of America serve and pursue the interests of masses of people and can legitimately favour its own people in any calculation of policy objectives. Indeed public officials such as elected politicians accept special obligations upon accepting office, for example the President of the United States takes an oath of office upon being elected President. Elected politicians who hold high office are under a duty to protect the population of their country even if this means getting 'morally dirty hands'. Politicians who hold high office have to accept what Nagel calls 'the prominence of consequentialism', the fact that what matters in politics is not abstract moral principles but the outcome, the result, the consequences of a decision.

We have outlined the many moral risks to the character of politicians and also discovered that some ruthlessness, some hardness is actually required for political life and also for political decision in order to fulfill the duties of high political office. However, apart from a certain ruthlessness (and we do not want our politicians to be too ruthless as our liberties and the lives of foreigners could be in danger) what other qualities of character do we seek in politicians? Bernard Williams in his 1983 interview with *The Center Magazine* comments about the qualities of character a politician should have:

> 'a sense of judgment about importance and a considerable measure of courage and a disinclination to being bullied are important to politicians.'

The historian Robert Blake in his history of the Conservative Party commented on the character of Margaret Thatcher, Prime Minister 1979–1990. Blake commented:

> 'Personally Margaret Thatcher emerged as a figure with the characteristics which people look for in a Prime Minister. She had courage, clarity of mind, determination and guts. She may not have inspired great affection but she was admired as a leader and respected as someone who knew what she was trying to do and who meant what she said. She had been lucky in various ways but luck was what Napoleon looked for in his Marshals and it may be a synonym for some personal if indefinable quality which leads to success ... Disraeli had a measure of luck, but the test of a political leader is his ability to exploit his luck.'

Indeed Blake mentions a factor of political life that is not a character quality namely 'luck' or 'chance'. Quentin Skinner in his book on Machiavelli comments:

> 'Machiavelli ends on a fatalistic note. Since our circumstances vary, while our natures remain fixed, political success is simply a matter of having the good fortune to suit the spirit of the age.'

Machiavelli, the great sixteenth century Florentine political thinker said:

> 'I believe that we are successful when our ways are suited to the times and circumstances, and unsuccessful when they are not.'

However despite mentioning the influence 'luck' or 'chance' has in political life Machiavelli in his work *The Prince* (1532) mentions attributes that a political leader should avoid and attributes that a political leader should cultivate. Machiavelli commented that what tended to make a political leader 'despised' by the population was if he was considered any of the following:

'changeable, frivolous, effeminate, cowardly and irresolute.'

In contrast a political leader should strive to make everyone recognise in his actions:

'greatness, spirit, dignity and strength.'

Those qualities of a political leader desired by Machiavelli: 'greatness, spirit, dignity and strength' can perhaps be summed up by the phrase 'natural authority'. A political leader should not solely rely on the 'prestige' of his political office for authority but should augment the authority of his high office with a 'natural authority'. The historian Andrew Roberts in his biography of Lord Salisbury, the late nineteenth-century Prime Minister comments:

'Salisbury was a natural leader to whose authority men yielded. He had an entirely self-contained personality.'

However, in addition to courage, natural authority and luck, a political leader needs will-power, an ability to sustain where other people would give up. Archibald Wavell the British Second World War General in a 1941 book *Generals and Generalship* commented:

'the first essential of a general to be the possession of the quality of robustness, the ability to withstand the shocks of war … a high margin over the normal breaking strain … very often, what was wanting when they failed was a sufficiently high margin over the normal breaking strain.'

Therefore 'a high margin over the normal breaking strain' is as much a necessary quality in politicians, who have to deal with very abnormal strain and stress, than it is for a General. A politician also needs the quality of being able to tell the public what it does not want to hear but is necessary for them to hear and understand for their long-term good.

A politician should not be 'sensitive to the marrow' but should have a nerve hardened against the insults and abuse of the world. Ashley Jackson in his biography of Churchill comments of Churchill's tough political 'skin':

'despite the rancour he attracted (at the beginning of his career), it was remarkable how little enmity he felt towards those who attacked him. He had the skin of a rhinoceros … his guileless disregard for what other people thought about his actions was one of his greatest political strengths.'

Having considered some of the qualities we might expect in politicians such as courage, judgment, will-power and insensitivity to ridicule we can conclude the discussion by examining what the earliest commentators on political character, the Ancient Greeks, notably Plato and Aristotle had to say on the matter. The Ancient Greeks perceived a direct link between good moral character and correct political action. Aristotle, in *Nicomachean Ethics*, contended that it is not easy to define in general rules which actions deserve moral praise and blame and that these matters require the judgment of the virtuous person. In other words Aristotle said that it requires the person of good moral character to judge with regularity and reliability what actions are the morally good ones. If there is one cardinal moral quality we expect of politicians who hold high office it is 'good judgment' since the politician has to make judgments affecting the lives of millions of people repeatedly over the course of many years. The Greek moralists such as Aristotle thought that it took someone of good moral character to determine with regularity and reliability what actions are appropriate and reasonable in changing and shifting political situations.

Indeed the advantages of good moral character for a politician go beyond the ability to make regular and reliable sound political judgments to actually being the precondition of being an effective political agent at all. A good moral character gives its possessor, thought Plato and Aristotle, psychic health and orderliness contrasted with the chaotic or even tyrannical character of an unjust soul. To be an effective political agent at all, a person must be just, moderate, courageous and wise. These were the four central virtues of the ancient classical world of Greece and Rome – courage, temperance (moderation in all things) justice and wisdom. Possession of these four cardinal virtues in the character of a politician gives their possessor a 'psychic health' which is a massive advantage for that politician as he has psychic 'balance' no matter how he or she is treated fairly or unfairly. Given that politics is a brutal and at times unfair business then the ability to stay stable under adverse and hostile conditions is a massive advantage for a politician. Therefore for Plato and Aristotle, the possession of good moral character by a politician (the virtues of courage, temperance, justice and wisdom) not only allows the possessor to make regular and reliable sound political judgments but also allows the politician with the moral virtues to act on the political stage with stability of character whatever happens in the changing seas of political life.

Plato argues that the possession of good moral character allows the politician to successfully master the human expertise of 'statecraft'. 'Statecraft' is distinguished from its closet skills or political arts such as the democratic arts of rhetoric (public political speaking) generalship (leading others) and judging by its knowledge of the 'correct timing' for the exercise and cessation of these other arts. Plato said that the statesman is wholly defined by the possession of that knowledge of when it is best to exercise the other political arts. Therefore 'statecraft' is a form of wisdom applied in the political sphere which will guide the politician is knowing when it is appropriate to speak and when it is wiser to stay silent, when to act decisively and when to forebear from acting, when to show anger and when to conceal anger.

In summary, the Ancient Greeks believed that good moral character was related to political life in at least three separate ways: (1) the politician of sound moral character could be expected to make regularly and reliably, sound political judgments; (2) a politician of sound moral character would possess 'psychic health' giving him or her the stability needed to cope with the brutal world of politics and (3) a politician of sound moral character would be able to master the skill or art of 'statecraft', having the judgment to know when to deploy the other political arts such as rhetoric, generalship and judging.

In a book entitled *Political Judgment* (2009) edited by Richard Bourke and Raymond Geuss, the view is put forward that: 'Politics must begin with the care of the self.' In other words an aspiring politician must first cure the serious defects in his own character before he enters politics, in the form of a psychological preparation for the slings of fortune. As the sixteenth century philosopher Montaigne (1533–1592) argued: 'not being able to control events, I control myself'.

Although the politician must learn to control himself and 'discipline his tongue' and have other virtues such as courage, the politician is not a moral teacher of the people, that is the role of clerics and imams. As Anthony Quinton argues in 'Of Men and Manners: Morals and Politics' (2011): 'A good ruler is not a moral teacher or a pioneer, he is the skilled practitioner of a technique, that of preserving public order, protecting the community against its rivals or enemies, and enhancing its prosperity.'

The fact that a political leader is not a moral teacher but rather the 'skilful practitioner of a technique' is illustrated by Anthony Quinton:

> 'As a ruler his motive will not be principally the moral improvement of the citizenry but the preservation of public order. In areas of lively moral controversy it is perfectly proper for him to sustain a law with whose moral correlate he does not agree, on the ground that it is necessary for the preservation of peace.'

Therefore a political leader might have private moral views which condemn abortion or homosexuality but for the sake of civil peace the wise political leader does not seek to change the laws allowing abortion or homosexual behaviour.

Political philosophy was in the doldrums in the post-Second World War period (1945–1970) until what can be called 'The Rawlsian resurrection' occurred with the publication of John Rawl's masterpiece *A Theory of Justice* in 1971. In 1974 Robert Nozick replied to Rawls's liberal egalitarianism with the anti-welfare state *Anarchy, State and Utopia*. However both Rawls and Nozick shared in common the following feature: they defined the conditions for the existence of fair and just political institutions without having anything to say about the character or virtue of either citizens or politicians who live under or work such 'fair' institutions. There was therefore an important 'gap' at the heart of 1970s American political philosophy. Bernard Williams commented in a January 1975 book review of Nozick's *Anarchy, State and Utopia* in the Times Literary Supplement that there were more virtues than simply 'justice' (which Nozick seemed obsessed by). Williams commented:

> 'We are reminded again of that richer range of moral resources, of the kinds of character that we want to have in society, which Mr.Nozick's treatment systematically leaves out.'

William Galston, in his 1991 book *Liberal Purposes: Goods, Virtues, and Diversity in the Liberal State* looked back 20 years to Rawls' *A Theory of Justice* and commented:

> 'liberalism has been understood by many as the articles of a peace treaty among individuals with diverse conceptions of the good but common interests in self-preservation and prosperity. On the level of basic institutions, the liberal constitution

has been regarded as an artful contrivance of countervailing powers and counterbalancing passions.'

Rawls and Nozick, while spending enormous intellectual energy on the political and social arrangements and institutions of the 'just' liberal state, do not say anything about the 'character', the moral virtue we want in citizens and politicians in the liberal constitutional state but as Galston comments:

> 'the liberal state must by definition be broadly inclusive of diversity, yet it cannot be wholly indifferent to the character of its citizens … the operation of liberal institutions is affected in important ways by the character of citizens and leaders … the viability of liberal society depends on its ability to endanger a virtuous citizenry.'

Galston lists the following character virtues that the liberal state should promote in its citizens: courage, law-abidingness, loyalty to the state, work ethic, respecting the rights of others. For political leaders in a liberal democratic state Galston lists the following: patience – the ability to accept, and work within, the constraints on action imposed by social diversity and constitutional institutions. Second, liberal leaders must have the capacity to forge a sense of common purpose in an individualistic and fragmented society. Third, liberal leaders must be able to resist the temptation to earn popularity by pandering to immoderate public demands. The liberal leader must, against the lure of the immediate future, insist on the requirements of the long-term future and through sound persuasion (rhetoric) the liberal leader tries to move the citizenry toward sound views. Galston quotes Thomas Jefferson one of the US founding fathers who saw popular elections as the best vehicle for discerning and selecting good leaders. Thomas Jefferson wrote to John Adams:

> 'There is a natural aristocracy among men. The grounds of this are virtue and talents … The natural aristocracy I consider as the most precious gift of nature, for the instruction, trusts, and government of society … May we not even say, that that form of government is the best, which provides the most effectively for a pure selection of these natural 'aristoi' into the offices of government? … I think the best remedy is exactly that provided by all our constitutions, to leave to the citizens the free election and separation of the "aristoi" from the "pseudo-aristoi".'

Therefore, according to Thomas Jefferson, the ultimate justification for democratic and free elections is their tendency to select political officeholders with the best appropriate character virtues.

William Galston in *Liberal Purposes* (1991) gives a warning that liberal states ignore the moral character of their citizens at their peril:

> 'the fact remains that political communities can move, and throughout history have moved, from health to disrepair for reasons linked to moral and cultural decay. In the face of this, I do not believe that contemporary American liberals can afford to be complacent. We cannot simply chant the mantra of diversity and hope that fate will

smile upon us. We must try as best we can to repair our tattered social fabric by attending more carefully to the moral requirements of liberal public life.'

William Galston's argument in *Liberal Purposes* reminds us that it is not just the moral character of political leaders that is an important philosophical issue but that the moral character of the mass of the citizens of liberal states may ultimately determine the survivability of those liberal democratic states.

It might be objected that a politician's character or indeed the character of a private citizen is the result of parental, educational and cultural forces that, in other words, a person does not deserve 'credit' or' censure' for having a good or bad moral character because given the peculiar matrix of their respective backgrounds, good or bad or indifferent in character is all they could ever be. However a long tradition of ethical thought stretching back to the ancient Greeks, Plato and Aristotle asserts that persons are to a significant degree responsible for their own characters. The argument of both the pagan Aristotleian tradition and the Roman Catholic orthodoxy represented by Tomas Aquinas is that a person shapes his or her own moral character through free moral choices. The first investigation of the virtues was made by Plato in such works as *Gorgias* and the *Republic*. The classical account of the virtues, however, to which all modern treatments refer, is that of Aristotle in *Nicomachean Ethics*. A modern account is likely to agree with Aristotle that virtues are dispositions of character, acquired by ethical training, displayed not just in action but in patters of emotional reaction. Aristotle said in *Nicomachean Ethics*:

> 'Moral virtues, like crafts, are acquired by practice and habituation ... we become just by performing just acts, self-controlled by performing self-controlled acts, brave by performing brave acts ... like activities produce like dispositions ... so it is a matter of no little importance what sort of habits we form from the earliest age–it makes a vast difference, or rather all the difference in the world.'[8]

---

8   Bernard Williams in his collection of essays *Moral Luck'* (1981) comments of 'character':

> 'the idea of one person's having a character, in the sense of having projects and categorical desires with which the person is identified ... he wants these things, finds his life bound up with them, and that they propel him forward, and thus they give him a reason for living his life ... differences of character give substance to the idea that individuals are not inter-substitutable.'

In his collection of essays *The Sense of the Past* (2006) Bernard Williams develops further the ancient Greek idea of forming one's own moral character through moral choice:

> 'In Nicomachean Ethics Aristotle raises the queswtion of how it can be true, as he claims it can be, that someone becomes (e.g. just) by doing just things: for how can someone do virtuous things without having the appropriate virtue? His answer Is that the things done by the learner, although they are in a sense virtuous things, do not yet fully display the virtue. We may say that they are minimally virtuous things: they are not done as the virtuous person does them ... the virtuous agent Is in a steady, unchangeable state ... Courageous or self-controlled things are not done "for their own sake", and doing them for their own sake would be something quite special: something like doing a certain thing in a certain situation to display or develop one's courage or self-control.'

continued

Aristotle gives a severe warning:

> 'A bad moral state, once formed, is not easily amended … it was at first open to the unjust and licentious persons not to become such, and therefore they are voluntarily what they are; but now that they have become what they are, it is no longer open to them not to be such.'

Modern philosophers would agree with Aristotle on the importance of moral choice to the formation of moral character. Harry Frankfurt in his collection of essays 'The Importance of What we Care About' argues of the crucial relationship between moral choice and the formation of moral character:

> 'Since it is most conspicuously by making a decision that a person identifies with some element of his psychic life, deciding plays an important role in the formation and maintenance of the self … it is apparent that making a decision is something that we do to ourselves.'

From the Roman Catholic 'natural law' tradition Robert George in his work 'In Defense of Natural Law' comments on the very close relationship between moral choice and character formation:

> 'free choices reflexively shape the personality and character of the chooser. In freely choosing we integrate ourselves around the principles of our choices. Thus, we constitute (or reconstitute) ourselves as particular sorts of persons. We construct (or reconstruct) our moral selves. Typically, this self-constitution or moral self-constitution is not the precise reason for our choosing; nevertheless, it is an unavoidable side effect of that choosing … precisely insofar as our choices are self-constituting they persist beyond the behaviour that executes them. Indeed, they persist in the personality and character of the chooser until, for better or worse, he repents of his prior choice and either makes a new choice that is incompatible with that prior choice or genuinely resolves not to repeat the choice he has now repudiated.'

....

continued

Bernard Williams also argues, following Aristotle, that a virtuous disposition is expressed in choice but is not only so expressed. The virtue is expressed in 'reason-structured responses' such as the emotions which link rational and non-rational aspects of the agent. So a virtue of character, such as courage, displays itself not only in choice and projects but also in emotional responses to situations. Bernard Williams comments in *The Sense of the Past* (2006):

> 'It is not untypical of the virtues that the virtuous person should be partly characterized by the way in which he thinks about situations and by the concepts he uses.'

It is interesting to note that for the Ancient Greeks 'wisdom' was the chief virtue but that for the more military-minded ancient Romans 'courage' was the primary virtue: see Shakespeare's Roman set play *Coriolanus* at Act 2, scene 3, lines 88–90: 'It is held that Valour is the chiefest Virtue, and Most dignifies the Haver.' The Scottish Enlightenment philosopher David Hume (1711–1776) argued that it was possible to make an inference about a person's moral character from specific instances of virtuous or vicious conduct. Hume said: 'If any action be either virtuous or vicious it is only as a sign of some quality or character.' ·

Robert George then offers a similar word of warning that Aristotle gave in *Nicomachean Ethics* that the formation of bad moral character is particularly difficult to rectify. In this way there is an asymmetry or difference between good moral character and bad moral character. Bad moral character is significantly harder to reform into good moral character than good moral character is to degenerate by bad moral choices into bad moral character. Robert George comments in *In Defense of Natural Law*:

> 'someone who has by his immoral choices constituted a wicked character can, with difficulty, reconstitute himself ... the constitution of a wicked character does not preclude the possibility of repentance and reconstitution around upright principles of action.'

However Robert George, similarly to Aristotle, argues there comes a point in a person's life when it is no longer possible for the wicked to become morally 'good' when in the words of Robert George there is 'complete integration' of the personality with evil, the wicked person fully accepts himself as evil, then the 'point of no return' is crossed and there is no possibility of a change to the good.

The tradition of ethical thought from Plato and Aristotle to modern-day philosophers such as Harry Frankfurt and Robert George accepts that whatever our background influences and personal advantages or disadvantages, we remain significantly responsible for our own moral characters: we shape ourselves through our own moral choices and therefore we are the agents of our own moral downfall or correct moral formation.[9]

NOTES

Thomas Nagel's essay on 'Ruthlessness in Public Life' is reprinted in his collection of essays *Mortal Questions* (1979). Bernard Williams examines 'Politics and Moral Character' in the collection of essays by Williams' entitled: *Moral Luck: Philosophical Papers 1973–1980* (1981). Robert George looks at the significance to a person's character of moral choice in *In Defense of Natural Law* (1999), pp. 119–120. Harry G Frankfurt in his philosophical essays *The Importance of What we Care About* (1988) in the essay 'Identification and Wholeheartedness'. The starting point for all discussions on 'virtue ethics' is Aristotle's *Nicomachean Ethics* (1976).

....

9   The tradition of fundamentalist Christian theology would assert that moral virtue as recommended by Aristotle is not the same thing at all as 'righteousness in the eyes of God'. Christian theologians such as Martin Luther and John Calvin would say that 'righteousness' comes from outside the person and is bestowed on a person by an act of divine grace by God after the sinner has repented his sins and exercised faith in Jesus Christ as the Son of God. The key difference between the pagan virtue of Aristotle and righteousness of Christians is that pagan virtue is developed 'within' a person by habits of virtue whereas Christian 'righteousness' is bestowed only by God as a gift to the believing and repenting sinner. In Aristotle's *Nicomachean Ethics* – characterised by Martin Luther as 'the worst of all books' – we encounter the idea that a person attains goodness by repeated practice of virtuous actions. For Luther and Calvin 'righteousness' is not inside a person to be built up by them through repeated practice of virtue but that 'righteousness' is bestowed from outside a person by God's grace. John Calvin argued that righteousness is neither the result of good works nor an internal quality but is literally 'outside us' bestowed by a merciful God.

7   Human Rights and Legal Theory

INTRODUCTION

'Human Rights' have become, in the early twenty-first century, a form of global secular religion. The spread of 'human rights consciousness' and effective protection for human rights in all countries of the world is seen as the ultimate goal of Western liberal ideology securing a safer and more just global community and guaranteeing basic rights for every person on earth. The promise of human rights ideology is that ultimately of a secular human 'paradise'. Charles Taylor, the philosopher and author of *A Secular Age* (2007), in an interview with the journal *The Utopian* in 2010 commented on the dominance in the Western democracies of the 'human rights' conception of politics and how other conceptions of politics such as 'civic republicanism' which seek to find in politics the common grounds for trust and co-operation have lost out to the dominance of the 'human rights' discourse. Taylor comments:

> 'there has been developed a very articulated human rights discourse, human rights law, and so on, concerned with individual rights, with equality and non-discrimination, with the promotion of democracy, so that a lot of people now look at politics in this framework. Is the polity (the state) violating this or that non-discrimination requirement, or this or that right? And this has come to eclipse the tradition of worrying about the collective creation of the common conditions of trust (the civic republican tradition) which alone make this kind of society possible.'

This chapter examines human rights on a much more narrow agenda than whether human rights discourse has gone too far in replacing other concerns such as the need for stability in the Western liberal democracies.

The questions considered in this chapter include: is it morally justifiable for a state to torture a terrorist in order to save many innocent lives? A question of some relevance after 9/11 in the United States. A related question is the extent to which the security of the citizens should be, as the ancient Roman orator Cicero (died 43 BCE) put it, 'the supreme law' for government.

Three questions give concrete examples of how human rights may or may not buckle under the weight of the demands of state necessity or state security: the infamous Abu Qatada case in the United Kingdom, the fate of the human rights movement in the United Kingdom in the post-9/11 age of hyper-terrorism and the historical precedent of the British Empire and the rule of law.

The last two questions in this chapter focus on the controversial issue of 'judicial review' of controversial legislation, and the extent to which the moral doctrine of 'utilitarianism' can provide a justification, if any, for the durability and non-derogability of fundamental human rights such as the right not to be tortured or subject to inhuman or degrading treatment – see **Art 3** of the **European Convention on Human Rights**.

Checklist

Make sure you are acquainted by the following topics:

- the moral acceptability of or moral prohibition on torture in the context of terrorism;
- the role national security concerns should play in human rights law;
- the issue as to whether 'strong-form' judicial review is acceptable;
- the issue of whether the moral theory of utilitarianism can account for human rights.

QUESTION 23

What does the well-known case of Abu Qatada (Othman) reveal about the ideology of the European Convention of Human Rights?

How to Answer this Question

This question focuses on one particularly high-profile case of both the UK courts and the European Court of Human Rights (ECtHR), the 'Abu Qatada' case, and asks what the case can tell us, from a jurisprudential perspective, of the wisdom or otherwise of having an institution of judges in Strasbourg who are free of the political pressures of our own judges in respect of important human rights decisions but are also free of the accountability of our own judges to the legal-political order of the UK state.

The answer should focus on, first, an accurate summary of the facts of the Abu Qatada case, why the case arose, its outcome etc., but then the answer should delve into wider jurisprudential territory of the functions of human rights documents, especially the **European Convention of Human Rights** (ECHR) and the political acceptability of 'supranational judges', namely judges who are beyond national boundaries but who nonetheless have authority in national legal systems. This is a profoundly important and profoundly relevant jurisprudential question.

Applying the Law

> The role of the ECtHR has been controversial in recent years as a court outside the legal and political life of the United Kingdom seeks to address matters which would seem especially within the remit of national state authorities, such as whether prisoners can have the vote or whether a judge can impose a 'whole life' tariff on a convicted murderer

↓

> The 'Abu Qatada' (Othman) case is a test case of the growing influence of the ECtHR on our existing UK legal system as the UK Government battled to have deported a terrorist suspect described by the Special Immigration Appeal Commission in 2007 as 'Osama bin Laden's right hand man in Europe' and a man with 'incalculable influence' over jihadist terrorist groups

↓

> Both Article 3, the prohibition on torture, inhuman and degrading treatment, and the totally separate Convention right Article 6, the right to a fair trial, were used to block Abu Qatada's deportation from the UK by the ECtHR

↓

> The ECtHR held that a 'real risk' of torture on returning to Jordan blocked Abu Qatada's deportation to Jordan from the UK

↓

> The Article 3 issue was resolved due to solemn promises made by the Jordanian authorities not to torture Qatada on his return

↓

> Article 6 was then invoked to block Qatada's deportation because he could not receive a fair trial in Jordan due to torture evidence possibly used against him at his future trial in that country

↓

> An international treaty was signed between UK and Jordan to cover the 'torture evidence' issue and Qatada went back to Jordan voluntarily

↓

> Qatada case raises issues about the wisdom or not of allowing a foreign court to adjudicate on human rights issues in the UK especially in the realms of national security as raised by Abu Qatada's continuing presence in the United Kingdom

ANSWER

The legal and political issues surrounding the deportation from the United Kingdom of foreign terrorist suspects is one of the most controversial aspects in the whole of UK law and politics today.

Indeed, such was the political pressure on the UK Government to arrange the extradition of the radical Jordanian-Palestinian cleric Abu Qatada to the Hashemite Kingdom of Jordan to face a trial on terrorism charges that the UK Government took the unprecedented step of concluding a binding international treaty with Jordan, signed by the Jordanian king and ratified by the Jordanian Parliament, promising not to use evidence obtained from torture at any trial in Jordan involving persons deported from the United Kingdom: see Treaty on Mutual Legal Assistance in Criminal Matters between the United Kingdom of Great Britain and the Kingdom of Jordan 2013. **Article 27(3)** states:

> 'Where there are serious and credible allegations that a statement from a person has been obtained by torture or ill-treatment by the authorities of the receiving State and it might be used in a criminal trial in the receiving State, then the statement shall not be submitted by the prosecution nor admitted by the Court in the receiving State…'

In the Abu Qatada case, both the ECtHR and the UK courts had accepted diplomatic assurances given by Jordan to the UK Government, called a 'Memorandum of Understanding' (MOU), that the Jordanians would not physically ill-treat or torture Abu Qatada himself upon his deportation to Jordan. This diplomatic assurance was important because of the very important rule laid down by the ECtHR in the case in 1996 of *Chahal v UK* that no person could be deported if there was a real risk of torture or inhuman or degrading treatment contrary to **Art 3** of the **Convention**. The *Chahal* ruling was importantly re-affirmed in the ECtHR case in *Saadi v Italy* (2008). The risk to national security that the terror suspect posed to the member state was a completely irrelevant factor in applying the *Chahal* test, said the ECtHR in the case of *Saadi*.

However, a separate argument was found by Abu Qatada's lawyers that evidence obtained from the torture of prosecution witnesses (Abu Qatada's alleged Islamist terrorist accomplices) could be admitted against Abu Qatada at trial in Jordan which meant that his trial would be 'flagrantly unfair' and a breach of Abu Qatada's right to a fair trial under **Art 6** of the **Convention**. The ECtHR in 2012 in a revolutionary judgment accepted that **Art 6** could be used to block Abu Qatada's deportation to the United Kingdom. In this case 'diplomatic assurances' by Jordan not to use torture evidence were not enough to satisfy the ECtHR nor enough to satisfy the Court of Appeal in the United Kingdom which also blocked Abu Qatada's deportation in March 2013 on the **Art 6** argument that the use of torture evidence from Abu Qatada's accomplices against Abu Qatada in Jordanian criminal proceedings would be a flagrant denial of his right to a fair trial. Indeed numerous legal documents around the world attest to the total unacceptability of the use of evidence from torture against a defendant in a criminal trial.

The **UN Convention against Torture 1984 Article 15** states that every state must ensure that any statement made under torture could not be invoked as evidence in any proceedings. The House of Lords ruled in *A v Secretary of State for the Home Department* (2005) that any evidence from anywhere in the world obtained by torture was automatically inadmissible in UK courts. The international consensus is that the use by the prosecution of evidence obtained from torture makes a fair trial impossible.

Therefore on the basis of this 'international consensus' against 'torture evidence', the ECtHR and the UK Court of Appeal were right to block Abu Qatada's deportation from the United Kingdom to Jordan under **Art 6** of the **ECHR**.

Following this international consensus on a total ban of evidence from torture being used in legal proceedings, the Special Immigration Appeals Commission (SIAC) in its November 2012 judgment *Mohammed Othman (Abu Qatada) v Secretary of State for the Home Department* robustly commented:

> 'The European Court of Human Right's case law established that an issue might exceptionally be raised under Article 6 by an expulsion or extradition decision in circumstances where the fugitive had suffered or risked suffering a flagrant denial of justice in the requesting country. The test was a stringent one and required a breach of the principles of a fair trial guaranteed by Article 6 which is so fundamental as to amount to a nullification, or destruction of the very essence of the Article 6 right to a fair trial.'

The question remains: why were the UK Courts and the ECtHR willing to accept the 'diplomatic assurances' from Jordan not to torture or physically ill-treat Abu Qatada on his return from the United Kingdom but those same courts rejected 'diplomatic assurances' from Jordan not to use evidence obtained from torture of prosecution witnesses at the trial in Jordan of Abu Qatada?

The answer to this question must be that for the Jordanians to have tortured Abu Qatada after giving the UK Government a 'diplomatic assurance' that the Jordanians would not torture him would be a serious breach of trust by the Jordanians and lead to a major diplomatic incident with the United Kingdom, whereas a breach of the promise not to use evidence already obtained from torture is nowhere near as serious a breach of trust as to torture Abu Qatada personally. In the SIAC judgment of November 2012 the court distinguished between the 'diplomatic assurance' not to torture Qatada and the 'diplomatic assurance' not to use 'torture evidence' at his trial. SIAC said:

> 'SIAC concluded that the United Kingdom could safely accept solemn assurances given by the Jordanian state and that those assurances removed the real risk that Qatada would suffer inhuman or degrading treatment at the hands of state agents in Jordan for two fundamental reasons: the close and friendly relations which have existed at all levels in the governments of both countries for many decades; and the general coincidence of interests of the two countries in those aspects of international affairs which affect them both. The Secretary of State has not satisfied us that there is no real risk that the impugned statements of the accomplices would be admitted against the appellant at trial.'

Therefore in concluding the international treaty with Jordan (the 'Abu Qatada' treaty) the United Kingdom has established in international law and Jordanian law that no evidence from torture can be used in Jordanian courts. This international treaty changes Jordanian law, which a 'diplomatic assurance' cannot do.

Abu Qatada has now left the UK jurisdiction and gone back to Jordan as of July 2013 as he was confident, in the light of the treaty, that he can receive a fair trial in Jordan but only the international treaty changing Jordanian law gave Abu Qatada and his lawyers that confidence so he could return home to Jordan.

However, the judgment in the Abu Qatada case by the ECtHR asserting his Art 6 right as a ground not to deport him can be criticised as an act of judicial imperialism seeking to expand the scope of the **European Convention of Human Rights** way beyond the intentions of its original framers in 1950. The ECtHR is widely regarded as expansionist on account of the court's view that the Convention is a 'living instrument' and can be applied ever more broadly to account for social and economic change.

There is also the point that domestic UK judges are, despite judicial independence, embedded in a legal-political system to which they owe allegiance. UK judges have an inescapable institutional responsibility to the UK state even if UK judges often make decisions against the government of the day. Judges in the ECtHR in Strasbourg have no institutional loyalty to the UK state and can deliver judgments from a detached Olympian height which have to be standardised enough to apply to all 47 Member States to the Council of Europe. These standardised detached judgments from Strasbourg may not be in the best interests of the individual member states such as the United Kingdom.

No reasonable person disagrees with the human rights established in the **ECHR** such as **Art 3**, the prohibition on torture, or **Art 6**, the right to a fair trial. The existence of the basic rights is not in serious question, rather it is the imperialistic use by judges of those unquestionable human rights in novel and controversial ways through overly imaginative judicial interpretivism that is the controversial question.

Establishing the principle in the Abu Qatada case that the 'real risk' of a 'flagrantly' unfair trial shall ban deportation opens up the possibility in some future case of a ruling that the real risk of an 'unfair trial' in itself can block deportation. However, this is to open up a hornet's nest of problems: what counts as an unfair trial? What counts as a flagrantly unfair trial?

An example of 'judicial imperialism' under the ECtHR is provided for by **Art 8**, the right to a family and private life, home and correspondence. In the case of *Marckx v Belgium* in 1979, ECtHR judge Sir Gerald Fitzmaurice commented on the original 'anti-totalitarian' nature of **Art 8**:

> 'the main, if not indeed the sole object and intended sphere of application of Article 8 was that of "domiciliary protection" of the individual. He and his family were no longer to be subjected to the four o'clock in the morning rat-a-tat on the door; to domestic intrusions, searches and questionings.... In short the whole gamut of fascist and communist inquisitorial practices ... It was for the avoidance of these horrors, tyrannies and vexations that "private and family life, home and correspondence" were to be respected.'

However, **Art 8** and the rest of the Convention rights have been transformed by the long passage of time since 1950 from a European legal pact against totalitarianism into something quite different, namely an ever-expanding European Bill of Rights. The Convention is viewed by the ECtHR as a 'living instrument' and **Art 8** has been the testing ground on which the battle over competing views of the Convention have been fought: whether the **European Convention of Human Rights** is a merely list of basic rights against totalitarian government or rather capable of stretching beyond that conception under the engine of judicial imperialism in Strasbourg.

It might in theory be a sound idea to have an ultimate human rights appeal court that is supra-national, a court beyond the pressures of domestic states' bitter controversies over human rights issues. Judges in such a 'removed' environment could approach legal issues over human rights insulated from political pressures.

However, a foreign court under the influence of the potent drug of 'judicial imperialism', with a strong judicial desire to see the Convention extended and unrolled even further into member states' national lives, could in theory also bring the human rights project, as reflected in the ECHR, into serious disrepute in Member States.

This is simply because action to protect the UK national interest such as the attempted deportation of dangerous terrorists is perceived in the United Kingdom to be seriously inhibited by extreme interpretations of the ECHR by Strasbourg judges.

NOTES

The continuing status of the **Human Rights Act 1998** remains unclear under the present Conservative Government with initial plans to repeal the Act for the time being shelved.

The wider issue of whether the United Kingdom remains a member of the Council of Europe, the institutional body of which the ECtHR is a part, remains a matter of great political controversy in the United Kingdom.

QUESTION 24

Is it morally justifiable for a state to torture a terrorist in order to save many innocent lives?

How to Answer this Question

This question poses a fundamental moral question that was made much more relevant following the 9/11 terrorist attacks in the United States by al-Qaeda. Three basic positions on the moral legitimacy of the torture of terrorists may be outlined:

(1) An absolute-eternal ban on torture: torture is never to be justified, not even in what is called 'ticking time bomb' scenarios where a terrorist in the custody of the security services refuses to divulge the whereabouts of a ticking bomb that

could kill thousands of innocent civilians. This is the approach of the **European Convention of Human Rights** (ECHR) which prohibits torture under **Art 3** and does not allow it even in a national emergency under **Art 15**. On this view, torture is a moral outrage that can never be justified, whatever the cost of absolute prohibition.

(2) A second, more modified, position holds that the torture of terrorists is generally morally wrong but could be justified in extreme circumstances, a 'national emergency' where thousands of innocent lives are threatened; indeed, a political leader who refused to authorise torture in these circumstances could be said to have failed in his 'duties of office' to protect the public.

(3) A third, utilitarian position which says that whether torture is permissible demands a 'cost–benefit' analysis that would often rule out torture since the costs of torture (including the psychological harm to the torturers and the psychological and physical harm to the tortured person) would outweigh any benefits in terms of intelligence data obtained from the tortured terrorist. However, this 'utilitarian' approach to torture, weighing costs and benefits, might justify the torture of a terrorist beyond a 'national emergency' which is the threshold for position (2) on the permissibility on torture. The 'utilitarian' approach to torture might justify torture not to save thousands of lives directly but to obtain intelligence material on the organisational structure of a terrorist organisation.

Applying the Law

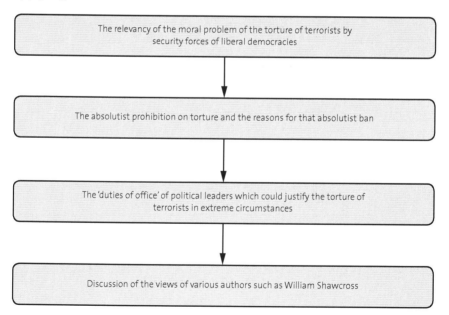

The relevancy of the moral problem of the torture of terrorists by security forces of liberal democracies

The absolutist prohibition on torture and the reasons for that absolutist ban

The 'duties of office' of political leaders which could justify the torture of terrorists in extreme circumstances

Discussion of the views of various authors such as William Shawcross

ANSWER

It is a truism of the post-9/11 age that the world now lives in an 'age of terror'. There were terrorist threats before 9/11, but what distinguishes the present threat is a combination and interplay of four deadly factors: (1) the willingness to employ suicide attackers to inflict mass casualties; (2) a so-called 'religious' justification to inflict mass casualties; (3) a transnational and trans-continental network of sympathetic groups dedicated to the Islamist cause; and (4) the obtaining and use of weapons of mass destruction against civilian targets as a so-called 'religious duty'. Given the scale of the current terrorist threat to modern Western democracies there has arisen what is known in legal and political philosophical circles as the TBS, or 'ticking bomb scenario'. The TBS postulates a situation where the security services of a Western democratic country have in their custody a known terrorist who boasts that he knows the whereabouts of a small nuclear bomb in the capital city of that country and that bomb is primed to explode in the next 24 hours. The moral dilemma for the security services and the government which controls it is: 'should the government authorise the torture of the known terrorist by the security services in order to locate the precise location of the atomic bomb so that it can be disarmed?'

Before we embark on a discussion of some of the issues involved in the TBS, it is necessary to remind ourselves that the leading Western democratic state, the United States, has used methods of torture officially sanctioned by the then President, George W Bush,[1] against a very small number of terrorist detainees. William Shawcross, in his book *Justice and the Enemy* (2011), comments:

> 'The "enhanced interrogation techniques" approved by President Bush were carried out by C.I.A. officers … included sleep deprivation, slapping, forced nudity, and prolonged wall standing. Most contentious of all was "waterboarding". In the method employed by the C.I.A., the prisoner is strapped with his head down on a tilted board; his face is wrapped in damp cloths onto which water is poured for twenty to forty seconds. This gives the sensation of drowning, causing a reflexive feeling of suffocation and panic. The rules stated that waterboarding could take place only with a physician present to monitor the prisoner's reaction.'

Waterboarding was, in fact, employed by the United States against only three suspected terrorists. However, if such techniques of interrogation are morally impermissible then their use against even one suspect would be a grave moral crime by the United States. Shawcross comments that the US intelligence community claimed that the 'waterboarding' of Khalid Sheikh Mohammed, the alleged 'no. 3' in the al-Qaeda leadership, yielded important intelligence information. Shawcross comments:

> 'The whole argument came to the fore once again after Osama bin Laden was found and executed by U.S. Navy SEALs in May 2011. Former officials of both the Bush administration and some serving members of the current Obama administration suggested

---

1 George W Bush (President of the United States 2000–2008) has said he would authorise again, if he could, the 'waterboarding' of terrorist suspects if that was necessary to protect the American people.

that important parts of the intelligence that eventually led to his hiding place in Abbottabad, Pakistan, had originally derived from enhanced interrogation of detainees including Khalid Sheikh Mohammed ... In 2010, Bush was still unrepentant: "Yeah, we waterboarded Khalid Sheikh Mohammed. I'd do it again to save lives."'

The starting point of the discussion as to whether torture of suspected terrorists is ever morally justifiable should start with a realisation of the particular problems of political office. The political theorist Michael Walzer, in a very influential essay, 'Political Action: The Problem of Dirty Hands' (1973), commented that a politician who holds high public office has 'duties of his office' which impose on the serving politician a considerable responsibility for consequences and outcomes. The serving politician, Walzer argues, 'acts on our behalf, even in our name'. Therefore getting morally 'dirty hands' to protect the public and so measure up to the duties of his office is 'a central feature of political life'. An individual who does not want to get 'dirty hands' in the pursuit of the public good or public safety is advised to remain in academia and not to take up the responsibilities of political office. Examples of political 'dirty hands' where the duties of political office might dictate a morally dubious course of action include: (1) the detention without trial of suspected enemy aliens or terrorist suspects; (2) the use of unmanned but computer-controlled drone attacks to drop high explosives on target suspected terrorists in foreign countries which could be viewed as political assassinations with the added risk of the deaths of innocent civilians; (3) the violation of Pakistani national territorial sovereignty by the United States in the attack on the Abbottabad compound housing Osama Bin Laden; and (4) the use of torture including 'waterboarding' by state agencies against suspected terrorists.

Given that political office necessarily involves the choosing of the morally dubious to protect the public, does this include and extend to political sanctioning of the use of torture as a legitimate method in extreme situations? Some commentators are prepared to rule out completely and absolutely the use of torture by the state and its security agencies. However, as Walzer points out, we would not want to be governed by people who would never ever be prepared to use torture. If I was living in a city where terrorists had planted a nuclear bomb I would hope that the politicians and security services would, in this extreme situation, authorise torture to discover the location of the bomb before it went off. However, even this scenario is a moral sell-out for some commentators committed to an absolute and eternal ban on the use of torture by the state. Eliza Manningham-Buller was Director of the British secret service MI5, and after her retirement she gave a series of talks for the BBC Reith Lectures in 2011 on 'Securing Freedom'. Lecture 2 was delivered in Leeds and broadcast on 13 September 2011 on BBC Radio 4. Manningham-Buller cannot be dismissed as one of the 'ivory tower academics' who in their lives have had no important decisions to make affecting the lives of millions of citizens. Manningham-Buller was in the front line of the fight against international Islamist terrorism and therefore her opinions carry great weight. She issued a strong condemnation of torture as a tool of government:

'Torture is illegal in our national law and in international law. It is wrong and never justified. It is a sadness and worse that the previous government of our great ally, the United States, chose to water-board some detainees. The argument that life-saving intelligence was thereby obtained, and I accept it was, still does not justify it. Torture should be utterly rejected even when it may offer the prospect of saving lives.'

This view expressed by Manningham-Buller may be termed the 'absolute and eternal' rejection of torture and is indeed reflected in **Art 3** of the **ECHR** to which the United Kingdom is a treaty member and which finds expression directly in UK law through the **Human Rights Act 1998, Art 3**. **Article 3** gives a non-derogable right not to be subject to torture or inhuman or degrading treatment. The **Art 3** right admits of no exceptions, not even for the gravest national emergency.

Manningham-Buller draws a historical parallel to justify her espousal of an absolute ban on torture:

'I am proud my Service refused to turn to the torture of high-level German prisoners in the Second World War, when in the early years, we stood alone and there was a high risk of our being invaded and becoming a Nazi province. So if not then, why should it be justified now?'

Manningham-Buller is adamant that the United States was wrong to torture terrorist detainees:

'I believe that the acquisition of short-term gain through water-boarding and other forms of mistreatment was a profound mistake and lost the United States moral authority and some of the widespread sympathy it had enjoyed as a result of 9/11. And I am confident that I know the answer to the question of whether torture has made the world a safer place. It hasn't.'

Manningham-Buller accepts that torture can get results:

'It's not the case that torture always produces false information, and that actually it's clear that torture can contribute to saving lives. But I don't think that's the point. I think the point is that it's not something that is right, legal or moral to do ... compromising our own integrity and decency as human beings by subjecting them to that sort of treatment?'

The need for the state itself not to compromise its own moral integrity by engaging in torture, even if very exceptionally, is a theme running through justifications for 'absolute-eternal' prohibitions on torture. However, Manningham-Buller also comments that the use of torture to obtain information from terrorists is very likely to be counter-productive in the long run:

'You might get short-term gain, but for every piece of information you might get from doing it, you radicalise, disenchant, disgust, turn to terrorism a lot of other people.'[2]

---

2   It was often said by critics of the British Government's policy of 'internment' of suspected Irish Republican terrorists detained without trial was 'the best recruiting sergeant' that the IRA (Irish Republican Army) ever had.

Another 'absolute-eternal' position concerning the rejection of torture is provided by Yuval Ginbar in his 2008 book, *Why Not Torture Terrorists?* Ginbar argues that

> 'the introduction of torture may shake the very foundations of a democratic state … to the extent that terrorists actually want to change the world, it may reasonably be argued that they would have scored an important victory if the taboo on torture were to be officially and legally lifted worldwide. The world would have, by taking that step, endorsed in principle part of their ends-justify-all-means philosophy, and in practice ensure the kind of no-holds-barred conflicts in which terrorists thrive.'

Ginbar argues that to sanction torture is to sanction 'an institution' which would morally pollute all participants and, as such, 'may breed self-perpetuation'. In a non-torturing state, the state may not be able to guarantee us absolute safety from the terrorists, but no torturing state has been able to do that either, and at least in the non-torturing state we will all be absolutely safe from torture abuse by our own state. Ginbar, though, does not base his total opposition to the use of torture by the state on the morally polluting effects torture would have on a state that adopted torture or on the insecurity caused to citizens knowing that their state engaged in torture. As important as these considerations are for Ginbar, the ultimate argument against torture is an argument based on humanity: in everything the state does there should be a 'speck of humanity'. Ginbar comments:

> 'nations, groups and individuals will never agree unanimously on what goals they should pursue – the ideal form of government, the ideal life, the true faith etc. What I believe humans may be able to agree, indeed should agree, is that in pursuing any goals whatsoever, they maintain that little speck of humanity at all times … which in turn means never to torture or otherwise ill-treat another human being, whatever the circumstances.'

Certainly the current law of both the United Kingdom and the **ECHR** reflect the absolutist rejection of torture explained by Eliza Manningham-Buller and Yuval Ginbar. **Article 3** of the **ECHR** is so strong a provision that the Grand Chamber of the European Court of Human Rights held in *Chahal v United Kingdom* (1996) that where there is a real risk that a non-national might be subject to torture or inhuman or degrading treatment in his own country he cannot be deported, even if his deportation is required on national security grounds. The European Court of Human Rights held:

> 'Whenever substantial grounds have been shown for believing that an individual would face a real risk of being subjected to treatment contrary to Article 3 if removed to another state, the responsibility of the contracting state to safeguard him or her against such treatment is engaged in the event of expulsion.'

This hardline approach against torture has manifested itself in the UK courts as well, no doubt influenced by the jurisprudence on torture of the European Court of Human Rights. Indeed under the **Human Rights Act 1998, s 2**, the UK courts must take into account decisions of the European Court of Human Rights when assessing convention rights. In the House of Lords case of *A v Home Secretary* (2005) the highest court in the UK legal system emphatically laid down a rule, described by Lord Bingham as a 'constitutional rule', that all evidence obtained by torture, wherever the location of that torture in the world, was automatically inadmissible as evidence in all UK courts. This constitutional rule was absolute in that it applied no matter how reliable that 'torture evidence' was and no matter how important the case was to the national security of the United Kingdom and no matter that UK security agencies had no part whatsoever in the torture. Lord Bingham referred to the English common law's rejection of evidence from torture in *A v Home Secretary*:

> 'in rejecting the use of torture, whether applied to potential defendants or potential witnesses, the common law was moved by the cruelty of the practice as applied to those not convicted of crime, by the inherent unreliability of confessions or evidence so procured and by the belief that it degraded all those who lent themselves to the practice.'

In the case of *A and others v Secretary of State for the Home Department*, the Government argued that evidence obtained by torture abroad without the complicity of the British authorities could be considered by the Special Immigration Appeals Commission. The House of Lords extended the common law's ban on torture evidence from UK security services to a ban on torture evidence obtained worldwide. Lord Carswell commented:

> 'the duty not to countenance the use of torture by admission of evidence so obtained in judicial proceedings must be regarded as paramount and … to allow its admission would shock the conscience, abuse or degrade the proceedings and involve the state in moral defilement.'

Whilst it can be accepted that as *a judicial* principle the courts should never allow into evidence material obtained by torture wherever in the world the torture was perpetrated, as a *political* choice it is much harder to accept that torture can never be morally justified, not even when the suspected terrorist admits he knows where a hidden nuclear device is and that it is soon to detonate. Lord Bingham, in his book *The Rule of Law* (2010), comments of torture that there are 'some practices so abhorrent as not to be tolerable, even when the safety of the state is said to be at risk … There are some things which even the supreme power in *the* state should not be allowed to do, ever'. However, it is by no means clear that it would *always* be morally wrong for a serving politician to order the torture of a suspected terrorist, for example to discover the whereabouts of a hidden nuclear bomb in a city. William Shawcross in his book *Justice and the Enemy* (2011) has two useful quotations which suggest that no responsible politician, responsible for the safety of millions of his fellow citizens, should ever rule out the use of torture in all circumstances. Shawcross quotes Dean Acheson, who said:

> 'No people in history have ever survived who thought they could protect their freedom by making themselves inoffensive to their enemies.'[3]

---

3 The failed policy of 'appeasement' of Hitler's Nazi regime in the 1930s is often derided and politicians such as Neville Chamberlain associated with the policy have a poor historical reputation. 'Appeasement' involved taking a conciliatory and non-warlike stance to Hitler's expansionist goals.

Shawcross then quotes Reinhold Niebuhr's warning that

> 'we take and must continue to take, morally hazardous actions to preserve our civilization.'

NOTES

William Shawcross's book, *Justice and the Enemy* (2011), is balanced and recommended on this topic. Yuval Ginbar's book, *Why Not Torture Terrorists?* (2008), is a good modern restatement of the absolutist position on torture. For the 'utilitarian' view that torture may be morally permitted beyond a 'national emergency', see WL Twining and PE Twining, 'Bentham on Torture' (1973), Northern Ireland Legal Quarterly 24.

QUESTION 25

National security should be the supreme law, or as Cicero put it, 'the safety of the people is the supreme law'.

▶ Discuss the validity of this opinion.

How to Answer this Question

The tradition of thought going back to the Roman politician Cicero holds that the first and second duties of government is to secure the safety of the population of the nation. Indeed, as Lord Donaldson recognised in *Cheblak* (1991), the securing of national security is the prerequisite for the enjoyment by citizens of all other human rights. In 'failed' states such as Somalia or the Democratic Republic of Congo citizens have little protection against murder, rape, kidnapping, extortion and robbery because there is no national security, no sense of living in a well-ordered society. Indeed, because of its vital importance 'national security' concerns can be carried too far and can be used to justify unfair behaviour by the state: for example, the mass detention of persons of Italian and German descent under the infamous regulation 18B during the Second World War in the United Kingdom, and similar mass detentions of people of Japanese origin in the United States following the attack by Japan on the United States in December 1941. However, the pendulum can swing too far the other way against 'national security' concerns and in favour of human rights. Arguably, the decision in *Chahal* (1996) confirmed in the case of *Saadi* (2008) by the European Court of Human Rights (ECtHR) puts too little emphasis on the urgent needs of national security by preventing a state such as the United Kingdom from deporting a suspected or known foreign terrorist back to their country of origin if there is a real risk of that person being tortured. It should always be remembered that a state signed up to the **European Convention of Human Rights** (ECHR) has a duty under **Art 2** to protect the 'right to life' of each citizen potentially threatened by a mass terrorist attack.

Applying the Law

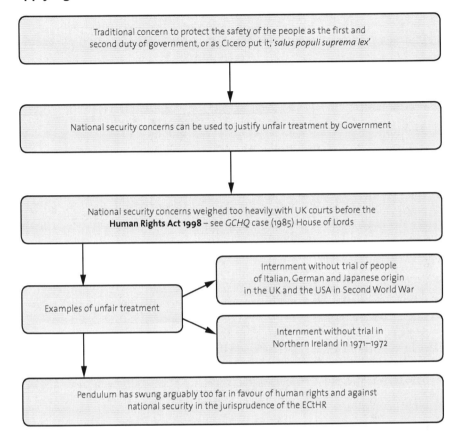

Traditional concern to protect the safety of the people as the first and second duty of government, or as Cicero put it, *'salus populi suprema lex'*

National security concerns can be used to justify unfair treatment by Government

National security concerns weighed too heavily with UK courts before the **Human Rights Act 1998** – see *GCHQ* case (1985) House of Lords

Examples of unfair treatment

Internment without trial of people of Italian, German and Japanese origin in the UK and the USA in Second World War

Internment without trial in Northern Ireland in 1971–1972

Pendulum has swung arguably too far in favour of human rights and against national security in the jurisprudence of the ECtHR

ANSWER

The first duty of any responsible and decent government is to protect the citizens of that state. Indeed, for writers such as Hobbes and Locke there is a mutual bond of obligation between ruler and ruled. Hobbes argued that the citizens of a state had the right of rebellion only when the sovereign power could no longer give effective protection for the lives and property of its citizens. If the sovereign power could guarantee protection to citizens then Hobbes thought this grounded an absolute obligation on citizens to obey the sovereign power – what Hobbes termed 'The Leviathan', the awe-inspiring sovereign power. Locke, in distinction to Hobbes (and one reason why Locke, not Hobbes, is the father of liberalism), believed in a much wider power of rebellion in citizens to the central authority such as the sovereign's interference with the liberties of the subject. However, for Locke as for Hobbes, a significant failure of a sovereign to guarantee protection of the life and property of the citizen gave citizens the right to overthrow the sovereign and replace it with a more effective new sovereign. The creation, preservation and continuance of the 'pact of protection and obedience' between citizens and state is therefore at the heart of the founding fathers of modern political philosophy in the seventeenth century: namely Hobbes and Locke.

An earlier thinker, Machiavelli, also made an absolute priority for the security of the state but in a very different way from Hobbes and Locke. Machiavelli pointed out that the traditional Christian virtues of humility, forgiveness and meekness were admirable in the private sphere of life but, given the evil of the world and the wicked hearts of men, then the ruler, be it Christian or otherwise, had to learn to occasionally do the opposite of what Christian theology teaches in order to safeguard the security and stability of the state. In other words, for Machiavelli, Christian principles and effective political leadership were not always compatible. Machiavelli argued that:

> 'A man who wishes to profess goodness at all times will come to ruin among so many who are not good. Therefore, it is necessary for a prince who wishes to maintain himself to learn how not to be good, and to use this knowledge or not use it according to necessity.'

Machiavelli believed that the wise ruler to safeguard his country must generally be virtuous, and not only seem to be virtuous, but to actually possess this quality. However, when necessary, and only when necessary to maintain the state, the wise ruler must quickly change from Christian principles to pagan severity, harshness, deceit and cunning. Machiavelli thus advances a thesis that the political ruler (unlike the private citizen who must cleave to Christian virtue), to safeguard his state from those who would wish to harm or destroy it, should act:

> 'against his faith, against charity, against humanity. And so it is necessary that he should have a mind ready to turn itself according to the way the winds of Fortune and the changing circumstances command him. And he should not depart from the good if it is possible to do so, but he should know how to enter into evil when forced by necessity.'

Machiavelli's lesson to the modern world is that if the government is to fulfil its primary duty to protect the people of the state, it cannot always abide by Christian principles, which although admirable in private life, are not always suited to the harsh and brutal environment of politics and international politics. A simple illustration to show the discontinuity between Christian ethical principles and realism in political life is to focus on the Christian duty not to deceive and lie to others. In order to protect its citizens, the government of a state must often withhold information from the public lest it fall into the wrong hands or cause panic. The responsible government may have to go beyond withholding information to actually publishing false information if, during wartime, such information would seriously confuse and distract the enemy. As the modern philosopher Bernard Williams comments:

> 'a moderate version of Machiavelli's thesis: the responsibilities of government are sufficiently different from those of private individuals to make governmental virtue a rather different matter from that of private individuals – or rather (and this is very much the point) from that of individuals who are being protected by a government. In particular, any government is charged with the security of its citizens, a responsibility which cannot be discharged without secrecy, and which it will be lucky if it can discharge without force and fraud.'

However, there has been something of a cultural shift in Western Europe over the last few decades driven by the human rights movement and human rights law such as the **ECHR** which has significantly watered down the idea that claims of national security should be the pre-eminent value in deciding the legitimacy of government action in fields such as deportation, anti-terrorist laws and the use of evidence obtained by torture. Perhaps because the severe human rights abuses of the Second World War era were often justified by an appeal to 'state or national security', and oppressive regimes both before and since the Second World War have often tried to justify repression and human rights abuses by appeal to national security (the Syrian regime of Assad in 2012 did exactly that), when it comes to democratic states some judges have refused to allow national security claims by government to trump all claims of human rights. A good illustration of some Western European judges prioritising human rights law above claims of national security concerns **Art 3** of the **ECHR**. This article forbids, without any exception, the use of torture, inhuman or degrading treatment. It might be accepted, with reservations, that no state signed up to the **ECHR** should ever use torture on anyone, but the ECtHR gave an added and, to some politicians, an unwelcome twist to the scope of **Art 3**. In the case of *Chahal v United Kingdom* (1996) the ECtHR held that **Art 3** obliged states not to remove a person to another state where he or she would face a real risk of torture or inhuman or degrading treatment, notwithstanding any threat the person might pose to public safety or national security. As Lord Bingham comments in *The Rule of Law* (2010):

> 'That the decision [*Chahal*] is a very unwelcome impediment to government action cannot be doubted. Dr. John Reid (then Home Secretary) described the judgment as "outrageously disproportionate"'.

This statement by John Reid in May 2007 attacking the *Chahal* decision 10 years earlier is a reflection of some politicians' anger at some judges prioritising human rights above national security concerns. Indeed the British Government tried to get the decision in *Chahal* amended but the attempt failed in the case of *Saadi v Italy* (2008). Indeed, since the decision in *Chahal* in 1996, the security situation in Europe has deteriorated rapidly in the wake of the September 11, 2001 terrorist attacks, with serious incidents in Istanbul in 2003, in Madrid in 2004 and London in July 2005, as well as other, less dramatic attacks. In the case of *Saadi v Italy* (2008) the UK Government intervened to try to persuade the ECtHR to recant in a case in which a Tunisian resident in Italy was threatened with deportation back to Tunisia, where he faced a risk of torture. The European Court of Human Rights strongly reaffirmed its approach in *Chahal*. The ECtHR said in *Saadi v Italy*:

> 'states face immense difficulties in modern times in protecting their communities from terrorist violence. It (the Court) cannot therefore underestimate the scale of the danger of terrorism today and the threat it poses to the community. That must not, however, call into question the absolute nature of Article 3.'

Of course, **Art 3**, in itself, only prohibits the use of torture, inhuman or degrading treatment but does not involve, on its own terms, an act of deportation by a signatory state of a foreign person considered to be a threat to national security to a country where there is a possibility, but not a certainty, that he will be tortured. However, in *Saadi v Italy* the

ECtHR emphasised that national security concerns had no weight whatsoever in this area of ECtHR jurisprudence. The UK Government, intervening, argued that the decision in *Chahal* failed to give proper weight to the public's right to life under **Art 2, ECHR** or to national security. The UK Government argued that the test in the *Chahal* case should be modified to allow a degree of risk of torture to be balanced against the threat posed to the public or state; and that, where a state presented some evidence of a threat to national security, the person alleging a risk of torture should have to prove that it was more likely than not to eventuate.

The Court's Grand Chamber unanimously rejected these arguments. It robustly reasserted the absolute character of **Art 3** and the test was 'was there a real risk that the person concerned will be subjected in the receiving country to treatment prohibited by Article 3'.

For some commentators, the decision in *Saadi* reaffirming *Chahal* was to be welcomed. David Feldman in July 2008's Cambridge Law Journal commented: 'The judgment in Saadi reaffirms fundamental values of humanity: a society which fails to treat terrorism suspects with more respect than terrorists have for society forfeits the moral justification for defending itself.'

Mr Feldman misses the point, however: the issue is whether national security and the safety of the public should have some role in this area of the law and not be excluded altogether as the cases of *Chahal* and *Saadi* assert. To give some weight to national security and the safety of the people is not to treat terrorists with the same lack of respect with which terrorists treat society. It is true that before the cultural change brought about by the **Human Rights Act 1998** in British judicial attitudes towards human rights and the competing claims of national security, UK judges used to be very 'executive minded' about national security. In other words, earlier generations of judges, before the **Human Rights Act** era, used to defer to the Government over national security claims and largely allowed national security claims by government to override civil liberties. However, in 2012, the pendulum has swung arguably too far the other way in favour of human rights and against genuine concerns of national security. UK judges, heavily influenced by the human rights 'citadel' of the European Court of Human Rights, arguably do not defer enough to the needs of national security expressed by the executive. Professor Finnis, in his 2011 collection of essays *Human Rights and Common Good*, comments that 'the power to admit, exclude and expel aliens was among the earliest and most widely recognized powers of the sovereign state'. Finnis argues that unless this power of sovereign states to exclude undesirable aliens is understood to be 'a constitutional principle ... the power will crumble', eroded by human rights law. Finnis argues that 'the power of exclusion ... needs to be understood as one of those elements of the common good which the law of our constitution articulates and promotes'. Specifically of the ruling of the ECtHR in *Chahal v UK* (1996), Finnis is critical of its lack of concern for legitimate national security interests:

> 'The absoluteness of a state's obligation not to engage in torture and other practices contrary to Article 3 in no way entails that the person with such an absolute right has thereby the right not to be subjected to any form of treatment (e.g. deportation) that

might have the foreseeable but unintended and unwelcome side effect of his being tortured or ill-treated by some other persons ... It is one thing for a state to deliver persons to another state *so as* to enable the latter to torture them and quite another matter to remove/deliver them to another state with all practically possible precaution against their being tortured thereafter and with the sole object of removing the real threat their presence poses to the lives of people in the removing state. Chahal's Article 3 ruling treats the intentions of the removing state as completely irrelevant and declares that the deportee's activities however undesirable or dangerous cannot be a material consideration. Taking into account Article 3's extension beyond torture to "degrading treatment" and the breadth of that concept in recent European Court of Human Rights jurisprudence, Chahal's ruling on Article 3 is juridically unsound by over-breadth, and shocking to conscience by its *indifference to the human rights threatened by the would-be deportee*. The same is regrettably true of the European Court of Human Rights Grand Chamber's unanimous ratification of Chahal in Saadi v Italy (2008) ... on all the main points the submissions of the United Kingdom, intervening, were sound but rejected by the European Court of Human Rights with the mantra that Article 3 is absolute.'

The overly 'executive minded' nature of the UK judiciary before the **Human Rights Act** era has been noted by many commentators. Adam Tomkins, in a collection of essays entitled *The Legal Protection of Human Rights* (2011), comments:

'It is well established that, in the twentieth century, British courts were routinely weak in judicially reviewing the legality and reasonableness of government actions alleged to have been taken in the interests of national security.'

Tomkins goes on to allege that 'The [UK] courts notoriously failed to enforce the rule of law in a whole series of war-time and peace-time decisions concerning such issues as internment and deportation.'

The classic cases usually quoted to show old-time judicial bias in favour of national security at the expense of human rights include *Liversidge v Anderson* (1942), *R v Secretary of State for Home Affairs, ex parte Hosenball* (1977) and *R v Secretary of State for the Home Department, ex parte Cheblak* (1991). In *Liversidge v Anderson* (1942) the House of Lords held that the Secretary of State during wartime acted in good faith in ordering the internment of an individual under **reg 18B** of the **Defence Regulations 1939**. In the order the minister recites that he has reasonable cause to believe a person to be of hostile associations, then the court cannot inquire whether in fact the Secretary of State had reasonable grounds for his belief. The House of Lords in declining to review the minister's decision to order internment said that the matter is one for the executive discretion of the Secretary of State. This case reflects a general abdication of judicial responsibility when the 'magic words' national security were uttered by the Home Secretary. As Lord Justice Sedley said with reference to pre-**Human Rights Act** judicial attitudes to government claims of national security in his collection of essays *Ashes and Sparks* (2011): 'the Home Secretary had only to say the magic words "national security".'

In the case of *Cheblak* (1991) the British Government decided to deport the applicant, a Lebanese citizen, at the time of the first Gulf war against Iraq in January 1991. The Home Secretary decided to deport Cheblak under the **Immigration Act 1971** on the ground that his deportation was conducive to the public good for reasons of 'national security'. The legislative scheme precluded any right of appeal against the decision of the Home Secretary, although the applicant might make representations to an independent, non-statutory panel established by the Home Secretary to advise him on such cases. The Court of Appeal said that, as long as the Home Secretary was acting in good faith, the Court would not investigate his grounds for believing that the deportation of the applicant was necessary to national security. The Court of Appeal held:

> 'that since national security was the exclusive responsibility of the executive, and since the Secretary of State was empowered to decide when deportation of a foreign national would be ordered, the exercise of his discretion being confined only by the requirement that he should act in good faith, the court was required to accept his evidence … there were no grounds for granting leave to apply for judicial review.'

UK governments post-**Human Rights Act 1998** must look back to cases like *Cheblak* in 1991 and think that life was so much easier then. If the Government wanted to deport a foreign national as a security risk then, assuming they were acting in good faith, the Government could rely on the courts to defer to the decision of government and put up no legal resistance. Now the position is radically different and both the ECtHR and the UK courts can deny the Government the right to deport a foreign national as a security risk if there is a 'real risk' that the person to be deported might be tortured in their country of origin (*Chahal* (1996), *Saadi* (2008)).

However, what is sometimes overlooked by commentators on the *Cheblak* case in 1991 is the comment by Lord Donaldson, Master of the Rolls, who observed:

> 'In accepting, as we must, that to some extent the needs of national security must displace civil liberties … it is not irrelevant to remember that the maintenance of national security underpins and is the foundation of all our civil liberties.'

Lord Donaldson makes a cogent point that is often overlooked. If civil society collapses into significant anarchy due to widespread terrorist attacks then citizens' right to life (**Art 2**), right not to be tortured or subject to inhuman or degrading treatment (**Art 3**), right to liberty and security (**Art 5**) and right to a private and family life (**Art 8**) are all under threat if mob rule takes over in a society. It is usually the most vulnerable in society who suffer the most when 'security' breaks down, the most vulnerable being the ones most in need of human rights protection by the state. Lord Donaldson is right – national security under the rule of law is the foundation stone of all other human rights. Lord Donaldson understood that justice does not exist in a vacuum, but in a political order which inspires confidence in the citizens and deters destructive elements from both within and outside the country from attacking the political order of the country.

The case which probably represented the high water mark of judicial deference to claims by the executive of 'national security' in civil liberties/human rights cases is the judgment of Lord Denning, Master of the Rolls, in *R v Secretary of State for Home Affairs, ex parte Hosenball* (1977). An American journalist, hardly an ongoing threat to national security, was ordered to be deported on those grounds because in the past he had published articles on how the UK Government used electronic surveillance in security matters. Hosenball appealed against the deportation order by the Home Secretary by way of judicial review in the UK courts as there had been breach of the rules of natural justice in the refusal to supply him with particulars of the allegations he had to meet. The Court of Appeal held that where national security was involved, the ordinary principles of natural justice were modified for the protection of the realm. The left-wing commentator Professor JAG Griffith commented that 'Lord Denning seemed to accept that the courts had no part to play [in cases involving national security] because the government never erred'. In what Professor Griffith labelled 'a remarkable passage' (and not in a good way), Lord Denning said in *Hosenball*:

> 'There is a conflict between the interests of national security on the one hand and the freedom of the individual on the other. The balance between these two is not for a court of law. It is for the Home Secretary. He is the person entrusted by Parliament with the task. In some parts of the world national security has on occasion been used as an excuse for all sorts of infringements of individual liberty. But not in England. Both during the wars and after them successive ministers have discharged their duties to the complete satisfaction of the people at large ... They have never interfered with the liberty or the freedom of movement of any individual except where it is absolutely necessary for the safety of the state.'

Obviously such judicial complacency about the 'wisdom' of central government as expressed in *Hosenball* (1977) can be easily mocked. However, Lord Denning's comments do reveal how far modern UK judges have come, perhaps too far, in being sceptical of government claims in a court of law to 'national security'. Lord Denning in *Hosenball* also commented:

> 'It is a case in which national security is involved: and our history shows that when the state itself is endangered, our cherished freedoms may have to take second place. Even natural justice itself may suffer a set-back ... times of peace hold their dangers too. Spies, subverters and saboteurs may be mingling amongst us, putting on a most innocent exterior. If they are British subjects, we must deal with them here. If they are foreigners, they can be deported. The rules of natural justice have to be modified in regard to foreigners here who prove themselves unwelcome and ought to be deported.'

As Lord Justice Sedley remarks in *Ashes and Sparks* (2011), in the 1985 House of Lords case, *Council of Civil Service Unions v Minister for the Civil Service*, the Prime Minister eventually uttered the 'magic words' 'national security' and walked away from court a winner. As Sir Stephen Sedley commented in the February 2012 *London Review of Books*: 'when, at the last minute, the government produced national security as its reason for banning trade unions at GCHQ, its surveillance headquarters, in 1984 the courts backed off without demur.'

In this case, the *GCHQ* case, in 1984 the Government under Mrs Thatcher suddenly banned trade union activity at its top-secret listening headquarters, GCHQ, without consulting the unions about the change of policy. The reason for this abrupt change of government policy to ban unions at GCHQ was national security concern – a fear that strike action might disrupt vital security work at GCHQ as it had been disrupted by union-led strike action in the past. Lord Fraser said in the *GCHQ* case:

> 'The decision on whether the requirements of national security outweigh the duty of fairness in any particular case is for the Government and not for the courts; the Government alone has access to the necessary information, and in any event the judicial process is unsuitable for reaching decisions on national security.'

The House of Lords did insist on a minimum procedural protection in the *GCHQ* case: namely that the Government was under an obligation to produce evidence that the decision was, in fact, based on grounds of national security (see the case of *The Zamora* (1916)). Lord Scarman said in the *GCHQ* case:

> 'I would dismiss this appeal for one reason only. I am satisfied that the respondent has made out a case on the ground of national security … the respondent refused to consult the unions before issuing her instruction because she feared that, if she did, union-organised disruption of the monitoring services of GCHQ could well result.'

Lord Diplock said in the case of *GCHQ*:

> 'the crucial point of law in this case is whether procedural propriety must give way to national security … national security, for which the executive government bears the responsibility and alone has access to sources of information that qualify it to judge what the necessary action is … To that there can, in my opinion, be only one sensible answer. That answer is "Yes."'

Summing up, we can observe that pre the **Human Rights Act**, when confronted by executive claims of 'national security', the courts backed off, insisting only that the Government produce 'some evidence' of the need to act in the interests of national security, with the judges always willing not to scrutinise too far the plausibility of that 'evidence' produced by the Government. What has happened post the **Human Rights Act 1998** are the following two developments: (1) a willingness by the UK courts sometimes not to allow claims of national security to outweigh the claims of human rights; and (2) a much more sceptical attitude by the UK courts to the claims of the UK Government to be acting in the interests of 'national security'.

We need to examine the possible reasons for the two judicial developments to 'national security' claims mentioned above. There has been a discernible change in judicial culture since the **Human Rights Act 1998** in which UK judges have heightened awareness of their role in protecting fundamental human rights from the claims of the executive government. Lord Bingham, in his book *Lives of the Law* (2011), comments of this change in judicial culture: 'a heightened awareness among judges of the sensitivity of the judicial role … a heightened sense of the judges' duty to respect and defend fundamental principles.'

Lord Justice Sedley, in *Ashes and Sparks*, comments similarly to Lord Bingham of a sea change in judicial culture in the United Kingdom brought about by the incorporation of the **ECHR** in the **Human Rights Act 1998**: 'most of [the Convention] has deepened our own jurisprudence and sharpened our judicial standards.'

We have explained the change in judicial attitudes to government claims of national security in UK court cases but there has been a parallel development with UK courts being much more sceptical than before about the evidence the Government purports to show the courts of the 'national security' concerns. This judicial scepticism has emerged following highly publicised examples where the Government was proved wrong about its intelligence information, especially the erroneous intelligence information presented by Tony Blair's New Labour Government to justify the invasion of Iraq in 2003 concerning alleged weapons of mass destruction held by Saddam Hussein. David Feldman comments in the Cambridge Law Journal 2005:

> 'The Human Rights Act 1998 and well publicised weaknesses in the evaluation and use of intelligence material by the Secret Intelligence Service and the Government in seeking to justify the second Gulf War combined to ensure that heightened scrutiny where human rights are engaged … would henceforth be a reality.'

Similar arguments were made by Adam Tomkins in Current Legal Problems (2011), in an article entitled 'National Security and the Due Process of Law'. Tompkins argues:

> 'courts must be alert to guard against the possibility that they may be dazzled by overblown Government claims as to sensitivity, risk and security. For the record shows that such claims may often be exaggerated and are sometimes wholly spurious.'

Tompkins, reflecting the new judicial mood, argues that 'the first maxim of our national security law' should be as follows:

> 'If national security comes to court, as come to court it will, it is not the court, its values, its decision-making, and its processes that must give way in the face of Government claims about what is required in the name of security. It is these claims that must give way if, on examining the evidence, they do not satisfy the court. Decision-making in national security and law-making in national security should be evidence based and evidence driven. If we stick to that as our starting point, we can surely strive for a national security law that is fair and just, and that gives legal process its due.'

The key turning point case in the UK courts' new attitude to national security claims by the UK Government was the House of Lords decision in *A v Secretary of State for the Home Department* (2004), also known as 'the Belmarsh case'. The case concerned a number of foreign nationals detained in Belmarsh prison, London, without charge or trial, indefinitely, on suspicion that they were involved in terrorism. The legal authority to so detain them was derived from legislation called the **Anti-Terrorism, Crime and Security Act 2001** passed after the atrocities of 9/11 in New York, Washington and Pennsylvania. The Belmarsh detainees could not be deported to their home countries since the case of *Chahal* (1996) decided by the ECtHR forbade the deportation of foreign nationals to countries where there was a real risk of torture in the country they were deported to – and that was the risk which awaited the Belmarsh detainees if deported to their home countries. Lord Bingham, one of the leading judges in 'the Belmarsh case', comments in his book *Lives of the Law* (2011):

> 'a strong majority [of judges in the case] held the Act to be incompatible with the Convention rights of the detainees on two grounds. The first of these was that the Act discriminated against the detainees on the ground of their nationality since they as foreign nationals were subjected to long-term incarceration without charge or trial whereas no such penalty could be imposed on British nationals similarly suspected. Secondly, the measure was held to be irrational because if the detainees were really regarded as serious potential terrorists it made very little sense to allow them, if they could, to go to other countries in which they could pursue their terrorist designs.'

The House of Lords in *A v Secretary of State for the Home Department* (2004) used **s 4** of the **Human Rights Act 1998** to declare the detention without trial provisions of the **Anti-Terrorism Act 2001** incompatible with **Art 14** (prohibition on discrimination) read with **Art 5** (the right to liberty). The UK Government was not, under the **Human Rights Act 1998**, legally obliged to change the legislation declared incompatible by the House of Lords but did repeal the offending legislation and replaced indefinite detention without trial by a system of house arrest called 'control orders' introduced by the **Prevention of Terrorism Act 2005**. Lord Bingham in *Lives of the Law* comments of the dramatic outcome of 'the Belmarsh case': 'it was on any showing a very bad result for the government … perhaps as serious a reverse as any of our governments has ever suffered in our domestic courts.'

Other commentators attest to the iconic status of the 'Belmarsh case' where the House of Lords allowed claims of human rights to trump purported government claims of the necessity of the legislative measures for 'national security'. David Feldman, in the Cambridge Law Journal (2005), commented that the decision in the Belmarsh case 'was perhaps the most powerful judicial defence of liberty since … Somerset v Stewart (1772)'.

Conor Gearty in Current Legal Problems (2005) commented that the decision of the House of Lords in the Belmarsh case was 'the finest assertion of civil liberties that has emerged from a British court since at least Entick v Carrington (1785)'.

Somerset v Stewart (1772) involved a decision by Lord Mansfield to order the freedom of a black slave kept in chains in a ship on the River Thames destined for the slave plantations of Virginia, United States. Lord Mansfield, on a writ of habeas corpus, ordered Somerset to be freed in an iconic judicial decision of the anti-slavery movement. In *Entick v Carrington* (1785), Lord Camden denounced the use of general search warrants by agents of the state and found for the claimant against the Government in an action for trespass. The fact that the 'Belmarsh case' is compared by commentators to legal icons such as *Somerset's* case and *Entick v Carrington* is an illustration of how quickly iconic the judicial decision of the House of Lords in the 'Belmarsh case' became. Lord Bingham commented in his 2010 book *The Rule of Law*: 'detaining suspects indefinitely without charge or trial [is] a practice formerly regarded as the hallmark of repressive authoritarian regimes'.[4]

It is hardly surprising, in the light of the above comment by Lord Bingham, that he and the other Law Lords found that the detention without trial provisions of the **Anti-Terrorism Act 2001** violated the **Human Rights Act 1998**. A contrary view would have been to accept that detention without trial of terrorist suspects is in normal times unacceptable but that detention without trial is a necessary if regrettable measure in times of national emergency, such as a sustained terrorist onslaught against society.

However, Lord Bingham and the other Law Lords were prepared to accept that the system of house arrest known as 'control orders', introduced to replace detention without trial, was legitimate in terms of the **Human Rights Act 1998**. Lord Bingham explicitly referred in his judgment in the case of '*MB*' (2007) to the human rights of the public under **Art 2**, the right to life – to be free of the threat of terrorist attack on their lives and the UK Government's duty to ensure the **Art 2** rights of the public. Lord Bingham said in '*MB*':

> 'States are under the obligation to take the measures needed to protect the fundamental rights of everyone within their jurisdiction against terrorist acts, especially Article 2 – the right to life. This positive obligation justifies States' fight against terrorism in accordance with present guidelines.'

Therefore the 'control orders' regime of house arrest introduced by the **Prevention of Terrorism Act 2005** was held legitimate by the House of Lords judges – indeed, given the needs of national security the senior judges could hardly have declared the 'control orders' scheme incompatible with human rights legislation after declaring the previous attempt at protecting the public, detention without trial, as incompatible under **s 4** of the **Human Rights Act 1998**. Parliament itself abolished the 'control orders' regime and replaced it with similar, modified provisions in the **Terrorism Investigatory Measures Act 2011**.

....

4 Arguably Lord Bingham is not quite accurate when he claims that the 'hallmark' of 'repressive authoritarian regimes' is detention without trial. The British Government in the period 1940–2001 has used detention without trial on three occasions yet can hardly be described as a 'repressive authoritarian regime'. The three occasions were: (1) using Regulation 18B during the 1939–1945 war to detain without charge or trial 'enemy aliens' such as people of Italian or German descent; (2) the use of 'internment' to detain without trial hundreds of republicans in Northern Ireland in 1971; (3) the 'detention without trial' of foreign terrorist suspects under the **Anti-Terrorism, Crime and Security Act 2001**. The 'hallmark' of repressive authoritarian regimes is not detention without trial, although it is a common practice of 'repressive authoritarian regimes'. The hallmarks of 'repressive authoritarian regimes' can be reduced to two core practices: (1) the execution (the murder) of political, religious and ethnic opponents of the regime: whether throwing people out of aeroplanes hundreds of miles out into the South Atlantic as practised in Argentina during the 1970s 'dirty war' or feeding political opponents to the crocodiles as practised by Idi Amin in Uganda in the 1970s; (2) the routine use of torture against detainees or against the families of detainees as practised by regimes from Iran to North Korea.

It is important to note that it is not only the courts but Parliament itself that has asserted the priority of human rights over national security concerns when national security concerns are felt to be inflated and exaggerated. Lord Bingham comments in *The Rule of Law*:

'there has been gradual erosion of one of the most fundamental safeguards of personal liberty in this country: the limit on the time a person suspected of having committed a terrorist crime may be held in custody without being charged or released. In 1997 the period was four days. In 2000 it was raised to seven days, in 2003 to fourteen days, in 2006 to twenty-eight days (Schedule 8 to Terrorism Act 2000, as amended by section 23 Terrorism Act 2006). But this was not enough. In late 2005 the government sought to raise the limit to ninety days. This bid was roundly defeated in the House of Commons. Undeterred, the government attempted to increase the period to forty-two days, narrowly succeeding in the House of Commons and abandoning the attempt only after an overwhelming defeat in the House of Lords on 15 October 2008.'

There is a concern in some quarters that some judges both at the ECtHR and in the UK jurisdiction are so embedded in the culture of 'human rights' that they neglect the importance and the legitimate weight of the claims of national security. The *Sunday Telegraph* (1 April 2012) reported adversely on a decision by the Court of Appeal concerning the refusal of entry to the United Kingdom of a Russian national suspected of being a contract killer. The *Sunday Telegraph* commented:

'One of the many astonishing aspects of a Court of Appeal decision that we report today is that the three judges … gave no weight at all to the issue of national security. The case involves a Russian individual, identified as "E1" who, as MI5 testified, is almost certainly involved in planning the assassination of a Chechnyan exile living in Britain. E1 is already thought to have played a significant role in the murder of another Chechnyan exile living in Britain. Not surprisingly the Home Secretary decided that E1's presence in Britain would not be conducive to the public good. Assassinations carried out by foreigners on British soil are not only bad in themselves: they also pose a real risk of harm to innocent bystanders. The Court did not even mention national security when explaining why it was going to overrule the Home Secretary's decision not to allow E1 into Britain. Instead, the judges focused on whether being excluded from Britain could have harmed E1's ability to mount an effective appeal. The Appeal Court decided that the Home Secretary's decision should be overturned. This is the kind of decision that could only be given by judges who have insulated themselves from the considerations that any reasonable person would put at the top of their list. It would not have violated any fundamental legal principles for the judges to decide that considerations of national security outweighed E1's right to be present at his appeal. That was what the judge in the lower court decided. His judgment was a model of good sense. We hope that the judges of the Supreme Court will take a more reasonable view of the importance of national security, and overturn the decision.'

In this case, *E1 v Secretary of State for the Home Department* (2012) Court of Appeal, whilst E1 was abroad the Secretary of State directed that he should be excluded from the United

Kingdom on the grounds that his presence was not conducive to the public good for reasons of national security. The decision gave notice to E1 of his out-of-country right of appeal to the Special Immigration Appeals Commission within 28 days, and indicated that he should not seek to return to the United Kingdom as he would be refused entry. The judge in the High Court said that the applicant agreed he could travel readily to Istanbul and give evidence to his appeal freely by means of a live television link. The Court of Appeal overruled the decision of the lower court and said that the appellant had been deprived of a valuable right – the right to pursue his appeal in-country.

The European Court of Human Rights also upset those with national security at the top of their priorities in the decision in the case of *Othman (Abu Qatada) v UK*, 17 January 2012. The ECtHR said that Qatada, a well-known radical Islamic cleric and al-Qaeda sympathiser, could not be deported to his own country of Jordan. This was because some of the evidence to be used against him for his trial in Jordan (for being part of a plot which blew up a hotel in Amman, the capital of Jordan) could have been obtained by the torture of prosecution witnesses. Therefore the ECtHR said that **Art 6** of the **Convention**, Qatada's right to a fair trial (a trial not in the United Kingdom but in Jordan), meant he could not be deported from the United Kingdom without a breach of his **Convention** rights, notably **Art 6** – the right to a fair trial. The argument of the ECtHR was that a trial based partly on evidence obtained from torture could not be fair given the great potential unreliability of evidence obtained by torture. The argument was not that Qatada himself was at risk of being tortured (the **Art 3** argument) since the ECtHR accepted the Jordanian Government's assurances to the UK Government that Qatada would not be tortured himself in Jordan. The argument against deportation was founded on **Art 6**, Qatada's right to a fair trial, since no trial could be fair based on prosecution witness evidence which might have been obtained from the torture of prosecution witnesses. Again the question remains: are legitimate national security concerns of the United Kingdom being given enough weight by such decisions of the ECtHR exemplified in the 'Qatada case'?

However, in the eyes of many, the European Court of Human Rights redeemed itself somewhat from accusations of 'human rights fanaticism' over the interests of national security by allowing the deportation by the UK Government of five alleged Islamist terrorists to the United States for trial. The five had tried to argue that their **Art 3** rights not to be subject to inhuman or degrading treatment would be violated by deportation to the United States where after conviction they faced incarceration for life without hope of parole in a 'supermax' prison in Colorado, where they would be in solitary confinement in a prison cell for 23 hours a day for the rest of their lives with only one hour a day solitary exercise period. The ECtHR held that their **Art 3** rights would not be violated by deportation from the United Kingdom to the United States.

In the case of *Babar Ahmad and Others v the United Kingdom* (2012), the ECtHR has ruled that there would be no violation of **Art 3** of the **ECHR** as a result of conditions of detention at ADX Florence prison in Colorado, if Ahmad, Ahsan, Abu Hamza, Bary and Al-Fawwaz were extradited to the United States; and, no violation of **Art 3** of the **Convention** as a result of the length of their possible sentences if Ahmad, Ahsan, Abu Hamza, Bary and

Al-Fawwaz were extradited. The Court adjourned its examination of Aswat's application as it required further submissions from the parties. The Court also decided to continue its indication to the UK Government that the applicants should not be extradited until the judgment became final or until the case was referred to the Grand Chamber at the request of one or both of the parties.

NOTES

Lord Bingham explores the tension between human rights and national security concerns in *The Rule of Law* (2011), particularly the chapter on 'Terrorism and the Rule of Law'. Bingham writes:

> 'The advent of serious terrorist violence, carried out by those willing to die in the cause of killing others, tests adherence to the rule of law to the utmost: for states, as is their duty, strain to protect their people against the consequences of such violence, and the strong temptation exists to cross the boundary which separates the lawful from the unlawful.'

Professor Griffiths in *The Politics of the Judiciary* (1997, 5th edition) refers to the 'executive-minded' attitude of UK judges before the **Human Rights Act** and judicial deference to government claims of 'national security'. The tension between human rights and national security concerns is examined in a collection of essays entitled *The Legal Protection of Human Rights: Sceptical Essays* (2011), edited by Tom Campbell, KD Ewing and Adam Tompkins.

QUESTION 26

Discuss how the 'rule of law' in the British Empire depended upon the concept of 'racial geography'.

How to Answer this Question

This question asks the student to identify what the 'rule of law' means and its importance in British legal and political life since the mid nineteenth century.

However, the question also asks the student to go beyond description and to take a very critical approach to the way British colonial authorities in countries as diverse as Jamaica and India abandoned the rule of law when faced with a perceived need to restore colonial authority in the face of threats to that imposed authority from indigenous local people in 1865 in Jamaica and in 1919 in India.

Applying the Law

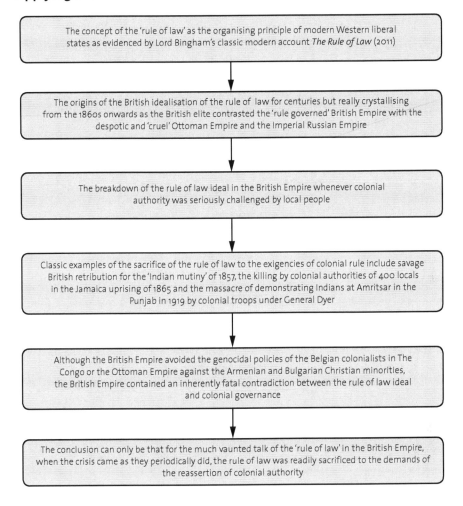

The concept of the 'rule of law' as the organising principle of modern Western liberal states as evidenced by Lord Bingham's classic modern account *The Rule of Law* (2011)

The origins of the British idealisation of the rule of law for centuries but really crystallising from the 1860s onwards as the British elite contrasted the 'rule governed' British Empire with the despotic and 'cruel' Ottoman Empire and the Imperial Russian Empire

The breakdown of the rule of law ideal in the British Empire whenever colonial authority was seriously challenged by local people

Classic examples of the sacrifice of the rule of law to the exigencies of colonial rule include savage British retribution for the 'Indian mutiny' of 1857, the killing by colonial authorities of 400 locals in the Jamaica uprising of 1865 and the massacre of demonstrating Indians at Amritsar in the Punjab in 1919 by colonial troops under General Dyer

Although the British Empire avoided the genocidal policies of the Belgian colonialists in The Congo or the Ottoman Empire against the Armenian and Bulgarian Christian minorities, the British Empire contained an inherently fatal contradiction between the rule of law ideal and colonial governance

The conclusion can only be that for the much vaunted talk of the 'rule of law' in the British Empire, when the crisis came as they periodically did, the rule of law was readily sacrificed to the demands of the reassertion of colonial authority

ANSWER

The hallmark of a modern civilised civil society is its adherence to the 'rule of law'.

Often when commentators, political leaders or journalists want to say that a country's legal system is in 'bad shape', they will tend to say that it lacks, or lacks significantly, 'the rule of law'.

The core of the existing principle for Lord Bingham in his leading work *The Rule of Law* (2011) is:

> 'that all persons and authorities within the state, whether public or private, should be bound by and entitled to the benefit of laws publicly made, taking effect in the future and publicly administered by the courts.'

The origins of this modern-day 'secular religion' in Britain that is called 'the rule of law' can be largely traced back to the Victorian British of the nineteenth century, for whom 'legality' was the touchstone of British imperial civilisation separating Britain from the brutal and despotic regimes of imperial Russia, the Turkish Ottoman Empire and the barbarities of other European colonial regimes, most notably the Belgians in the Congo from the 1880s.

RW Kostal, in his important book *A Jurisprudence of Power: Victorian Empire and the Rule of Law* (2005), writes:

> 'The English were a law-loving people, at least in the sense that their political elites were steeped in the idea that even the most exalted and powerful were liable to legal constraints and penalties.'

In the 1860s and beyond the English thought their country was the most civilised in the world. The hallmark of this moral superiority was the established common law and statutory law which made England great, the bearer of 'civilizational order' to the colonies.

The deep legal-mindedness of the mid-Victorian English elite was summed up by the great mid-nineteenth-century lawyer, Sir James Fitzjames Stephen, who commented of 'the English gospel of Law'.

However, when it came to the use of force to maintain 'civilizational order' in the colonies, then the 'rule of law' so beloved of the English was seriously subverted, if not overthrown in the interests of 'iron colonial law and order'.

The two archetypal or symbolic examples from British colonial history are India in 1857 and again in 1919, and Jamaica in 1865.

The British in India tried to give at least the appearance of the rule of law through, for example, a series of landmark statutes aimed at modernising the Indian legal system, and the work of Sir James Fitzjames Stephen between 1869 and 1872 in creating the **Indian Evidence Act**, **Indian Criminal Procedure Act** and **Indian Contract Act**. As Thomas Metcalf argued in *Ideologies of the Raj* (1995): 'Reformed codes of procedure represented a commitment to the "rule of law".'

However, when confronted by challenges to colonial power by the Indians in 1857 during the 'mutiny' or, as it is now called, 'the first war of Indian independence', the British behaved as barbarically as the Indian mutineers with massacres, collective punishments of Indians and cruelly bizarre forms of capital punishment such as firing captured Indians from British army canons.

The Amritsar massacre of April 1919 was, in the words of the historian Denis Judd in his 2004 book *The Lion and the Tiger: The Rise and Fall of the British Raj*, 'one of the most brutal episodes in the history of the British Raj in India'.

At the end of the First World War in 1918 the British Raj decided to pass legislation, embodied in the two 'Rowlatt' Acts, that extended into peacetime the restrictive legislation of the wartime period.

The 'iron fist in the velvet glove' of British colonial rule was never clearer in action than on 13 April 1919 at Amritsar in the Punjab. The Punjab was wracked by serious civil disorder during the spring of 1919. News of the arrest of several nationalist leaders in the city of Amritsar sparked rioting, during which five English colonialists were killed. The colonial army under Reginald Dyer opened fire without warning upon an estimated 20,000-strong crowd. For 10–15 minutes the firing continued, killing 379 unarmed Indians and wounding 1,200 more. The army immediately withdrew, leaving the dead, dying and wounded unattended. The massacre did immediately restore law and order in the Punjab but at terrible cost to Britain's reputation in India as the 'law-abiding British'.

The army's action in firing on the unarmed crowd met with widespread support throughout the armed forces in the British Empire and more generally in England, where General Reginald Dyer, who ordered the shooting, was acclaimed by the House of Lords and made the beneficiary of a fund which raised some £26,000 for Dyer's retirement fund.

The use of unrestrained force on unarmed demonstrators was hardly compatible with the proud commitment of the British in India to the rule of law.

One of the standard justifications for British imperialism was that it brought colonial territories and their inhabitants within the rule of law. Until the British Empire was dismantled in the second half of the twentieth century, this justification continued to be regularly offered as a counter to the anti-colonial movement.

However, it was in the 1860s, at the height of both the 'zeal for Empire' (Queen Victoria was later created Empress of India in 1877) and the secular religion of the 'rule of law', that the tensions between racial-colonial governance and the rule of law exploded in Jamaica in 1865.

The occasion was the violent suppression in 1865 under martial law of a supposed insurrection in the Morant Bay area of Jamaica, which had been a British colony since the days of Oliver Cromwell in the 1650s.

For the British governor of Jamaica, Edward Eyre, the rioting in eastern Jamaica by a few hundred black people was seen as an existential threat to white British colonial rule on the island. Nearly 500 people were either shot dead or hanged by Eyre's troops and many more were flogged as punishment for their insubordination to British colonial authority.

The action of Eyre that perhaps symbolises his complete break with the rule of law in 1865 in Jamaica was his treatment of one of the leaders of the revolt, George William Gordon. Governor Eyre had Gordon arrested in Kingston, which was under ordinary civil law, and had him forcibly transferred to Morant Bay for court martial under military law. George Gordon was hanged after a military tribunal sentenced him to death.

Although Edward Eyre had his supporters, such as Thomas Carlyle, who believed that Eyre had saved Jamaica for the empire, for some in England Eyre's actions brought the rule of law into contempt.

The radical lawyer Frederic Harrison commented: 'The contagion of lawlessness spreads fast. What is done in a colony today may be done in Ireland tomorrow, and in England thereafter.'

Walter Bagehot commented of Governor Edward Eyre's actions: 'In causing Mr. Gordon to be hanged, Eyre's greatest offence is that he put an affront on the majesty of law and, for a time, cancelled the ripest fruits of our civilization.'

In both 1865, at the time of the Jamaica Morant Bay uprising, and in 1919, the time of the Amritsar massacre, the British governing elite was defined partly by its ideology that the mark of a truly great civilisation was the accountability of offices of state and individuals to law.

AV Dicey, the great Victorian constitutional writer, commented in 1885, in his *Introduction to the Study of the Constitution*, that in Britain everyone from the prime minister to the lowest tax collector was subject to the law and liable to criminal punishment or civil action for breach of the law. Dicey commented that the English law reports were full of cases of officials being made answerable to the law for their actions.

However, 'out in the colonies' these platitudes were much harder to maintain with sincerity as the needs of colonial 'law and order' subverted a purported British allegiance to the rule of law.

In perhaps the single key sentence which sums up the contradictions between the rule of law ideal and iron colonial rule in the British Empire, Kostal comments:

> 'the rule of law was contingent upon racial geography.'

NOTES

The modern classic account of the 'rule of law' concept is given by Lord Bingham in *The Rule of Law* (2011, Penguin Books).

RW Kostal provides the central account of the rule of law in the mid-Victorian era and the Jamaican massacre of 1865 in *A Jurisprudence of Power: Victorian Empire and the Rule of Law* (2005, Oxford University Press).

A good modern account of the British imperial rule in India, 'The Raj', is provided by Denis Judd in *The Lion and the Tiger: The Rise and Fall of the British Raj* (2004, Oxford University Press).

QUESTION 27

Critically discuss how the 'human rights' movement in the United Kingdom has faltered in the 'age of terror' post-9/11/2001.

How to Answer this Question

This question is difficult because it not only requires you to discuss the subject of universal human rights as evidenced by the **United Nations Universal Declaration of Human Rights** in 1948, their origins in the post-Second World War reaction to the horrors of genocide in the 1939–1945 world conflict, but also asks for an appraisal of the human rights movement in the 'age of terror' post-9/11.

The question should be approached in two parts: first, an account of the post-1945 universal 'world conscience' human rights movement evidenced by the 1948 UN declaration, the 1966 **International Covenants on Civil and Political Rights** and the establishment of the International Criminal Court in 2002 by the **Treaty of Rome 1998**. The second part of the answer should focus on how the global international terrorist jihad movement, symbolised by the 9/11 attacks in the United States, brought the issue of national security back to occupy the same public space that the human rights movement had seemed to dominate pre-9/11.

Applying the Law

The growth of the human rights movement post-Second World War as evidenced by the 1948 **Universal Declaration of the Human Rights of Man**

↓

The sense that the Second World War was a turning point in the history of the human rights movement, that the 'filmed' atrocities in the Nazi concentration camps by liberating Allied forces led to the cry 'never again'. It is the horror of the Second World War that gives the human rights movement its traction and strength in the Western world today

↓

There is a narrative around the 'human rights' story which saw an eventual 'future' triumph of a global order on the basis of rule of law and human rights observance which would progress from the UN **Universal Declaration of Human Rights** to the more detailed covenant on Civil and Political Rights and finally to enforcement through the International Criminal Court

↓

The fall of the Berlin Wall in 1990 and the consequent collapse of communism in Eastern Europe in 1991 fed into and substantially strengthened the narrative of the eventual triumph of a global order based on the rule of law and human rights

↓

However, cutting across this narrative was the attack of 9/11 and the emergence of hyper-terrorism

↓

Human rights and their enforcement no longer seemed as unproblematic as before 9/11. National states had to consider national security against the 'new terrorism' as seriously as they had promised to respect the human rights of everyone in their jurisdiction

↓

Human rights advocates such as Professor Ronald Dworkin perceived that the human rights project was under threat in the post 9/11 'age of terror' and that Thomas Hobbes' *Leviathan* (1651) had suddenly become relevant again after slumbering since 1945, the years of relative peace and security in Western Europe until 9/11/2001

ANSWER

It is certainly possible to speak of a 'human rights' story or 'narrative' from the eighteenth-century Enlightenment to the present era, in which the idea of 'rights' became universalised and the notion of a human rights-respecting 'new world order' seemed to be on the cusp of delivery in the 1990s, to be only cut across by the events of 9/11/2001. 'The Twin Towers' attack of that September and everything after in terms of global jihad and the so-called 'war on terror' made it impossible to argue that respect for human rights was always an unqualified good.

The first point to note in the growth of human rights as an ideology, especially since the Second World War, is the 'internationalisation' and 'universalisation' of human rights, at least in theory even if far from practice, to every human on the planet. The French Revolutionaries limited their 'rights' to citizens of the new Republic, and the Americans in their Constitution of 1787 gave constitutional rights to US citizens but definitely not to slaves who made up the bulk of the US population at the time.

It is instructive to compare these old, 'national' views of human rights with the very modern views of the human rights activist and Director of 'Liberty' (the human rights organisation), Shami Chakrabarti, in her book *On Liberty* (2014): 'I am an internationalist, not least because I believe human rights to be universal and human beings to be of equal worth and entitled to protection whatever the accidents of birth, history and geography.' Such sentiments have been used to heavily criticise US military 'drone strikes' in Pakistan, Yemen and Somalia which have killed innocent civilians as well as terrorist suspects. Such 'internationalist' views of human rights do potentially call into question the legitimacy of any military action which might injure innocent civilians at all.

The high water mark of human rights in the United Kingdom was the passage of the **Human Rights Act 1998**. Clayton and Tomlinson, in their book *Tom Bingham and the Transformation of the Law* (2009), comment:

> 'When the Human Rights Act came into effect, Lord Bingham observed that its implementation "has assumed something of the character of a religious event: an event eagerly-sought and long-awaited but arousing feelings of apprehension as well as expectations, the uncertainty that accompanies any new and testing experience".'

They also comment:

> 'the Human Rights Act has become an established feature of the legal landscape. It has penetrated every aspect of private and public law … English law has absorbed "rights discourse" without cataclysmic upheaval. As a result of the enactment of the Human Rights Act, rights jurisprudence has taken firm root in the legal landscape.'

If the **Human Rights Act 1998** was the statutory high water mark of human rights discourse in the UK legal system, then the judicial counterpart to the **Human Rights Act** was the decision of the House of Lords in *A v Home Secretary* (2004) using the **Human Rights Act s 4** to declare 'incompatible' Labour's 'detention without trial' scheme, directed at 19 alleged foreign terrorist suspects, introduced in November 2001 following the 9/11 attacks in the United States. The Belmarsh detainee system was on a much smaller scale, but similar in its offensiveness to human rights activists' nostrils to 'Guantanamo Bay' in Cuba, run by the United States to detain about 10,000 terror suspects without trial from 2002. As Chakrabarti comments in *On Liberty*: 'foreign nationals are always politically the easiest to detain without charge or trial.'

Chakrabarti comments in *On Liberty*:

> 'In 1998, a New Labour government took a bill through parliament with significant cross-party support incorporating the ECHR articles into UK Law. Now they could be enforced in local courts with a greater understanding of domestic culture and context and without claimants having to make the sometimes decade-long hike to Strasbourg. This was an incredibly important moment for the United Kingdom. The Human Rights Act provided our modern Bill of Rights. It is the short but essential list of protections for the vulnerable against the State ... the "declaration of incompatibility" is very powerful. This says that the Act of Parliament cannot possibly be reconciled with human rights. This is very powerful. It has moral, political and persuasive effect in any democracy that respects the rule of law. Despite this moral force, the bad legislation stays in place unless Parliament chooses to change it.'

However, literally 'out of a blue Manhattan sky', the attack on the Twin Towers 'changed the atmosphere' irrevocably over human rights since September 11, 2001. No longer did human rights seem to be an unqualified good when the needs of national security demanded tough government action to deal with terrorist suspects and terrorist threats from home and abroad. There was after 9/11 a serious re-emergence of Hobbesian questions raised long ago in *Leviathan* (1651) about the role of 'protection' and 'security' by the state and the trade-off with liberty. A serious failure to protect the citizens from terror attack can seriously weaken a state's legitimacy. Chakrabarti comments in *On Liberty*:

> 'these are challenging times for human rights. The ill-judged and misnamed "War on Terror" has morphed into a permanent state of exception becoming the rule. Some have readily decided that the rule of law is too exacting and human rights principles too expensive in times of insecurity. As I write some senior figures in the Conservative Party and UKIP propose abolishing the Human Rights Act and withdrawing from the European Convention on Human Rights.'

Conor Gearty, in the Hamlyn Lectures 'Can Human Rights Survive?' (2005), comments of the seeming unstoppable velocity of the human rights movement before the events of 9/11:

> 'Since the end of the Cold War, human rights as a subject of political discourse has really taken off, with more and more of the peoples of the world embracing this language as a way of organising political debate and of informing their relations with

the world…. So all-embracing has been the language of human rights of late that it has seemed at times impossible to articulate a vision of the future without lapsing into its vernacular. Where once we had ideas like "socialism", "social justice" and "fairness", nowadays increasingly "human rights" is being called upon to do all the moral work.'

However, Gearty recognises a number of recent clouds over this 'human rights utopia' which seemed to be being born in the 1990s:

'first, there is the crisis of authority. Why is it that human rights has moved onto so much ethical territory, to the exclusion of other moral notions that have done useful work in their day? Neither religion nor reason has the hold that each once had. Human rights are a set of values for a Godless age. The human rights idea is "half pre-modern, half modern." However as post-modern uncertainty embeds itself more deeply in our culture, and as our memory of religious and Enlightenment time fades, so our commitment to the benign relic of both periods can be expected to begin to recede.'

In other words, with regard to the foundations of human rights, do they actually exist? And if they do, upon what grounding exactly? Both are questions which have not received fully satisfactory answers.

As if to illustrate the fragility of human rights even in our supposedly enlightened Western cultures, Gearty refers to an extraordinary contradictory period of Blair's Labour Government from 1998 until 2001.

Gearty writes of the absurdity of a Labour Government (1997–2005), introducing detention without trial of foreign terrorist suspects and then replacing this measure after three years with further draconian measures, namely 'house arrest'/control orders in the **Prevention of Terrorism Act 2005**.

All this 'repression' whilst Blair's Government was, in the words of Gearty, 'publicly devoted at the same time to establishing a human rights culture' which can be seen in the **Human Rights Act 1998** and the later **Equality Act 2010**. Gearty wonders in amazement: 'How have such draconian attacks on the basic DNA of human rights – dignity, legality, democracy – been able to take place in a society presided over by a human-rights respecting administration?'

For Gearty, 'the human rights movement' is 'one of the great civilising achievements of the modern era', but 'there is something else going on here as well revealed by my title "Can Human Rights Survive?"': there is, in 'an age of terror and anxiety', 'no certainty of a happy ending' for the human rights story.

It looked for a time before the Islamist world jihadist wave swept onto the historical dial on 9/11 that the human rights story had a chance of winning. The 1990s were the supposed beginning of the fulfilment of the 'world wide human rights project', with the Rome statute of 1998 setting up the 2002 International Criminal Court following temporary international criminal courts for war crimes for the former Yugoslavia and Rwanda.

The attacks of 9/11 put an end to the narrative of the triumph of a global order on the basis of the rule of law and human rights observations that was holding sway at the end of the twentieth century – the idea that the new post-Second World War legal order would progress from the UN Universal Declaration of Human Rights in 1948 to the more detailed Covenant on Civil and Political Rights in the mid-1960s and finally to enforcement through the International Criminal Court. Instead, hyper-terror emerged, terror with a 'divine' or 'holy' mandate that could not be compromised with by the Western world. In consequence the politics of national sovereignty and national security reasserted themselves over the tom-tom beat of human rights. The Syrian civil war and its fallout has 'changed everything again' with the emergence of the hyper-brutal 'Islamic State' in 2014.

The United Kingdom has brought in eight separate anti-terrorist statutes since 2001 from the **Anti-Terrorism, Crime and Security Act** of that year to the most recent **Counter-Terrorism and Security Act 2015**. For some jurisprudential writers such as Professor Dworkin, these are troubling times for human rights in the United Kingdom. Human rights need to be reasserted in this 'age of terror and anxiety about security'. The 'Leviathan' of Hobbes, the mighty state demanding obedience from citizens in return for protection from terrorist threats needs to be reminded of the fundamental importance of human rights.

Dworkin wrote an important defence of the human rights project in the United Kingdom in the *Guardian* in 2006. It is worth quoting from it extensively, for it represents the view on the human rights project in the United Kingdom in the 'age of terror' of the leading jurisprudential scholar of the last 40 years. Professor Dworkin wrote:

> 'This is a dangerous time for freedom in Britain. The country's most powerful politicians have joined its irresponsible press in a shameful attack on the idea of human rights. Tony Blair says that the nation needs to re-examine what he calls the "philosophy" behind the Human Rights Act so as to change the balance it strikes between individual freedom and the community's security.
>
> …
>
> The balancing metaphor is dangerous because it suggests no principled basis for deciding how much torture we should facilitate, or for how many years we should jail people without trial. It leaves that decision up to politicians who are anxious to pander to the tabloids. The metaphor is deeply misleading because it assumes that we should decide which human rights to recognise through a kind of cost–benefit analysis, the way we might decide what speed limits to adopt. It suggests that the test should be the benefit to the British public, as Blair declared in his "Let's talk" speech, when he said that "the demands of the majority of the law-abiding

community have to take precedence". This amazing statement undermines the whole point of recognising human rights; it is tantamount to declaring that there are no such things.

…

It might well be in the public interest to lock up people who the police think dangerous even though they have committed no crime, or to censor people whose opinions are offensive or unwelcome, or to torture people who we believe have information about impending crimes. But we do not do that, at least in ordinary legal practice, because we insist that people have a right to a fair trial and free speech and not to be tortured. We insist on these rights even though the majority would be safer and more comfortable if we ignored them.

…

Of course it is terrible when deluded terrorists or criminals on probation kill innocent people. But the increased risk that each of us runs is marginal when we insist on enforcing human rights rather than abandoning them just because they have proved inconvenient. It is one of Britain's most honoured traditions to accept the marginally increased risk as the price of respect for individual human dignity. That is what self-respect requires. It is dangerous gibberish to say that the public has a right to as much security as it can have; no one has a right to security purchased through injustice.

Simon Jenkins, in the *Sunday Times*, recently declared his enthusiasm for the 18th-century philosopher Jeremy Bentham who said that all that matters is the greatest happiness of the greatest number, and that the whole idea of human rights is therefore "nonsense upon stilts". But Europe, led by Britain, rejected Bentham's utilitarianism after the second world war when it established the European human rights convention. The 20th-century tyrannies have taught us that protecting the dignity of human beings, one by one, is worth the increased discomfort and risk that respecting human rights may cost the public at large. The Human Rights Act, which makes that convention part of Britain's own law, was one of the great achievements of this government. It is sad that Blair's political weakness has tempted him to rubbish ideals of which he and the country should be proud.'

NOTES

Two modern classic accounts lamenting the decline of the human rights movement post-9/11, especially in the United Kingdom, are:

Conor Gearty, *Can Human Rights Survive?* (2005, Cambridge University Press)
Shami Chakrabarti, *On Liberty* (2014, Penguin Books)

QUESTION 28

Should the UK Supreme Court have the legal power to declare certain legislation as 'unconstitutional' and therefore legally invalid as is the practice with the United States Supreme Court?

How to Answer this Question

Judicial power to rule as invalid 'unconstitutional' legislation has existed as a power in the United States Supreme Court since 1803. Between 1880 and 1935 more than 170 statutes – state and federal – were struck down by American courts even though those statutes attempted to improve working conditions for American workers. The central case in this era was *Lochner v New York* (1905) in which the United States Supreme Court held that a New York statute limiting working hours for bakers to ten hours a day was an 'unreasonable, unnecessary and arbitrary interference with the right and liberty of the individual to contract'. This period is usually called 'the Lochner era' and it must give pause to those who think that 'strong-form' judicial review is an integral part of any constitutional liberal democracy. The United Kingdom has 'weak-form' judicial review in the form of **Human Rights Act 1998, s 4** which allows judges of the High Court, Court of Appeal and Supreme Court to declare UK legislation as 'incompatible' with Convention rights under the **European Convention of Human Rights**. Such a 'declaration of incompatibility' crucially in legal theory does not suspend or invalidate the offending legislation: see **Art 4(6)** of the **Human Rights Act 1998**. However, in the 12 years since the **Human Rights Act** has been in force (October 2000) the UK Parliament has never ignored a judicial 'declaration of incompatibility' but has always repealed or amended the offending legislation. The question then arises of the chasm between legal theory and legal reality, the gap between the 'law in the books' and the 'law in practice'. If 'declarations of incompatibility' invariably lead to reforming measures by Parliament, could 'weak-form' judicial review be sliding into a version of US-style 'strong-form' judicial review? Certainly the European Court of Human Rights in the case of *Burden v UK* (2008) thought that in the future the **s 4, Human Rights Act** 'declaration of incompatibility' power could provide an 'effective remedy' for breach of Convention rights. In any case, apart from **s 4, Human Rights Act**, certain academic and judicial voices have mooted the possibility of a common law change to the principle of unlimited parliamentary sovereignty. Professor Dworkin in his book *Justice for Hedgehogs* (2011) suggested that the time was ripe to question traditional parliamentary sovereignty, and three Law Lords in the 2004 *Jackson* case suggested that legislation which sought to displace the rule of law could be ignored by the judges in the future. However, Lord Bingham in his much-lauded book *The Rule of Law* (2010) doubted the competency of common law judges to change the principle of parliamentary sovereignty. In any case strong-form judicial review can be criticised as an affront to democracy. As Lord Devlin once said: 'Power resides in the last word' and strong-form judicial review gives a few unelected privileged ex-lawyers (judges) the 'final word' over legislation passed by the elected representatives of millions and millions of citizens.

Applying the Law

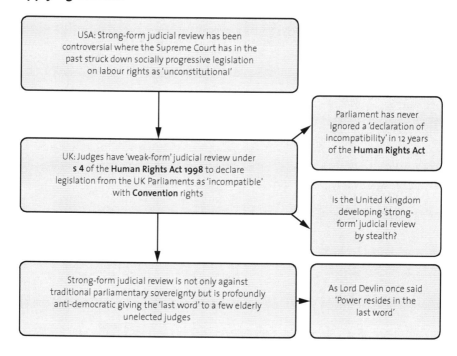

USA: Strong-form judicial review has been controversial where the Supreme Court has in the past struck down socially progressive legislation on labour rights as 'unconstitutional'

UK: Judges have 'weak-form' judicial review under **s 4** of the **Human Rights Act 1998** to declare legislation from the UK Parliaments as 'incompatible' with **Convention** rights

Parliament has never ignored a 'declaration of incompatibility' in 12 years of the **Human Rights Act**

Is the United Kingdom developing 'strong-form' judicial review by stealth?

Strong-form judicial review is not only against traditional parliamentary sovereignty but is profoundly anti-democratic giving the 'last word' to a few elderly unelected judges

As Lord Devlin once said 'Power resides in the last word'

ANSWER

Roger Cotterrell points out in *The Politics of Jurisprudence* (2003):

'In the United States … law has remarkable cultural centrality.'

One of the reasons for the cultural centrality of law in the United States is the role of the Supreme Court. The Supreme Court has since 1803[5] had the power to strike down legislation as 'unconstitutional'. In other words, the Supreme Court has the 'last word' concerning the validity of legislation. Writing in 2000, Cotterrell comments in *Common Law Approaches to the Relationship between Law and Morality* that in the United States the Supreme Court judges are central to the negotiation and working out of law's relation to morality because the Supreme Court in the United States has ultimate authority to interpret a written constitution and bill of rights which are, themselves, seen as the repository of political and moral values. Cotterrell argued that the centrality of the judge to the working out of law's relation to morality was 'much harder to maintain in the legal environment of Britain than in that of the United States'. Cotterrell argued that in the

---

5   The Supreme Court in *Marbury v Madison* (1803) granted itself the power to declare legislation in the United States as 'invalid'. *Marbury v Madison* (1803) is a landmark case in US constitutional law that formed the basis for the exercise of judicial review under **Article 3** of the **United States Constitution**. The landmark decision helped define the boundary between the constitutionally separate executive and judicial branches of the American form of government.

United Kingdom it was in Parliament rather than in the courts that the interface of law and morality was worked out through legislation.

However, since the coming into force of the **Human Rights Act 1998** in October 2000 it is plausible to maintain that the UK courts have become as central as Parliament to the working out of law's relation to morality in the form of human rights law. One example will suffice for present purposes. The UK judges have since the introduction of the **Human Rights Act 1998** had the power under **Art 8** of the **European Convention of Human Rights** to overrule decisions of the Government to deport individuals from the country back to their country of origin because the judges hold that to do so would violate the **Art 8** right to a private and family life if the person to be deported has made family ties in the United Kingdom. This means that the UK judges are at the forefront of adjudicating on important moral-political rights such as the **Art 8** right to a private life. In the case of *VW (Uganda) v Secretary of State for the Home Department* (2009) the Court of Appeal allowed the appeal of VW against the Government's decision to order her removal to Uganda as an illegal immigrant. The Court of Appeal, accepting that VW had strong family ties in the United Kingdom, held that the enforced break-up of the family of VW by her intended deportation was not justified by the legitimate demands of immigration control. This approach of the UK courts to **Art 8** and deportation orders by the Government follows the lead of the European Court of Human Rights. In the case of *AA v United Kingdom* (2011) the European Court of Human Rights blocked the intended deportation of AA, a Nigerian, by the UK Government.

AA, a Nigerian national, arrived in the United Kingdom in 2000 to join his mother. In 2002, at the age of 15 he was convicted of rape and released on licence in 2004. He was served with a deportation order while still in detention. The European Court of Human Rights blocked the deportation on ground that it violated AA's right to a private life; the Court held the following:

> 'that the totality of social ties between settled migrants and the community in which they were living constituted part of the concept of "private life" within Article 8 and the expulsion of a settled migrant constituted an interference with his right to respect for private life; that having regard in particular to the nature and seriousness of the offence committed (an offence committed by a minor which required regard to be had to the best interests of the child), the length of his stay in the UK (eleven years), the time which had elapsed since that offence (nine years) and his conduct during that period (no further offences and conduct that appeared exemplary) and the solidity of his social, cultural and family ties with the United Kingdom (lived with his mother and had a close relationship with two sisters and an uncle, completed further education in UK and had employment with a local authority and was a member of a church community) the intended deportation would be disproportionate to the legitimate aim of the "prevention of disorder and crime" and would therefore not be necessary in a democratic society.'

Therefore UK judges, following the lead of the European Court of Human Rights, have become since the enactment of the **Human Rights Act 1998** interpreters of crucial moral-legal concepts such as the right to a private life in the context of deportation cases, for example. It is true that even before the **Human Rights Act 1998** the UK judges were using old common law powers of judicial review to monitor and strike down executive decisions that did not comply with public law principles. However, the scope of judicial review at common law was limited and did not extend to the broad moral-political evaluation and criticism of executive action employed by the judges under the **Human Rights Act 1998**. The history of the growth of judicial review as a check on executive action (but not on legislation itself – there is no power under judicial review at common law or under the **Human Rights Act** to declare legislation legally invalid) is an interesting one. Sir Stephen Sedley in *Ashes and Sparks* (2011) comments: 'while other areas of substantive law have become landmasses of statute, our constitutional law remains a common law ocean dotted with islands of statutory provision.'

Sedley comments that after the Second World War, from the early 1950s, the judges began to use judicial review, common law powers, to supervise the use of statutory powers by civil servants and central and local government. It is not surprising that as government power grew after the Second World War (the welfare state, expansion of police powers and resources, for example) and expressed itself through a massive increase in statute law, then the judges responded by increasing the scope of the common law in judicial review.

Sedley quotes Lord Diplock in *R v Inland Revenue Commissioners, ex parte National Federation of the Self-Employed* (1982) – looking back at legal developments in that case in 1982, Lord Diplock said:

> 'like most of English public law the rules for judicial review are not to be found in any statute. They were made by judges, by judges they can be changed, and so they have been over the years to meet the need to preserve the integrity of the rule of law despite changes in social structure, methods of government and the extent to which the activities of private citizens are controlled by governmental authorities ... those changes have been particularly rapid since World War 2.'

Therefore in response to the growth of the state since the Second World War, expressed through increased legislation, and also the fact that the government of the day controls Parliament, then the judges have expanded common law judicial review to protect the citizen from abuse of power by the state.

Sedley believes that 'the judiciary have moved into the space created by the democratic deficit' and by 'a methodological enlargement of the doctrines of judicial review between 1952 and 1982', and at p. 81:

> 'By the time the executive had fully woken up to what was happening, which was not until the end of the 1970s, it was too late. The judges had occupied areas of constitutional high ground which government had come to believe, and the public had come to fear, were beyond the reach of the law, and the judges were now directing fire on entrenchments of the local and central state.'

Sedley says that the existence of judicial review remedies go back to the late nineteenth century but from the 1950s onwards 'what was new was the judicial will to find, use and expand them. In this process judicial energy has been everything'.

Therefore we have in the modern flowering of public law judicial remedies a body of law entirely judge-made used to match the growth of state intervention since the Second World War. This is one part of the common law that has not retreated but expanded since the Second World War, but it has expanded precisely because the state through legislation has expanded since then. Lord Bingham in his book *Lives of the Law* (2011) tells a similar story to Lord Justice Sedley about the growth of judicial review in the years since the Second World War. Lord Bingham comments about the 'sudden surge' in the use of judicial review of executive decisions which can be explained as due to:

> 'a strong public wish to challenge official decisions affecting their lives … If people feel hard done by, they are much readier than they were to go to law in search of a remedy … [Another] reason is found in the immense and complex reach of the modern State in all its manifestations … the huge reach and immense activity of the state, built on a mass of complex and very detailed legislation and regulation, inevitably gives rise to a number of grievances which people are now much readier to raise than they once were.'

The crucial questions is: should UK judges have powers that go far beyond the judicial review of executive decisions to have full judicial review of legislation itself? At the moment judges can only judicially review governmental decisions under statute for (1) irrationality, (2) unreasonableness and (3) procedural unfairness (see Lord Diplock's classic threefold classification of the heads of judicial review in the 1985 *GCHQ* case). Judges of the High Court, Court of Appeal and Supreme Court in the United Kingdom can at the moment issue a 'declaration of incompatibility' under **Human Rights Act 1998, s 4** which signals to Parliament that legislation is incompatible with a **Convention** right or rights as determined by the judges under the **Human Rights Act**. It is very important to make clear that in strict legal and constitutional theory a 'declaration of incompatibility' by the senior UK judges does not suspend or invalidate the legislation declared incompatible: see **Human Rights Act, s 4(6)**. However, it is also important to be realistic here as well: in the 12 years since the **Human Rights Act** came into force in 2000 no UK Government has ever ignored a 'declaration of incompatibility' by the UK judges. Jonathan Morgan argues in *The Legal Protection of Human Rights: Sceptical Essays* (2011):

> 'if Parliament refused to amend the legislation, the losing party would proceed to the European Court of Human Rights in Strasbourg, and almost certainly win. The government would then have little option but to pass remedial action … It is the threat of what amounts to an appeal to Strasbourg against post-declaration inaction that makes the Human Rights Act potent.'

The political reality, whatever the strict legal position, is that a 'declaration of incompatibility' by the judges against a piece of legislation invariably leads to remedial action by the UK Government against the offending legislation. The UK Parliament has never once stood up to the judges when a declaration of incompatibility has been issued. The Ministry of Justice reports that between the **Human Rights Act 1998** coming into force on 2 October 2000 and 23 May 2007, a total of 24 declarations of incompatibility have been made by domestic courts under **Human Rights Act 1998, s 4**. In none of those instances has Parliament ignored the judges. It may well be that a 'convention' or constitutional understanding is developing that 'declarations of incompatibility' will be followed by remedial fast-track legislation under **Human Rights Act, s 10**. Jonathan Morgan argues that there is a '*de facto* bindingness' emerging of declarations of incompatibility so that 'weak-form' judicial review of legislation which **Human Rights Act 1998, s 4** originally represented is collapsing over the years into 'hard line' US-style judicial review of legislation through the emergence of a constitutional convention that a 'declaration of incompatibility' by the courts is always followed by remedial legislation. Mark Tushnet, in *Weak Courts, Strong Rights* (2008), has an argument that 'weak-form' judicial review is inherently unstable and either develops into strong-form systems of judicial review such as the United States because weak-form judicial review judges mimic strong-form systems of judicial review of legislation or weak-form judicial review reverts back to strong parliamentary sovereignty. What we have witnessed over the last 12 years in the United Kingdom is the slow emergence of 'strong-form' judicial review of legislation from an initial claim in 2000 by the Government that 'declarations of incompatibility' did not threaten parliamentary sovereignty: see **Human Rights Act 1998, s 4(6)**.

Indeed, the European Court of Human Rights in Strasbourg seems to be encouraging the development of **Human Rights Act s 4** ('the declaration of incompatibility') by the UK judges as a strong-form power of judicial review of UK legislation. In *Burden v UK* (2008) the Grand Chamber of the European Court of Human Rights held that **Human Rights Act 1998 s 4** does not provide an 'effective remedy' for violations of **ECHR** rights because a declaration of incompatibility formally 'places no legal obligation on the executive or the legislature to amend the law'. However, the Grand Chamber went beyond the logic of the formal legal position, arguing that the passage of time could see **s 4** developing into an 'effective remedy' for violation of **Convention** rights. The Grand Chamber declared:

> 'it cannot be excluded that at some time in the future the practice of giving effect to the national courts' declarations of incompatibility by amendment of the legislation is so certain as to indicate that section 4 of the Human Rights Act is to be interpreted as imposing a binding obligation.'

Although this has not evolved, as of 2012 the Grand Chamber in *Burden v UK* (2008) noted 'with satisfaction that in all the cases where declarations of incompatibility have to date become final, steps have been taken to amend the offending legislative provisions'.

Jonathan Morgan, in *The Legal Protection of Human Rights*, comments that:

> 'The European Court of Human Rights makes it very clear that while Parliament might have the theoretical freedom to ignore a declaration of incompatibility, the UK's Convention obligation to provide an effective remedy for invasions of rights entirely negates that freedom.'

Indeed, short of the **s4** 'declaration of incompatibility' being legally binding on Parliament (which could evolve some time in the future as the European Court of Human Rights adverted to in *Burden v UK*), Morgan comments that the 'political pressure' exerted on Parliament by a 'declaration of incompatibility' is 'extraordinarily potent'. Morgan comments: 'De facto the courts require the politicians to amend the statute, with the looming threat of condemnation in the European Court of Human Rights as the sanction for recalcitrance.'

It is necessary to point out that before the judges can issue a **s4** declaration of incompatibility against legislation, the judges have a prior duty under **s3** of the **Human Rights Act** to so interpret legislation so as to make the legislation compatible with **Convention** rights. Only if the judges cannot so interpret legislation in that way can they then issue a 'declaration of incompatibility' under **s4**. The **s4** declaration of incompatibility is therefore a 'measure of last resort', as the House of Lords said in *Ghaidan* (2004). However, the **s3** 'interpretive duty' is a duty that goes far beyond the usual duty of judges in the interpretation of legislation outside of the **s3 Human Rights Act** context. Lord Bingham said in *Sheldrake v Director of Public Prosecutions* (2004) House of Lords:

> 'the interpretative obligation under section 3 is a very strong and far reaching one, and may require the court to depart from the legislative intention of Parliament.'

James Allan writes in *The Legal Protection of Human Rights: Sceptical Essays* (2011):

> 'The Human Rights Act has not left us with parliamentary sovereignty in any substantive sense – not when judges can rewrite legislation they happen to think infringes the enumerated rights and not when every single Declaration of Incompatibility, without exception, is met by the capitulation of the elected branches.'

For some writers such as James Allan and Jonathan Morgan, the combined effect of **ss3 and 4** of the **Human Rights Act** is to leave little room for traditional parliamentary sovereignty. Under **s3** the judges in attempting to make legislation fit convention rights can rewrite legislation, and where this is not possible judges can issue a declaration of incompatibility which is always followed by remedial legislation passed by Parliament to correct the judicially declared incompatibility. Morgan argues that **s3** should be repealed and replaced with a provision that makes clear that interpretation cannot distort the meaning of statutory language. Morgan argues that **s4** should be repealed and not replaced. Allen concludes that 'we should be angry' from a democratic legitimacy perspective of how the **Human Rights Act** has turned out in practice:

> 'The United Kingdom is the textbook example of how weak-form judicial review under a statutory bill of rights can collapse, into something functionally indistinguishable from strong-form judicial review under an entrenched, constitutionalized bill of rights.'

The opposition to 'strong-form' judicial review – the legal right of unelected judges to strike down legislation passed by a democratically elected legislature – is usually based on arguments from democratic legitimacy. Jeremy Waldron, in 'Judicial Review of Legislation' (in *The Routledge Companion to Philosophy of Law* (2012)) comments of strong-form judicial review:

> 'in a system of strong-form judicial review, those who make the final decisions act as though the views they happen to hold – which of course they think right – are entitled to a great deal more respect than the views that I happen to hold or any one of my millions of fellow citizens happen to hold. In other words, the issue comes down to fairness and the principle of political equality. It is worth dwelling on the basis of the affront to political equality that judicial review involves. People fought long and hard for the vote and for democratic representation. They wanted the right to govern themselves, not just on mundane issues of policy, but also on the high matters of principle.'

Waldron points out that leaving the final word 'on the high matters of principle' to judges and not the elected legislature is wrong because 'judges are not elected to their office and they are not accountable publicly for their decisions'. As a result, Waldron believes that strong-form judicial review:

> 'is a massive violation of the principle of political equality, which is fundamental to democracy. In matters of which the people of a society disagree in good faith, matters important to their lives and to their life together, strong-form judicial review gives immeasurably greater weight to the views of appointed judges than it gives to ordinary citizens … there is substantially greater amount of political fairness in the way decisions are made in a system of legislative supremacy than there is in a system of strong-form judicial review.'

Those in favour of strong-form judicial review, with judges given the power to strike down 'unconstitutional' legislation, might well argue that the protection of the human rights of minorities in society or unpopular groups such as criminals or illegal immigrants need to be protected by unelected judges free from the popular clamour which often influences the legislature. In other words, marginalised groups which might suffer at the hands of a democratically elected legislature need the assurance of their rights being protected by an elite group not beholden to the popular will, namely the judiciary.

However, the question remains: could strong-form judicial review come the way of the UK legal system? We have already seen that **s 4** of the **Human Rights Act** could well turn into a form of strong judicial review in the future, but there is another possibility as well and that is that the common law could itself develop to modify the traditional rules that Parliament can legislate on any subject it likes and that no court may question any Act of Parliament.

Professor Dworkin in his latest work in 2011, *Justice for Hedgehogs*, remarks that when he was a law student more than half a century ago he was told that in the United Kingdom, unlike the United States of America, Parliament was supreme and that this was 'a cardinal example of unchallengeable law'. As Dworkin comments: 'it went without saying.'

Dworkin, perceiving a sea change in judicial attitudes, says that parliamentary sovereignty does not go without saying now. Dworkin comments:

> 'Many lawyers, and at least some judges, now believe that Parliament's power is indeed limited. When the government recently floated the idea of a bill that would oust the courts of jurisdiction over detainees suspected of terrorism, these lawyers claimed that such an act would be null and void … The status of Parliament as lawgiver, among the most fundamental of legal issues, has once again become a deep question of political morality.'

Dworkin in his jurisprudential role as incitor to judicial mutiny over the unchallengeability of statute law had in a lecture in Cambridge called on the judges to declare a clause in an asylum bill, which would have closed off judicial review, as unconstitutional and to treat the clause as invalid. The Government thought better of it and dropped the offending clause in the asylum bill.

For Dworkin, the reason for the change in lawyers' attitudes to parliamentary sovereignty that sees it as 'no longer evidently just' is due to the legal culture of human rights which has turned UK lawyers and judges into 'working political philosophers of a democratic state'. Despite the academic rhetoric, Dworkin is right to highlight the change in legal culture in the United Kingdom since the introduction of the **Human Rights Act 1998** which has entrenched the idea of human rights as 'trumps' against executive action in the legal culture. The influence of Professor Dworkin in this regard should not be underestimated. Both in a speech at Cambridge and in his recent book, *Justice for Hedgehogs*, Dworkin has called on senior English judges to declare invalid legislation which violates fundamental human rights or violates the rule of law significantly. Although American, Dworkin is described by Lloyd's *Introduction to Jurisprudence* (2008) as 'the most significant jurist of our times'. It appears that some, but not all, senior judges are inclined to follow Dworkin's call to insurrection against traditional parliamentary sovereignty.

A number of English senior judges in the twenty-first century have suggested that common law control of draconian anti-human rights statutes could emerge in the legal future in the United Kingdom.

In the House of Lords case of *Jackson v Attorney-General* (2006) Lord Steyn said the following potentially legal revolutionary comment:

> 'The classic account given by Dicey of the doctrine of the supremacy of Parliament, pure and absolute as it was, can now seem to be out of place in the modern United Kingdom. Nevertheless, the supremacy of Parliament is still the general principle of our constitution. It is a construct of the common law. The judges created this principle. If that is so, it is not unthinkable that circumstances could arise where the

courts may have to qualify a principle established on a different hypothesis of constitutionalism. In exceptional circumstances involving an attempt to abolish judicial review or the ordinary role of the courts, the Appellate Committee of the House of Lords or a new Supreme Court may have to consider whether this is a constitutional fundamental which even a sovereign Parliament acting at the behest of a complaisant House of Commons cannot abolish.'

In similar prophetic vein, Baroness Hale commented in the *Jackson* case:

'The courts will treat with particular suspicion (and might even reject) any attempt to subvert the rule of law by removing governmental action affecting the rights of the individual from all judicial scrutiny.'

The argument for recognising a judicial power at common law to declare in exceptional cases certain statutes invalid seems to be as follows: since parliamentary sovereignty is a creation of common law then common law can evolve to recognise a more limited principle of parliamentary sovereignty in a different era from Dicey's late-nineteenth-century era. If the Supreme Court of the United Kingdom did in the legal future assume such controlling powers over statutes, even if in exceptional circumstances, then the UK Supreme Court would be much nearer in spirit with its namesake the US Supreme Court than at present. However, the late Lord Bingham, in his last published book *The Rule of Law* (2010), vigorously dissented from the views of Lords Steyn, Hope and Baroness Hale in *Jackson* (2004). Lord Bingham unambiguously announces: 'I cannot for my part accept that my colleagues' observations are correct.'

Lord Bingham insisted that there was no common law power to modify the principle of parliamentary sovereignty and that it was a confusion to reason that because parliamentary sovereignty had been recognised by judges that therefore the judges had created the principle of parliamentary sovereignty. Lord Bingham is keen to reject any judicial attempt to modify unilaterally the traditional principle of parliamentary sovereignty:

'the principle of parliamentary sovereignty has been recognized as fundamental in this country not because the judges invented it but because it has for centuries been accepted as such by judges and others officially concerned in the operation of our constitutional system. The judges did not by themselves establish the principle and they cannot, by themselves, change it.'

The principle of traditional parliamentary sovereignty was not a creation of the common law, argues Lord Bingham, and therefore the common law has no jurisdiction to modify the principle. Lord Bingham's strong contrary view clearly indicates that the 'new' view of parliamentary sovereignty, and the concomitant proposed role of the common law in extreme cases in controlling statutes that significantly violate the rule of law, is going to face a tough road before it is accepted widely in the legal community. However, as Lord Bingham admitted, the statements of the three judges challenging traditional parliamentary sovereignty in the *Jackson* case were 'welcomed in some quarters'.[6]

Aim Higher

The 'weak-form' judicial review of the UK legal system whereby the senior judges can under **s4 Human Rights Act 1998** declare legislation 'incompatible' with **Convention** rights is arguably inherently unstable. There is a strong tendency for the Government to think that morally and politically remedial legislation should be introduced if the judges think that legislation is incompatible with **Convention** rights even after straining to interpret the legislation so as to be compatible with the **Convention** under **s3 Human Rights Act 1998**. Therefore there is an inherent tendency for 'weak-form' judicial review to slide into or collapse into strong-form judicial review by parliamentary deference to declarations of incompatibility. Indeed, the possibility of **s4** 'declarations of incompatibility' becoming US-style 'strong-form' judicial review was canvassed by the European Court of Human Rights in *Burden v UK* (2008).

NOTES

Lord Bingham examines and then rejects calls for traditional parliamentary sovereignty to be modified in favour of strong judicial review of legislation in *The Rule of Law* (2011), in Chapter 12, 'The Rule of Law and the Sovereignty of Parliament'. Professor Dworkin calls for strong-form judicial review of legislation in the United Kingdom in *Justice for Hedgehogs* (2011) at pp. 413–414. Jeremy Waldron takes a critical view of strong-form judicial review in his essay 'Judicial Review of Legislation', in *The Routledge Companion to Philosophy of Law* (2012), edited by Andrei Marmor. Lord Justice Sedley analyses the growth of judicial review at common law in *Ashes and Sparks: Essays on Law and Justice* (2011) in Chapter 25, 'The Moral Economy of Judicial Review'. The subject of judicial review of both 'strong' judicial review and weak varieties is examined in the collection of essays entitled *The Legal Protection of Human Rights: Sceptical Essays* (2011), edited by Tom Campbell, KD Ewing and Adam Tompkins.

QUESTION 29

Is utilitarianism an acceptable foundation for justice and human rights?

How to Answer this Question

Utilitarianism has been a very influential theory since its origins with David Hume (1711–1776) and Jeremy Bentham (1748–1832). However, serious doubts persist as to

---

6   Professor Dworkin, the distinguished American jurist, welcomed the opinion of the three judges in the *Jackson* (2004) case, that traditional parliamentary sovereignty could be modified by common law judges: see Dworkin's book *Justice for Hedgehogs* (2011).

whether even sophisticated versions of utilitarianism can account for the importance, persistence and absolute quality of fundamental human rights in Western societies. The appeal of utilitarianism has rested on its egalitarian and consequentialist features, but the theory has been accused, with some justification, of ignoring 'the separateness of persons'. The two most influential modern attacks on utilitarianism as a moral and political theory have been by John Rawls in *A Theory of Justice* (1971) and Robert Nozick in *Anarchy, State and Utopia* (1974). These two anti-utilitarian masterpieces seek to develop principles of justice for the organisation of the state that are totally independent of any 'utilitarian' calculation. A skeleton plan is given:

Applying the Law

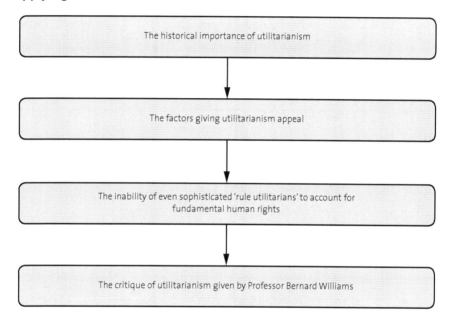

The historical importance of utilitarianism

The factors giving utilitarianism appeal

The inability of even sophisticated 'rule utilitarians' to account for fundamental human rights

The critique of utilitarianism given by Professor Bernard Williams

ANSWER

Until about 1970 the governing theory of political philosophy in the Western world was some version of utilitarianism. In 1971 John Rawls published his anti-utilitarian masterpiece, *A Theory of Justice*, which rejected utilitarianism as an acceptable foundation for principles of justice. The early 1970s saw further insightful assaults on utilitarianism as a political philosophy in the form of Bernard Williams's anti-utilitarian essay published in 1973 in *Utilitarianism: For and Against* and, most critical of all, in Robert Nozick's 1974 *Anarchy, State and Utopia*, which claimed that utilitarianism ignored the basic fact of human life – namely, our 'separate existences'.

However, utilitarianism as a form of political theory had a remarkably long shelf-life and, therefore, the theory must have some form of intuitive appeal. The core idea behind utilitarianism is that political arrangements are sound when they are organised so as to produce the greatest happiness or satisfaction of the greatest number of persons. Indeed, this is the rough-and-ready rule of thumb which is the background justification of most government policy in liberal democracies concerning education, social services and health policies, for example. However, the question is not whether a utilitarian calculus should play some part in government calculations, but whether the pursuit of utilitarian goals by government should be qualified by 'side-constraints' in the form of fundamental non-negotiable human rights that should block the pursuit of utilitarian policies where these infringe individual human rights. So utilitarianism cannot be dismissed out of hand as a political philosophy; it has a legitimate space in government calculations. The crucial question is whether it occupies all the space in political philosophy and political decisions.

Utilitarianism has two central appealing features: (1) it aims to maximise human satisfaction or happiness; and (2) it is fundamentally egalitarian in structure in that in the utilitarian calculation 'everybody to count for one, nobody for more than one' (see this utilitarian slogan mentioned in John Stuart Mill's *Utilitarianism* (1863) taken from Bentham's *Rationale of Judicial Evidence*). There is no recognition or bias in utilitarian philosophy for caste, class, race or religion. The 'democratic' nature of utilitarianism, as opposed to 'aristocratic' or 'hereditary' forms of political organisation, may account for the long-term appeal of utilitarianism as ideas of democracy and egalitarianism grew in the West from the late eighteenth century (the French Revolution, for example, in 1789, whose slogan was 'liberty, equality, fraternity'). Indeed, in 1776 the English lawyer–philosopher, Jeremy Bentham, had written that both government and the limits of government were to be justified by reference to the greatest happiness of the greatest number of citizens (see Bentham's *A Fragment on Government* (1776)). This, at first sight, seems to be an intuitively attractive theory: for the promotion of the well-being of as many citizens as possible within the constraints of reality would seem to be a natural aim of government. Indeed, as a background theory of government, utilitarianism has been and continues to be influential. Utilitarianism can be viewed most favourably as a version of 'a common good' (*commune bonum*) theory of political theory. However, government must have much more in mind than utilitarianism to be politically acceptable. Yet the principle of utility formulated by Bentham claims to be the only principle that can provide an objective foundation for morals and legislation as opposed to other principles, such as the law of nature, law of reason, natural justice and natural equity, for example.

Utilitarianism has mutated into many different forms as sympathetic philosophers have tried to defend the theory against attack from hostile philosophers, exemplified by Rawls (1921–2002) and Nozick (1938–2002). The main criticism directed against utilitarianism is that it fails to provide a sufficiently secure foundation of human rights. However, some sophisticated versions of utilitarianism do claim, with some, if not complete, persuasiveness, that utilitarianism can account for the existence, extent and fundamental importance of human rights in modern liberal democracies. Indeed, the lack of 'fit' between utilitarianism and the persistence and importance of human rights in the Western world has been used to discredit utilitarianism as an acceptable political theory. Sophisticated utilitarians, such as the British philosopher, RM Hare (see *Moral Thinking* (1981)), argue that refined versions of utilitarianism can justify and support many of the basic human rights valued and protected in the West.[7] For example, protecting freedom of speech and freedom of the press is very likely in fact to lead to the maximisation of human happiness through (a) a better informed and educated population, which, in turn, will lead to the election of more competent political leaders; and (b) the scrutiny and 'watchdog' effect of the media on government, which is likely to lead to better and more honest government.

Therefore, a 'rule of utility' supporting freedom of speech and the press, even when that is inconvenient to utility in individual cases, can explain the persistence and importance of the human right of free speech in the West. Indeed, the 'rule utilitarian' can argue that his justification for human rights – to promote utility in the long run – is a much more stable and understandable justification for 'human rights' than anti-utilitarian justifications of human rights based on such nebulous, and arguably empty, concepts such as 'equality'

---

7   RM Hare, in an article published in 1979 in *Philosophy and Public Affairs* entitled 'What Is Wrong with Slavery', attempts to show how a utilitarian can account for our intuition that slavery is always wrong. RM Hare gives an account of the two essential features of slavery: (1) slavery is first a *status* in society: the 'slave is so called first of all because he occupies a certain place in society, lacking certain rights and privileges secured by the law to others, and subject to certain liabilities from which others are free'; (2) a slave has a *relation* to a master who could be an individual or the state.

The status of a slave was defined by the Ancient Greeks in terms of four freedoms which the slave lacks. These are: (1) a legally recognised position in the community, conferring a right of access to the courts; (2) protection from illegal seizure and detention and other personal violence; (3) the privilege of going where he wants to go; and (4) that of working as he pleases. These features are present in a document from Macedonia dated about 200 years before the birth of Christ. In Ancient Greece and Rome it was possible for a citizen to lose his legal rights and become a slave by sentence of a court for some crimes. Bernard Williams in *Shame and Necessity* (1993) points out that in Ancient Greece and Rome the institution of slavery was not seen as 'just' or 'unjust' but as an economic necessity if those societies were to function. The attitude of the Ancient world was that it was just 'bad luck' or 'bad fortune' to have been captured in war and turned into a slave. Williams comments: 'a paradigm of bad luck throughout the ancient world was being taken into slavery by military conquest'. Williams comments:

> 'The Greeks had the institution of chattel slavery, and their way of life, as it actually functioned, presupposed it … free people in the Greek world were able to see what an arbitrary calamity it was for someone to become a slave. What they found it much harder to do, once they had the system, was to imagine their world without it … they had nothing to put in the place of the system … being captured into slavery was a paradigm of disaster, of which any rational person would complain … slavery, in most people's eyes, was not just, but necessary. Because it was necessary, it was not, as an institution, seen as unjust either.'

Slaves were considered to be victims of bad luck but there the sympathy of the free to the slaves stopped.

> 'Manumission', the process in Ancient Greece and Rome by which a former slave became a citizen with legal rights, involved in Bernard Williams's phrase 'an extraordinary transition': 'by manumission the freed slave was transformed from an object to a subject of rights, the most complete metamorphosis one can imagine.'

(Dworkin – see *Taking Rights Seriously* (1977)), 'the separateness of persons' (see Nozick) or 'fairness' (see Rawls's *Justice as Fairness*).[8]

Another example of rule utilitarianism at work justifying fundamental human rights concerns the universal prohibition in liberal democracies on the use of torture by the police to obtain evidence or intelligence. The rule utilitarian would say that an absolute ban on the legitimate use of torture by the police would serve utilitarian aims of promoting the greatest happiness of the greatest number in the following ways: (a) prohibiting torture by the police is likely to maximise utility because citizens will not suffer anxiety in case they or their family members are arrested and may suffer torture at the hands of the police; (b) the police will use more reliable methods in solving crime rather than rely on the unreliable fruits of torture; and (c) the morale and self-respect of the police as an organisation will be improved by a rule prohibiting the torture of suspects.

Therefore, for these compelling reasons based on utility, the state should adopt a strict rule prohibiting the torture of suspects by the police. However, despite the persuasive nature of these subtle arguments, the 'rule utilitarian' fails to account for the following strong counter-arguments:

(a) The torture of suspects by the police is wrong in itself independent of any argument based on utilitarian consequences. Torture of suspects by the state is intuitively a moral wrong in itself independent of the utilitarian calculus. Of course, a utilitarian such as Bentham would denounce such an argument as 'nonsense upon stilts', but the utilitarian has no convincing explanation of our deep intuition that torture is wrong in itself other than to deny our intuitions as valid.

(b) It may be that in certain cases the torture of suspects would improve utility, such as where a terrorist could be tortured by police to find out the location of a bomb that would kill thousands of innocent persons. Many reasonable persons would believe torture to be justifiable in such circumstances and agree with the utilitarian to carve out an exception to the prohibition on torture in such 'ticking bomb' situations. However, the utilitarian cannot therefore adequately account for the absolute and non-derogable nature of many prohibitions on torture in many liberal democratic states (see, for example, **Art 3** of the **European Convention on Human Rights** which allows for non-derogation on the absolute prohibition on torture).

....

8   RM Hare attempts to show in the article referred to in the footnote above that a utilitarian would always say that in 'real life' slavery should always be forbidden because the costs will always massively outweigh the benefits. Hare not only refers to the great suffering and constant fear of abuse and torture of those persons unfortunate enough to be in slavery status but also to the 'effect on character' of the exploiters (the slave owners) themselves. RM Hare in his article aims to show how slavery is wrong in terms of the intense human suffering of the slaves and the degradation of the slave owners themselves. Hare claims to have *shown* what is wrong with slavery rather than, as non-utilitarians do, merely protesting that slavery is wrong based on an 'intuition' that slavery is wrong. Against Hare, though, is another intuition: do we really need to be shown how slavery is wrong? Is it not just wrong that one person can legally 'own' another human being?

The ultimate failure of even sophisticated versions of utilitarianism, such as 'rule utilitarianism', to account for our intuitions about the moral wrongness of violations of rights such as the state torture of suspects has led political philosophers to develop non-utilitarian theories of rights and justice, the two most celebrated being *A Theory of Justice* (1971) by John Rawls and *Anarchy, State and Utopia* (1974) by Robert Nozick. The contingent or 'everything depends on the circumstances' feature of utilitarianism has been a too slippery slope for the foundation of fundamental human rights. Before we examine the political philosophy of the two American giants, Rawls and Nozick, we should consider the devastating critique of utilitarianism given by the English philosopher Bernard Williams (1929–2003) in his 1973 work *Utilitarianism: For and Against*. Williams gave the following graphic illustration of the deficiencies of utilitarianism as a moral theory by using the imaginary account of 'Jim in the jungle'.

'Jim in the jungle' has become a standard stock phrase and example for critics of utilitarianism. The story is as follows. Jim finds himself in the central square of a small South American town at a time in the early 1970s when dictatorship blighted that continent. Tied up against the wall is a row of 20 native Indians, most terrified, a few defiant, and in front of them several armed men in uniform. A heavy man turns out to be the captain in charge and, after establishing that Jim is not a spy but an innocent tourist, the captain explains that the captured Indians are from an area where there has been a revolt against the Government. The 20 captured Indians are to be executed by firing squad so as to deter further revolts against the Government by the native Indian population. However, the captain of the execution squad informs Jim that, since he is an 'honourable foreign guest', the captain will spare the lives of 19 of the Indians if Jim himself shoots dead one of the captives. If Jim refuses his grisly task then, says the captain, all 20 Indians must be executed immediately. This dilemma facing Jim confronts us with the limitations of utilitarianism as a moral theory, for the utilitarian would reply to the dilemma by urging Jim to kill one lone Indian captive in order to save 19 lives. The calculus of utility would demand that Jim carries out the captain's offer and himself kill one Indian in order to save 19 Indians from certain death. Utilitarianism would always prefer one dead to 20 dead. However, the moral equation is more complex than utilitarianism would allow.

As Professor Williams argues, it is not obvious that Jim should kill the one Indian in order to save the other 19 Indians from certain death at the hands of the captain and his troops, for utilitarianism cannot account for the moral point that each one of us is especially responsible for what he does rather than for what other persons do. This is, says Professor Williams, an idea closely connected with the value of integrity. Utilitarianism makes the moral value called integrity unintelligible. The crucial point overlooked by utilitarianism is that by shooting one captive Indian in order to save 19 Jim becomes a murderer and, as a result, his moral character in the eyes of himself, other persons and God is changed forever. His view of himself and what is important to himself is changed forever, even though he was trying through the murder of one innocent to save 19 other innocents. If Jim refuses the captain's offer to kill and then the captain orders his troops to kill 20 Indians, Jim has not himself killed anyone, he has merely refused an immoral offer. It is the captain's choice to kill 20 and the captain had the power to choose mercy or to kill.

Jim's decision to refuse to kill one is indeed a cause of the deaths of 20 but it is not the significant or substantial cause which is, in fact, the captain's order to his troops to execute the 20 Indians.

Utilitarianism fails as a moral theory because it has the effect of depriving human life of all that makes it worthwhile, failing sufficiently to take account of each person's integrity, the projects central to their lives, and the especial obligations and loyalty owed to family and friends. By judging human actions in terms of their consequences for utility only, utilitarianism makes human agency of only secondary and derivative importance, whereas, for example, deontological (duty-based) moral theories, such as those expounded by Immanuel Kant (1724–1804), make human agency the central aspect of morality. For Kant, the morality of an action is to be judged not by the consequences of that action as utilitarianism does, but by the intention or will which motivates that human action. The idea of personal integrity and personal responsibility is a 'golden thread' that runs through the Judaeo-Christian tradition and which cannot be accounted for in utilitarian moral theory. As is reported by St Paul in the Epistle to the Philippians, 2: 12: 'Work out your own salvation with fear and trembling.'

The American philosopher Thomas Nagel has another telling point to make against utilitarianism. Nagel writes in *Equality and Partiality* (1991):

> 'moral rules by which murder and torture are always wrong, confer a certain status on persons which they do not have in a moral or legal system in which murder and torture are regarded merely as great evils – so that sometimes it may be permissible to commit them in order to prevent even more of the same. Faced with the question whether to murder one to save five from murder, one may be convinced that fewer people will be murdered if one does it; but one would thereby be accepting the principle that anyone is legitimately murderable, given the right circumstances. This is a subtle but definite alteration for the worse in everyone's moral status. Whereas if one refuses, one is saying that all murders are illegitimate, including of course the five that one will have refused to prevent. To preserve the status of every person as someone that it is never legitimate to murder … is vitally important, and its recognition by a society is an enormous good in itself, apart from its consequences.'

The pervasive 'moral blindness' of utilitarianism has led some political philosophers to develop sophisticated non-utilitarian theories of justice. It is proposed to sketch briefly the non-utilitarian based theories of justice developed by John Rawls and Robert Nozick.

The political philosophy of Rawls is driven by certain facts – historical facts about modern Western liberal democratic states. In a 1987 article called 'The Idea of an Overlapping Consensus' (in Oxford Journal of Legal Studies) Rawls asks, given that modern society is made up of deep divisions between religious, social and political groups, what political principles to organise civil society could be formulated that could be given the assent of reasonable persons who otherwise fundamentally disagree about religion, morality or politics? The Rawlsian 'overlapping consensus' represents those fundamental principles to organise society which could be agreed upon by persons who disagree with each other about much else in life. The need to achieve social stability and unity over fundamental political principle in deeply divided societies in the Western world has been a major theme of the more recent work of Rawls, who has said: 'The Problem of Stability is Fundamental to Political Philosophy' (see Rawls, *Political Liberalism* (1993)).

'Political liberalism', as Rawls terms his most recent theory, accepts, as it must, the existence of reasonable but incompatible doctrines in society (for example, Roman Catholicism and atheism) which do not reject the essentials of a liberal democratic regime (society, for example, contains democratic persons who do and who do not believe in God). Of course, society may contain unreasonable, irrational or even mad elements (such as political or religious terrorists) and Rawls says that the issue for society here is one of containment and suppression of such groups, for as Rawls comments: 'In their case the problem is to contain them so that they do not undermine the unity and justice of society.'

The basic idea of Rawls is to devise principles of justice that govern the constitutional structure of the state which can obtain the consent of the differing reasonable groups in society (that is, an 'overlapping consensus'). How to discover these basic principles which will form the basis of the 'overlapping consensus' and so obtain the 'holy grail' of political philosophy – namely, social stability in a liberal democracy? Rawls has a version of 'social contract' theory to discover the basic constitutional principles. Rawls, in his original work in 1971, *A Theory of Justice*, asked the reader to imagine a situation in which rational individuals do not know how rich or poor they are, where they do not know where they come in the socio-economic index of society. Behind this 'veil of ignorance' (as Rawls terms this position of 'blind choice') rational individuals choose what principles of justice should govern society. The 'original position' is meant to model conditions of fairness as the rational individuals will not be able to choose those principles of justice which reflect their actual position in society – hence, the self-description of Rawls of his own theory as 'justice as fairness'. It should be noted that no consideration of any utilitarian calculations enter the theory and therefore Rawls's theory is a non-utilitarian theory of justice. At the outset of *A Theory of Justice* Rawls explains why he calls the theory 'justice as fairness' by reference to the hypothetical social contract, 'the original position' which is the foundation of Rawls's theory. Rawls comments:

> 'the original position is, one might say, the appropriate initial status quo, and thus the fundamental agreements reached in it are fair. This explains the propriety of the name "justice as fairness": it conveys the idea that the principles of justice are agreed to in an initial situation that is fair.'

The initial 'original position' is fair since the rational choosers of the 'principles of justice' are screened from any information about themselves which might unfairly influence their choice of principles for society. Rawls claims that a rational person in the 'original position' would choose the following two principles of justice, given that it could turn out that the rational chooser was at the bottom, middle or top of the socio-economic index of society. Those two principles of justice are:

(a) Each person has an equal claim to a fully adequate scheme of equal basic rights and liberties, which scheme is compatible with the same scheme for all persons in society.

(b) Social and economic inequalities in society (and so Rawls is neither a socialist nor a Marxist) are to satisfy two conditions: (i) all positions and offices are open to all persons under conditions of fair equality of opportunity, and (ii) the inequalities in society are to be justified if those inequalities work for the benefit of the least advantaged members of society.

The American philosopher, Thomas Nagel, in a 1997 article, 'Justice and Nature' (in Oxford Journal of Legal Studies), comments that the complete absence of distinguishing information under the veil of ignorance of the choosers in Rawls's theory in the 'original position' would require that all inequalities in society be justified by reference to their contribution to everyone's interest. This is because no chooser could not guarantee that he would be at the bottom of the socio-economic index in society. So 'justice as fairness' would allow for socio-economic inequalities as long as that system worked for the benefit of the worst off in society. Indeed, it is possible to make too much of the principle of equality which, although justifying the important value of equality of opportunity, can be taken to absurd extremes. As Nagel points out, it seems a mindless abuse of the ideal of equality that advocates for the physically handicapped have blocked the installation of free-standing pay toilets on Manhattan streets in New York (of the kind that are common in Europe) unless they could all be large enough for wheelchair access.[9]

Much ink has been spilt by philosophers as to whether the two principles of justice which Rawls says would be chosen in the 'original position' would in fact be chosen behind 'the

---

9 On the topic of equality, the philosopher Harry Frankfurt has written in his collection of essays *The Importance of What We Care About* (1988) that what is important is that people have enough for what they need in life and that talk of 'equality' only produces life-destroying 'alienation' in those who have less wealth than others in society. Frankfurt comments:

> 'To the extent that people are preoccupied with equality for its own sake, their readiness to be satisfied with any particular level of income or wealth is guided not by their own interests and needs but just by the magnitude of the economic benefits that are at the disposal of others. In this way egalitarianism distracts people from measuring the requirements to which their individual personal circumstances give rise. It encourages them instead to insist upon a level of economic support that is determined by a calculation in which the particular features of their own lives are irrelevant. How sizeable the economic assets of others are has nothing much to do, after all, with what kind of person someone is. A concern for economic equality, construed as desirable in itself, tends to divert a person's attention away from endeavouring to discover – within his experience of himself and of his life – what he himself really cares about and what will actually satisfy him … Exaggerating the moral importance of economic equality is harmful … because it is alienating.'

Harry Frankfurt concludes that the mistaken belief that economic equality is important in itself distracts people from concentrating on leading their own fulfilled lives. The mistaken belief that economic equality is important in itself influences them to take too seriously, as though it were a matter of great moral concern, a question that is inherently rather insignificant: how their economic status compares with the economic status of others: 'in this way the doctrine of equality contributes to the moral disorientation and shallowness of our time.'

veil of ignorance' (see, for example, the criticisms of the 'original position' by Thomas Nagel in *The Philosophical Review* (1973)). In more recent writings (such as his restatement of his views in his 1993 book, *Political Liberalism*), Rawls argues primarily not that his two principles of justice would be chosen in the 'original position' (as he argued in 1971) but rather that his two principles of justice are most likely to gain acceptance, the sought-after 'overlapping consensus', in conflict-ridden modern Western liberal democratic societies such as the United States of America. The hypothetical 'original position' in the more recent Rawlsian writings has taken a back seat to the more pressing problem of achieving consensus in actual liberal democratic Western societies. It is important to note that Rawls's 'principles of justice' are not formulated as 'universal' principles of justice aimed at all societies whatever the historical period or geographical location. Rawls is explicit that his 'theory of justice' is aimed at the modern Western state with its respect for and tradition of democracy, the rule of law and equality of opportunity for all citizens. Rawls can be criticised, therefore, for holding up merely a 'mirror' to liberal democratic states since the Rawlsian two principles of justice are likely to gain acceptance as reflections of current ideals in those liberal democratic states.

Rawls comments in *Political Liberalism*:

> 'the aim of "justice as fairness" then is practical: it presents itself as a conception of justice that may be shared by citizens as a basis of a reasoned, informed and willing political agreement. It expresses their shared and public political reason. It should be independent of the opposing and conflicting philosophical and religious doctrines that citizens affirm.'

Rawls, in his writings in the 1980s and 1990s, is keen to stress 'the idea of society as a fair system of co-operation' (*Political Liberalism*). This 'fair system of co-operation' crucially depends on principles of political arrangement that each reasonable participant can accept provided that, likewise, everyone else accepts them. Rawls has a noble dream for Western liberal democracies: the idea of a well-ordered society as a society effectively regulated by a public political conception of justice. Whether in the light of factors such as pervasive human evil manifesting in rising crime rates and civil disorder, religious and political terrorism, and factors such as global warming, food shortages and energy crises, the 'well-ordered' liberal political society of Rawls's imagination can be maintained in the long run, only history will tell.

However, Rawls is insistent that his two principles of justice are practicably realisable and that they are not utopian:

> 'the most reasonable political conception of justice for a democratic regime will be liberal. It will protect the familiar basic rights and assigns them a special priority; it also includes measures to ensure that all persons in society have sufficient material means to make effective use of those basic rights. Faced with the fact of pluralism, a liberal view removes from the political agenda the most divisive issues (such as religion or morality), reduces serious contention and conflict which must undermine the bases of social co-operation.'

For Rawls, his liberalism is 'political' only in that his 'two principles of justice' can be supported by a wide range of persons with conflicting religious, moral and ideological viewpoints. Rawls's 'two principles of justice' form the 'overlapping consensus' which is realisable in otherwise deeply divided liberal democratic societies.

Robert Nozick published his *Anarchy, State and Utopia* (1974) partly as a response to Rawls's *A Theory of Justice* and also to refute utilitarianism as any acceptable theory for government. Nozick is even more hostile to utilitarianism than Rawls was in *A Theory of Justice*. Nozick seriously doubts the intelligibility of the utilitarian calculation balancing the happiness and pains of all persons in society. Nozick comments that there is no social entity with a good that undergoes some sacrifice for its own good. There are only individual people, different individual people, with their own individual lives. Nozick continues that using one of these persons for the benefit of others, as utilitarianism allows, uses that person and benefits the others. Nothing more. What happens is that something is done to him for the sake of others. Talk of an overall social good covers this up. To use a person in this way does not sufficiently respect and take account of the fact that he is a separate person, that his is the only life he has. Nozick, therefore, doubts whether utilitarianism is intelligible as a moral theory and that the existence of fundamental human rights reflects the crucial metaphysical and sociological fact of our separate existences from each other. This root idea for Nozick – namely, that there are different individuals with separate lives and so no one may be sacrificed for others – underlies the existence of the fundamental human rights and leads to the rejection of utilitarianism as a moral theory with its talk of 'balancing' the pleasures and pains of different persons so as to produce a 'utilitarian' calculation. The individual rights that we enjoy (indeed, the very first sentence of *Anarchy, State and Utopia* states: 'Individuals have rights, and there are things no person or group may do to them without violating their rights') reflect the basic insight that persons have 'separate existences' (as Nozick comments, we should remind ourselves 'of how different people are' from each other).

From this metaphysical and psychological fact about our separate existences Nozick savages utilitarianism as a political and moral philosophy and builds his own 'theory of the state' which does respect individual persons and their rights – namely, the 'minimal state'. Nozick argues that only the minimal state is morally legitimate as it treats us as inviolate individuals who may not be used in certain ways by others as means or tools or instruments or resources: the 'minimal state' treats us as persons having individual rights with the dignity this constitutes. Treating us with respect, says Nozick, by respecting our rights, the 'minimal state' allows us, individually or with whom we choose, to choose our life and to realise ends and our conception of ourselves aided by the voluntary co-operation of other individuals possessing the same dignity. The 'minimal state' of Nozick's imagination would be different from the United States and United Kingdom in important respects. Nozick is not an anarchist, he believes in the legitimacy and necessity of a central authority with a monopoly on the use of legitimate coercion. This central authority is necessary to protect individuals against the violence and theft of others. No individual, no matter how wealthy, can match the crime-fighting resources of a modern state. Therefore, some taxation to support the 'minimal state' is necessary.

However, Nozick is insistent that any redistributive taxation to support the poor and needy is impermissible as it treats the wealthy as a resource to be used to support others and, therefore, violates the sanctity of the cardinal principle for Nozick, 'the separateness of persons'. As Nozick comments, every person is entitled to all that they have acquired provided they gained their possessions justly. The state must do no more than enforce contracts, prevent crime and safeguard the country from external attack. It is for individuals, through charitable donations and voluntary bequests, to help the poor and needy. Enforced taxation of the rich to help the poor is not legitimate for Nozick. The state is too dangerous an entity to be trusted with power beyond that which is required by the 'minimal state'. Nozick can be viewed as the father of right-wing free-market and anti-welfarism political philosophy, which denies utilitarianism as both a dangerous egalitarian and potentially socialistic philosophy and which threatens, in its treatment of persons as 'units' of utility, the sacred rights of inviolable individuals.

However, Nozick's views can be criticised in the light of Professor Hart's criticisms in an essay entitled 'Between Utility and Rights' (in *Essays in Jurisprudence and Philosophy* (1983)). Hart comments that it is a distortion of language to suggest that some taxation of the rich to help the poor and needy is inevitably a violation of the rights of the rich. As Hart comments: 'Can one man's relief from great suffering not outweigh a small loss of income imposed on another to provide it?' Therefore, as a fair society we accept some redistributive taxation so long as the level of taxation on the rich is reasonable and fair. Nozick wants to shield the rich from any redistributive taxation to relieve the poor. This seems intuitively unreasonable and no serious politician today would assert such an extreme position. Moreover, Nozick's concern for freedom seems to extend only to those who have the resources to exercise it. As Hart comments:

> 'It is, of course, an ancient insight that for a meaningful life not only the protection of freedom from deliberate restriction but opportunities and resources for its exercise are needed. Except for a few privileged and lucky persons, the ability to shape life for oneself and lead a meaningful life is something to be constructed by positive marshalling of social and economic resources … Nothing is more likely to bring freedom into contempt and so endanger it than failure to support those who lack, through no fault of their own, the material and social conditions and opportunities which are needed if a man's freedom is to contribute to his welfare.'

The consequences of the 'minimal state' envisaged by Nozick could well lead to social and economic resentment from the mass of individuals denied economic help through redistributive taxation, leading possibly to civil disorder and revolution and disturbing the security of the rich which Nozick was so keen to protect. The key point which Professor Hart makes in his criticism of Nozick is that, in constructing his theory, he sought to derive too much from the idea of the 'separateness of persons' and that other values are relevant to a moral and political theory. As Hart comments:

> 'Why should there not be included a basic right to the positive service of the relief of great needs or suffering or the provision of basic education and skills and why should property rights have an absolute, permanent, exclusive and unmodifiable character?'

It is arguable that Nozick has made in *Anarchy, State and Utopia* as much a false idol of the idea of 'the separateness of persons' as utilitarianism made of the slogan 'the greatest happiness of the greatest number'. Perhaps, to use a phrase coined by Professor Hart, the truth in political philosophy lies 'between utility and absolute rights'.

Common Pitfalls

Students can avoid the pitfall of thinking that utilitarianism cannot provide a theory of human rights. Sophisticated utilitarians, such as RM Hare, argue that utility is nearly always served by strict adherence to fundamental human rights: therefore there can be a 'utility of rights'. Students can gain extra marks by arguing that even the most sophisticated versions of utilitarianism cannot account for the absolute and persisting nature of fundamental human rights.

NOTES

The section on utilitarianism by Rawls in *A Theory of Justice* (1971) is the best starting point for learning about the criticisms of utilitarianism. Heavier reading is provided by Nozick in *Anarchy, State and Utopia* (1974), but the reader should refer also to Professor Bernard Williams's critique of utilitarianism in *Utilitarianism: For and Against* (1973) with JJC Smart. Nozick's extreme anti-utilitarian theory is itself critiqued by Professor Hart in 'Between Utility and Rights' in *Essays in Jurisprudence and Philosophy* (1983).

8 Common Law and Statute

INTRODUCTION

Common law and statute law are the two most important sources of law in the Anglo-American legal systems so this topic should have an inherent appeal for students of jurisprudence. However the common law and statutory law are both a useful lens through which to view legal theorists, as different legal theorists tend to focus on common law or statute law and give one of them pre-eminence in their legal theories depending on the focus of their own theory of law. For example, Bentham was implacably hostile to the common law but saw his ideal form of law in the comprehensive codification of law namely statutory law.

Modern legal positivists such as Professor Raz and Professor John Gardner view the essence of law as being an exercise of authority to change the normative position of others, so there is an emphasis on the finality of legislation as a legal source. Professor Dworkin has concentrated in his legal theory on judicial adjudication so the common law tends to be the focus of his legal theory.

Checklist

Ensure that you are acquainted with the following topics:

- Bentham's hostile attitude towards the common law;
- the theory of classical common law;
- the role of experience in the formation of the common law;
- the reasons for the domination of legislation as the primary legal source in the Anglo-American legal systems;
- the extent to which the common law is a 'conservative' institution;
- what 'leading cases' can tell us about the nature of the common law;
- the historical significance of the writ of habeas corpus;
- the significance of the leading common law case of *Somerset v Stewart* (1772).

QUESTION 30

Explain the dominance of legislation as the primary source of modern law.

How to Answer this Question

This question seeks to explore the reasons why legislation, statute law has become the dominant legal source leading to the subordination of common law. The circumspection of the modern judiciary, with regard to their law-making powers (with exceptions, most notably Lord Denning) compared to the golden age of the common law under Lord Mansfield in the late eighteenth century, partly explains the rise of the statute but legislation itself offers many advantages to the modern policy maker in terms of rapid response, finality and the ability of legislation through extremely detailed Codes of Practice to minutely regulate areas of social life, such as police work (see **the Police and Criminal Evidence Act 1984** and its ever updated complex codes of practice) or health and safety.

Applying the Law

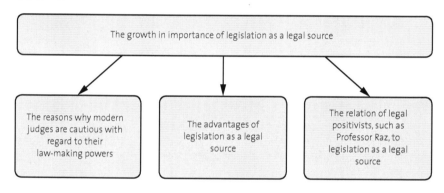

ANSWER

In his biographical note for Lord Scarman in the *Oxford Dictionary of National Biography* Stephen Sedley[1] comments:

> 'One of the long term processes which the twentieth century witnessed in the legal system of England and Wales was the transition from the common law dominated system of the nineteenth century to the statute dominated system of the twenty-first.'

Perhaps the eclipse of the common law as a legal source and the rise of the statute owes something to the democratic impulse. The unaccountable law-making power of unelected judges raises a democratic legitimacy deficit in contrast to the inherent democratic legitimacy of Parliament produced statute law. The legitimacy of European Union derived legislation raises whole new areas of democratic concern which we will not examine.

---

1   Sir Stephen Sedley is perhaps the best judicial author on the law alive today. Lord Bingham died in 2010 and authored three classics on the law: *The Business of Judging* (2000), *The Rule of Law* (2010) and *Lives of the Law* (2011). Sir Stephen Sedley with his collection of essays *Ashes and Sparks* (2011) could well fill the vacuum left by Lord Bingham.

Certainly judges in the present era are more careful in their use of their law-making powers than in previous eras and overly activist judges such as Lord Denning are frowned upon; indeed Lord Denning positively gloried in the judicial law-making role.

Lord Bingham, the former senior Law Lord, in an essay entitled 'The Judge as Lawmaker: An English perspective' outlines the many restrictions that a judge in England should recognise as impinging upon his law-making powers:

(1)   where reasonable and right-minded citizens have legitimately ordered their affairs on the basis of a certain understanding of the law. As Lord Reid put it:

> 'People rely on the certainty of the law in settling their affairs, in particular in making contracts or settlements. It would be very wrong if judges were to disregard or innovate on what can fairly be regarded as settled law in matters of that kind.'

(2)   where, although a rule of law is seen to be defective, its amendment calls for a detailed legislative code, with qualifications, exceptions and safeguards which cannot be feasibly be introduced by judicial decisions. Such cases call for a rule of judicial abstinence, particularly where wise and effective reform of the law calls for research and consultation of a kind which no court of law is fitted to undertake;

(3)   where the question involves an issue of current social policy on which there is no consensus in the community;

(4)   where an issue is the subject of current legislative activity. If Parliament is actually engaging in deciding what the rule should be in a given legal situation, the courts are generally wise to await the outcome of that deliberation rather than to pre-empt the result by judicial decision;

(5)   where the issue arises in a field far removed from ordinary judicial experience.

Lord Bingham, having outlined these major general reasons why a judge should be circumspect in her use of her law-making powers, offers some further reasons which should act as a check on judicial law-making:

(a)   On the whole, the law advances in small steps, not by giant bounds … If judges make too free with existing law, or are too neglectful of precedent, the law becomes reprehensibly uncertain and unpredictable.

(b)   Lord Denning's glorification of judicial law-making is dangerous because then too much of the law depends on the temperament and predilections of individual judges.

(c)   A judge who works to a predetermined law reform agenda necessarily deprives himself of the capacity to respond to the merits of the particular case as it unfolds before him.

(d)   Judges are, by and large, not fitted to be law reformers but are trained to interpret and apply the law.

The courts are unlikely to change the law where the change in a particular area does not cohere with the law generally, as was said by McHugh J. in *Burnie Port Authority v General Jones Pty Ltd* (1994):

'A judge-made rule is legitimate only when it can be effectively integrated into the mass of principles, rules and standards which constitute the common law and equity. A rule which will not "fit" into the general body of the established law cannot be the subject of judge-made law.'

Legislation can ride roughshod over existing legal principle and forge out a new direction for the law[2] such as bringing in a ban to stop smoking in public places, but the common law does not progress in so aggressive a fashion – it builds slowly upon a 'reef' of existing legal principle.

This judicial caution of the present era with regard to their law-making powers would not in itself explain the modern domination of legislation as a legal source. There must be powerful reasons why statute law has become such a powerful agent for the governmental steering of society. However, in earlier times, government was much more reluctant to employ legislation as the 'catch all' solution to social problems that it has become today. Lord Liverpool, Prime Minister 1812–1827, pessimistically observed in the House of Lords when discussing the limitations on governmental action:

'This was a doctrine that could not be too often or too strongly impressed on the people of this country. They ought to be taught that evils inseparable from the state of things should not be charged on any government; and, on enquiry, it would be found that by far the greater part of the miseries of which human nature complained were in all times and In all countries beyond the control of human legislation.'

However Lord Liverpool's pessimistic assessment of the effectiveness of legislation to 'control' the 'miseries of which human nature complained' has not prevailed and especially since the Second World War, there has been an ever-increasing burden of legislation.[3]

The following reasons are suggested for the fact that we now live in the 'age of statutes':

(1)   Legislation is the deliberate production of law, the presentation of new legal norms as a direct exercise of authority. The common law, judge-made law, is in a sense accidentally produced through the chance occurrences of litigation. If the essence of law is that it involves an exercise of authority to change another's normative position then it is hardly surprising that legislation rather than common law has become the

. . . .

2   Examples of legislation forging out new directions for the law and overturning overnight established modes of thought and legal practice include: **The Abortion Act 1967** legalising abortion under certain circumstances, the decriminalisation of homosexual activity between consenting adults in **The Sexual Offences Act 1967** and **The Hunting Act 2004** making fox hunting illegal.

3   The massive growth in legislation since 1945 in the United Kingdom has been matched by a corresponding increase in the scope of judicial review of executive action as judges attempted to keep an eye on government and its ever-increasing sphere of operations. For discussion of the reasons for the growth in judicial review see Question 28, Chapter 7 of this book.

primary legal source. As the state has expanded and deepened into the social fabric in the massive growth of the state in England since the Second World War, then **it is** not surprising that legislation has grown in importance in parallel, as the state seeks to penetrate deeper into, and regulate the social fabric. As the philosopher Anthony Quinton notes in *The Politics of Imperfection* (1978) the state has expanded its reach into areas formerly occupied by other social institutions:

> 'it has seemed not merely convenient, but imperative, for government to take on itself all sorts of functions that were previously discharged by other institutions, such as the Church or the family, or in a private, non-institutional way.'

(2) Legislation is proactive, identifying social problems and addressing them directly, whereas judicial decisions are reactive dependent on legal problems being brought forward for decision.

(3) Legislation is seen in contrast to judicial common law as an explicitly political process, statute law is the result of overt political conflict or debate. Statute law thus embodies policy, defined collective goals for the management of complex modern societies. Common law judges often defer to Parliament on policy matters for the forensic process is ill-equipped for the broad consultation and debate process required to deliver policy-driven law.

(4) Legislation can be viewed of as a process aiming at a certain finality – a conclusive clarity in legal expression. Judge-made law is provisional in a way that legislation is not. The common law is always 'work in progress', by its very nature 'a barrier reef' in which deletions and additions are continually made by the surge of the common law wave. Of course, legislation can be repealed by other legislation but, at least in intention, legislation is meant to enjoy some permanence. Case law is always being restated in updated form, by contrast legislation aims at finality and even code-like comprehensiveness in an area of law. Legislation, by aiming at finality, fits with the essence of law as perceived by thinkers from Thomas Hobbes in *Leviathan* (1651) to Raz in *Between Authority and Interpretation* (2009). For Raz:

> 'it is in the nature of law that it claims authority ie that it claims to be authoritative, and that means that it claims to have settled moral and other social issues.'

The law then is an exercise of authority to achieve finality in disputed social or moral matters or to achieve finality where there is no controversy but a decision is still required as to some matter. Legislation is, on this model of law, the paradigm of law-making with the common law a secondary source of law. Raz has commented on why legislation is so important given the nature of modern, pluralistic democratic societies. In 'The Politics of the Rule of Law' in *Ethics in the Public Domain* (1994) Raz comments:

> 'The reason for the importance of legislation in modern societies is that democratic legislation seems essential for the adequate government of a pluralistic society in a continuous process of social and economic change … Only democratic politics can be sufficiently sensitive to the results of change, and only democratic politics can respond adequately to the different interests and perspectives of different subcultures.'

Raz adds that although legislation is the primary legal source in today's society:

> 'Mine is not the theory that courts should have no share in making and developing the law. I am an advocate, not an opponent, of both judicial discretion and judicial power to set precedents, which between them give the courts considerable law-making power.'

NOTES

An excellent account of the reasons why modern English judges are very cautious about using their law-making powers at common law is given by Lord Bingham (who held the three top judicial posts in the English legal system: Lord Chief Justice, Master of the Rolls, Senior Law Lord) in an essay entitled 'The Judge as Lawmaker: An English Perspective' in a collection of essays called *The Business of Judging: Selected Essays and Speeches* (2000).

The reasons as to why legislation has become the dominant legal source are examined by Roger Cotterrell in *Living Law* (2008) at pp. 344–349.

QUESTION 31

Is the common law a 'conservative' institution?

How to Answer this Question

The common law certainly has strong conservative elements within its structure. Common law has a concern with 'precedent' both vertically (between the same level of court so that a court must generally abide by its own decisions, e.g. The 1966 'Practice Statement' by the House of Lords) and horizontally (lower courts must follow the decisions of higher 'precedent-making' courts). The especial concern for precedent that the common has reflects the need for certainty and predictability in the law as well as the need for 'integrity' – that the common law shall speak with the same moral voice (see Dworkin, *Law's Empire* (1986)). The common law is sometimes criticised for moving too slowly and this is primarily because the common law is reactive responding to the chance effects of litigation but also because modern day judges do not see their role as to bring in large scale comprehensive reforms (see Lord Bingham 'The Judge as Law-maker 'in *The Business of Judging* (2000)). Legislation in contrast to common law is not bound by precedent or the accidents of litigation but can chart whole new legal territories for the law to move into. However the common law can move with the times, if only cautiously, as the case of *R v Raghip* (1991) shows.

Applying the Law

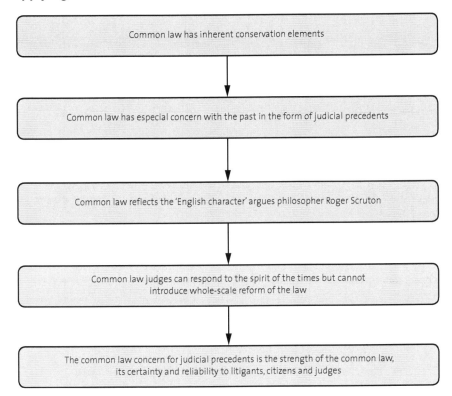

Common law has inherent conservation elements

Common law has especial concern with the past in the form of judicial precedents

Common law reflects the 'English character' argues philosopher Roger Scruton

Common law judges can respond to the spirit of the times but cannot introduce whole-scale reform of the law

The common law concern for judicial precedents is the strength of the common law, its certainty and reliability to litigants, citizens and judges

ANSWER

It is important at this stage of the discussion to distinguish between authoritarians and conservatives. Authoritarians such as Thomas Hobbes, the author of *Leviathan* (1651), believe in strong non-divisible central authority. Hobbes was hostile to the common law partly because he saw it as outside the authority of the sovereign power. Authoritarians cannot readily tolerate any system of authority that is in any way a challenge to the central sovereign authority. Indeed common law lawyers have on occasion suggested that the common law is a system of law outside the authority of the central sovereign power. The main theme here is that conservative political ideology has an affinity with the common law and that generally speaking radicals of both left-wing and right-wing will tend to favour legislation as their method of forcing through the changes required by their varied utopian ideologies.

Bentham the radical reformer of the late Enlightenment, detested the common law and sought its replacement with statutory codification and put his faith in legislation to achieve mighty social and political reforms. Indeed Galligan in *Law in Modern Society* (2007) claims Bentham should be called the *'icon'* of modern Western legal orders since modern legal orders in Western democracies use legislation as the usual means to achieve great social goals. However Galligan does not comment on the fact that Bentham favoured well-thought out, carefully considered, well-drafted legislation and he would not have approved of much modern legislation which is often rushed, poorly drafted and far too heavy in volume to be well absorbed by the judicial system. As Lord Bingham recently noted in his last book *The Rule of Law* (2010) there are:

> 'concerns aroused, from a rule of law perspective, by the torrent of legislation which we have witnessed in recent years … it must be questioned whether the current volume and style of legislation are well suited to serve the rule of law even if it is accepted, as it must be, that the subject matter of much legislation is inevitably very complex.'

Accepting that much modern legislation falls short of the Benthamite ideal of well-thought out, well-drafted codes of law it is still the case that radicals and social progressives will look to legislation and not the common law as their vehicle for change.

Conservatives generally dislike radical change and this is why the common law, with its step-by-step slow incremental change is more suited to the conservative temperament than legislation. Lord Salisbury (1830–1903)[4] Conservative Prime Minister, can be seen as an archetypal conservative who believed in delaying reform until change was absolutely necessary. Professor Roger Scruton, himself a conservative thinker discussed later, once in the early 1980s edited 'The Salisbury Review' dedicated to Lord Salisbury. Roger Scruton has said of Lord Salisbury:

> 'I think for someone to have been prime minister for almost 20 years and hardly anyone to have heard of him is a sign of a successful prime minister. It meant that he didn't change anything or do anything. He was the perfect conservative.'

Lord Salisbury praised the constitution of the United States because of its safeguard of the Supreme Court against hasty or radical legislation. Ramsden comments:

> 'Salisbury had the eminent Liberal jurist Sir Henry Maine's word for it that had any American legislature passed a measure similar to the Irish Land Act, the Supreme Court would have annulled it as unconstitutional.'

Salisbury told a Watford assembly in the 1880s: 'though I do not exclude the necessity of organic change when that necessity is clearly proved' such reform measures had to be proven to be 'directly to the benefit of the nation'. Organic change in the light of proven experience is the very essence of the common law, utopianism the preserve of legislative schemes. Lord Salisbury was fond of the saying: 'A gram of experience is worth a ton of theory' and indeed the experience driven common law fits neatly with this conservative philosophy of Lord Salisbury. The biographer of Salisbury, Andrew Roberts comments:

---

4 Lord Salisbury has a place in the textbooks on constitutional law as he was the last Prime Minister to hold office whilst having a seat in the House of Lords in 1902. Since then a 'constitutional convention' has arisen that the Prime Minister always sits in the House of Commons since the House of Commons is the 'fulcrum of the nation' the elected house.

'Salisbury's distinctive philosophy ... one that viewed with intense scepticism any concept of liberty not steeped in precedent ... and secular schemes for the improvement of Mankind as hopelessly utopian. Despairing of projects based upon lofty ideals rather than practical, day-to-day experience.'

Lord Salisbury once said 'hostility to Radicalism, incessant, implacable hostility, is the essential definition of Conservatism' and that 'the use of Conservatism was to delay changes 'til they became harmless'. Such a conservative philosophy of government makes Salisbury a natural ally of the common law not legislation.

The common law has always had a particular concern for property rights and indeed the saying 'An Englishman's home is his castle' has been judicially quoted with approval by the Lord Chief Justice in the Court of Appeal as recently as 1994. Lord Taylor in *R v Khan* (1994), a case concerning the placing by police of a surveillance device on the side of a man's house suspected of involvement of supplying heroin, commented:

'"An Englishman's home is his castle" is a tenet jealously held and widely respected. It is, in our view, at least worthy of consideration as to whether the circumstances in which bugging a private home by the police can be justified should be the subject of statutory control.'

Lord Coke had said in 1626 in 'The Institutes of the Laws of England': 'For a man's house is his castle and each man's home is his safest refuge' this principle although not a rule of law, meant that the law gave householders the right to prevent entry to their homes without lawful authority to do so. In the nineteenth century the common law developed the remedies of the tort of nuisance and the rule in *Rylands v Fletcher* to preserve the enjoyment of property. In the late nineteenth century Lord Salisbury at the Carlton Club in 1883 commented on the defence of property rights as a sacred part of conservative philosophy:

'I do not for a moment admit that the Conservative party has no other duties than the defence of property. It has many other important duties; but undoubtedly as the institution by which industry is able to work, by which numbers are able to live, by which the power of Empire is sustained, property is the special object and care of the Conservative party, and the defence must be carried where the attack is strongest.'

Lord Salisbury believed not only in limited government but in private initiative and self-help especially for the poorest classes of persons. When opening a convalescent home near Bradford in October 1877 Salisbury said that charity should never 'diminish the sense of freedom, independence and self-help which is an essential portion of the character of the British working man'. This self-reliance that Salisbury saw as so important is also built in to the very fabric of the common law. The common law can be seen as a set of remedies that depend on the litigant making the effort to assert his rights in court. In contrast legislation can bestow benefits on individuals without them even asking for them, whether it is legislation creating a new motorway or airport or the creation of a conservation area or an increase in state welfare payments. Lord Salisbury above all detested radicalism and ill-considered change and put his faith in the wisdom of established institutions such as The Established Church, the House of Lords, the landed aristocracy, the monarchy. There is scarcely a more venerable and historic English institution than the thousand-year-old common law and as the historian of the common law Brian Simpson comments: 'judicial decision is apolitical. Politics are the evil. Those of the political right have a tendency to fall in love with the classical common law' (from *Leading Cases of the Common law* (1995)).

One contemporary self-described conservative philosopher who most definitely 'fell in love' with the common law is the Professor of Philosophy at St Andrews University, Roger Scruton. In his 2001 book *England: An Elegy* Professor Scruton does not hesitate to heap the common law of England with gilded praise:

> 'a vision of law ... provided a paradigm of natural justice ... the noble aspiration which had always guided it, namely, to do justice in the individual case, regardless of the interests of power.'

In even more purple prose Professor Scruton serves up an almost mystical connection between the common law and the English character:

> 'the common law endorses custom and tradition ... a familiar companion, an unspoken background to daily dealings, an impartial observer who can be called upon at any time to bear witness, to give judgement and to bring peace. The common law therefore played an important part in the sense of England as a home. It was the root cause of the law-abidingness of the English, and of their ability to live side by side as strangers in a condition of trust. England ... was a society of reserved, reclusive, eccentric individuals who constantly turned their backs upon one another, but who lived side by side in a common home, respecting the rules and procedures like frosty members of a single club.'

Professor Scruton believes that it is the common law that is the root of the traditional English love of freedom:

> 'Often, when the English tried to put into words the enchantment that lay over their country, they would describe England as "the land of the free". But the particular kind of freedom that the English enjoyed was a creature of the common law. English freedom existed because it was protected; the common law stood like a shield between the individual and the sovereign power.'

For Professor Scruton, unlike legislation which traditionally was understood by Hobbes, Bentham and Austin as 'the commands of the sovereign,' the common law involved a different paradigm of law. As Professor Scruton remarks 'the conception of law as the subject's defence rather than the sovereign's command'.

In a later article from 2008 'The Forbidding of England', Scruton develops the theme that the common law offers a very different paradigm or model of law to that offered by statute law. Scruton argues that the common law holds the ground between citizens and the state and citizens and other citizens. The common law is a mediator and not the expression of raw power that legislation represents. For Scruton the common law speaks in the same tone of voice to citizens and sovereign and insists that justice not power will prevail. If the nerve of legislation is legitimate authority then the nerve of the common law is justice for Scruton. Scruton comments:

> 'The common law of England is not imposed from above by sovereign powers that hope to control us, but is built from below by judges striving to resolve our conflicts. It is a bottom-up form of legal order, a legal order designed to protect the subject from his oppressors.'

However Scruton identifies dark clouds swelling over the glorious common law of his native land:

> 'But we should not believe that the common law is a permanent possession. Indeed, it has been the most important casualty of the EU's relentless dictatorship, which has been concerned at every step to create centralized legislation and courts empowered to enforce it. At every point, now, our judges find themselves hampered by regulations, by vast tomes of dictatorial edicts.'

The major theme in this essay has been to trace how conservative political thought can be traced in certain themes of the common law. However the common law cannot be characterised as a wholly conservative institution. The common law does move 'with the times' and two major impulses driving the common law forward are improvements in medical science and public concern with a particular issue that calls for common law reform. In *Page v Smith* (1996) Lord Lloyd commented: 'As medical science advances, it is important that the law should not be seen to limp too far behind.'

A good example of the common law reforming itself to keep up with scientific advances and understanding lies in the field of the admissibility at criminal trial of expert psychological testimony concerning the potential unreliability of the accused's confession.

The traditional approach of the common law to the evaluation of witness credibility was to rely on the forensic test of cross-examination and the reaction of the witness in terms of demeanour and confidence in response to cross-examination. Therefore attention would be paid in court to how the witness gave evidence under cross-examination: confidently or evasively, without hesitation or haltingly and with prevarication. The witness's credibility could also be tested in terms of internal consistency or self-contradiction, consistency or inconsistency with what the same witness has said on previous occasions, consistency with other credible witnesses, consistency with undisputed facts such as medical testimony. The court would also give attention to the inherent plausibility of the witness's story, did it have 'the ring of truth' about it? The witness's credibility could also be assessed in the light of any striking omission which her account in court had. Finally the credibility of the witness could be assessed in terms of any previous criminal record, motive for bias or history of any mental or physical illness or disability which could affect the credibility of the testimony of the witness.

At court the defendant's confession could be assessed for truthfulness by the jury using the following forensic techniques: did the defendant's confession display any 'special knowledge' which only the perpetrator of the crime could have known such as the actual position of the body of the murder victim? Did the defendant's confession contain any striking omissions of detail which a reasonable person would expect to be mentioned in the confession? Did the defendant's confession show internal consistency or any internal contradiction? Did the defendant's confession show any significant consistency or significant inconsistency with other credible witness testimony or undisputed documentary or scientific evidence? Was the defendant treated in an appropriate manner by those in authority questioning him before he produced the confession; for example was the defendant threatened with violence by the police or offered an inducement as a result of which he may have made a false confession? Did the defendant have a possible motive to falsely confess to protect the real culprit, perhaps a family member or a close friend? Was the defendant intoxicated under the influence of alcohol or drugs at the time he made the confession? Was the defendant mentally ill or mentally handicapped which could have led him to make a false confession?

However with regard to the accused's psychological vulnerabilities in terms of suggestibility or compliance whilst making his confession in the police station, the common law had been very slow to keep up with scientific developments which could identify psychological vulnerabilities of the defendant under police interrogation. These were not vulnerabilities based upon mental illness or mental handicap which a police doctor could detect. A police doctor could not, without special training and the application of certain psychometric tests to the suspect, detect psychological vulnerabilities such as suggestibility of the suspect in the face of police questioning. These psychological vulnerabilities of the defendant principally, suggestibility and compliance, could lead to a false confession being made by the defendant whilst a suspect under caution in police interrogation.

The crucial point is that without expert psychological defence testimony before it, a jury could convict upon unreliable confessions where the reason for the unreliable confession resides largely in the undetected psychological weaknesses of the defendant. In other words the usual methods of assessing confession evidence at court are totally inadequate to identify these complex psychological weaknesses such as suggestibility which could lead to a false confession being made. Only expert psychological testing of the defendant and expert psychological testimony in court can alert the jury to the potential unreliability of certain confessions.

By the 1980s these psychological vulnerabilities of suspects could be assessed by scientifically valid psychometric tests but the common law was initially very reluctant to admit such evidence given by psychologists for the defence at trial. No doubt this judicial reluctance to admit psychological expert testimony on the defendant's psychological vulnerabilities to make false confessions was due to certain judges at common law being suspicious of the value of 'psychologically' based expert testimony as opposed to the well accepted and well respected methods of psychiatry. One of the pioneers of psychological research in terms of psychological vulnerabilities of suspects and other witnesses is

Professor Gisli Gudjonsson of the Institute of Psychiatry, King's College London. Gudjonsson's ground breaking monograph 'The Psychology of Interrogations, Confessions and Testimony' appeared in 1992, but Gudjonsson had been developing his now world renowned psychometric tests for interrogative suggestibility since the 1980s.

In a 2010 paper for The British Psychological Society, Gudjonsson relates how, in 1988, during the appeal of the 'Tottenham three' convicted of murdering PC Blakelock during the Broadwater farm riot in north London of 1985, Lord Lane in the Court of Appeal refused to allow Gudjonsson to give important psychological evidence for the defence concerning unreliable confession evidence. Indeed 1988 was not a good year for British justice and Lord Lane's subsequent reputation because not only did Lord Lane rule inadmissible Gudjonsson's testimony in the 'Tottenham three' case, but in January 1988 Lord Lane had dismissed the second appeal of the Birmingham Six in words which stand as a monument to judicial inertia:

> 'The longer this hearing has gone on, the more convinced this court has become that the verdict of the jury was correct.'[5]

Gudjonsson comments that the judicial 'atmosphere' with regard to false confessions and expert psychological testimony for the defence changed radically after October 1989:

> 'The acquittal of the "Guildford Four" in October 1989 "opened the gates" for other cases of miscarriage of justice in the UK involving disputed confessions … Since that time there has been a growing number of other cases where appellants have had their convictions overturned on the basis of unsafe confessions.'

The common law was led by events (the revelations of miscarriage of justice cases on false confessions from 1989 onwards) and 'the continually growing scientific knowledge in police interviews' to adopt a much more tolerant attitude to the admissibility of defence expert psychological testimony especially in the field of false confessions. Gudjonsson comments on the landmark case of *Raghip* (1991) which signalled a change in common law attitudes to expert defence psychological testimony on false confessions from the rather dismissive attitude of the previous common law approach to such expert testimony on false confessions:

> 'that view was to change in 1991 when Raghip and his two co-appellants had their convictions for the murder of P.C. Blakelock overturned after successful submissions by defence counsels and the expert testimony of three clinical psychologists. The ruling in the case broadened the criteria for admissibility and acceptance of psychological testimony in cases of disputed confessions to include borderline IQ and personality traits related to interrogative suggestibility and compliance. Importantly, the Court of Appeal judges warned that high suggestibility and intellectual deficits could not satisfactorily be detected by observations of the defendant's performance in the witness box.'

....

5   The Birmingham Six were finally freed after having their convictions quashed at their third appeal hearing in March 1991.

Professor Gudjonsson comments on how, in effect the common law redeemed itself, by changing to bring itself into line with advances in medical and scientific knowledge in the field of psychological vulnerability of suspects under police interview and false confessions. The case of *Raghip* (1991) was key to the rehabilitation of the common law in this area:

> 'This case was the first of its kind and delivered the most important judgment for the psychology profession in the UK. It has influenced the admissibility of expert psychological testimony in many other cases.'

The other concern identified pulling along the common law apart from developments in scientific understanding, is public concern. An example of this concerns the problems of misidentification in criminal cases with consequent miscarriages of justice. In *R v Long* (1973) the Court of Appeal left the issue as to how to direct a jury on the issue of possible misidentification at the discretion of the individual trial judge. In 1976 the Devlin committee on visual identification evidence, set up to deal with public concern over miscarriages of justice concerning visual identification, reported recommending statutory changes which would radically affect the admissibility of visual identification. Although it should be noted that the Devlin Committee was influenced by improved scientific knowledge of the potential fallibilities of visual identification evidence. The Court of Appeal was goaded by this public concern over mistaken visual identification in criminal cases to radically change the common law regime on the admissibility of visual identification. The results of the Court of Appeal's significant change to the common law in this area of visual identification evidence can be seen in the case of *R v Turnbull* (1977) which removes judicial discretion in this area of the law and establishes almost a 'common law statute' for the judge to deal with disputed visual identification evidence.

There is therefore a tension inherent in the common law between the demands of certainty and adaptability. Lord Justice Sedley in his Hamyln Lectures (1999) observes:

> 'the common law, like the god Janus, is for ever facing both the future and the past … the common law likes to travel back to the future, looking constantly for precedents that will blunt the edge of the anxiety that it is sacrificing stability on the altar of innovation.'

The importance of precedent in the common law is that it seeks to mediate between what Sedley calls 'the equal and opposite pulls of adaptability and certainty'. The common law can break new ground but as an extension of what has gone before not a complete revolution in legal doctrine. Legislation is the ground for legal revolutions not the common law. Therefore the common law judge's search for precedent is not cosmetic or a hollow cover for judicial legislation. The earnest judicial search for precedent reflects the law's search to reconcile two incompatible things – certainty and adaptability. Frederick Schauer in a chapter entitled 'Precedent' in *The Routledge Companion to Philosophy of Law* (2012) comments that the common law's obsession with precedent (*stare decisis*) 'are all located in the vicinity of the related ideas of stability, reliance and proportionality'. The ability of citizens to count on the law is important and outweighs the advantages of giving judges a right to ignore precedent and find the decision which is best in the individual case. Schaeur comments:

> 'the positive advantages of consistency will in some domains outweigh the potential advantages of allowing each judge to try to improve on the results reached by his or her predecessor.'

The need for certainty and consistency in the common law and thus the importance of precedent will arise particularly in those areas of the common law that citizens plan their lives by such as wills and inheritance, contract law, commercial law, for example. Those like Bentham (1748–1832) who view law as a tool for social progress and societal change will tend to minimise the role of precedent-driven common law and give a much enhanced role to the rapid effects of legislation. Schauer comments that, in addition to the value of stability, the doctrine of precedent in the common law can foster the kind of cross-temporal (across time) integration that Ronald Dworkin refers to as 'Integrity'. The demand by Dworkin that judges interpret the common law so that it 'speaks' with the same moral voice of principle has been a consistent theme of his legal writings in for example *Law's Empire* (1986).

A conservative will tend to favour the doctrine of precedent in the common law not only because it promotes certainty and stability, both conservative virtues, but because in addition the doctrine of precedent makes it possible to unite the past with the present. Schauer comments:

> 'what stare decisis (precedent) does, may be a way of making a community cohesive across time, and may even be part of why we can say we are members of the same community as those who are long dead. If the very fact that what has been done in the past is a reason to do it again, a link is forged between the past and the present that may not otherwise have existed.'

NOTES

Roger Scruton addresses how the common law reflects the English 'character' in *England: An Elegy* (2000). Lord Bingham examines common law and statute in *The Rule of Law* (2011). Lord Justice Sedley examines the common law in his 1999 Hamlyn lectures: 'Freedom, Law and Justice'. Frederick Schauer in an article entitled 'Precedent' examines the common law's especial concern with precedent in *The Routledge Companion to Philosophy of Law* (2012), edited by Andrei Marmor.

QUESTION 32

'The life of the law has not been logic: it has been experience'. Oliver Wendell Holmes. Discuss.

How to Answer this Question

This question involves discussion of the strengths of the common law as a source of law.

The great advantage of the common law is that it presents a vast reservoir of human wisdom as contained within judicial precedent. Given the conservative belief concerning the radical intellectual imperfection of the human individual (see Anthony Quinton, *The Politics of Imperfection* (1978)) then judges should trust the historically accumulated wisdom of the community as expressed in the common law rather than their own imperfect judgment. This is the essence of Holmes's dictum that 'the life of the law has not been logic: it has been experience'. The message of the common law is that where logic points one way for the law to go, and experience points in another direction for the law then the law should rather follow experience. There is a discussion of the common law method of reasoning, which is the slow incremental development of the law rather than sudden breaks and turns in the law which characterises much legislation.

Applying the Law

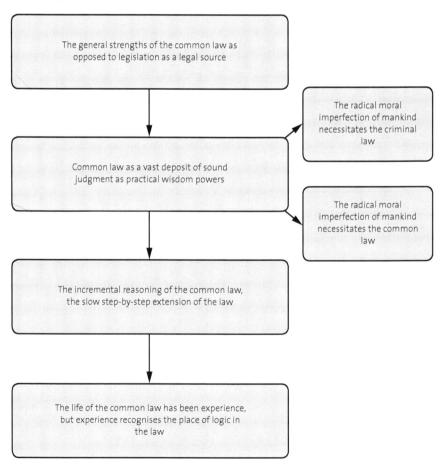

The general strengths of the common law as opposed to legislation as a legal source

Common law as a vast deposit of sound judgment as practical wisdom powers

The radical moral imperfection of mankind necessitates the criminal law

The radical moral imperfection of mankind necessitates the common law

The incremental reasoning of the common law, the slow step-by-step extension of the law

The life of the common law has been experience, but experience recognises the place of logic in the law

ANSWER

However much the common law has taken a back seat to statute in the present era there is still something to be said for the view that the common law represents a form of collective wisdom to be set against the tide of often rushed, ill-considered legislative measures. Roger Cotterrell in *Living Law* (2008) writes of modern statute law's 'transience, disposability and moral emptiness' and 'the endlessly pragmatic adjustment of regulation to increasing social complexity'. Compared to this gloomy vision of modern statute law, the common law, built upon incremental steps set down by generations of judges, seems positively attractive.

The great strength of the common law is that it is a repository of the collective experience and wisdom of a nation's judiciary over centuries. Statute law, on the other hand, is 'of the moment' – the result often of temporary political expediency. The great American jurist and future Supreme Court judge Oliver Wendell Holmes put the point succinctly about the strength of the common law when he wrote in his 1880 work *The Common Law*: 'The life of the law has not been logic: it has been experience'.

Holmes used the above saying to demonstrate the limitations of using 'logic' as a guide to the doctrines of the common law. Holmes commented:

> 'The law embodies the story of a nation's development through many centuries, and it cannot be dealt with as if it contained only the axioms and corollaries of a book of mathematics.'

Holmes reflected further on the common law in his article 'The Path of the Law' (1897 Harvard Law Review), drawing an analogy between the growth of a plant and the organic growth of the common law based on experience:

> 'The development of our law has gone on for nearly a thousand years, like the development of a plant, each generation taking the inevitable next step, mind, like matter, simply obeying a law of spontaneous growth.'

Specifically on the law of contract as part of common law doctrine Holmes writes in *The Common Law*:

> 'the distinctions of the law are founded on experience, not on logic.'

Perhaps Holmes overstated the point about the role of experience in the formation of the common law for the life of the law has a place for logic as well as experience: the common law should be a result of logic tempered by experience and experience checked by logic. However, the strength of the common law resides in the fact that when it is considered necessary to follow experience then logic must give way to experience. Two famous common law cases *Ibrahim v R* (1914) and *R v Howe* (1987) will illustrate the point mentioned in the previous sentence.

In the Privy Council case of *Ibrahim v R*, the great judge of the First World War period, Lord Sumner (described as the 'benevolent malevolence' by Lord Goddard) considered the common law rule that a confession was inadmissible as evidence if obtained by a person in authority who held out the fear of prejudice or hope of advantage to the suspect. Lord Sumner commented that 'logically' the fact that a confession was obtained under circumstances of hope or fear induced in the suspect by those in authority should go to the weight of the confession before the jury and not its admissibility. Lord Sumner in *Ibrahim* commented that in an action for tort (such as false imprisonment heard before a civil jury) the fact that a defendant had made a confession as a result of threats or promises would not make the confession inadmissible in the tort action. As Lord Sumner commented:

> 'in action of tort, evidence of this kind could not be excluded when tendered against a tort-feasor, though a jury might well be told as prudent men to think little of it.'

Given this civil law position what then justified the rule in criminal cases that a confession obtained by threats or promises by those in authority was inadmissible at trial? Logic said admit the confession for the jury's consideration, as in civil cases, but experience in criminal cases pointed another way. Judicial experience over the centuries considered that in criminal cases where the prospects of an innocent man being imprisoned (or, before 1965, hanged to death for murder) on the basis of dubious confessions was too great a risk to take and therefore, since 1783 the common law had erected a rule in criminal cases preventing the jury from hearing evidence of a confession obtained by threats or promises of those in authority. The Eleventh Report of the Criminal Law Revision Committee in 1972 was composed of some eminent judges such as Lord Justice Lawton, Lord Edmund-Davies and Mr Justice James who justified an exclusionary rule for some confessions obtained by the police. Drawing on judicial experience the Report concluded:

> Persons who are subjected to threats, inducements or oppression may confess falsely; juries are particularly apt to attach weight to such a confession even though the evidence of the threat, inducement or oppression is before them; consequently they must be prevented from knowing of the confession.

In the case of *R v Howe* (1987), House of Lords logic pointed one way but judicial experience pointed in a different direction for the law. The case concerned the dramatic legal and moral issue as to whether the common law defence of duress was available on a charge of murder. The defence of duress was available at common law for many offences, such as manslaughter and causing grievous bodily harm with intent to do so, an offence that is only a heartbeat away from murder. Logic would therefore argue that duress should be available on a murder charge. Lord Hailsham in *R v Howe* (1987) successfully resisted the argument from logic by insisting that judicial experience, dating back to Hale in the seventeenth century and Blackstone in the eighteenth century, had always maintained that a man should sacrifice his own life when threatened with death rather than taking the life of an innocent to save his own life. Lord Hailsham commented of the arguments on the other side for allowing duress as a defence to murder:

'First, among these is the argument from logic and consistency. A long line of cases, it is said, carefully researched and closely analysed, establish duress as an available defence in a wide range of crimes'

and therefore logic pointed to the availability of duress as a defence to murder.

However, despite this argument from 'logic and consistency' Lord Hailsham denied that logic should have the last word in shaping the common law and said of the common law, especially that branch concerned with the deterrence of criminal conduct:

'Consistency and logic, although inherently desirable, are not always prime characteristics of a penal code based like the common law on custom and precedent. Law so based is not an exact science.'

Lord Hailsham quoting long judicial experience going back to Lord Hale and Sir William Blackstone – 'an unbroken tradition of authority' said that duress was not available at common law to murder since, in the words of Sir William Blackstone:

'a man under duress ought rather to die himself than escape by the murder of an innocent.'[6]

Judicial experience suffused with Christian morality, as expressed in the common law, did not allow the murder of an innocent in order for a man to escape with his own life.[7]

Indeed the very nerve of the common law is judicial experience[8] given the incremental organic development of the common law refracted through case law over the centuries. Legislation, statute law often brings in sudden breaks and new starts in the law (e.g. the smoking ban in public places introduced in July 2007) but the common law method is one of careful, slow incremental growth.

....

6 Duress is a defence to all charges except murder (*R v Howe* (1987)) and attempted murder (*R v Gotts* (1992)).

7 The idea of the judge at common law reflecting community morality, a 'spokesperson' for community standards and wisdom probably made sense at an earlier time when England was culturally homogeneous and much smaller in population. However in multicultural societies, especially of the massive size and diversity of the United States of America, it is much less clear how the judge could be a 'spokesperson for community values' – which community and which values? Roger Cotterrell writes in *Living Law* (2008): 'In a nation as large as the United States, for example, "contemporary community standards" in defining "obscenity" might well, as the United States Supreme Court once decided, have to be considered in relation to a variety of overlapping communities, whose standards differ radically: see *Miller v California* (1973) noting that "our nation is too big and too diverse" for a single national standard to apply. Standards of what is "obscene" will be different in New York City compared to rural Kentucky.'

8 It has to be accepted that experience can sometimes be a bad guide even judicial experience can be a bad guide. For an infamous example of the defective 'wisdom' of the common law was the 'marital rape immunity'. Up to 1991 the common law believed a man could not in law be guilty of raping his own wife, a common law 'fiction' overturned by the Court of Appeal in *R v R* (1991).

In an essay entitled 'Judicial Legislation' (1989) Lord Oliver outlined the traditional common law method of judicial law-making by examining Lord Atkin's formulation of a general principle of liability in the tort of negligence in the very famous case of *Donoghue v Stevenson* (1932):

> 'The way in which he arrived at his decision was by a careful review of previous cases, the extraction from them of a number of propositions and an extrapolation from those propositions to the broad general proposition of the foundation of liability … The case is an excellent example of the way in which English judges develop the law by extension from what has gone before, each decided principle being used as the stepping stone to a further step forward by way of what at least is claimed to be a logical progression. *Donoghue v Stevenson* certainly resulted in the establishment of a joint broad general proposition, but it was not one which, at any rate in the intention of its author, was conceived as a massive step forward in the legal development.'

Lord Oliver, building on his theme of the inherent 'incrementalism' of the common law, comments of the general common law method:

> 'The process is essentially an incremental one built up from case to case, the conclusion being reached by deduction from what has gone before. Lord Atkin was not inventing a principle. He was merely stating in terms which had not previously been universally perceived, the principle which he was able to deduce from the previously decided cases.'

The common law is like a carpet weaved by many hands and it is only when the carpet reaches a certain stage of development that certain motifs can be discerned, as Lord Atkin discerned a general principle of tort liability in *Donoghue v Stevenson*. In the weave of the carpet can be discerned reason and logic but also the guiding hand of experience.

Aim Higher

Students can gain extra marks by noting that the strength of the common law is that it relies on the collective wisdom of the past, set against the intellectual imperfections of people of any given human era. Given the intellectual imperfections of any individual the common law's strength is as the accumulated wisdom of the community. Respect for the common law is therefore a feature of 'conservative' thought which emphasises attachment to, or reverence for, established customs and institutions. Given man's moral and intellectual imperfections conservatives place their trust in the social wisdom of established institutions such as the common law.

NOTES

Roger Cotterrell in *Politics of Jurisprudence* (2003) discusses the common law and the theory of classical common law thought at pp. 21–48. The common law is also extensively discussed in *Common Law Theory* (2007) edited by Douglas Edlin. The most comprehensive discussion of the thought of Oliver Wendell Holmes is to be found in *The Path of the Law and its Influence: The Legacy of Oliver Wendell Holmes* (2000) edited by Steven J Burton.

QUESTION 33

What can the phenomenon of leading cases tell us about the nature of the common law?

How to Answer this Question

The phenomenon of 'leading cases' in the common law is interesting because it tells us the following: (1) the existence and glorification of 'leading cases' is illustrative of the legal profession's collective faith in the common law method (2) 'leading cases' are an ideological device to illustrate the wisdom, moral superiority and humanity of the common law and common law judges (3) 'leading cases' tend to stand out by their possession of high blown even 'sermon-like' rhetoric of the judges. However the common law does show a history of defending liberty, see the history of the writ of *habeas corpus*.

Applying the Law

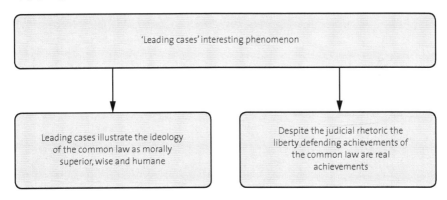

'Leading cases' interesting phenomenon

Leading cases illustrate the ideology of the common law as morally superior, wise and humane

Despite the judicial rhetoric the liberty defending achievements of the common law are real achievements

ANSWER

One established part of the traditional lexicon of the common law is that of the 'leading case'. 'Leading cases' as Allan Hutchinson points out: 'stand as reminders of the legal community's collective faith in the common law tradition or method'.

Brian Simpson, another historian of the common law comments that 'leading cases are the very stuff of which the common law is made'. Common law 'landmark' cases help to perpetuate an ideology of the appeal court judges as the supreme guardians of the sacred and fundamental rights of the British citizen, a judicial role boosted significantly by the requirement on judges to be the guardians of the **Human Rights Act 1998**.

Amongst lawyers and educated laymen the 'leading' cases of the common law become totemic or symbolic of judicial activism at common law on the side of the underdog in the face of oppression, whether state oppression: see *Christie v Leachinsky* (discussed below) or the oppression of a slave master: see *Somerset's* case (discussed below). The ideological function of 'leading cases' is to establish and perpetuate the 'humanity' 'decency' and inherent 'fair mindedness' of the senior English judiciary and hence of the common law itself.

The common law was a source of national pride and 'leading cases' played their part in this ideological construct too. Conservative political thought also takes a pride in country for example as Scruton comments 'conservatives regard society as an achievement'. The common law has traditionally been one source of pride in country and society. Lord Bingham[9] comments in *The Rule of Law* (2010) that the common law's prohibition on evidence obtained by torture was a source of national pride to Englishmen in that the practice of torture to obtain proof was prevalent in continental Europe under the Roman-canon models of justice employed there:

> 'from a very early date, not later than the fifteenth century, the common law of England adamantly set its face against the use of torture and the admission of evidence obtained by torture. Its rejection of this abhorrent practice was indeed hailed as a distinguishing feature of the common law, and was the subject of proud claims by a series of the greatest English writers, including Fortescue, Coke and Blackstone, who contrasted it with the practice adopted in Europe. The English rejection of torture was also the subject of admiring comment by authorities such as Voltaire.'

Lord Bingham in *A and others v Secretary of State for the Home Department* (2005) put a very positive spin on the common law's rejection of torture as an evidence gathering device:

> 'In rejecting the use of torture, whether applied to potential defendants or potential witnesses, the common law was moved by the cruelty of the practice as applied to those not convicted of crime, by the inherent unreliability of confessions or evidence so procured and by the belief that it degraded all those who lent themselves to the practice.'

It is true that torture was practised on defendants until 1640 in England but this was only pursuant to the exercise of the royal prerogative which could override the common law. In 1640 with the abolition of the Court of Star Chamber, where torture evidence had been received, lawfully sanctioned torture in England ceased.

In the case of *A and others v Secretary of State for the Home Department* (2005) the Government argued that evidence obtained by torture abroad without the complicity of the British authorities could be considered by the Special Immigration Appeals Commission, a United Kingdom judicial body. The House of Lords unanimously and strongly rejected the Government's argument and laid down a common law rule of exclusion that any evidence obtained by torture is automatically inadmissible in proceedings in the United Kingdom, regardless of where, by whom, and against whom the torture was committed. The use of torture anywhere in the world renders inadmissible at common law any evidence obtained thereby for use in UK courts. The House of Lords in so ruling did in effect extend the common law. Lord Bingham and the other Law Lords no doubt thought that

---

9   Lord Bingham was perhaps the greatest judge of his generation as well as a distinguished writer on the law. Lord Bingham held the three most senior judicial roles in the England and Wales legal system: Master of the Rolls, Lord Chief Justice and Senior Law Lord. He died in 2010 aged 76.

their judgment, in ruling inadmissible at common law in United Kingdom courts the evidential fruits of torture from anywhere in the world, was in line with the ideology of the common law, namely that the common law is civilised, humane, just and wise. As Lord Carswell commented in the 2005 case on torture evidence:

> 'the duty not to countenance the use of torture by admission of evidence so obtained in judicial proceedings must be regarded as paramount and … to allow its admission would shock the conscience, abuse or degrade the proceedings and involve the state in moral defilement.'

The ideology propounded in this judicial pronouncement by Lord Carswell is of the common law judges as moral guardians of the conscience of the United Kingdom state.

One theme in leading common law cases, as a way of upholding the ideology of common law decision making, is to contrast the liberties enjoyed by the English under the common law with less fortunate countries. In *Christie v Leachinsky* (1947) a landmark case of the common law which established that on arrest a citizen was entitled to know from a police officer on what grounds he is being arrested, Lord Simonds contrasted English practice with lands under tyranny:

> 'Blind, unquestioning obedience is the law of tyrants and of slaves: it does not yet flourish on English soil. I would, therefore, submit the general proposition that it is a condition of lawful arrest that the man arrested should be entitled to know why he is arrested.'

In the case of *R v Borron* (1820) a case concerning the criminal offence of misconduct in a public office, Abbott CJ distinguished Britain from 'enslaved people':

> 'To punish as a criminal any person who, in the gratuitous exercise of a public trust, may have fallen into error or mistake belongs only to the despotic ruler of an enslaved people, and is wholly abhorrent from the jurisprudence of this kingdom.'

It is also part of the traditional rhetoric of the common law that all citizens of the country are equal under it and subject to it, no matter how rich or powerful. Thomas Fuller, the clergyman, stated in the seventeenth century: 'Be Ye Ever So High, The Law Is Above', a phrase beloved of common law lawyers such as Lord Denning. Indeed Lord Denning used Thomas Fuller's phrase in 1977 in the Court of Appeal case of *Gouriet v Union of Post Office Workers*. Lord Denning sent out a judicial warning to a British society plagued by militant and unlawful trade union activity:

> 'To every subject in this land, no matter how powerful, I would use Thomas Fuller's words over 300 years ago: "Be you ever so high, the law is above you".'

The *Gouriet* case involved the Union of Post Office Workers who had called on their members not to handle mails to South Africa in response to a call from the International Confederation of Free Trade Unions to its member unions for protest action against the South African Government's policy of 'apartheid'. The plaintiff, Gouriet, sought an injunction to restrain the Union of Post Office Workers from soliciting or endeavouring to procure any person to detain or delay any postal packet in the course of transmission between England and Wales and the Republic of South Africa.

The distinguished commentator on the law and leading human rights and media barrister, Geoffrey Robertson, comments in 'The New Statesman' journal of Lord Bingham's and Lord Denning's[10] favourite aphorism from the seventeenth-century writer Thomas Fuller: 'Be you ever so high, the law is above you.'

In the ideology of the common law in the eighteenth century, the execution of Lord Ferrers in 1760 after a trial in the House of Lords, for the murder of his own steward, was for many decades later used as material for the ideological claim of the ruling elites that all men stood equal under the law of England. The conviction and execution of the Reverend William Dodd in 1777 for capital forgery at the Old Bailey despite the recommendation of mercy by the jury and strong public pressure for a reprieve again showed to the masses that the law of England was formally indifferent to status and power of people before the law. Lord Bingham in *Lives of the Law* comments:

> 'There was strong support for a reprieve, which led Dodd to believe that he would not be executed, but this may have been counter-productive and have caused Lord Mansfield to oppose the grant of mercy, believing that it might be dangerous to give in to such pressure. On 27 June 1777 Dodd was hanged at Tyburn, a rare if not unprecedented fate for a beneficient clergyman of the Church of England.'

The historian Douglas Hay comments in his classic 1975 article 'Property, Authority and the Criminal Law':

> '"Equality before the law" implied that no man was exempt from it. It was part of the lore of politics that in England social class did not preserve a man even from the extreme sanction of death. This was not, of course, true. But the impression made by the execution of a man of property or position was very deep.'

Of the judicial execution by hanging in 1760 of the aristocrat Lord Ferrers for the murder of a social inferior, Hay comments: 'the event was often recalled as an irrefutable proof of the justice of English society'.

Douglas Hay writes of the ideological significance of the common law's claim to protect all Englishmen without reference to wealth, social position or political power:

> 'An extremely pervasive rhetorical tradition, with deep historical roots … The law was held to be the guardian of Englishmen, of all Englishmen. Gentlemen held this as an unquestionable belief: that belief, too, gave the ideology of justice an integrity which no self-conscious manipulation could alone sustain.'

....

10 Lord Denning was Master of the Rolls from 1962–1982 and perhaps was the most famous judge of the post-war years. He died in 1999 aged 100 years. He published a number of best-selling books on the law.

Professor Hay uses as a famous historical example of the common law's protective shield of the individual Englishman against even the government, the celebrated political trial in 1765 of *Entick v Carrington*.

In this celebrated constitutional case, the court declared that general warrants issued by the government to search property and seize goods were invalid and that therefore government agents had trespassed on the plaintiff's property. *Entick v Carrington* established the general and fundamental constitutional principle that the executive, the government, had to exercise its powers under clear legal authority. However Douglas Hay is wrong to say that 'Lord Mansfield' found against general warrants in 1765. In fact it was Lord Camden, Lord Chancellor who gave the famous judgment in *Entick v Carrington*. Lord Mansfield appeared in another celebrated common law case a few years later, *Somerset's* case in 1772.

It is of note that Lord Denning, who was described in his Oxford Dictionary of National Biography entry as: 'a great master of the common law', liked to utilise *Somerset's* case (1772) to establish the strength and independence of the common law from outside pressure and also as an exemplar of the common law's strong leaning towards liberty.

Somerset's case was a case where upon a writ of *habeas corpus* brought by his English friends, a black slave in a ship moored in the Thames and destined for Jamaica was freed by the common law judge, Lord Mansfield. *Somerset's* case has been described in these terms by Alan Watson: 'probably the most famous decision in English law is that of Lord Mansfield in *Somerset v Stewart* in 1772'. As a 'leading case' *Somerset v Stewart* fits the common law ideology, of inherent English moral superiority, as it involves the contrast between the fate of slaves under the liberty favouring common law and the fate of slaves in countries not governed by English common law.

One noticeable aspect of 'leading' cases is the frequent judicial use of strong rhetoric or resonant language to convey the essential moral 'rightness' of the common law. A famous example of the use of resonant judicial language to convey the essential moral 'rightness' of the common law is the Lord Chancellor Lord Sankey's 'golden thread' speech in *Woolmington v DPP* (1935):

> 'Throughout the web of the English Criminal Law one golden thread is always to be seen, that it is the duty of the prosecution to prove the prisoner's guilt.'

Christie v Leachinsky (1947) has already been noted as an example of resonant judicial rhetoric, but a further example of judicial high flown rhetoric to vindicate the common law is to be found in the dramatic late Victorian case of *R v Dudley and Stephens* (1884).

The facts of *Dudley and Stephens* (1884) really need no repetition for as Brian Simpson comments; 'no leading case in the common law is better known than that of *R v Dudley and Stephens*'. However the basic facts of this notorious case of late Victorian cannibalism were these: in 1884 Tom Dudley was employed to sail the fifty-foot yacht Mignonette from England to Sydney, Australia. The yacht, with a crew of four, foundered in the South Atlantic a 1,000 miles from land. After the eighteenth day, when they had been seven days without food, and five without water, Dudley and Stephens killed and ate Richard Parker the weakest of the crew and the unfortunate cabin boy of the ship. Rescued four days later and back in England, Dudley and Stephens made no secret of how they had survived. The two cannibalistic seamen were convicted of murder and sentenced to death but the sentence was commuted to six months hard labour. In the High Court, upholding the convictions for murder, Lord Coleridge in the high moralistic tone of late Victorian England gave a 'secular sermon' and said:

> 'To preserve one's life is generally speaking a duty, but it may be the plainest and the highest duty to sacrifice it. War is full of instances in which it is a man's duty not to live, but to die ... The duty, in case of shipwreck, of a captain to his crew, of the crew to the passengers, of soldiers to women and children, as in the noble case of the Birkenhead; these duties impose on men the moral necessity, not of the preservation, but of the sacrifice of their lives for others, from which in no country, least of all, it is to be hoped, in England, will men ever shrink, as indeed, they have not shrunk.'

In this passage of judicial rhetoric we have, apart from the high moral tone, an appeal to standards of decency and courage in England which do not necessarily pertain in other countries.

Brian Simpson, in his study of this case *Cannibalism and the Common Law* (1984) comments that Lord Coleridge's language strikes modern critics as 'pompous' and 'expressed in a style appropriate to a sermon'. Judicial rhetoric can sometimes disguise the moral complexity of a situation and indeed, as Brian Simpson points out, 'maritime survival cannibalism, preceded by the drawing of lots and killing, was a socially accepted practice among seamen until the end of the days of sail'.

As Simpson concludes on Lord Coleridge's 'sermon-like' judgment in *Dudley and Stephens*: 'the opinion therefore presented the seafaring community with an exhortation to noble and self-sacrificial behaviour or a recipe for total inactivity in the face of a crisis'. Lord Coleridge in his high-flown moralising judicial rhetoric condemning the killing of another to save oneself and others, overlooked the 'custom of the sea' by which maritime survival cannibalism was widely socially acceptable in the seafaring community.

However the foregoing criticism of the high flown rhetoric of some judges in some common law cases should not detract from the real achievements of the common law in protecting liberty such as the development of the writ of *habeas corpus* which has become a great symbol of liberty throughout the world. The idea of 'leading cases' became particularly important in the United States where at Harvard Law School Professor Langdell pioneered the 'case system' of instruction which came to dominate legal education in American law schools after the 1870s. Langdell thought that if law students were given a selection of leading cases to study in class under the supervision of a professor, students could learn how to tease out the principles from the cases and how to apply them in complex litigation. The 'case class system' of legal education in American law schools continues to this day, so that 'leading cases' are also an 'educational technique' to teach students as well as an 'ideology' of the common law.

NOTES

On 'leading cases' a good introduction is Allan Hutchinson's book *Is Eating People Wrong?: Great Legal Cases and How They Shaped the World* (2011). A W Brian Simpson's book *Leading Cases in the Common Law* (1995) shows how, at Harvard Law School, the idea was developed of teaching law through the study of leading cases. Brian Simpson's classic account of the 1884 *R v Dudley and Stephens* case and its background is explored in *Cannibalism and the Common Law: A Victorian Yachting Tragedy* (1984).

9 Liberalism, Toleration and Punishment

INTRODUCTION

This chapter examines the issue of how liberalism, the dominant ideology of Western democracies since 1945 is best justified. Also examined is the issue of the historical journey of toleration in Western liberal democratic states from religious toleration after the wars of religion, (the original 'liberalism of fear') to toleration of political views and sexual lifestyles.

Checklist
Ensure that you are acquainted with the following topics:
■ the two meanings of the phrase 'the liberalism of fear';
■ the historically sensitive, non-utopian justifications for liberalism of Judith Shklar and Bernard Williams;
■ the basis of toleration in liberal democratic states;
■ the main justifications for the punishment of criminal offenders in liberal democratic states.

QUESTION 34

Explain what is meant by the 'liberalism of fear'.

How to Answer this Question

This question examines the justification for liberalism, the dominant ideology of the Western liberal democracies. Traditional justifications for liberalism have appealed to the existence of 'pre-state' 'natural rights' which the state exists to enforce: see John Locke (*A Second Treatise on Civil Government* (1690)) and Robert Nozick (*Anarchy, State and Utopia* (1974)). Another justification for liberalism is found in the value of personal autonomy and personality development through freedom and choice: see JS Mill, *On Liberty* (1859) and Joseph Raz, *The Morality of Freedom* (1986). John Rawls in *A Theory of Justice* (1971) attempted to show how the basic principles of liberalism would emerge from the conditions of fair and rational choice hence the title for his theory 'justice as fairness'. However a more recent strand of thinking within liberalism represented by Judith Shklar and Bernard Williams reject such attempts to base liberalism on disputable theses such as 'alleged' 'natural rights', or disputed theories of human personality: does human nature require liberalism? Williams also rejects any attempt to argue that liberalism is the natural result of reason or rationality for if that were so why did no-one before the modern period also recognise liberalism as 'rational?' Liberalism, as Williams says, spectacularly lacks an explanation of why persons in earlier ages did not turn to liberalism. Shklar and Williams argue that liberalism is best justified by an appeal to the 'facts of history'. Shklar emphasises the cruelty and oppression often visited upon the weak by the powerful and that official power, given this 'historical memory' must be limited by strict legal upholding of fundamental human rights. Bernard Williams emphasises another aspect of historical consciousness – the fact that persons in 'modernity' the current 'age' do not accept old 'legitimation' stories for authority prevalent in earlier ages such as a 'God given' right to rule. Williams say that in a reflective, sceptical era such as ours all authority and is distrusted and therefore a much greater presumption in favour of letting the citizen fulfil his own desires is given by government than was the case in earlier eras. Bernard Williams says that all legitimate authority must satisfy the 'Basic Legitimation Demand' (the BLD) which requires government to create and maintain the conditions necessary for 'order, trust, peace and co-operation' between citizens. Williams says it may have been the case that in the past the 'BLD' could have been satisfied by an authoritarian government but in the conditions of our sceptical, reflective authority-distrusting age only a liberal state can satisfy the BLD. Williams has a crude but effective visual device to show how liberalism is the only realistic ideology for our age:

BLD + Modernity= Liberalism.

The Basic Legitimation Demand added to the fact of 'modernity' (the present sceptical age) leads to one conclusion, the liberal state.

Liberalism is the dominant ideology of the Western democratic states. There are debates within liberalism of which prominent examples are: (1) The extent to which the taxation of the rich is justified to redistribute wealth through a 'welfare state'. John Rawls famously argued in *A Theory of Justice* (1971) that economic inequalities could only be justified if they worked for the benefit of the worst off in society therefore some sort of welfare provision through taxation of the rich is justified. Robert Nozick argued that because of our 'separate existences' to take legitimately acquired wealth from one person and redistribute to another through taxation is a form of 'forced labour' and is therefore unjust. (2) The United States Constitution protects under the First Amendment to the Constitution free speech and this extends to racially offensive 'hate speech' which would not be tolerated in the laws of the United Kingdom. (3) There is a debate within liberalism as to whether the death penalty for murder is consistent with liberal principles against 'cruel and unusual punishments'. The liberal countries of the European Union have set their faces firmly against the death penalty but in the United States the death penalty was ruled 'constitutional' by the Supreme Court in 1976 (after a suspension ordered by the Supreme Court in 1972) and continues to be practised by certain states in the Union such as Texas.

Apart from these debates within liberalism as to what liberalism requires there is perhaps a more fundamental debate that liberalism has with its external enemies such as right-wing authoritarianism, Marxism, Islamic fundamentalism and various forms of modern-day anarchistic philosophy. Liberalism has to try to defend itself against such ideological threats and the question therefore is: What are the securest foundations of liberalism? Bernard Williams and Judith Shklar would say the foundations of liberalism are best dug around the 'lessons of history'.

Applying the Law

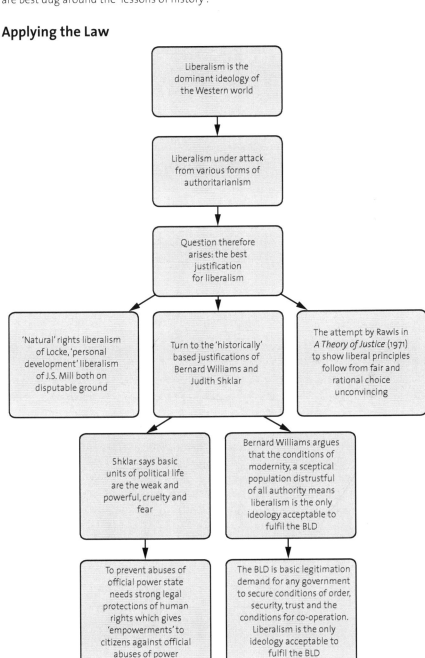

Liberalism is the dominant ideology of the Western world

Liberalism under attack from various forms of authoritarianism

Question therefore arises: the best justification for liberalism

'Natural' rights liberalism of Locke, 'personal development' liberalism of J.S. Mill both on disputable ground

Turn to the 'historically' based justifications of Bernard Williams and Judith Shklar

The attempt by Rawls in *A Theory of Justice* (1971) to show liberal principles follow from fair and rational choice unconvincing

Shklar says basic units of political life are the weak and powerful, cruelty and fear

Bernard Williams argues that the conditions of modernity, a sceptical population distrustful of all authority means liberalism is the only ideology acceptable to fulfil the BLD

To prevent abuses of official power state needs strong legal protections of human rights which gives 'empowerments' to citizens against official abuses of power

The BLD is basic legitimation demand for any government to secure conditions of order, security, trust and the conditions for co-operation. Liberalism is the only ideology acceptable to fulfil the BLD

ANSWER --

Liberalism of one kind or another is the dominant political tradition of Western culture and as such has been under attack from the authoritarian right wing and authoritarian left-wing for decades as well as newer attacks from Islamist radicalism. However despite attacks from without liberalism there has been a debate going on within liberalism about how best to justify the characteristic practices and beliefs of liberalism. What are those characteristic practices and beliefs of liberalism? They can be listed as follows:

(1) A strong commitment to the rule of law.[1]
(2) A strong commitment to the 'separation of powers' between executive, legislative and judicial branches of government.
(3) A strong commitment to some form of representative democracy.
(4) A strong commitment to the legal guarantee of fundamental human rights.[2]
(5) A strong commitment to a free and independent press and media. It can be said that a free society is one in which we cannot defame the government because there is no such offence.
(6) A strong commitment to a large degree of individual freedom for citizens from governmental control.[3]

These can be considered the 'core' liberal commitments. Outside of this list liberals can disagree amongst themselves. To give a very famous example of disagreement amongst liberals concerns the provision of a welfare state for the vulnerable in society funded by compulsory taxation of wealth earners. John Rawls in his classic liberal text *A Theory of Justice* (1971) argued for a welfare state funded by taxation on the basis of a principle of justice that economic inequalities in society could only be justified in society if those inequalities worked for the best benefit of the economically worst off in society. Therefore, Rawls argued, the existence of the rich could be justified if through taxation a part of their wealth helped to fund a welfare system for the worst off. Robert Nozick, a very different kind of liberal, in his reply to Rawls, *Anarchy, State and Utopia* (1974) argued that redistributive taxation on the wealthy to pay for the welfare of the poor was illegitimate, a kind of 'forced labour' in which the legitimately gained wealth of the rich was required by government to be handed partly over to the poor. However Rawls, the egalitarian liberal and Nozick the libertarian liberal.would agree on the core liberal commitments such as the rule of law and a free press and media. Another example of debates within liberalism about what liberalism should include involves the limits of free speech, the right to freedom of expression (see for example **Article 10, European Convention of Human Rights**). It is well known that the United States Constitution protects forms of 'hate speech' against racial and other groups that are not tolerated in the United Kingdom and are outlawed. For political philosophers such as Bernard Williams the protection of 'hate speech' under the United States constitution is not part of the 'core' liberal commitments but is a 'cultural peculiarity' of the United States not tolerated in Western Europe.

....

1   On the topic of the 'rule of law' and its meaning and value see Question 4 in Chapter 2 of this book.
2   On the topic of human rights see Questions 27, 28 and 29 in Chapter 7 of this book.
3   On the topic of the justifications for liberalism see Questions 34 and 35 in Chapter 9 of this book.

Bernard Williams discusses in *In the Beginning was the Deed* (2005) the difference between 'basic' human rights such as the right not to be tortured, total censorship by the state which infringes the right to freedom of expression and more 'marginal' rights such as freedom for 'hate speech'. Williams says that the foundation for the basic human rights need rest on no greater theory that it is 'self-evident' that persons should not be tortured or have their freedom of expression totally curtailed. In other words protection for the basic or fundamental rights are not the product of a liberal culture (as is sometimes argued by opponents of liberal rights) but reflect historical awareness of how governments in the past have abused citizens. However Williams says that for rights which are not fundamental such as the protection of hate speech by the United States Constitution, 'elaborate philosophical distinctions are required to define and establish these rights'.

The fact that, according to Bernard Williams, 'elaborate philosophical distinctions' are needed to justify the protection of 'hate speech' shows that such a right is not a fundamental human right such as general freedom of expression. Williams then notes that the obsession in the United States with protecting hate speech (which in the United Kingdom would be unlawful) is in fact a cultural feature of United States life and not an aspect of a fundamental human right. Williams comments:

> 'It is simply a fact that many European liberals, fully respectable in their liberal convictions, find it a quaint local obsession of Americans that they insist on defending on principle the right to offer any form of odious racist insult or provocation so long as by some argument it can be represented as a form of speech.'

Bernard Williams concludes that the American obsession with free speech is 'partly the product of a culturally injected overdose of the First Amendment'.

There is not only a debate within liberalism over such issues as the legitimacy of the welfare state or the constitutional protection of 'hate speech' but there is a debate within liberalism as to how exactly the core liberal commitments (listed 1–6 above) are to be justified. Two leading political philosophers – Judith Shklar and Bernard Williams – have both argued that it is wiser to give the core liberal commitments a basis in the facts of human history and 'historical memory' rather than try to erect elaborate theoretical or utopian foundations for the core liberal commitments. This is because if we want to defend the core liberal commitments and spread their usage throughout the world then arguments based on abstract theory or utopian ideology can always be attacked and countered with opposing argument but it is much harder to argue with the 'facts of history'. Judith Shklar, in an article entitled 'The Liberalism of Fear' in *Liberalism and the Moral Life* (1989) edited by N Rosenblum, argues that liberalism has only one overriding aim:

> 'to secure the political conditions that are necessary for the exercise of personal freedom.'

The justification for this liberal aim is the project of Shklar's article. She considers two historical attempts to justify liberalism: (1) an appeal to natural rights; (2) an appeal to the importance of liberty to the development of human personality. Shklar says of the natural right justification for liberalism:

'there is the liberalism of natural rights which looks to the constant fulfilment of an ideal pre-established normative order, be it nature's or God's, whose principles have to be realized in the lives of individual citizens through public guarantees.'

Examples of such 'natural rights' justification of liberalism, natural rights which pre-exist society include the God-given natural rights theory of John Locke (seventeenth century) and the rights theory of Robert Nozick in *Anarchy, State and Utopia* (1974). Nozick assumes natural rights exist as reflecting 'the separateness of persons'. Shklar then examines another historical justification of liberalism: 'the liberalism of personal development'. The argument here is that freedom is necessary for personal as well as social progress. We cannot, the argument goes, make the best of our potentialities unless we are free to do so. JS Mill in his work *On Liberty* (1859) argued of:

'the importance to men and society of giving full freedom to human nature to expand itself in innumerable and conflicting directions.'

Shklar comments of the 'liberalism of natural rights' and the 'liberalism of personal development':

'It would not be unfair to say that these two forms of liberalism have their spokesmen in Locke and John Stuart Mill respectively.'

However Shklar notes of these two justifications of liberalism that neither draws on 'strongly developed historical memory, and it is on this faculty of the human mind that the liberalism of fear (Shklar's form of liberalism) draws most heavily'.

So what exactly is 'the liberalism of fear' which Shklar claims is by far the strongest justification for the core liberal commitments? Shklar starts her analysis by noting the 'realities' the 'facts' of political life. The basic facts of political life are not reflective citizens contemplating their natural rights or their personal development but rather the basic units of political life:

'are the weak and the powerful. And the freedom liberalism wishes to secure is freedom from the abuse of power and intimidation of the defenceless that this difference invites.'

According to Judith Shklar:

'The liberalism of fear ... worries about the excesses of official agents at every level of government, and it assumes that these are apt to burden the poor and weak most heavily.'

Drawing explicitly on the historical experience of humankind Shklar comments:

'The assumption, amply justified by every page of political history, is that some agents of government will behave lawlessly and brutally in small or big ways most of the time unless they are prevented from doing so.'

Differences in public power allow for the deliberate infliction of physical, and secondarily emotional, pain upon a weaker person or group by stronger ones in order to achieve some end. It is against the usage of cruelty by public officials that the 'liberalism of fear' invokes the core commitments of liberalism. Shklar is arguing that liberalism is justified not by arguable and highly contestable theories of natural rights or personal development but by the brute realities of power and the abuse of it and the sufferings of those abused by it. Shklar is very clear what lies at the base or justification of liberalism:

> 'What liberalism requires is the possibility of making the evil of cruelty and fear the basic norm of its political practices and prescriptions.'

By using the 'Kelsen' (Hans Kelsen, the Austrian jurist) term 'the basic norm', Shklar is arguing that the fear of official abuses of power is the absolute bedrock and foundational justification of liberalism and its core commitments. The 'liberalism of fear' is 'anti-utopian' because it does not rest on any contestable theory of the human personality, it is 'reductionist' because it is based on the physical suffering and fears of ordinary human beings rather than on some complex theory of what society should be like. The 'liberalism of fear' in Shklar's words is 'based on common and immediate experiences'. Shklar then goes on to show how some of the core commitments of liberalism relate to the fear of the official abuse of power (the 'liberalism of fear'):

> 'It is at this point that the liberalism of fear adopts a strong defense of equal rights and their legal protection. It cannot base itself upon the notion of rights as fundamental and given, but it does see them as just those licenses and empowerments that citizens must have in order to preserve their freedom and to protect themselves against abuse.'

In addition to strong protection of equal human rights Shklar argues for a clear 'separation of powers': 'multiple centers of power and institutionalised rights' and that 'democracy' is a 'necessity':

> 'because without enough equality of power to protect and assert one's rights, freedom is but a hope.'

In addition, Shklar mentions as part of 'the liberalism of fear's' defences against the official abuse of power: 'an accessible, fair and independent judiciary open to appeal'.

In summary, Judith Shklar has provided a non-utopian, non-theoretical justification of the core commitments of liberalism grounded in the memory of the abuse of official power and the ever-present threat of its return. In a similar way to Shklar, Bernard Williams in his 2005 book *In the Beginning was the Deed* has put forward a practically based non-theoretical defence of liberalism. Williams referred to the 'only certain universals' of politics: 'power, powerlessness, cruelty and fear' and said that the first question of all in politics was the problem of securing order and security. If the state cannot guarantee order and security then all other protections for citizens will count for nothing. Williams criticises Rawls who, in *A Theory of Justice* (1971), had written:

> 'Justice is the first virtue of social institutions.'

Bernard Williams denies this, although justice is important to any well-run society, the first virtue of politics is order not justice and justice purchased at the expense of order is likely to prove self-defeating. Interestingly, towards the end of his life as a political philosopher, John Rawls changed emphasis somewhat and argued that the 'securing of social stability' was the basic task of politics and political philosophy. Rawls said in *Political Liberalism* (1993):

> 'the problem of stability is fundamental to political philosophy.'

Therefore Bernard Williams and, to the end of his life, John Rawls accepted 'Thomas Hobbes's question' as the fundamental one for politics and political philosophy: how to achieve order, security and stability over a mass of people? However Bernard Williams at this point parts company with Thomas Hobbes (the author of the great masterpiece of political philosophy *Leviathan*). Hobbes had argued for a very strong indivisible central sovereign power called 'The Leviathan' to keep men 'in awe and fear' and thereby secure peace and order. For Bernard Williams an over-mighty state can become part of the problem of 'fear' as much as the solution. Williams comments:

> 'the circumstances of Hobbesian fear don't merely represent the absence of government, or even the breakdown or partial breakdown of government. They may be caused by the activities of government.'

Williams agrees with Hobbes that putting a stop to disorder requires the effective use of state power. But if the state has no scruples then the solution to 'fear' will become the problem as those subject to state power will lose their freedom and even their lives. For Williams therefore the securing of order is not enough, the state has to secure the conditions of 'trust, safety, and the conditions of co-operation'. This is what Williams calls the 'Basic Legitimation Demand' (BLD). For Bernard Williams, no state can ever be justified unless it can conform to the BLD – the 'basic legitimation demand' of citizens to live in 'order, trust and security'. Williams accepts that there have been societies in the past that have not been 'liberal' in the modern understanding of the concept but have still been legitimate because they have met the BLD, by providing all citizens with the conditions of 'order, trust and security'. Indeed, Williams accepts that even today in the modern world it could be possible to have a non-liberal authoritarian government which met the BLD – by being the only government who could stop a civil war or ethnic cleansing.

However, Williams says that given the 'fact of modernity', the fact that people expect a high level of personal freedom and do not believe that their rulers have any 'natural' or 'God-given' right to rule, then 'liberalism' is the only type of government which can meet the BLD – the basic legitimation demand. Williams's argument for liberalism can be summed up by the following equation: BLD (basic legitimation demand) + Modernity = Liberalism.

Williams is hostile to those versions of liberalism which argue that the principles of liberalism are 'rational' or the natural product of 'reason'. John Rawls argued in *A Theory of Justice* (1971) that the outlines of a liberal constitutional society would be chosen rationally by choosers in conditions of perfect rational choice (Rawls' 'veil of ignorance').

Bernard Williams is extremely sceptical of such an argument by thinkers such as Rawls that liberal principles are somehow the only 'rational' or 'reasonable' ones to choose. Williams says that liberal theorists cannot plausibly explain why no one in the history of humanity before liberalism could see that 'reason' demanded liberal principles. Williams prefers to base arguments for liberalism on (1) the historical facts of modernity; and (2) the 'liberalism of fear' – that liberalism is the best antidote we have got to the official abuse of power. In *Ethics and the Limits of Philosophy* (1985) Bernard Williams says that Rawls retains more radical hopes 'born of the Enlightenment' to give a justification for liberalism based on the desire that the basic principles governing the institutions of a liberal society should be 'transparent' to all. Rawls shares the Enlightenment commitment that all members of the liberal society should understand how the foundations of a liberal society are justified 'publicly' that is that the requirements, the values, of a liberal society are represented in a set of stateable principles. The requirement that Rawls sets himself of arriving at a set of publicly stateable principles is, Williams argues, a legacy of the Enlightenment of the Eighteenth Century. Indeed Rawls produced two publicly stated principles in *A Theory of Justice* for the justification of liberal constitutional society: (1) the principle that each citizen is to enjoy the maximum degree of liberties consistent with the same enjoyment of liberty as others; (2) that all public offices are to be open equally to all and that economic inequalities are to be justified to the extent that they work for the benefit of the worst off in society.

Bernard Williams thinks that the best justification of liberalism is not as Rawls locates it, in abstract non-historical principles but rather liberalism must be understood first of all as a 'historical phenomenon' and therefore the justification for liberalism must be historically based to citizens 'around here and now' as Bernard Williams puts the need for an historically sensitive justification for liberalism. Rawls's abstract production of his governing principles for liberal society in *A Theory of Justice* (1971) might as well be addressed to the 'founding fathers' of the American constitution in the late eighteenth century but Rawls' account lacks explanatory power of how we got to liberalism in the first place, the intellectual and historical processes which made 'liberalism' the dominant ideology of modern Western civilisation. Bernard Williams aims to supply that historically astute interpretation of liberalism.

Williams is clear that given the 'facts of modernity' non-liberal states do not now in general meet the BLD. Williams says 'it is a manifest fact that some kind of democracy, participatory politics at some level, is a feature' of legitimate rule 'for the modern world. One need look no further than the worldwide success of the demand for it'.

Williams says that 'modernity' is a basic category of social and hence of political understanding and so therefore a politically useful construction of liberty for us should take the most general conditions of modernity as given. The significant point for us 'here and now' says Williams is that we do not accept the old legitimation stories that our rulers have a 'natural' or 'God-given' right to rule us. We, the people of modernity, see these old stories which used to legitimate authority as ideology, designed to obscure the truth in the self-interest of the rulers. For example in the early nineteenth century in England the ideology was that only the 'aristocracy' the ruling elite had the education, character and 'breeding' to be the rulers and therefore 'aristocratic' (from the Greek meaning 'rule of the best') rule by men such as Lord Liverpool or the Duke of Wellington was presented as 'natural'. In classical Greece, Plato argued that the best form of government was rule by 'philosopher-kings' and fear of the 'mob', the masses of the ruled was a fear of ruling elites from classical antiquity until the nineteenth century. In Shakespeare's most political play called *Coriolanus*, set in ancient Rome, the patrician ruling elite refers to the mass of the people as 'the beast with many heads' or the 'many-headed multitude'. Indeed the Roman writer Horace in 'Epistles' refers to 'beluamultorumcapitum' literally 'the monster with many heads' referring to the 'mob' of the populace with their ignoble and shameful intentions. A good example of early nineteenth century aristocratic attitudes to the masses of the ruled can be found in the distinguished personage of the national hero of Waterloo, the Duke of Wellington. The Duke of Wellington was Prime Minister 1828–1830 and had defeated Napoleon at Waterloo in 1815. The French Revolution of 1789–1794 had inspired Wellington's hatred of the mob and its vindictive executions of the French aristocracy, and Wellington feared that the extension of the franchise (the vote) in England to the lower classes would lead to the loss of aristocratic power, privileges and most importantly protection from the destructive and vengeful actions of the class hatred of the 'mob'. The Duke of Wellington wrote to a friend in 1832 at the time of the **Great Reform Act 1832** which extended voting rights:

> 'We have now educated the lower orders. They now say why should they not associate with us? They wanted to resort to our private houses, our entertainments; have the run of our kitchens and dance with our wives and daughters … They would shortly afterwards discover that they are better qualified to be Legislators, Ministers, Generals, Holders of Large Properties than we are.'

For the Duke of Wellington and men like him, aristocratic rule was based on two concepts: (1) a belief that the aristocracy, and the aristocracy only were fitted to govern the country; (2) aristocratic rule was based on a strict sense of 'duty' which put the interests of the country far head of personal discomfort or personal loss. Wellington was the archetype of aristocratic rule based on unswerving duty in that he was incorruptible, dedicated to public service (he became Prime Minister against his own wishes in 1828), dedicated to the service of his country and he expected the same high standards from his own class. Wellington commented that it would be better for Parliament to do its duty than to try to bring Parliament 'to a greater degree under popular influence'. When the Duke of Wellington lost patience with fellow aristocrats, it was because their behaviour violated the standards he expected his class to conform to, Wellington believed rights reflected responsibilities, and duty justified authority. A cavalry officer who sought to transfer into another regiment in order to avoid going on active service was told starkly by Wellington that he should go into active service or leave the army, as Wellington told him: 'he must sail or sell (his commission)'.

The distrust and fear of the destructive power of the masses exhibited by ruling elites and the related claim that only 'the aristocracy' had the duty and detachment necessary to rule the country, may be dismissed as ideology – the ruling elites putting up a smokescreen about 'mob rule' to justify their own narrow class-based ruling privileges but the Duke of Wellington knew from the experience of the French Revolution across the Channel what the fate could be of aristocrats who succumbed too quickly to popular rule.

Another ideological justification for the dominance of elites in the pre-modern period was the so-called 'Divine Right of Kings'. In the reign of King James 1st of England and Scotland (1603–1625) and before him, the ideology was that the King ruled on God's behalf, the King was a kind of 'little God' who sat on his throne to rule other people as God's anointed deputy: see King James's own political work *Basilikon Doron* (1598) and Shakespeare's *Richard II* where the King is referred to as 'God's deputy'. The Biblical justification for the 'Divine Right of Kings' was primarily to be found in St Paul's letter to the Romans Chapter 13 where he states that all political authority on earth derives from God's mandate to the rulers.

These old ideological justifications for authority are no longer believable in modernity and can never be believable again. Bernard Williams, in *Ethics and the Limits of Philosophy* (1985), uses a quotation from Thomas Paine to illustrate that once insight and knowledge are gained in a culture then people cannot be returned to a condition of ignorance in which old legitimacy myths for the exercise of hierarchical authority such as 'the divine rights of kings' or the 'naturalness' of aristocratic rule could be re-established. Thomas Paine said in 'The Rights of Man':

> 'When once the veil begins to rend, it admits not of repair. Ignorance is of a peculiar nature; and once dispelled, it is impossible to re-establish it. It is not originally a thing of itself, but is only the absence of knowledge and though man may be kept ignorant, he cannot be made ignorant.'

Given the distrust we have of authority in modernity then as Williams argues:

> 'In interpreting and distributing liberty we allow each citizen a stronger presumption in favour of what he or she certainly wants, to carry out his or her own desires.'

Therefore Williams argues that understanding our historical condition helps us to understand the value that liberty has for us. The fact of 'modernity' as the German sociologist Max Weber (died 1920) understood it involved 'the disenchantment of the world' as Western people lost faith in God and therefore God-based explanations of political authority. Modern Western citizens retreated from believing that the order of how people should treat one another is somehow inscribed either in them or in the universal realm. One effect of this 'scepticism' of modern people is an associated tendency to hold up various traditional sources of authority to question; it is a notable feature of modernity, says Williams, that we do not believe the traditional legitimation stories of hierarchy and inequality. Williams concludes that because citizens in the 'modern' age have doubts about authority we allow each citizen a strong presumption in favour of carrying out his or her own desires. Williams comments in *Ethics and the Limits of Philosophy* (1985):

> 'the modern world is marked by a peculiar level of reflectiveness … reflective consciousness.'

Williams argues:

> 'there is no route back from reflectiveness … this phenomenon of self-consciousness together with the institutions and processes that support it, constitute one reason why past forms of life are not a real option for the present … where we see them as wrong was in the myths that legitimated their hierarchies.'

Williams comments that the modern 'naturalistic' conception of society without reference to supernatural elements such as God, was 'expressed by Hobbes and Spinoza at the beginning of the modern world' representing one of the ways in which in Max Weber's famous phrase 'the magic has gone from' the world. Any realistic account of liberalism must take into account the historical process by which we arrived at liberalism as the dominant ideology of Western culture and civilisation. Bernard Williams supplies such an historical account of liberalism.

On the subject of human rights Williams again looks for a justification that is not based on highly contestable theoretical views but on the brute facts of human history and life:

> 'It seems to me sensible, both philosophically and politically, to make our views about human rights, or at least the most basic human rights, depend as little as possible on disputable theses of liberalism or any other particular ideology.'

Bernard Williams argues that the abuses with which fundamental human rights guard us against are 'self-evidently' evil, the abuse of fundamental human rights are 'unmediated coercion', by which Williams means they are naked abuses of power. Of course, all states use coercion against citizens but when a person is sentenced to a long period of imprisonment or even (as in the United States) execution it is done after a fair public trial, in other words the state' coercive powers are 'mediated' they can only occur after a certain procedure has been fulfilled. However when an agent of the state tortures a detainee or someone is put in prison without trial for their political beliefs there is no 'mediation' of the coercion, it is an evil which must be guarded against by the rigorous legal protection of fundamental human rights.

> Bernard Williams distinguishes between a strongly moralised conception of liberalism as based on ideals of individual autonomy such as characterise the work of Rawls, Nozick, Dworkin and Raz and a 'more sceptical, historically alert' version of liberalism as exemplified by Bernard Williams and Judith Shklar. Williams says that the 'more sceptical, historically alert' version of liberalism of himself and Judith Shklar offers: 'the best hope for humanly acceptable legitimate government under modern conditions.'

We have been discussing so far how best to justify the core commitments of the modern liberal state which at the outset of the discussion we identified as:

(1) A strong commitment to the rule of law.
(2) A strong commitment to the 'separation of powers' between executive, legislative and judicial branches of government.
(3) A strong commitment to some form of representative democracy.

(4) A strong commitment to the legal guarantee of fundamental human rights.
(5) A strong commitment to a free and independent press and media.
(6) A strong commitment to a large degree of individual freedom for citizens from governmental control.

However, beyond these core commitments of liberalism, a decent liberal government has a further duty and that is not to forfeit or put in danger what gains have been made over the decades in terms of social stability and public order through the ill-considered political strivings for far-reaching social improvements or social experiments. In assessing the long-term effects of policies, political leaders must never assume that a public good secured (such as law and order) is secured for good. Old evils such as civil disorder can reappear in surprisingly new contexts. Therefore a politically realist government will understand that 'preventing the worst' is the first duty of political leaders. The supreme function of statesmanship is to guard against preventable evils but the besetting temptation of all politics to concern itself with the immediate present at the expense of the future and therefore a politically realist government will not pursue social policies which threaten the long term stability of the society in question.

Aim Higher

The term 'liberalism of fear' has meaning in two quite different contexts. The first meaning of the 'liberalism of fear' refers to the historical explanation for the emergence of religious toleration then political toleration in Western Europe from about 1700 onwards. The religious wars between Catholics and Protestants such as in France and wars between different kinds of Protestant (see the English civil war of the 1640s) convinced thinkers like John Locke that the only possible alternative to unending civil war was religious toleration. Therefore religious toleration grew out of a 'fear' the fear of religious wars. Therefore it is possible to speak of the 'liberalism of fear,' liberal toleration of different religious faiths based on a 'fear' of the old intolerance and wars. The more modern usage of the phrase the 'liberalism of fear' refers to a contemporary justification for liberalism especially the entrenched protection of fundamental human rights. This 'liberalism of fear' points out that the basic units of political life always have been and always will be the weak and the strong, the fearful and the powerful. The 'liberalism of fear' refers to the' fear' of the weak of the official abuse of power given that it is the weak and vulnerable who bear the weight of such abuses.

NOTES

Judith Shklar, in an article entitled 'The Liberalism of Fear' in *Liberalism and the Moral Life* (1989), edited by N Rosenblum, has written the key article for the 'liberalism of fear'. Bernard Williams' views on the 'historical' non-theoretical justification for liberalism is to be found in *In the Beginning was the Deed: Realism and Moralism in Political Argument* (2005), especially Chapters 1, 2, 5, 6, 7 and 10.

QUESTION 35

What is the modern philosophical basis of toleration in liberal democratic states?

How to Answer this Question

The issue of whether, and to what extent, the state should tolerate so-called victimless immoralities has been of concern to philosophers at least since the publication of John Stuart Mill's *On Liberty* (1859). The roots of toleration, at least in the religious context, can be traced back to Locke's analysis in *A Letter Concerning Toleration* (1667). Modern debate was re-ignited with the Hart-Devlin debate in the 1950s and 1960s over proposals to decriminalise homosexuality in England.[4] Modern theorists, such as Dworkin and Raz, have sought to give strong foundations to liberal toleration but their approach is opposed by a continuing strand of 'natural law' thought which seeks to emphasise the continuing relevance of man's sinfulness in the eyes of God and the need to suppress immoral conduct. The debate between liberals and conservatives on this matter could not be of more relevance today.

Applying the Law

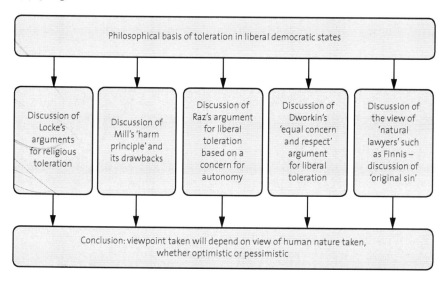

Philosophical basis of toleration in liberal democratic states

Discussion of Locke's arguments for religious toleration

Discussion of Mill's 'harm principle' and its drawbacks

Discussion of Raz's argument for liberal toleration based on a concern for autonomy

Discussion of Dworkin's 'equal concern and respect' argument for liberal toleration

Discussion of the view of 'natural lawyers' such as Finnis – discussion of 'original sin'

Conclusion: viewpoint taken will depend on view of human nature taken, whether optimistic or pessimistic

---

4 Homosexual acts by adults over 21 years of age in private were decriminalised by the **Sexual Offences Act 1967**. As late as 1964 jail sentences were still being handed down by judges for this offence. It is interesting to note the cultural influence of the film 'Victim' (1961) on law reform here. In that film Dirk Bogarde played a barrister being blackmailed for his homosexuality. The idea that the law against homosexuality was a 'blackmailer's charter' certainly influenced the decision of the Government to allow Leo Abse's private members bill decriminalising adult homosexual acts to pass in 1967 although this was a full ten years after the Wolfenden Committee had recommended liberalisation of the law in this area in the 1957 Wolfenden Report. As Roy Jenkins, Home Secretary 1965–1967, observed in his 1991 autobiography *A Life at The Centre*: 'a liberal hour had struck' in the mid 1960s in Britain. It is important to remember, however, that the **Sexual Offences Act 1967** was originally an act of 'toleration' not 'approval' of adult homosexual acts in private although in the early twenty-first century in the UK homosexuality is viewed as the full equal of heterosexuality: but that is not how the **Sexual Offences Act 1967** was viewed at the time.

ANSWER

The question of how far and on what basis the state should tolerate so-called 'victimless' immoralities, such as drug abuse, homosexuality and suicide, has been a source of great philosophical inquiry for many jurists and philosophers.

The starting point for the historical origin of toleration is often taken to be John Locke's (1632–1704) *Letter Concerning Toleration* (1667) which was later joined by a Second Letter and a Third Letter. Between 1642 and 1649 there was a civil war in England partly arising from conflicting religious beliefs. When the dust of conflict had settled, and Charles II was restored to the throne in 1660, philosophers such as Locke naturally asked the questions: 'How is civil society even possible between those of different faiths?' and 'What can conceivably be the basis of religious toleration?'

The alternative to religious toleration was unpalatable: unending civil war. Therefore, the historical origin of political liberalism is the seventeenth century in England, something like the modern understanding of liberty of conscience and freedom of thought, began then. It is possible to speak of 'the liberalism of fear' born out of the fear associated with religious persecution and cruelties. The historical origin of political liberalism is then the cruelties of the wars of religion and the toleration towards other people's faith which was the only alternative to never-ending religious war. Modern writers such as Judith Shklar in her celebrated 1989 article 'The Liberalism of Fear' tend to use the phrase 'the liberalism of fear' to mean the fear by ordinary citizens of the official abuse of power in all contexts. Such fear of the weak against official abuse of power then is used by Shklar to justify rigorous human rights law and the constitutional protections of the modern liberal state.

However John Rawls gives a different meaning to the phrase 'liberalism of fear'. Rawls in his historical explanation of the emergence of liberalism in *Political Liberalism* (1993) uses the phrase 'liberalism of fear' to signify the growth of religious and then political toleration arising in reaction from the 'cruelties of the religious civil wars' of the sixteenth and seventeenth centuries. John Locke, in 1667, wrote *A Letter Concerning Toleration* in which he argued:

> 'God has given no man authority over another, no man can abandon the care of his own salvation to the care of another, a church is a voluntary society, and no man is bound to any particular church and he may leave it as freely as he entered, only faith and inward sincerity gain our salvation with God.'

In England in the 1660s there was a widespread belief that civil order and tranquillity required religious uniformity. Locke argued for the opposite conclusion: freedom of religious worship. Locke had two main arguments, which were original to Locke, for religious toleration: (1) the true faith cannot be forced, and (2) the government has no more reason to think that it is right in religious matters than anyone else.[5]

Locke thought that any attempt to force a particular religion onto persons was inconsistent with the true ends of religion for, as Locke commented, 'the way to salvation not being any forced exterior performance, but the voluntary and secret choice of the mind'. This is an explicitly religious argument to justify religious toleration and Locke argues that neither the example of Jesus nor the teaching of the New Testament suggests that the use of force is a proper way to bring persons to salvation. Locke gives another more philosophical argument for religious toleration: that the identity of the true religion was itself a matter of dispute and that the government has, in the words of Locke, 'no more certain or more infallible knowledge of the way to attain it than I myself'. This observation that governments may be wrong about which is the true religion is bolstered by the observation that governments are motivated by the quest for power, not truth, and are therefore unlikely to be sound in the pursuit of religious truth. History is full of examples of the use of religion by government for political ends.

As a result of these observations, Locke believed that 'in religious worship every man hath a perfect liberty which he may freely use without or contrary to the magistrate's command'.

It is possible to see, in the context of religious freedom advocated in Locke's writings, the origin of freedom of opinion which is the hallmark of modern democratic liberal states.[6]

....

5   The fact that government is no more likely to be correct than anyone else about the 'true' religion is attested to by Locke through showing the changing allegiances of the English Crown from the reign of Henry VIII to Elizabeth I. Henry VIII was a reformed Roman Catholic establishing the national Church in England. Henry VIII's son Edward VI was a strict Protestant. Edward VI was succeeded by the staunchly Roman Catholic Queen Mary whose sister, Elizabeth I reverted back to Protestantism. John Locke in *A Letter Concerning Toleration* said:

> 'our modern English history affords us fresher examples, in the reigns of Henry 8th, Edward 6th, Mary, and Elizabeth, how easily and smoothly the clergy changed their decrees, their articles of faith, their form of worship, every thing, according to the inclination of those Kings and Queens.'

6   John Rawls, the famous American political philosopher in his book *Political Liberalism* (1993) quotes Kalven who said that a free society is one in which it is impossible to defame the government – in other words the offence of 'seditious libel' which used to exist in England no longer exists in a free society: it is impossible to 'defame' the government by criticism or ridicule because the government of a free society no longer takes legal action against those who criticise or ridicule the government. Rawls quoting Kalven asserts:

> 'The absence of seditious libel as a crime is the true pragmatic test of freedom of speech. This I would argue is what free speech is about. Any society in which seditious libel is a crime is, no matter what its other features, not a free society. A society can, for example, either treat obscenity as a crime or not a crime without thereby altering its basic nature as a society. It seems to me it cannot do so with seditious libel. Here the response to this crime defines the society.'

The history of the use by governments of the crime of seditious libel to suppress criticism and dissent and to maintain their power demonstrates the great significance of this particular liberty. As long as the crime of seditious libel exists the public press and free discussion cannot play their role in informing the electorate. Rawls comments of the 'great importance' of the Supreme Court decision in the United States in the case of *New York Times v Sullivan* (1964) in which the Supreme Court rejected the crime of seditious libel and declared the **Sedition Act of 1798** unconstitutional as against the First Amendment guaranteeing free speech.

The next landmark in philosophical writings concerning toleration was published in 1859 by John Stuart Mill, *On Liberty*. Mill stated the view that the only justification for the intervention of the state through the criminal law restraining an individual's actions was 'to prevent harm to others'. The individual's own physical or moral welfare was not a sufficient reason for state intervention. Of course, an individual's family and friends could use moral persuasion and psychological pressure to dissuade any individual from pursuing a course of conduct harmful to himself, but the state could only intervene if there was 'harm to others'. Mill bases his doctrine, 'the harm principle', on the value of freedom in itself to human beings:

> 'The only freedom which deserves the name is that of pursuing our own good in our own way so long as we do not attempt to deprive others of theirs, or impede their efforts to obtain it.'

There are serious problems, though, with the 'harm principle' as a rational basis for toleration in modern Western society:

(1)　As Professor Hart pointed out in *Law, Liberty and Morality* (1962), the psychology of a human being employed by Mill is defective, in that Mill's conception of a human being was endowed with the settled temperament and character of a middle-aged middle-class man not unlike Mill himself. However, many individuals need protection from their own foolish choices, such as addiction to opiates, and therefore some 'paternalism' in the state is needed. The fundamental point that Mill overlooked is that not every individual is the model of rationality and maturity envisaged by Mill in *On Liberty*.

(2)　Mill's theory also has to answer the fundamental objection 'what is to count as "harm to others"?' Does 'harm' include only physical harm or does it include harm to the ethical environment of the community?

As Professor Dworkin has commented in a 1989 article ('Liberal Community' in California Law Review) some liberals have thought that liberal tolerance can be fully justified by John Stuart Mill's 'harm principle', which holds that the state may properly restrain someone's liberty only to prevent his harming others, not himself. This, it is argued, rules out legislation making homosexual acts criminal. However, as Dworkin points out, this argument is sound only if we limit harm to physical harm to person or property. Every community has an ethical environment, and that environment makes a difference to the lives its members can lead. A community which tolerates homosexuality, and in which homosexuality has a strong presence, provides a different ethical environment from one in which homosexuality is forbidden, and some people believe themselves harmed by the difference.

The failure of Mill's 'harm principle' to provide a satisfactory foundation for liberal toleration has led to the development of other theories. Professor Raz, a believer in liberal toleration, writes in 'Liberalism, Scepticism and Democracy' (1989, Iowa Law Review) that toleration springs from a concern with the well-being of citizens based on a respect for personal autonomy. The state should be careful in the means it adopts to promote virtue.

Those means should not infringe a person's autonomy, which is the foundation of his or her well-being. Government should neither criminalise nor employ coercion to discourage victimless immoralities. Raz argues that, by attaching the stigma of criminal conviction, by disrupting a person's life through the process of trial and conviction, criminal coercion affects the general control people have over the course of their lives. Such an infringement of personal autonomy may be justified by the need to protect the autonomy of others. However, when the matter concerns victimless offences, then respect for the autonomy of the individual dictates a policy of toleration by government.

Therefore, for Raz, liberal toleration stems from a concern with the well-being of citizens in that the criminal conviction and punishment for victimless immoralities can interfere substantially with the control (the autonomy) that a person has over his own life.

Professor Dworkin has deployed a number of arguments over the years to argue for 'liberalism', but the most celebrated justification was the argument based on 'equal concern and respect' which is found, for example, in the article 'Liberalism' (reprinted in *A Matter of Principle* (1985)). The argument is that the state has a fundamental duty to treat its citizens with equal concern and respect and this includes respecting the lifestyle choice of citizens, including homosexuality. As Dworkin writes in 'Liberalism': 'The constitutive morality of liberalism is a theory of equality that requires official neutrality amongst theories of what is valuable in life.' This is in distinction to the 'conservative' or 'perfectionist' view that society must help its members to achieve what is in fact good. A proponent of 'perfectionism' is the natural lawyer, Professor Finnis (whose leading work is *Natural Law and Natural Rights* (1980)) severely criticises Dworkin's 'equal concern and respect' argument for liberal toleration. Finnis denies that laws prohibiting drug abuse (for example, opiates such as heroin), suicide or homosexuality violate a person's self-respect or denies that citizen 'equal concern and respect'. Finnis comments in his 'Maccabean Lecture' for the British Academy in 1985:

> 'the phenomenon of conversion (repentance) or, less dramatically, of regret and reform, shows that one must not identify the person (and his worth as a human being) with his current lifestyle. A person prevented from using illegal drugs, committing suicide or engaging in homosexual acts on this view cannot think that the law does not treat him as an equal for the justifying concern of the law is an effort to uphold morality for the good, the worth and the dignity of everyone without exception. To condemn and prohibit the sin is not to manifest contempt for the sinner in classic Catholic theology.'

Therefore, Finnis argues that legislation prohibiting homosexuality may be based on a sense of equal concern and respect – the equal worth and human dignity of those persons whose conduct is outlawed precisely on the ground that such immoral conduct as homosexuality actually degrades human worth and dignity. The tradition in Western Christian thought from Aquinas (1225–1273), and supported by Finnis, is that persons who are prone to vice and resistant to verbal persuasion not only can be restrained from depraved actions by coercive threats but also can be led by an acculturation (called 'habituation' by natural lawyers) to make willingly, through their own authentic free choice, the good choices which earlier they made only under coercion and threats. Therefore, Finnis argues that the concept of the state showing 'equal concern and respect' to citizens can lead to the prohibition of homosexuality rather than the same concept leading to the legalisation of homosexuality, as Dworkin argues.

The natural lawyers' view of a 'paternalistic state' prohibiting possession of drugs, suicide and homosexuality is based on a concept found in the Bible itself. The key concept for natural lawyers of 'original sin' can be traced back to the Old Testament (see Psalm 51, verse 5) and was endorsed by St Augustine (354–430) in the fifth century (see Augustine's monumental work, *The City of God*, for his views on 'original sin'). The view of 'original sin' is that man in his natural non-religious state is inherently sinful and prone to evil conduct and that this is an 'inherited' characteristic of every human being who is not saved by Divine grace. Pelagius, a monk of the fifth century, famously disagreed with Augustine's notion of original sin and argued that man is born with a natural tendency towards goodness and charity. However St Augustine's view of the universality of 'original sin' has been very influential and supports the natural lawyers' view that the state needs to use coercion to enforce morality. Ultra-conservative 'Augustinians' believe that the individual is incapable of behaving well without the repressive intervention of the state and its laws, and that 'sins' such as abortion, homosexuality and suicide need to be rigorously suppressed. The authoritarian state is an Augustinian construct. The Augustinian view of 'original sin' was ratified by the Council of Carthage in 418 AD. The criminal law of England was broadly Augustinian before the 1960s, but has become increasingly Pelagian from the mid-1960s with the decriminalisation of homosexuality, attempted suicide, abortion and more tolerant legal attitudes towards the possession of illegal drugs. Lord Devlin, the Law Lord (1905–1992), in his book *The Enforcement of Morals* (1965), can be viewed as taking a traditional 'natural law' approach to the issue of the toleration or suppression of activities such as homosexuality when he wrote that 'the suppression of vice is as much the law's business as the suppression of subversive activities'. This echoes the comment of Oliver Cromwell (1599–1658) as Lord Protector in 1656 that 'the suppressing of vice and encouragement of virtue' was on a par with the security of the peace of the nation as the ends of his government (Cromwell quoted in *Cromwell and the Interregnum*, edited by David L Smith (2003)).

The view of the prevalence of 'original sin' in human beings is supported by the great natural law thinker St Thomas Aquinas, who is quoted by Finnis (in *Aquinas* (1998)) as holding:

> 'there is in us a natural inclination towards what is appealing (*conveniens*) to bodily feelings (*carnali sensui*) against the good of practical reasonableness (*contra bonum rationis*).'

As Finnis comments, like all great exponents of natural law and moral objectivity, Aquinas expects immoral customs and practices to predominate. This belief in the pervasiveness of 'original sin' was challenged by the men of the Enlightenment in the eighteenth century. Indeed, as Professor Henry Chadwick comments in his book, *St Augustine* (1986), the men of the Enlightenment thought the actual perfecting of man was hindered by belief in original sin and disliked Augustine very much. The men of the Enlightenment were displeased when the Enlightenment philosopher, Immanuel Kant (1724–1804), decisively assented to the belief that human nature is distorted by a pervasive radical evil. Kant had asserted that from the crooked timber of humanity nothing completely straight can be made. The doctrine of 'original sin' was well expressed by the great Bible translator, William Tyndale (1494–1536) in his work *A Pathway to the Holy Scripture* (1530) when he wrote:

> 'By nature through the fall of Adam are we the children of wrath, heirs of the vengeance of God by birth, yea and from our conception … so are we hated of God for that natural poison which is conceived and born with us before we do any outward evil.'

As the great Puritan thinker of the mid-seventeenth century, John Owen (1616–1683), commented in his book *The Holy Spirit* (1674): 'Original sin is the habitual inconformity of our natures to the holiness of God.'

The recognition of 'original sin' as a pervasive human characteristic will generally lead to the adoption of conservative or even authoritarian views on the state and the enforcement of morals. This is the view of the classical 'natural lawyers', such as Aquinas and Finnis. The rejection of the 'original sin' doctrine (Pelagianism) will lead to an optimistic view of human beings and a rejection of the concept of 'sin' at all, leading to 'liberalism' in the enforcement of morals and toleration of homosexuality, abortion and suicide. This is the view of Raz and Dworkin. Ultimately, the question as to whether, and to what extent, the state should enforce morality will depend on which view of human nature is taken by the theorist, whether pessimistic or optimistic.

Common Pitfalls

Students can avoid the pitfall of thinking that JS Mill's 'harm principle' is in itself a workable theory for defining the limits of state power over the individual and his lifestyle choices, since everything depends on what counts as 'harm'. In other words 'the harm principle' has to be embedded in a normative theory of what counts as relevant 'harm' to others – for example is it just physical harm or harm to the social environment? Students can gain extra marks by pointing out that legal theorists such as Raz and Dworkin, who take a permissive attitude towards abortion, homosexuality and illegal drug use, are in fact, in the tradition of eighteenth-century Enlightenment thinkers such as Rousseau and William Godwin who argued against institutions which repress the innate moral goodness of persons.

NOTES

The views of Locke concerning religious toleration can be found in *The Stanford Encyclopedia of Philosophy* website entries on Locke (http://plato.stanford.edu/), especially Alex Tuckness's essay 'Locke's political philosophy'. For a general discussion of Locke's arguments concerning religious toleration, see *John Locke: an Essay Concerning Toleration*, edited with an introduction and notes by JR Milton and Philip Milton (2006). The 'Everyman' edition of JS Mill's *On Liberty* contains a useful interpretive essay by the philosopher, Isaiah Berlin.

Dworkin's views are reflected in the essay 'Liberalism' (1978), collected in *A Matter of Principle* (1985). The view of Raz on liberal toleration can be found in *The Morality of Freedom* (1986). The conservative views of Professor Finnis can be found in the 1985 Maccabean lecture on Jurisprudence to the British Academy and in the approving reference Finnis gives to the concept of 'public morality' in Chapter VIII of *Natural Law and Natural Rights* (1980). The views of St Thomas Aquinas on human immorality can be found in Finnis's work *Aquinas: Moral, Political and Legal Theory* (1998).

Index